# PRISON EPISTLES:

## EPHESIANS, PHILIPPIANS, COLOSSIANS & PHILEMON

# Cover Photo Description

(Front Cover) Paul wrote four letters as a prisoner in Rome for 2 years, about A.D. 60-61. During this time in chains, Paul was always guarded by at least one Roman soldier. In these years he was not in a dungeon as he was at other times. Rather, as he awaited his trial, Rome allowed the apostle to live in a house he rented (Acts 20:16, 30). The Roman government provided no meals, clothes, or services for prisoners. So whatever necessities Paul received came only from friends.

Years spent as a prisoner were tough times, but Paul made the most of them. Day by day, Paul practiced looking up to heaven, and rejoicing in the Lord for all His blessings. So even as an innocent prisoner in chains, during these unjust years Paul wrote four glorious letters—the Prison Epistles—that have blessed the Church for 2,000 years!

(Back Cover) Paul wrote in Greek, using a pen made from a reed, and ink that was a mixture of water, soot, gum, and the black that came as a lamp burned. He wrote on dried paper or parchment made from dried papyrus reeds, or animal skins.

The picture of the mountain illustrates the relation of a doxology (Eph. 3:20-21), to the first and second halves of Ephesians. Praise be to God for His great power at work in us. For through this power of the Spirit, God is able to do much more than we can ask or imagine. Amen! Through the power of His Spirit, He has redeemed us (Eph. 1–3), and He enables us to live worthy of His blessings and our calling to be His children (Eph. 4–6). So like Paul, let us live day by day, looking up, and depending on the power of God's Spirit, rather than on ourselves. For God's Spirit in us is the source of all the power we need to praise Him and live in ways that please Him.

 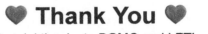 

♥ **Thank You** ♥

Special thanks to BGMC and LFTL
for helping fund the Faith & Action Ministry.

# Contact Information

Address: Faith & Action Team
429 U.S. Hwy 65
Walnut Shade, Missouri 65771 U.S.A

Telephone: (417) 881-4698
E-mail: Orders@FaithAndActionSeries.org
Web: www.FaithAndActionSeries.org

# Prison Epistles:
## EPHESIANS, PHILIPPIANS, COLOSSIANS & PHILEMON

## Student Manual

## by Dr. Quentin McGhee

### Instructional Design by
### Dr. Quentin McGhee, Senior Editor

PUT YOUR FAITH TO WORK!

## Faith & Action Series

Faith & Action
429 U.S. Hwy 65
Walnut Shade, Missouri 65771 U.S.A.

# Copyright Information

# Components That Complement This Book

Visit www.FaithAndActionSeries.org to see components with this book:

**eVisuals**— project all figures in color with captions. Download from our website.

**2 Kindle** color versions from Amazon: Matches the printed book for your computer or large tablet. Or for your tablet, phone, or computer www.amazon.com (search Faith & Action Team)

**Teacher's Guides**—To purchase a TG submit our online form for approval as a teacher, pastor or administrator.

www.faithandactionseries.org/teachers.html

First Edition 2017

*Faith & Action Series*—Prison Epistles: Ephesians, Philippians, Colossians & Philemon; First Edition
©2017 Faith & Action Team

Course # BIB2052
ISBN: 978-1-60382-062-2
Item # 4411-25E0

# Table of Contents

**Chapter—Lesson**

## Unit 1:
## Exploring Ephesians and Colossians—Part 1

## Unit 2:
## Exploring Ephesians and Colossians—Part 2

## Unit 3:
## Exploring Philippians and Philemon

# List of Figures

# Faith & Action Series Overview

| Bible | Theology | Church Ministries |
|---|---|---|
| Survey of the Old Testament | Theology 1: The Bible, God & Angels | Evangelism & Discipleship |
| Survey of the New Testament | Theology 2: Man, Sin, Christ & Salvation | Marriage & Family |
| Pentateuch | Theology 3: The Holy Spirit & the Church | Pastoral Ministry |
| Historical Books | Hermeneutics 1: General Principles for Interpreting Scripture | Ministerial Ethics |
| Poetic Books | Hermeneutics 2: Interpreting Genres of Scripture | Homiletics 1: Preparing Biblical Messages |
| Major Prophets | Unlocking the Treasures of Your Fire Bible | Homiletics 2 |
| Minor Prophets | | Principles of Teaching |
| Synoptic Gospels: Life & Teachings of Christ | | Biblical Counseling |
| Gospel of John | | Children's Ministry |
| Acts of the Holy Spirit | | Youth Ministry |
| Romans & Galatians | | Missions 1 |
| First & Second Corinthians | | Missions 2: Cross-Cultural Communications |
| Prison Epistles | | Teaching Literacy: Read the Light |
| Paul's Eschatological & Pastoral Epistles | | Leadership 1: Loving God & People |
| Hebrews | | Leadership 2: Skills to Empower, Govern & Administrate |
| General Epistles | | Church History 1: Christ to Reformation |
| Revelation & Daniel | | Church History 2: Reformation to Present |

# Faith & Action Series
# Three-Year Bible School Plan (95 credits)

## First Year

### First Semester

| Course # | Title | Credits |
|---|---|---|
| BIB1013 | Survey of the New Testament | 3 |
| BIB1023 | Pentateuch | 3 |
| BIB1033 | Synoptic Gospels: Life & Teachings of Christ | 3 |
| THE1012 | Theology 1: The Bible, God & Angels | 2 |
| THE1023 | Hermeneutics 1: General Principles for Interpreting Scripture | 3 |
| MIN3023 | Children's Ministry | 2 |
| | | 16 |

### Second Semester

| Course # | Title | Credits |
|---|---|---|
| BIB1043 | Survey of the Old Testament | 3 |
| BIB1052 | Gospel of John | 2 |
| BIB1063 | Acts of the Holy Spirit | 3 |
| THE1032 | Theology 2: Man, Sin, Christ & Salvation | 2 |
| MIN1013 | Homiletics 1: Preparing Biblical Messages | 3 |
| MIN1033 | Evangelism & Discipleship | 3 |
| | | 16 |

## Second Year

### First Semester

| Course # | Title | Credits |
|---|---|---|
| BIB2013 | Romans & Galatians | 3 |
| BIB2023 | Historical Books | 3 |
| BIB2072 | Hebrews | 2 |
| MIN2012 | Church History 1: Christ to Reformation | 2 |
| MIN2023 | Missions 1 | 3 |
| MIN3073 | Marriage & Family | 3 |
| | | 16 |

### Second Semester

| Course # | Title | Credits |
|---|---|---|
| BIB2043 | First & Second Corinthians | 3 |
| BIB2052 | Prison Epistles | 2 |
| BIB2062 | Poetic Books | 2 |
| MIN2032 | Church History 2: Reformation to Present | 2 |
| THE2042 | Theology 3: The Holy Spirit & the Church | 2 |
| MIN2042 | Leadership 1: Loving God & People | 2 |
| THE2033 | Hermeneutics 2: Interpreting Genres of Scripture | 2 |
| | | 15 |

## Third Year

### First Semester

| Course # | Title | Credits |
|---|---|---|
| BIB3012 | Paul's Eschatological & Pastoral Epistles | 2 |
| BIB3022 | General Epistles | 2 |
| BIB3033 | Major Prophets | 3 |
| MIN3012 | Pastoral Ministry | 2 |
| MIN1032/ MIN1042 | Teaching Literacy/ Unlocking the Treasure of Fire Bible | 2 |
| MIN3033 | Missions 2: Cross-Cultural Communications | 3 |
| MIN3043 | Homiletics 2 | 2 |
| | | 16 |

### Second Semester

| Course # | Title | Credits |
|---|---|---|
| BIB3043 | Revelation & Daniel | 3 |
| MIN3053 | Biblical Counseling | 3 |
| BIB3053 | Minor Prophets | 2 |
| MIN3063 | Principles of Teaching | 2 |
| MIN3072 | Ministerial Ethics | 2 |
| MIN3082 | Youth Ministry | 2 |
| MIN3092 | Leadership 2: Skills to Empower, Govern & Administrate | 2 |
| | | 16 |

# About This Book

1. **The Lesson Headings** divide each chapter into several parts. Each of these lessons focuses on principles related to one theme. We number the lessons consecutively throughout the book.

2. **The Lesson Goals** are listed at the beginning of each chapter. Also, when a lesson begins, the goal for that lesson is printed there. You will find that there is at least one goal for each lesson.

3. **Key Words** are defined in a section called "Definitions" at the end of the book. The symbol * comes before all words that are defined. To help some students, we have also defined a few words that are not key words.

4. **Teaching Method:** These courses are designed for the *guided discovery* method of learning. This method focuses on the student, rather than the teacher. When this course is used in a classroom, lectures are not intended. Rather, most of the class time should be used for students to discuss the questions in the margins and related questions from the teacher and other students. At least 25 percent of the student's grade should be on how faithfully the student has tried to answer questions *before* class.

   It is VERY important for each student to own his or her book. We encourage Bible schools to require students to buy their texts at the time they pay tuition. It is a shame for students to leave school without their books, because they need them for a lifetime of ministry. Owning the book enables a student to write notes in it and underline important ideas. Also, when students own their books, they do not waste class time by copying things that are already written in the text. Rather, they spend their time discussing questions related to the Bible and ministry.

   In a classroom the teacher and students should discuss key questions together. The best teachers never answer their own questions. Some students will complain at first when the teacher requires them to think, read, and search for answers. But a good teacher knows that children who are always carried never learn to walk. And students who are always told the answer learn to memorize, but not to think and solve problems. In many ways, a good teacher is like a coach—guiding others to succeed.

   The questions in this course are like a path that leads straight to the goal. If the questions are too hard for a student, the teacher can ask easier questions that are like stairs toward harder questions. Also, the teacher should ask questions that guide students to apply the text to local issues. Often, a good teacher will add a story or illustration that emphasizes a truth for students.

5. **Schedule:** This *Faith & Action Series* course is for two credits. For a Bible school course, it is good to plan 26 contact hours between the teacher and students. This allows one lesson for a class hour.

6. **The Questions:** Most questions in the margins are identified by the hammer ⟍ and nail ⟍ symbols. Questions are steps toward a goal. As a student answers the questions, he or she is sure to reach the goals. The hammer introduces *content questions* and the nail precedes *application questions*. Our logo for this book includes the hammer hitting the nail. A student must grasp content before being able to apply it. The answers to all content questions are in the text, near the question. We encourage students to answer nail or application questions from their local settings.

   In some books there is the symbol of a shovel ⟍ before certain questions. Questions beside the shovel symbol are *inductive questions*. The word *induce* means "to lead." These questions lead students to discover truth for themselves.

7. *Sabio* is a Spanish word that means "wise man." This symbol in the margin signifies a proverb or wise saying.

8. **The Illustrations,** such as stories and examples, are preceded by the candle symbol.

9. **Figures** include pictures, photos, charts, and maps. We number the figures in order throughout the chapter. For example, the first three figures in chapter one are numbered 1.1, 1.2, and 1.3. There is a list of significant figures near the front of the book.

10. **The Test Yourself** questions come at the end of each chapter and are indicated by the balance symbol ⚖. There are always ten of these questions. As a rule, there are two test questions for each goal in the chapter. If students miss any of these questions, they need to understand why they missed them. Knowing why an answer is right is as important as knowing the right answer.

11. **Essay Test Topics** are at the end of each chapter, indicated by the pencil symbol ✏. Note that these essay topics are the lesson goals of the chapter. A student should be able to summarize these goals, writing 50-100 words on each one. These essay topics test students at a much higher level than the multiple choice, Test Yourself questions.

12. **Sample Answers** to the hammer questions, some comments on the nail questions, and answers for the Test Yourself questions and Essay Topics are in the Teacher's Guide. Students should answer questions so they will grow and become strong in their mental skills.

13. **Bible quotations** are usually from the New International Version (NIV). We also use the New American Standard Bible (NASB) and the King James Version (KJV). We encourage students to compare biblical passages in several versions of the Bible.

14. **The Scripture List** includes key Scripture references in this course. It is located near the back of the book.

15. **The Bibliography** is near the endnotes page. It is a complete list of books to which the authors refer in this course. Some students will want to do further research in these books.

16. **Endnotes** identify the sources of thoughts and quotes. They are listed by chapter at the end of the book.

17. **The Unit Exams and Final Exam** are in the Teacher's Guide. In the Teacher's Guide there are also other useful items for the teacher and potential projects for the students.

18. **Course Description (BIB2052):** A thorough study of Paul's four Prison Epistles—Ephesians, Colossians, Philippians & Philemon. Examining each of these letters includes an analysis of the biblical author, date, readers, historical setting, purpose, themes, special features, and outlines. Also, studying each epistle involves the exegesis and analysis of each paragraph, with an emphasis on the two hermeneutical questions: What did the text mean to the first readers? How does it apply to us? Continuing to the top of the hermeneutical ladder, each lesson identifies timeless, cross-cultural principles, for every paragraph of the biblical text. Interactive questions, case studies, and illustrations guide students to evaluate and apply these principles to the situations believers face today. (This course is designed for two credits, based on 16 class hours per credit.)

19. **Global Goals:**

| F&A Chapter | Prison Epistles | Global Goals |
|---|---|---|
| 1 | Eph. 1–3 | • List the Prison Epistles, and explain their title, author, his setting, and date of writing.<br>• Summarize the background, readers, purposes, and outline of Ephesians.<br>• Explain and illustrate our 8 blessings in Christ (Eph. 1:3-14).<br>• Analyze and apply 3 aspects of Paul's prayer for believers (Eph. 1:15-23).<br>• Explain the mystery in Ephesians 2–3.<br>• Sketch and explain the relationship of Ephesians 1–3 and 4–6 to the doxology of Ephesians 3:20-21. |
| 2 | Eph. 4:1–5:20 | • Relate the need to live worthy—to the roles of love, unity, and serving in Christ.<br>• Contrast 6 types of things to put off, and put on.<br>• Explain how being filled with the Spirit brings assurance, victory over sin, and power for service.<br>• Summarize 5 keys to living filled with the Spirit. |
| 3 | Eph. 5:21–6:24 | • Analyze responsibilities for each group in God's family.<br>• Summarize aspects of spiritual warfare in Ephesians 1–6, and explain the armor we need.<br>• Analyze praying in the Spirit, occasions and types of prayer. |
| 4 | Col. 1-2 | • Analyze the authorship, date, city, purposes, theme, and outline of Colossians.<br>• Summarize 6 errors of the Colossian heresy.<br>• Explain ways Christ is Supreme as Creator and Reconciler (Col. 1:15-23). Apply these.<br>• Examine the cost, message, purpose, and power of spiritual ministry (Col. 1:24–2:5). |

| 5 | Phil. 1–4 | • Analyze the authorship, date, recipients, city, purposes, outline, themes, background, and setting of Philippians.<br>• Sketch and explain a diagram of Paul's prayer (Phil. 1:9-11).<br>• Make a chart of key events in Acts 21–28, showing Paul's path to Rome.<br>• Explain and illustrate 3 doors that are always before us in difficult times.<br>• State the principle of Philippians 2:4, and illustrate it 7 times from Philippians 1–2. Sketch and explain the contrast between legalists, followers of Christ, and libertines (Phil. 3).<br>• Summarize factors of joy and peace (Phil. 4). |
| 6 | Phm. 1 | • Analyze the problem of slavery in Paul's day, and the biblical solution.<br>• From Philemon, explain, illustrate, and apply 12 principles for resolving conflict. |

## 20. Author

**Dr. Quentin McGhee** is the founder and senior editor of the *Faith & Action Series*. He earned a B.A. from Southwestern College in Oklahoma City, and a B.S. from Oral Roberts University (ORU), Tulsa, Oklahoma. Later he completed an M.Div. at the Assemblies of God Theological Seminary, where he taught beginning Greek. He earned a D.Min. from ORU in 1987. Dr. McGhee and his wife, Elizabeth, pioneered a church in Oklahoma. They went on to serve as missionaries in Kenya for 15 years. There they helped start many churches, developed an extension Bible school for full-time ministers, and assisted in curriculum development. Currently, Dr. McGhee serves as Director for the *Faith & Action Series*, while Elizabeth assists with graphics, desk-top publishing, website development, translations, and sales.

## 21. Contributors and Reviewers

**Dr. Steve D. Eutsler** has a rich ministerial background as a teacher, pastor, preacher, and writer. He serves as a mentor for students of Global University in the areas of Bible and Practical Theology. Steve has served as adjunct professor at Central Bible College and Evangel University for 12 years, teaching courses on Bible, practical ministry, and preaching. He has pastored 18 years; serves as a Dale Carnegie trainer; is the author of several books; and his sermon outlines often appear in *Enrichment Journal* and *Pulpit Helps*. He earned his Doctor of Ministry degree at Assemblies of God Theological Seminary, Springfield, Missouri. In this course Dr. Eutsler contributed significant research, notes, suggestions for and evaluation of biblical principles.

**Dr. John Wesley Adams** is Professor of Biblical Studies at All Nations Training Center—Kansas City, Grandview, Missouri. He has four earned degrees in biblical and theological studies: a B.A. from Southern Nazarene University, Bethany, Oklahoma; an M.A. also from Southern Nazarene University; an M.Div. from Nazarene Theological Seminary, Kansas City, Missouri; and a Ph.D. from Baylor University, Waco, Texas. Dr. Adams is a contributing author to the *Beacon Dictionary of Theology*, co-author and associate editor of the *Full Life Study Bible*.

**Dr. French L. Arrington** has ministered in evangelical and Pentecostal circles around the world. He has served as a pastor and for 17 years at Lee University, where he was chairman of the Bible and Theology Dept., Professor of New Testament Greek and Pauline Studies; and received the Excellence in Teaching Award. He has lectured in seminaries in Korea, Puerto Rico, Guatemala, Philippines, Indonesia, Ecuador, Virgin Islands, China, and Russia. He also ministers at seminars, conferences, and local churches. Dr. Arrington is an ordained bishop in the Church of God; and served as Professor of New Testament Greek and Exegesis at the Pentecostal Theological Seminary from 1981-2002, where he is now Professor Emeritus. In 2017 he was asked to serve full time again at the Church of God Pentecostal Theological Seminary, as the first Chair of the Restoration of the Tabernacle of David.

His education includes B.A. degrees from Lee College and the University of Chattanooga; an M.Div. and a Th.M. from Columbia Theologica Seminary; and a Ph.D in biblical languages from St. Louis University. He has authored and edited too many books to list here. Pathway Press published his three-volume work *Christian Doctrine: a Pentecostal Perspective*. His latest commentary is: *The Greatest Letter Ever Written: A Study of Romans*. He was a general editor of the *Life in the Spirit New Testament Commentary*.

**Dr. James Hernando** has earned the following degrees: B.S. in Education (State University of New York), B.A. in Bible (Northeast Bible College), M.S. in Education (State University of New York), M.Div. (Assemblies of God Theological Seminary), M.Phil. and Ph.D. (Drew University, 1990). Jim and his wife, Moira, have three sons: Matthew, Eric, and Daniel.

Jim taught at Trinity Bible College and served as Chair of Biblical Studies (1980–1986). He has been Associate Professor of New Testament at AGTS from 1990–2014, and Chairs the Biblical Theology Department. Jim has preached and taught Hermeneutics and New Testament Theology in Ukraine and Costa Rica.

His recent publications are: 2 Corinthians in *Full Life Bible Commentary to the New Testament* (Zondervan), *Dictionary of Hermeneutics: A Concise Guide to Terms, Names, Methods and Expressions* (Gospel Publishing House), *Studies in the Letters of Paul* (Global University), and *First and Second Corinthians* (Faith & Action Series).

Jim has been awarded many honors, such as: Who's Who in American High Schools, Who's Who in American Colleges and University, FTE Hispanic Doctoral Scholarship, Outstanding Alumnus of Valley Forge Christian College, Member of the Advisory Board for the Foundation of Pentecostal Scholarship, and Assemblies of God Distinguished Educator's Award for 25 years of service.

# Dedication

This book—*Prison Epistles: Ephesians, Philippians, Colossians, Philemon*—was made possible by a generous donation from Dr. Daniel T. and Bonnie Sheaffer.

Daniel Thomas Sheaffer was born November 29, 1929 to Reverend Gerald and Jeanette Sheaffer. Dan was named after his uncle, Daniel Thomas Muse, a bishop of the Pentecostal Holiness Church.

Malawi, East Africa

Dan first began preaching at the age of 17. Like many Pentecostal pioneers, when he didn't have a church to speak in, he preached on street corners, or used schools to hold revivals.

In 1950, at the age of 21, Dan married Bonnie Rose Benson, who became his faithful companion for the next 60 years. They conducted evangelistic meetings for several years, and Dan was ordained by the Assemblies of God Oklahoma District in 1958.

Dan and Bonnie pastored First Assembly of God in Miami, Oklahoma from 1961–1969. Then they accepted the pastorate of a small AG church in Oklahoma City. This proved to be a step of destiny into a ministry that would impact multitudes of people in many nations of the world. In the first 3 years, from 1969 to 1971, the small church grew from 42 to 1250 members, in a new building. Then in 1979 the Sheaffers led the congregation to build Crossroads Cathedral, located on two major highways. This was one of the first and largest mega-churches in the Assemblies of God. It seated about 6,000 people each Sunday morning, contained more than 200,000 square feet, and was built debt free—partly because the Sheaffers founded a successful business to build homes and do general contracting to expand their ministry.

Thousands of people came to Christ in this strategic megacity church at the crossroads. But as Assemblies of God General Superintendent (2007-2017), Dr. George O. Wood noted, Dan and Bonnie Sheaffer had a heart for Oklahoma City and the world. Their generosity is a legend. Here are a few of the projects made possible by their ministry and the millions of dollars they gave:

- The *Faith & Action* books: *Romans & Galatians, 1 & 2 Corinthians, General Epistles,* and *Gospel of John,* which more than three million students will study worldwide;

- Churches they founded and built in Liberia, Kenya, Nigeria, South Africa, Paraguay, Colombia, Jamaica, Chile, and Burundi;

- 1,000 churches they funded in Malawi, and sponsorships that helped the Malawi AG Church grow from 200 to 4,000 churches with 800,000 members;

- Malawi Assemblies of God School of Theology that trains students from across Africa;

- The Sheaffer Full Life Center at Southwestern Assemblies of God University (SAGU) in Waxahachie Texas. This building has 111,000 square feet, and contains a cafeteria, classrooms, offices, an athletic center, two gymnasiums, and a chapel;

- Participation in the construction of Bridges and Teeter Hall on the SAGU campus;

- The financial undergirding of the Doctor of Ministry program at Assemblies of God Theological Seminary (AGTS) in Springfield, Missouri;

- The Assemblies of God Center for Holy Land Studies, funded during their final pastorate at Harvest Assembly of God Church, Oklahoma City;
- Initial funding for the Daniel T. Sheaffer Chair of Practical Ministry at AGTS.

Dan held degrees from Oklahoma City Southwestern College, Oklahoma City University, East Central State University, Tulsa University, Luther Rice Seminary, and Southwestern Assemblies of God University. Pastor Sheaffer and Bonnie hosted the popular Trinity Broadcasting Network program, *The Answer* for 17 years, and were frequent hosts and guests of TBN's "Praise the Lord" program. Dan authored two books of Bible questions and answers and a church growth book entitled, *Together We Grow*.

To Dan and Bonnie Sheaffer, we gratefully dedicate this book. Their legacy endures forever. And we express our thankfulness to their daughter, Terri, and her husband, Gary King; and their son, Mike, and his wife, Starla, who continue to fulfill the Great Commission as Dan and Bonnie cheer from heaven.

# Unit 1:
# Exploring Ephesians and Colossians—Part 1

**Ephesians 1–3**, like the left side of a mountain, rises in praise for two reasons: *first,* for all the spiritual blessings God has poured out on us in Christ (Eph. 1:3-14); and *second,* for redeeming and uniting Jews and Gentiles into one body, one family, and one temple (Eph. 2–3 see Figure 1.60).

Likewise **Ephesians 4–6** rises, like the right side of a mountain, as the praise of our response—as we *live worthy* of all our Father has done for us in Christ. We live worthy of God's blessings as we take off (like dirty clothes) 6 types of sins, and replace them with 6 virtues. God enables us to live worthy in society, in our homes, at work, and in spiritual warfare.

The top of a mountain is its most glorious, inspiring point. The peak of Ephesians is the doxology of **3:20-21**. These verses glorify God. They shout glory to God from the mountain top—because God *"is able to do immeasurably more than all we can ask or imagine, by his power that is at work within us"* (Eph. 3:20). As the peak of a mountain relates to both side, Ephesians 3:20-21 relates to the two parts of Ephesians. By *His power* at work in us God has done all of Ephesians 1–3. He has poured out His blessings on us—redeeming and uniting Jews and Gentiles into one body (Eph. 1–3). And by the power of that same Spirit who works in us, God enables us to live worthy—causing us to rejoice as we obey the 35 commands of Ephesians 4–6. *By His power!* This is the key. So let us praise Him, and depend on the power of His Spirit for both sides of the mountain of salvation—for redemption and spiritual unity (Eph. 1–3), and for living worthy (Eph. 4–6). For *by His power* at work in us, He is able to do much more than we can ask or imagine.

As you study Unit 1 with us, here are some goals we will help you reach:

## Chapter 1: Ephesians, Powerful Doctrine—Our Riches in Christ (Eph. 1–3)
- *List the Prison Epistles, and explain their title, author, his setting, and date of writing.*
- *Summarize the background, readers, purposes, and outline of Ephesians.*
- *Explain and illustrate our 8 blessings in Christ (Eph. 1:3-14).*
- *Analyze and apply 3 aspects of Paul's prayer for believers (Eph. 1:15-23).*
- *Explain the mystery in Ephesians 2–3.*
- *Sketch and explain the relationship of Ephesians 1–3 and 4–6 to the doxology of Ephesians 3:20-21.*

## Chapter 2: Live Worthy of Your Calling, in the Church and in the World (Eph. 4:1–5:20)
- *Relate the need to live worthy—to the roles of love, unity, and serving in Christ.*
- *Contrast 6 types of things to put off, and put on.*
- *Explain how being filled with the Spirit brings assurance, victory over sin, and power for service.*
- *Summarize 5 keys to living filled with the Spirit.*

# Chapter 1:
# Ephesians: Powerful Doctrine— Our Riches in Christ

## (Eph. 1–3)

Have you ever met someone who always wants something new and different? Yet this person has a home, a family, and so many blessings! Such an attitude can lead to discontent in the midst of plenty. In the Christian life a similar attitude of ingratitude is possible. Some Christians are always seeking higher spiritual experiences—as they overlook what we have in Christ. The tragedy is that as they want more and more, they forget to appreciate the spiritual riches God has poured out on us in Christ. Ungrateful believers open themselves to being deceived by false teachers—who are like clouds without water, promising what they cannot give. In contrast, Paul calls attention to what God has already done for us through His One and Only Son. For as we meditate on the love, grace, and mercy God has lavished on us, our hearts overflow daily with praise, and we live worthy of being God's children (Eph. 4:1).

Figure 1.1 Paul stayed 3 years in Ephesus (Acts 19). It was a time of great revival. New believers burned magic scrolls worth the wages of 1,000 men working 50 days! These **new believers were so thankful to be free from the slavery of sin and Satan—and to be children in the family of God!**

## Lessons:

### Brief Introduction to the Prison Epistles, and Fuller Introduction to Ephesians

**①**
**Goal A:** *List the Prison Epistles, and explain their title.*
**Goal B:** *Summarize the background of the city of Ephesus, and the Ephesian believers.*
**Goal C:** *Explain the purposes and outline of Ephesians.*
**Goal D:** *Identify and explain the 5 key phrases in Ephesians 1:1-2.*

### Our Spiritual Blessings "in Christ"—Part 1 (Eph. 1:3-8)

**②**
**Goal A:** *Clarify the roles of the Father, Son, and Spirit in providing salvation.*
**Goal B:** *Explain and illustrate blessings 1–4 that we have in Christ (Eph. 1:3-8).*

### Our Spiritual Blessings "in Christ"—Part 2 (Eph. 1:9-14)

**③**
**Goal C:** *Explain and illustrate blessings 5–8 that we have in Christ (Eph. 1:9-14).*

### Paul's First Prayer for the Ephesians: to Discern God's Purpose (Eph. 1:15-23)

**④**
**Goal:** *Explain, illustrate, and apply 3 aspects of Paul's prayer for believers (Eph. 1:15-23).*

### The "Before and After" of Those "in Christ"—Part 1 (Eph. 2:1-10)

**⑤**
**Goal A:** *Explain 5 ways we were hopeless before we were in Christ (Eph. 2:1-3).*
**Goal B:** *Summarize and illustrate 3 aspects of salvation that Christ provided (Eph. 2:4-10).*

### The "Before and After" of Those "in Christ"—Part 2 (Eph. 2:11-22)

**⑥**
**Goal C:** *Analyze these 3 relationships of Gentiles to Jews: included, united, made equal (Eph. 2:13-22).*

### The "Mystery of Christ" (Eph. 3:1-13)

**⑦**
**Goal A:** *Explain the mystery in Ephesians 3:1-13.*
**Goal B:** *Summarize 3 ways "the mystery of Christ" includes Jews and Gentiles (Eph. 3:6).*
**Goal C:** *List 4 responsibilities we have in response to "the mystery of Christ."*
**Goal D:** *Explain 2 purposes of "the mystery of Christ."*

### Paul's Second Prayer for Believers (Eph. 3:14-21)

**⑧**
**Goal A:** *Analyze the role of the Spirit in overcoming the flesh and the world, and how to live filled with the Spirit (Eph. 3:14-17a).*
**Goal B:** *Explain and illustrate the role of love in obeying the teachings of Jesus (Eph. 3:14-17a).*
**Goal C:** *Sketch and explain the relationship of Ephesians 1–3 and 4–6 to the doxology of Ephesians 3:20-21.*

**Prison Epistles**—the four letters Paul wrote as a prisoner in Rome, about A.D. 60-61; Ephesians, Colossians, Philippians, and Philemon

**in Christ**—the boundary, realm, and sphere of God's plan of redemption; salvation is available as we abide *in Christ*. *In Christ* occurs seven times in Ephesians and over 160 times in Paul's 13 letters.

**Trinitarian**—a person who believes the Father, Son, and Holy Spirit are equal and work together to provide salvation

**election**—the act or process of choosing; God elects or chooses all who choose to receive and follow Jesus.

**predestination**—to plan a destiny; God has planned for all who receive Jesus to become like Him and be with Him.

**adoption**—the legal process of bringing a person into a family, and giving that person all the status and privileges of sons and daughters who were born in the family

**Gentiles**—the ethnic groups and nations of earth; non-Jews

**redemption**—the act or process of buying back a person who has become a slave

**seal**—a mark, emblem, or other way to show validity or ownership; God put the Holy Spirit in us to assure us that His promises to us are valid, and to show that we belong to Him.

**deposit**—a partial, initial payment to assure that someone will receive the full amount; God deposited His Spirit in us to assure us that we will receive all He has promised.

**inheritance**—wealth and riches that one person gives to another; the inheritance of those who follow Jesus is all that God has promised us in Christ.

**doxology**—a word of praise to God; a song, prayer, or praise glorifying God, often at the end of a section of writing, or at the end of a church service

---

**Lesson 1**

## Brief Introduction to the Prison Epistles, and Fuller Introduction to Ephesians

**Goal A:** *List the Prison Epistles, and explain their title.*
**Goal B:** *Summarize the background of the city of Ephesus, and the Ephesian believers.*
**Goal C:** *Explain the purposes and outline of Ephesians.*
**Goal D:** *Identify and explain the 5 key phrases in Ephesians 1:1-2.*

---

### Introduction to the Prison Epistles

What should we think of Paul's time in prison? Was it a problem or a blessing? Would it have been better for all if Paul had stayed free? Would the Church have grown faster if he continued to travel? Or was it God's will for Paul to be in prison? These are hard questions to answer. But we know that Paul's time in prison was a blessing to many (Acts 28:30-31). It gave Paul time to write his *Prison Epistles: Ephesians, Philippians, Colossians, and Philemon.

*Q 1* Which letters are the Prison Epistles? How do they get their title?

### A. Author, date, and readers of Ephesians

**Author.** Each of these four letters begins with Paul's name, showing that he is the author. Also, all of these four letters refer to Paul's chains or bonds (Col. 1:24; Eph. 3:1; 4:1; 6:20; Phil. 1:1-13; Philem. 1, 9-10). Most believe that Paul wrote these letters from Rome. Although Paul was in chains and was guarded, the government allowed him to live in a house he rented for 2 years (Acts 28:16, 30). In contrast, during a later imprisonment in Rome (66–67 A.D.), Paul was in a cold dungeon (2 Tim. 4:13), again

*Q 2* Who wrote the Prison Epistles? Where were they written?

chained like a common criminal (2 Tim. 1:16; 2:9). Paul's final letter, 2 Timothy, was also written from prison, but it is grouped among Paul's pastoral letters.

Bible scholars have heaped high praise on this Epistle. Many consider it a crown of Paul's writing—which summarizes some of the apostle's key themes.[1] Liberals question whether Paul is the author, and have tried to tear the letter apart. But as a wise man said, trying to answer all the objections of unbelievers is like arguing with the waves of the sea—they never end. The authors of this course believe there is no good reason to question the Bible's claim that Paul is the author (Eph. 1:1). And we affirm that Paul's letter to the Ephesians is a mountain peak among Paul's letters.

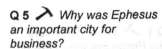

**Q 3** *When did Paul write the Prison Epistles?*

**Date.**    Paul probably wrote the four Prison Epistles about A.D. 60–61. His time in prison was difficult, but fruitful. In Rome, Paul was chained to a Roman soldier. He lived in a house he rented for 2 years, and he received visitors (Acts 28:30-31). This enabled him to hear reports from churches. As a result, he wrote letters to encourage, solve problems, teach, and guide believers. His ministry of prayer and evangelism continued in spite of his chains (Col. 1:3-14; Eph. 1:15-23; Phil. 1:3-6, 12-18; Philem. 4-6).

**Q 4** *Why are the words "in Ephesus" not present in some Old Greek copies of Paul's letter to the Ephesians?*

**Readers.**    In Ephesians 1:1 some early Greek manuscripts do not have the words *in Ephesus*. Although Paul wrote first to the church at Ephesus, perhaps others copied the letter and omitted the words *in Ephesus* as they passed it to several churches in the area. We know that scribes often copied letters that Paul wrote to churches—and circulated these letters to other churches. Over 5,000 ancient copies exist in Greek, containing the New Testament or parts of it! And over 19,000 ancient copies exist in other languages, such as Syriac, Latin, Coptic, and Aramaic.[2] Near the end of Paul's letter to the Colossians we find: *"After this letter has been read to you, see that it is also read in the church of the Laodiceans and that you in turn read the letter from Laodicea"* (Col. 4:16). Likewise, Paul's letter to the Ephesians was surely copied and sent to other churches. And his letters have even come through the centuries to us and to believers all over the world.

It appears that Paul sent letters to the Colossians and the Ephesians via Tychicus, a fellow servant of Christ:

> [21] *Tychicus, the dear brother and faithful servant in the Lord, will tell you everything, so that you also may know how I am and what I am doing.* [22] *I am sending him to you for this very purpose, that you may know how we are, and that he may encourage you* (Eph. 6:21-22).

## B. Background of Ephesus and the Ephesian believers

**Q 5** *Why was Ephesus an important city for business?*

Pergamum was the capital of Asia, but Ephesus was the most important city there. It was located on the eastern shore of the Aegean Sea. Some say 200,000 to a third of a million lived in Ephesus. Others think the city had a population of half a million people.

**Figure 1.2    This marble street at Ephesus led past businesses to the harbor of the Aegean Sea.**

The biggest ships in the world came to Ephesus. Also, major roads ended in this city. Some researchers have dug up the main street of Ephesus. It was 36 feet (11 m) wide, 1,735 feet (529 m) long, and made of marble. The street ended at the sea. There were businesses and shops all along the main street.[3]

Ephesus was also famous for the temple of the Greek goddess *Artemis. It was four times bigger than the *Parthenon at Athens. Her temple was one of the seven wonders of the Old World. In all the earth, there was no other Greek temple so great. It was 425 feet (130 m) long, 220 feet (67 m) wide, and had 120 stone pillars that were each 60 feet (18 m) high. People traveled to Ephesus from all over the Roman Empire. There they bowed down to the idol of Artemis.

Some refer to Artemis by her Roman name, Diana. People worshiped her as the goddess of the moon. She was also linked with childbirth. Local craftsmen made statues of the goddess. These statues had many breasts. The Ephesians believed that men communicated with Artemis through the prostitutes in the temple.[4] Paul's preaching lessened the sale of idols. Recall the great riot in the city during Paul's ministry (Acts 19:23-41). Businessmen, such as Demetrius, became angry when people began to turn from Artemis to Jesus. Opposition to the gospel was never greater than at Ephesus. Paul learned many things on his first two trips. No doubt this prepared him for the spiritual warfare in Ephesus on his third trip. Remember that even apostles grow in grace.

Q 6 ⊼ How did the gospel affect the worship of Artemis in Ephesus?

**Figure 1.3   Ruins of the temple of Artemis (Diana) in Ephesus**

The Bible contains much related to Ephesus.

- Paul left Priscilla and Aquila to minister in Ephesus near the end of his second trip (Acts 18:18-19). There they taught Apollos, the great Jewish speaker (Acts 18:24-26).

- Later, Paul returned to Ephesus on his third trip. His greatest revival was there. Paul ministered 3 years in Ephesus—longer than in any other city (Acts 20:31). He preached the gospel in the synagogue, in the school of Tyrannus, in homes, and in the marketplaces (Acts 19).

Q 7 ⊼ Explain 3 things that happened in Ephesus on Paul's third missionary trip.

- Twelve disciples were baptized in the Holy Spirit in Ephesus (Acts 19:1-7). Demons were cast out of others. The sons of Sceva had a race on the marble street (See Figure 1.2). In contrast, the anointing on Paul was so great that handkerchiefs that had touched his body brought healing. Converts burned magic books worth enough money to pay 1,000 men for working 50 days. Did the smoke from these books fill the main street and enter the temple of Artemis?

- Timothy became the first pastor or overseer of Ephesus. Paul left him there and wrote to him later (1 Tim. 1:3).

Q 8 ⊼ Complete Figure 1.4, identifying 9 churches in a circle around Ephesus.

| Direction From Ephesus | Churches Paul Planted |
|---|---|
| East | |
| West | |
| Northwest | |

**Figure 1.4   Practice identifying nine churches that circled Ephesus.**

Ephesus was Paul's base of ministry for 3 years (Acts 19:8-10; 20:31). It was in the center of the churches that Paul planted. East of Ephesus were the Galatian churches of Pisidian Antioch, Iconium, Lystra, and Derbe. West of Ephesus, across the Aegean Sea, were Athens and Corinth. And northwest of Ephesus were the churches of Philippi, Thessalonica, and Berea. Thus Ephesus was like the hub of a wheel; it was the center of

Q 9 ⊼ How did Ephesus serve as a base for Paul's ministry?

God's strategy for a big area. *To Ephesus,* the churches sent messengers to Paul with questions or offerings. And *from Ephesus,* Paul sent letters to the churches he planted. Therefore, Ephesus became a new center for God's mission to the Gentiles. It was second only to Antioch, Syria as a base for Gentile missions.

Ephesus is truly one of the most important cities of the Bible. In Revelation, John wrote first to the church in Ephesus (Rev. 2:1-7).

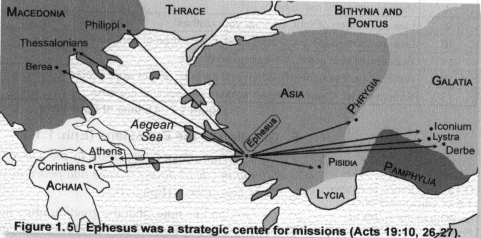

**Figure 1.5   Ephesus was a strategic center for missions (Acts 19:10, 26-27).**

## C. The purposes of Ephesians

**Q 10** *What is Paul's purpose in Ephesians 1–3?*

Paul's purposes in Ephesians are twofold: to clarify *doctrine* (Eph. 1–3) and *duty* (Eph. 4–6).

On *doctrine*, Paul begins by emphasizing that *in Christ* God has blessed believers with every spiritual blessing. Next, Paul explains the mystery hidden through the ages—that God's blessings are for both Jews and Gentiles, who become *one body in Christ*. We will explore this mystery in Ephesians 1–3.

**Figure 1.6   The rebuilt Celsus Library, next to the huge gates of the market at Ephesus**

On *duty*, Paul's purpose is to explain how Jews and Gentiles must reflect Christ—at home, at work, and in daily living. We will explore our response to Christ and our responsibilities in Ephesians 4–6.

**Q 11** *Doctrine without duty is a tree without _____. Duty without doctrine is a tree without _____.*

*Sabio* says: "Doctrine without duty is a tree without fruit. Duty without doctrine is a tree without root."

## D. Outline of Ephesians

**Q 12** *Which chapters in Ephesians emphasize our response to all God has done for us in Christ?*

The theme of Christ's provision and our responsibility dominates Ephesians. Ephesians 1–3 emphasizes *what* Christ did. Ephesians 4–6 stresses *so what* and *now what*—our response and responsibilities.

| Lessons | Topics | Ephesians |
|---|---|---|
| 1 | Greeting | 1:1-2 |
| | **I.  Doctrine: Our Riches in Christ** | **1–3** |
| 2 | Our spiritual blessings in Christ | 1:3-14 |
| 3 | Paul's first prayer: For believers to discern God's purpose | 1:15-23 |
| 4 | Our spiritual position: Made alive in Christ | 2:1-10 |
| 5 | Our spiritual position: Made one in Christ | 2:11-22 |
| 6 | Paul's ministry of the mystery of Christ | 3:1-13 |
| 7 | Paul's second prayer: For believers to fulfill God's purpose | 3:14-21 |
| | **II.  Duty: Our Responsibilities in Christ** | **4–6** |
| 8 | Walk in unity and maturity. | 4:1-16 |
| 9 | Live as children of light: Change your clothes! | 4:17-32 |
| 10 | Live as children of light: Imitate God, not children of darkness. | 5:1-20 |
| 11 | Reflect Christ at home: Wives and husbands | 5:21-33 |
| 12 | Reflect Christ at home: Children and parents; and at work: Workers and employers | 6:1-9 |
| 13 | Reflect Christ at war: Christian soldiers and spiritual enemies | 6:10-24 |

**Figure 1.7   Outline of Ephesians**

## E. Greeting to the Ephesians (Eph. 1:1-2)

*¹Paul, an apostle of Christ Jesus by the will of God, To the saints in Ephesus, the faithful in Christ Jesus: ²Grace and peace to you from God our Father and the Lord Jesus Christ* (Eph. 1:1-2).

**Q 13** *Complete Figure 1.8 as you study Paul's greeting to the saints at Ephesus.*

Dr. Gordon Fee notes that the greeting often hints at what is ahead in the letter. Let us look at some key topics Paul introduces in his greeting, Ephesians 1:1-2.

| Key Words and Phrases | Your Explanations and Comments |
|---|---|
| *Paul, an apostle* | |
| *saints, the faithful in Christ* | |
| *in Christ* | |
| *Grace and peace* | |
| *God our Father and the Lord Jesus Christ* | |

**Figure 1.8   Practice explaining key words and phrases in the introduction of Ephesians.**

- *"Paul, an apostle of Christ Jesus by the will of God."* These words identify Paul as the author of the letter to the Ephesians. He refers to himself as an apostle, *one sent by God*, to emphasize his authority. Believers should accept and obey his words, because he is an apostle sent by Christ. Apostles, like all of God's leaders, do not choose themselves. Rather, true apostles come only through *the will of God.* No person should take the honor of ministry upon himself (Heb. 5:4). God alone selects and calls true ministers—so we should pay attention to them.

- *"The saints in Ephesus, the faithful in Christ Jesus"* includes Jews and Gentiles (Acts 19). The word *saints* means "the holy." *Saints* are not perfect, but we are those who have become God's children, through repentance and a living relationship with Jesus Christ by faith. As small children mature into adults, *saints* grow in grace. And saints are *"faithful in Christ"*—*faithful* stewards of His grace, and *faithful* to practice His teachings. Paul will give many guidelines to help the *saints* at Ephesus mature in Christ (Eph. 4–6). And God's apostle will explain that Jesus unites all saints, Jews and Gentiles, into one body (Eph. 1–3).

- \**"In Christ"* is a key phrase for Paul. Jesus Christ is the boundary and sphere of God's plan of redemption. Christ is the door through which we enter the family of God. He is the Lamb who makes our redemption possible. We are acceptable to God as we abide in Christ. He is the vine, and we are the branches. He is the head to which all believers in the body are connected (Eph. 4:15). *In Christ* occurs seven times in Ephesians and over 160 times in Paul's 13 letters. *In Christ* and *in Him* are the key phrases of Ephesians 1:1-2, the focus of Ephesians 1:3-17. Throughout Ephesians, and all of Paul's letters, praise overflows for what God has done for us *in Christ.*[5]

- *"Grace and peace to you."* *Grace* is the Greek greeting and *peace* is the Hebrew greeting, so Paul is greeting both Gentiles and Jews. In all of Paul's letters, and in all of life, *grace* precedes *peace.* *Grace* is the love, mercy, kindness, and favor God gives us in Christ. *Peace*, with the biblical background of *shalom*, means "the absence of strife, the presence of God, and His provision for our needs." Grace is the root and peace is the fruit of our salvation. Grace is the foundation for the house of peace. Because of the grace God freely offers us, we can have peace with God and each other. We can only discover the peace of God when we accept the grace of God in Christ.

- *"From God our Father and the Lord Jesus Christ"* (Eph. 1:2). *Grace and peace* come to us from *God our Father and the Lord Jesus Christ.* Throughout Ephesians, Paul is \*Trinitarian—that is, he emphasizes that the Father, Son, and Holy Spirit are equal; and they work together to provide our salvation. In Ephesians 1:2, Paul mentions the Father and the Son. We will see the full Trinity in action in our next lesson (Eph. 1:3-14).

## Our Spiritual Blessings "in Christ"—Part 1 (Eph. 1:3-14)

**Goal A:** *Clarify the roles of the Father, Son, and Spirit in providing salvation.*
**Goal B:** *Explain and illustrate blessings 1–4 that we have in Christ (Eph. 1:3-8).*

In the Greek text, Ephesians 1:3-14 is one sentence of 202 words! Take a deep breath and try to read this sentence out loud. It is truly breathtaking! In Ephesians 1:3-14 Paul overflows with praise—for the eight blessings God has poured out on us in Christ. This long sentence is like a great waterfall of blessings, with praise splashing up to God.

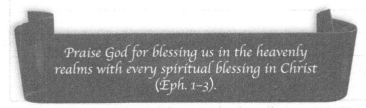

*Praise God for blessing us in the heavenly realms with every spiritual blessing in Christ (Eph. 1–3).*

**Figure 1.9**
**The banner over Ephesians 1–3 is praise for the spiritual blessings God has given Jews and Gentiles in Christ.**

**Q 14** ✎ *In Ephesians 1:3-14, how many times does Paul write "in Christ" or "in Him"? Underline them.*

**Q 15** ↗ *How is Ephesians 1:3-14 like a waterfall that flows down and splahes up?*

³*Praise be to the God and Father of our Lord Jesus Christ, who has blessed us in the heavenly realms with every spiritual blessing in Christ.* ⁴*For he chose us in him before the creation of the world to be holy and blameless in his sight.*

*In love* ⁵*he predestined us to be adopted as his sons through Jesus Christ, in accordance with his pleasure and will—* ⁶*to the praise of his glorious grace, which he has freely given us in the One he loves.*

**Figure 1.10    Ephesians 1:3-14 is like a great waterfall of blessings with praise splashing up to God.**

⁷*In him we have redemption through his blood, the forgiveness of sins, in accordance with the riches of God's grace* ⁸*that he lavished on us with all wisdom and understanding.*

⁹*And he made known to us the mystery of his will according to his good pleasure, which he purposed in Christ,* ¹⁰*to be put into effect when the times will have reached their fulfillment—to bring all things in heaven and on earth together under one head, even Christ.*

¹¹*In him we were also chosen, having been predestined according to the plan of him who works out everything in conformity with the purpose of his will,* ¹²*in order that we, who were the first to hope in Christ, might be for the praise of his glory.*

¹³*And you also were included in Christ when you heard the word of truth, the gospel of your salvation. Having believed, you were marked in him with a seal, the promised Holy Spirit,* ¹⁴*who is a deposit guaranteeing our inheritance until the redemption of those who are God's possession—to the praise of his glory* (Eph. 1:3-14).

| Source of Blessings | Blessings in Christ | Eph. 1 |
|---|---|---|
| **God the Father** | A. God blessed us in the heavenly realms with every spiritual blessing in Christ. | 1:3 |
| | B. God chose us to be holy and blameless in Christ. | 1:4 |
| | C. God predestined us to be adopted as His children through Christ. | 1:5-6 |

Figure 1.11    Continued on following page

Continued from previous page

| Source of Blessings | Blessings in Christ | Eph. 1 |
|---|---|---|
| | D. Jesus redeemed us through His blood, providing forgiveness. | 1:7-8 |
| God the Son | E. God revealed Jesus to us as the head over all things in heaven and on earth. | 1:9-10 |
| | F. Jesus is the One *in whom* we are chosen. Our salvation is *in Christ*. Our hope is *in Christ*. | 1:11-13a |
| God the Holy Spirit | G. The Holy Spirit is the *seal which shows that we belong to God. | 1:13b |
| | H. The Holy Spirit is the *deposit that guarantees our inheritance. | 1:14 |

**Figure 1.11   The entire Trinity unites to provide our salvation.**

After greeting the Ephesians, Paul bursts into praise for all of the blessings God has given us (Eph. 1:3-14). Many scholars note that this passage is a spiritual song with three parts (Figure 1.11). Each part emphasizes one member of the Trinity. And each part ends with a chorus such as, *"to the praise of his glorious grace"* (Eph. 1:6, 12, 14).

**Q 16** *In Figure 1.12, summarize the blessings that each member of the Trinity provides for our salvation.*

| Source of Blessings | Blessings in Christ | Eph. 1 |
|---|---|---|
| | A. | 1:3 |
| God the Father | B. | 1:4 |
| | C. | 1:5-6 |
| | D. | 1:7-8 |
| God the Son | E. | 1:9-10 |
| | F. | 1:11-13a |
| God the Holy Spirit | G. | 1:13b |
| | H. | 1:14 |

**Figure 1.12   Practice summarizing the blessings that the entire Trinity provides for our salvation.**

## A. God blessed us in the heavenly realms with great wealth—every spiritual blessing in Christ (Eph. 1:3).

³*Praise be to the God and Father of our Lord Jesus Christ, who has blessed us in the heavenly realms with every spiritual blessing in Christ* (Eph. 1:3).

We could title a sermon on Ephesians 1:3-14, "God's Wealthy Family." For this epistle speaks to us about the riches we have *in Christ*.

*Sabio* says: "Those who have Christ have everything. But those without Christ have nothing."

**Q 17** *In Ephesians, chapters _____ are about our wealth in Christ, and _____ are about our walk in Christ.*

If you visited Ephesus today, you would find a dead city. But the letter Paul wrote to the Ephesians lives. We could call the letter to the Ephesians "The wealth and the walk of believers." That is a good summary of the book, because in chapters 1–3 Paul writes about our wealth in Christ. And in chapters 4–6 he talks about our walk in the Lord.

We really need to understand our wealth in Christ before we talk about our walk. For if we try to live the Christian life *without* first appreciating who we are and what we have in Christ, we will not walk well. The enemy's strategy is to rob us of understanding

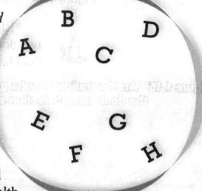

**Figure 1.13   In Ephesians 1:3-14 praise overflows for eight blessings God has poured out on us in Christ. In this lesson we will examine each of these eight blessings, A–H.**

**Q 18** *Why is it important to understand our wealth in Christ <u>before</u> we study our walk in Christ?*

our wealth in Christ so that we live poorly rather than richly. His strategy is to deceive us in our walk so that we do not walk in righteousness with God. Ephesians tells us how to live in God's wealth, and how to walk in the Lord's steps. Ephesians 1:3-14 reveals that God calls us to be a wealthy church—not necessarily wealthy in finances. But when we are wealthy, we have something to share with others. And Paul explains that we are to be wealthy in love, wealthy in the grace of God, wealthy in forgiveness, wealthy in healing, wealthy in compassion, wealthy in serving. We are wealthy in God— *"who has blessed us in the heavenly realms with every spiritual blessing in Christ"* (Eph. 1:3). So let us live as the spiritually rich: generous to our brothers and sisters in Christ, and sharing our faith with those outside the family of God.[6]

**Q 19** *Are all believers on earth wealthy? Explain.*

The Bible sometimes contrasts the earthly and the heavenly status of believers. God *"has blessed us in the heavenly realms with every spiritual blessing in Christ."* Yet, on earth we lack many of the blessings of those who are rich in this world. Peter said to the cripple, [6]" *'Silver or gold I do not have, but what I have I give you. In the name of Jesus Christ of Nazareth, walk.'* [7]*Taking him by the right hand, he helped him up, and instantly the man's feet and ankles became strong"* (Acts 3:6-7). We may lack earthly resources, but in Christ, we have more to offer than those with only money. Paul referred to himself as *"sorrowful, yet always rejoicing; poor, yet making many rich; having nothing, and yet possessing everything"* (2 Cor. 6:10). And Jesus said to the suffering church at Smyrna, *"I know your afflictions and your poverty—yet you are rich"* (Rev. 2:9). So although we may be poor by earthly standards, let us keep looking up. *"Do not be afraid, little flock, for your Father has been pleased to give you the kingdom"* (Luke 12:32).

**Q 20** *Complete Figure 1.14, answering questions on the ship illustration.*

## B  God chose us in Christ to be holy and blameless (Eph. 1:4).

[4]*For he chose us in him before the creation of the world to be holy and blameless in his sight* (Eph. 1:4).

| Aspects | Questions to Answer |
|---|---|
| The ship | What does the ship represent? Who chose the ship and bought it? |
| The Captain | Who is the Captain of the ship? |
| The passengers | Who can get on the ship? How are people elected/chosen to get on the ship? How much is the fare? Can people get off the ship? |
| Destination | Where is the ship predestined to go? |

**Figure 1.14   Practice answering questions about election and predestination.**

*Election and *predestination are important topics in Scripture. To understand these two doctrines, consider a great ship on its way to heaven. The ship represents the Church. God has chosen (elected) the ship. And He bought it to be His own possession. Christ is

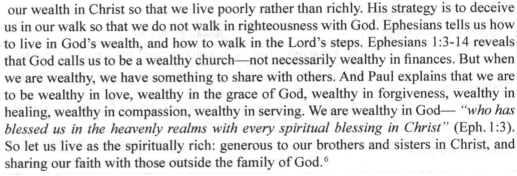

**Figure 1.15   An illustration about a great ship helps us understand the doctrines of election and predestination.**

the Captain of the ship. No one can pay to ride this ship. But all are welcome free. The only condition to come onto the ship is to be a friend of the Captain. As people develop a personal relationship with the Captain, they are chosen (elected) to come onto the ship. As long as people are on the ship, in a good relationship with the Captain, they are among the elect—the chosen. But if they choose to abandon the ship and its Captain, they cease to be part of the elect. Election is always in connection with the Captain and His ship. Predestination tells us about the ship's destination, and what God has prepared for those who remain on it. God has predestined all who receive Christ to be conformed to the Captain (Rom. 8:29). Likewise, God has predestined all who remain on the ship to reach heaven and receive the inheritance He planned (Eph. 1:14). God invites everyone to come onto the ship, through faith in and submission to the Captain.[7]

In Luke 15 read the parables of the lost coin, the lost sheep, and the lost son. These three parables illustrate one theme: There is joy in heaven when one sinner repents (Luke 15:7, 10, 32). All heaven rejoices when one sinner—of any age, from any nation— repents and agrees to what God has planned for humanity.

Why did God choose us to be in Christ? Paul emphasizes that God chose us to be *"holy and blameless in Christ"* (Eph. 1:4). Throughout his writings Paul explains that we are holy and blameless in three ways: in our position, in our actions, and in our condition. So Scripture refers to us as *saints*—based on the Greek word *hagios,* which means "the holy" (Eph. 1:1; Phil. 1:1; Col. 1:2). (Pronounce *hagios:* **haa**-gee-aas)

Q 21 ✎ *Complete Figure 1.16, explaining 3 ways we are holy and blameless in Christ.*

| Aspects of Holiness | Your Explanations |
|---|---|
| Position | |
| Actions | |
| Condition | |

Figure 1.16    Practice explaining three ways we are holy and blameless in Christ (Eph. 1:4).

## C. God predestined us to be adopted as His children through Jesus Christ (Eph. 1:5-6).

*In love ⁵He predestined us to be adopted as his sons through Jesus Christ, in accordance with his pleasure and will— ⁶to the praise of his glorious grace, which he has freely given us in the One he loves* (Eph. 1:5-6).

Notice that Ephesians 1:4 ends with the word *in love,* which connects verse 4 and 5. Recall that all of Ephesians 1:3-14 is just one sentence in the Greek. God loves the whole world. He loves every person in every nation. Our Heavenly Father has opened His arms wide, inviting everyone to become members of His family. He wants everyone to receive the full inheritance He offers to share with all people. As Paul wrote, God *wants all* to be saved (1 Tim. 2:4), so He gave His Son as a *ransom for all* (1 Tim. 2:6). As the sun shines on all people, the love of God radiates to every human. His plan includes everyone who will accept Christ as Savior and Lord.

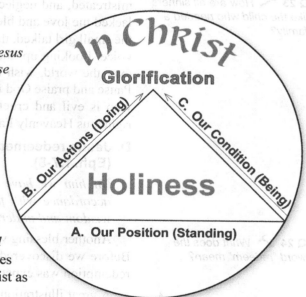

Figure 1.17   There are three aspects or sides of holiness in Christ.

Q 22 ✎ *Complete Figure 1.18, answering questions about adoption.*

For a fuller explanation of the three aspects of our holiness in Christ, see the *Faith & Action* course *Romans & Galatians,* Figure 5.4.

| Aspects of Adoption | Questions to Answer |
|---|---|
| Scope/width | Whom does God love and want to adopt? Explain and illustrate. |
| Background | Who could be adopted in Paul's day? |
| Meaning | What is adoption? |
| Method | How does the blessing of adoption come? |
| Purpose | What is a purpose of adoption? |
| Privileges | What are the privileges of adoption? |

Figure 1.18   Practice explaining adoption (Eph. 1:4).

The blessing God planned before the creation of the world is to adopt all as His children. *Adoption in the ancient world was used in a broad sense. Adoption included legally accepting a child as your own, who was not yours at birth. Slaves could also be adopted. Adoption is the legal process of bringing a person into a family—and giving that person all the status and privileges of sons and daughters who were born in the family. Adoption meant: to receive and place as a son (Rom. 8:15-17, 23; Gal. 4:1-7).[8]

How does the blessing of adoption come? Paul says adoption comes in the Father's love, through Jesus Christ—by God's pleasure and will, freely.

What purpose of adoption does Paul mention in Ephesians 1:6? That all will praise God for His glorious grace (Eph. 1:6). Through *adoption*, those who were once referred to as *children of wrath and disobedience* become *children of God* (Eph. 2:1-3; 5:6; Col. 3:6)!

A child has certain privileges. But wise parents know when children should receive their full inheritance. God in His love has already insured our inheritance through the deposit of the Holy Spirit in us. In Christ we are predestined to receive all the rights and privileges of God's children! Even now we enjoy many of the benefits of adoption, such as knowing God our Father—enjoying His love, peace, fellowship, and provision (Rom. 8:15-17, 23; Gal. 4:1-7).

**Q 23** *How are all sinners like the child who needed a family?*

Our daughter, Cheryti, and son-in law, Shawn, have adopted five children.[†] Cheryti works with the government to help families adopt children who have been abandoned, abused, or orphaned. Once she was counseling a child whom the government had sent to her. The child's parents did not care for her well. This child was poor, abused, mistreated, and neglected. She was raised in a home stained by many sins. The child lacked the love and blessings God planned to provide through a family. As Cheryti and the small girl talked, this child noticed the love in Cheryti's eyes and the kindness in her voice. Looking up, the child asked, "Would you be my mommy?" Many children, all over the world, wish they could have at least one parent who loves and wants them. Pause and praise God for adopting you. Give thanks that you no longer belong to Satan, who is evil and cruel. Rather, you have become the child of our loving, holy, and righteous Heavenly Father. Adopted! Praise the Lord!

### D. Jesus redeemed us through His blood, providing forgiveness (Eph. 1:7-8).

[7]*In him we have redemption through his blood, the forgiveness of sins, in accordance with the riches of God's grace* [8]*that he lavished on us with all wisdom and understanding* (Eph. 1:7-8).

**Q 24** *What does the word "redeem" mean?*

Another blessing we have in Christ is redemption. To *redeem* means "to buy back." Before we discovered freedom in Christ we were slaves of self, sin, and Satan. This redemption was expensive—it cost Jesus His life (1 Pet. 1:18-19)!

**Q 25** *How does the account of Hosea and Gomer illustrate redemption? Summarize the story.*

A great illustration of redemption is in the book of Hosea. This prophet lived in the final days of the Northern Kingdom of Israel in the 8th century B.C. These were dark and tragic times. Israel had turned away from God and was disobeying Him through sins such as cursing, lying, stealing, adultery, murder, and social injustice (Hos. 4:1-2). God commanded the holy prophet Hosea to marry a harlot named Gomer. This marriage represented the union of the holy God to the unfaithful nation of Israel. Even the names of their three children described the sad state of Isreal. After a few years of marriage, Gomer left, and eventually became a slave. Yet, showing compassion, Hosea redeemed Gomer, buying her at an auction of slaves (Hos. 3:1-5). Likewise, we have all disobeyed God, gone astray, and became slaves of sin. Yet the Lord has not dealt with us according to our sins. Rather, by His love and grace, He has redeemed us with the blood of Christ, forgiven our transgressions, and adopted us into His family.

**Q 26** *In what ways were you in slavery before you found freedom in Christ?*

Most of us have no idea what it would be like to be a slave—in bondage, without rights, without hope, and shown no mercy. Yet sin and Satan enslave millions with

---

†Cheryti is the daughter of Quentin and Elizabeth McGhee.

the same sad results. Jesus redeems, frees, and forgives us. What a blessing—such wonderful news!

## Lesson 3 — Our Spiritual Blessings "in Christ"—Part 2 (Eph. 1:9-14)

**Goal C:** *Explain and illustrate blessings 5–8 that we have in Christ (Eph. 1:9-14).*

**Q 27** ✎ *Summarize the four blessings in Christ (A–D) that you studied in Lesson 2.*

| Source of Blessings | | Blessings in Christ | Eph. 1 |
|---|---|---|---|
| God the Father | **A.** | | 1:3 |
| | **B.** | | 1:4 |
| | **C.** | | 1:5-6 |
| God the Son | **D.** | | 1:7-8 |
| | **E.** | | 1:9-10 |
| | **F.** | | 1:11-13a |
| God the Holy Spirit | **G.** | | 1:13b |
| | **H.** | | 1:14 |

**Figure 1.19   Practice summarizing the blessings that the entire Trinity provides for our salvation.**

### E. God revealed Jesus to us as the head over all things in heaven and on earth (Eph. 1:9-10).

⁹*And he made known to us the **mystery** of his will according to his good pleasure, which he purposed in Christ, ¹⁰to be put into effect when the times will have reached their fulfillment—to bring all things in heaven and on earth together under one head, even Christ (Eph. 1:9-10).*

Paul uses the word *mystery* as a secret—unknown in the past, but now revealed. In Ephesians 3:1-13 we will study the *mystery* of God bringing Jews and Gentiles together in one body, the Church, under Christ the head. But here in Ephesians 1:9-10, Paul soars into the heavens, using the word *mystery* in its broadest sense. On earth, creation groans in bondage to the problems of sin and chaos (Rom. 8:21). The *mystery* religions of Paul's time sought to discover the unifying principle of the cosmos. John reveals Christ as the *Logos,* the source and ruler of creation who became flesh so we could become God's children (John 1:1-18). In a similar way, Paul declares that God's mysterious plan is to exalt Christ as the Redeemer and Ruler over *"all things in heaven and on earth"* (Eph. 1:10). To the mind without God, life does not make sense. The natural mind does not understand the purpose of living, the struggle between good and evil, the wars, famines, hunger, and suffering on earth—all of these are a mystery to the carnal mind. As Solomon wrote, life under the sun, without God, is as meaningless as chasing the wind (Eccl. 1:14). Likewise, the world religions apart from Christianity are the empty story of people trying to save themselves by climbing ladders made by human hands. In contrast, in Christ, God takes the first step, offering salvation to us freely, rather than by our own efforts. And when Jesus returns, He will judge Satan, fallen angels, and sinners. God will reveal our full salvation, in His own time, and unite all the universe under

**Q 28** ↗ *What does Paul mean by "mystery"? What mystery will we study in Ephesians 3:1-13?*

**Q 29** ✎ *How does Paul use the word "mystery" in a broad way in Ephesians 1:9-10?*

**Q 30** ✎ *How is Christ the answer to what the religions of the world are seeking?*

Christ.[9] Christ, as the Creator and Ruler of all creation, is the One who came to bring harmony, love, and unity to the world and the universe.

Many people struggle to make sense of life. They are like King Solomon who tried everything without finding happiness in anything. For those who do not know God, life can be empty and meaningless. But God is the beginning and the end. He sent His Son to redeem us. And He will once again send His Son, when the time is right, to fulfill His plan for all of creation. Jesus is the One through whom God holds everything together (Col. 1:17). And He is the One who will redeem, restore, and unite the universe—according to God's will and good pleasure—*when the times will have reached their fulfillment*. So let us—the children of God—worship Him, submit to Him, and lean back in His promises and plan as we would rest in a comfortable chair.

*Q 31  How does Jesus fill your life with purpose, praise, and hope?*

> [15]*He is the image of the invisible God, the firstborn over all creation.* [16]*For by him all things were created: things in heaven and on earth, visible and invisible, whether thrones or powers or rulers or authorities; all things were created by him and for him.* [17]*He is before all things, and in him all things hold together.* [18]*And he is the head of the body, the church; he is the beginning and the firstborn from among the dead, so that in everything he might have the supremacy.* [19]**For God was pleased to have all his fullness dwell in him,** [20]**and through him to reconcile to himself all things, whether things on earth or things in heaven, by making peace through his blood, shed on the cross** (Col. 1:15-20).

### F.  Jesus is the One in whom we are chosen (Eph. 1:11-13a).

> [11]*In him we were also chosen, having been predestined according to the plan of him who works out everything in conformity with the purpose of his will,* [12]*in order that we, who were the first to hope in Christ,* **might be for the praise of his glory.** [13]*And you also were included in Christ when you heard the word of truth, the gospel of your salvation* (Eph. 1:11-13a).

*Q 32  In Ephesians 1:12, who was the first to hope in Christ—Jews or Gentiles?*

Paul continues to praise God for one blessing on top of another *in Christ*. His words remind us of the prologue of John's Gospel, where he writes about Jesus saying, *"From the fullness of His grace we have all received one blessing after another"* (John 1:16).

*Q 33  When were we chosen and included in God's plan? Explain.*

In point B of this lesson, we studied the blessing that God *"chose us in Christ to be holy and blameless"* (Eph. 1:4). Paul underlines this blessing again here in Ephesians 1:11-13, worshiping God for including Jews *and* Gentiles. Also note that here Paul explains more about God's purpose. Our Father chose us *to be holy and blameless in Christ* (Eph. 1:4), and *to be the praise of His glory* (Eph. 1:13). Later in this letter Paul will explain more about how the Church reflects the glory of God.

*Q 34  What are some purposes that led God to choose us to be in Christ (Eph. 1:4, 11-12)?*

In Ephesians 3:10, Paul explains the mystery of Jews and Gentiles being heirs together of the grace and riches of God. Paul writes:

> [10]*His intent was that now, through the church,* **the manifold wisdom of God should be made known to the rulers and authorities in the heavenly realms,** [11]*according to his eternal purpose which he accomplished in Christ Jesus our Lord* (Eph. 3:10-11).

*Q 35  What are some ways that you and your church bring praise and glory to God?*

On earth, the Church is the light of the world. And in the heavenly realms, the Church displays the wisdom of God to good and bad angels. So as we live day by day, let us remember that God chose us to display and reveal His glory in all we say and do. We are living letters from Christ to all people (2 Cor. 3:1-6) and even angels (Eph. 3:10-11).

How has this blessing of being chosen to reflect God's glory come to us? It has come *"according to the plan of him who works out everything in conformity with the purpose of his will"* (Eph. 1:11). God is sovereign—He is in control. He works out all things for His purpose and plan. So when life does not seem to make sense, continue to trust in God.

God is building His Church. Our few years on earth are like the mist that appears for a moment and then passes away (James 4:14). Our life is like a shadow that lasts only a few hours (Job 14:2). A thousand years of time on earth is like a day on the Lord's calendar (2 Pet. 3:8). And throughout eternity the Church will reflect God's glory (Eph. 1:12).

A beautiful painting is more than one color. It is a combination of many colors, painted by the hand of a skillful artist. God is the master painter. He is the One who paints the rainbow across the heavens. And in the Church, He is blending together the redeemed of all ages—from every age, race, and culture—to reflect His glory. Even now the glory of God shines through His Church (Eph. 3:8-11; 5:27). And the body of Christ will radiate God's glory in all its fullness, as this age on earth fades and the age to come reveals the full inheritance of the children of God.

**Q 36** ➤ *How is the Church like a beautiful painting?*

## G. The Holy Spirit is the seal showing we belong to God (Eph. 1:13b).

¹³*And you also were included in Christ when you heard the word of truth, the gospel of your salvation. Having believed, you were marked in him with a seal, the promised Holy Spirit* (Eph. 1:13).

**Figure 1.20**
In ancient times kings, government rulers, and each family had seals and signet rings that represented them. To show that a letter or document was official, people poured hot wax on the bottom of the document, or rolled it up and poured hot wax on the seam. Then they pressed their ring into the hot wax, to show the letter or document belonged to them.

In ancient times, seals were the highest form and proof of ownership. In Old Testament days, kings over nations and vast kingdoms pressed their signet rings into the hot wax on a document to show that it was official. A king's seal on a letter revealed that the power of the government was connected to the letter or law. Haman pressed the king's seal onto a document that made it legal to kill Jews and seize their property on a certain day (Esther 3:10-13). Roman Caesars sealed documents to show that the law of the kingdom flowed through the writing on a scroll or paper.

**Q 37** ➤ *What does Paul mean by the "seal" of the Holy Spirit (Eph. 1:13)?*

**Q 38** ➤ *How are seals used in the place where you live?*

**Q 39** ➤ *What hope and confidence do you have because of God's seal on you?*

**Q 40** ➤ *Complete Figure 1.21, summarizing key verses on the use of seals and signets in the Bible.*

| Reference | Your Summaries of Verses About Seals and Signet Rings That Showed Official Ownership |
|---|---|
| Gen. 38:18 | |
| Gen. 41:41-42 | |
| Exod. 39:14 | |

Figure1.21     Continued on following page

Continued from previous page

| Reference | Your Summaries of Verses About Seals and Signet Rings that Showed Official Ownership |
|---|---|
| Esther 3:10-13 | |
| Esther 8:2 | |
| Jer. 22:24-27 | |
| Dan. 6:17 | |
| Eph. 1:13 | |
| 2 Cor. 1:22 | |
| 2 Cor. 5:5 | |
| Rev. 5:1; 6:1 | |

**Figure 1.21    Practice summarizing verses about seals and signet rings that showed official ownership.**

Today, many still use seals to show that a certificate or contract is official and legal. But the use of seals for legal purposes is less common these days, so we believers can miss the deep meaning of Ephesians 1:13. Yet in this verse Paul is declaring that the Holy Spirit in us is the seal of Almighty God that we belong to Him. The presence of the Holy Spirit in us is precious and sobering. The Spirit in us shows that God has bought and redeemed us through the blood of Jesus. He has taken possession of us. The Spirit in us shows that we are officially the children of God, adopted into His family. This grand assurance of the Spirit's seal is at the peak of Paul's praise. Do not miss the significance of God's seal upon each true believer. Later in this letter, Paul will insist that we walk worthy of the King who has poured out all spiritual blessings on us in Christ. "Love so amazing, so divine, demands my soul, my life, my all."[10] Let us ponder this amazing truth and worship our Father in heaven. God wanted us so much that He gave His only Son to take us as His official possession forever, and share His glory and kingdom with us. Stand up straight. Lift up your head. Revel in the truth that God is proud to seal you as His own. Be thankful and act thankful. We are the children of the King of kings, and His seal is in and on us so that all will know we belong to Him.

**Q 41** ↗ *What does God's seal on you reveal? How must it affect your behavior?*

[19]*Do you not know that your body is a temple of the Holy Spirit, who is in you, whom you have received from God? You are not your own;* [20]*you were bought at a price. Therefore honor God with your body* (1 Cor. 6:19-20).

### H. The Holy Spirit is the deposit that guarantees our inheritance (Eph. 1:14).

[13]*And you also were included in Christ when you heard the word of truth, the gospel of your salvation. Having believed, you were marked in him with a seal, the promised Holy Spirit,* [14]***who is a deposit guaranteeing our inheritance until the redemption of those who are God's possession—to the praise of his glory.***

Ephesians 1:14 includes at least three key words: *deposit, inheritance,* and *possession.* Let us look at each of these three words.

**Q 42** ↗ *What is the purpose of a deposit? What deposit has God put in us?*

The Holy Spirit in us is a **deposit**—a down payment that guarantees we will receive our full inheritance *in Christ* (Rom. 8:15-17). God has big plans for us. He delights to share Himself and His kingdom with us. In this present age, we do not receive our full inheritance. Yet even now, God has given us a deposit, the Holy Spirit, to guarantee that He will fulfill all He has promised us in Christ.

**Q 43** ↖ *What are some of the things we will receive in our full inheritance?*

A deposit is not the full amount. Rather, it is just a small part of what someone is to receive. In many nations, if people want to buy a house, they enter into a contract and pay a deposit of about 5 percent of the amount the seller will receive. When the contract is complete, the seller who received the deposit receives the other 95 percent that the buyer pays. Paul uses the earthly concept of a deposit to emphasize that God is sincere. He has promised to give Himself to us in a relationship forever. He has promised to give us a new body, a new home, new joy, awesome fellowship, and a glorious relationship with Him for eternity. He has promised to come back and take us to heaven. The best is eschatological—yet to come! Even now though, to guarantee our future, God has given us the *deposit* of His Spirit within us.

The deposit, who is the Holy Spirit, assures our **inheritance**. Throughout the Bible, there is a great emphasis on inheritance. Parents leave an inheritance for their children as Abraham left all he had to Isaac. God's plan was for Israel to inherit the land of Canaan. Since many of the Israelites were unfaithful to God, they died in the wilderness and did not inherit the land that flowed with milk and honey. The history of Israel is a solemn warning that our inheritance depends on our faith and faithfulness to God (Heb. 3:6–4:14). Still, God gave the inheritance of the Promised Land to the children of the Israelites who died in the wilderness. The twelve tribes of Israel enjoyed the inheritance of Canaan from the time of Joshua (1400 B.C.) to the captivity of Judah (about 600 B.C.). And a small remnant returned to live in Canaan after the captivity. Today, there are about 12 million Jews who live in Israel. But the glory of Israel's inheritance has faded greatly since the days of kings such as David and Solomon. In contrast, God promises those in Christ an inheritance that will never fade (Eph. 1:11, 14; 1 Pet. 1:4).

**Figure 1.22 Some Israelites enjoyed the inheritance of Canaan from the time of Joshua through the kings.**

**Q 44** Complete Figure 1.23, summarizing verses about the inheritance God has promised to give those who overcome the world through following Christ in faith.

| Reference | Your Summaries of Verses About the Inheritance of God's Children |
|---|---|
| Luke 12:32 | |
| 1 Cor. 6:9-10 | |
| Gal. 5:19-21 | |
| Eph. 1:11, 14 | |
| 1 Pet. 1:4 | |
| Rev. 21:7-9 | |

**Figure 1.23   Practice summarizing verses about the inheritance God has promised to His children.**

Ephesians 1:14 contrasts the *inheritance* we receive from God and the **possession** God receives—which is us, the people He has redeemed through Christ. We are God's possession. He owns us, and He has put His seal upon us. Some scholars want to interpret Ephesians 1:13-14 to mean that we are the inheritance that God receives—but this is *out of harmony* with the way the New Testament uses the word *inheritance*.[11] Paul is emphasizing that God gives us an inheritance in Christ, and He receives us as His possession. God has given us the deposit of our inheritance—the Holy Spirit; and He will give us our complete inheritance. Although our inheritance involves a home in heaven and great riches, the emphasis is on relationship. God gives us Himself, beginning with the deposit of the Holy Spirit. He becomes our God, and we become His people.

**Q 45** Who receives an inheritance, us or God? Explain.

**Q 46** Are you growing and maturing in your relationship with Christ? Explain.

**Summary.**   Paul's heart overflows with praise as he thinks of all the rich, wonderful blessings of God "in Christ!" Paul's list of eight blessings is not a complete list, but it mentions some wonderful things God provides. The fact is, God has blessed His people with *every* blessing we can ever imagine in Christ Jesus (Eph. 1:3; 3:20)! Reflect on each of these wonderful blessings! No amount of money or effort can provide them. God graciously gives them to every believer "in Christ!" The key—the secret—is knowing and abiding in Christ! *"In him are hidden all the treasures of wisdom and knowledge"* (Col. 2:3).

**Q 47** ↘ *Summarize the eight blessings in Christ (A–H) that you studied in Lessons 2 and 3.*

| Source of Blessings | Blessings in Christ | Eph. 1 |
|---|---|---|
| God the Father | A. | 1:3 |
| | B. | 1:4 |
| | C. | 1:5-6 |
| God the Son | D. | 1:7-8 |
| | E. | 1:9-10 |
| | F. | 1:11-13a |
| God the Holy Spirit | G. | 1:13b |
| | H. | 1:14 |

**Figure 1.24    Practice summarizing the blessings that the entire Trinity provides for our salvation.**

## Lesson 4  Paul's First Prayer for the Ephesians: For Believers to Discern God's Purpose (Eph. 1:15-23)

**Goal:** *Explain, illustrate, and apply 3 aspects of Paul's prayer for believers (Eph. 1:15-23).*

¹⁵*For this reason, ever since I heard about your faith in the Lord Jesus and your love for all the saints,*

¹⁶*I have not stopped giving thanks for you, remembering you in my prayers.* ¹⁷*I keep asking that the God of our Lord Jesus Christ, the glorious Father, may give you the Spirit of wisdom and revelation, so that you may* **know him better**.

¹⁸*I pray also that the eyes of your heart may be enlightened in order that you may* **know the hope** *to which he has called you,* [know] *the riches of his glorious inheritance in the saints,*

¹⁹*and* [know] **his incomparably great power for us who believe**. *That power is like the working of his mighty strength,* ²⁰*which he exerted in Christ when he raised him from the dead and seated him at his right hand in the heavenly realms,* ²¹*far above all rule and authority, power and dominion, and every title that can be given, not only in the present age but also in the one to come.*

²²*And God placed all things under his feet and appointed him to be head over everything for the church,*

²³*which is his body, the fullness of him who fills everything in every way* (Eph. 1:15-23).

**Q 48** ↗ *Was Paul's letter only for believers in Ephesus? Explain.*

**Setting.**    There are some people that we would like to have praying for us. They are people of spiritual passion and power—who over the years have walked and talked with God. They are people who know God in a close, intimate relationship. Who would you want praying for you?

We all would like to have Paul praying for us. And his writings and prayers are for all—because the Spirit inspired them for all believers of all times. Paul was in Ephesus for a short time on his second missionary journey, about A.D. 52 (Acts 18:19-21). And he spent 2 to 3 years in Ephesus on his third missionary trip, about A.D. 55-57. So it may seem strange to us when Paul says *"I remember you in my prayers since I **heard** about your faith in the Lord Jesus"* (Eph. 1:15-16). Paul knew the believers he met at Ephesus when he was there. But by the time he wrote to them, about A.D. 61, no doubt the church had expanded. So there were some believers at Ephesus he had only heard about.

In prison, Paul heard a report about Colossian believers, and perhaps the Ephesians, through Epaphras (Col. 1:7). From Paul's prayer, we see that these believers at Ephesus knew God. But are there any believers anywhere, who do not need to know God better? Even the apostle Paul prayed that he might know God in an ever-increasing measure. Twenty-five years after his conversion, Paul testified

> [10]*I want to know Christ and the power of his resurrection and the fellowship of sharing in his sufferings, becoming like him in his death,* [11]*and so, somehow, to attain to the resurrection from the dead* (Phil. 3:10-11).

Prayer should be a way of life for us, like breathing. We should live each hour of the day in an attitude of prayer. Watchman Nee referred to this discipline as *practicing the presence of Jesus.* Paul prayed *before* he spoke or wrote. Sometimes when we face challenges, we are tempted to reverse Paul's order. We become aware of a need. Then we quickly send a message or speak words of concern. When we do this, we are always at risk. A wise habit is to *first* pray our concerns to God. Prayer will provide insights and spiritual help. Later, like Paul, we may feel led to share insights, through some form of communication. This is such an important lesson for all of us! We may be able to do more after we pray. But we can never do more until we pray.

Paul's prayer focuses on spiritual knowledge. Let us look at three requests (A–C) that Paul prayed for the Ephesians—and us—to know.

## A. We need to know God better (Eph. 1:15-17).

> [15]*For this reason, ever since I heard about your faith in the Lord Jesus and your love for all the saints,* [16]*I have not stopped giving thanks for you, remembering you in my prayers.* [17]*I keep asking that the God of our Lord Jesus Christ, the glorious Father, may give you the Spirit of wisdom and revelation, so that you may know him better* (Eph. 1:15-17).

Do not skip the words, *for this reason* (Eph. 1:15). What reason? Because God has blessed us in the heavenly realms with every spiritual blessing in Christ.

Paul joined praise with prayer. Ephesians 1:3-14 is praise for all God has blessed us with in Christ. *For this reason*, because of God's blessings, Paul prays that believers will know God better. Knowing *about* God and *what He has done for us* is not a substitute for knowing God. The Israelites knew all God had done to deliver them from Egypt. They had seen all the 10 plagues, and watched the world's most powerful army drown in the Red Sea. But these same Israelites knew God less and less, instead of more and more. So God did not fulfill His promise of bringing them into Canaan. Rather, He caused all of them over age 20, except Joshua and Caleb, to die in the wilderness—short of the promise. This is the same multitude who praised God and danced before Him in worship by the Red Sea, as Miriam played the tambourine. Yet neither Miriam, Aaron, Moses, nor anyone over 20 years of age entered the Promised Land. Not everyone praising God and talking about heaven will arrive there (Matt. 7:21).

Praising God is not enough. We must live in a relationship with God—knowing, loving, obeying, and serving Him. Paul wants believers to know God deeply, and live in the light of all God has done for us in Christ. Paul joined his praise with prayer. As Paul prayed, he gave thanks for the faith and love of Ephesian believers. He praised God that

**Q 49** What should spiritual leaders always do first when they are facing problems in the church? Why?

 **Sabio says:** A wise habit is to *first* pray our concerns to God.

**Q 50** What are the 3 things Paul wanted believers to know?

**Q 51** What reason caused Paul to pray for believers to know God better (Eph. 1:15-17)?

**Q 52** Why is praising God insufficient? Give an example.

**Q 53** What is the difference between knowing about God and His deeds, and knowing God?

they had faith toward God, and love for all the saints—those who are holy through the blood of Jesus, and the presence of the Holy Spirit. The Ephesian believers had made a good start. Still there was a reason Paul prayed for them. In Ephesians 1:3-14, Paul listed eight blessings of salvation that God the Father, God the Son, and God the Spirit have provided for us. God has loved us, redeemed us, forgiven us, and adopted us into His family. God has given us a deposit of our inheritance. But Paul wants all believers to grow in God and receive their full inheritance—and not lose the deposit. God Himself is our greatest inheritance. He has become our God and we have become His people (Rev. 21:3). We are spiritually rich beyond human imagination, even though our circumstances on earth do not show it. We are wealthy in Christ. We are rich beyond any level the human mind can conceive by itself. But only the Holy Spirit can reveal to us how wealthy we are in Christ. So Paul prayed: *"I keep asking that the God of our Lord Jesus Christ, the glorious Father, may give you the Spirit of wisdom and revelation, so that you may know him better"* (Eph. 1:17). The spirit of wisdom and revelation are possible only though the Holy Spirit, who is the personal Spirit of wisdom and revelation.[12] The more we know God now, the more of our inheritance we are receiving now. And the more we live in His presence and know Him better, the more sure we are of receiving our full inheritance. So let our motto be: "Forward ever, backward never." And may our life be a daily prayer that ascends to God, saying: "Lord, I want to know you more. May our relationship grow deeper, day by day. Teach me to enjoy your presence in all of life."

**Q 54** *What does Paul pray for and desire for all believers?*

A preacher named Charles Haddon Spurgeon published 62 books of his sermons. He is one of the most loved and appreciated preachers. Spurgeon was a man who knew God, and walked with Him. He once said that in the hours he was awake, there was never a period of 15 minutes that he did not enjoy the presence of God.[13] May all of us make it our goal to know God in a deep way, and to be aware that He is with us. This is Paul's prayer for us, our privilege, and God's invitation. (In Ephesians 5:18, we will explore how being filled with the Spirit is the key to knowing and experiencing God's presence in all we do.)

Paul prayed for the Holy Spirit, the Spirit of wisdom and revelation, to help us know God better. For Paul, knowing God is not just for the head, but for the heart, and the hands. Paul is praying for the Ephesians and us to know God in an intimate, deep, personal way. He is praying for us to know God as our Lord, King, and closest friend.

> PAUL PRAYED FOR THE HOLY SPIRIT, THE SPIRIT OF WISDOM AND REVELATION, TO HELP US KNOW GOD BETTER.

**Q 55** *According to 1 Corinthians 2:9-16, how does the Spirit help us know God?*

The Bible uses the word *know* to describe an intimate, personal relationship. In Genesis, *"Adam knew Eve his wife, and she conceived and bore Cain"* (Gen. 4:1 NKJV). This verse describes *knowledge* as the love, closeness, and oneness in marriage. Likewise, in Ephesians, Paul writes about the relationship between a husband and wife, and compares it to the relationship between Christ and His Church (Eph. 5:25-32). Paul writes about the love of Christ that passes *head* knowledge (Eph. 3:19). In other words, Paul wants us to have a spiritual knowledge of God—a knowledge we experience as His Spirit fills us. Later, Paul prays for us to live in a relationship with God that grows beyond knowledge (of the head), to knowledge that comes from being filled with His Spirit (Eph. 3:19-20; 5:18).

**Q 56** *What does Paul mean by "knowing God"?*

**Application.** How do we know that a person has a deep, inner knowledge of God? How does this spiritual knowledge of God reveal itself in the life of a person? Knowing God is experiential, spiritual knowledge. To know God is to be filled with the light and love of His presence. Such knowledge of God expresses itself through words that edify others, and actions that glorify God. Knowledge of God is a deep relationship with

**Q 57** *Why does Paul want believers to grow in the knowledge of God?*

Him that shows itself in the way we live. Spiritual knowledge of God comforts, cheers, strengthens, and guides. Spiritual knowledge of God demonstrates itself through the fruit of the Spirit. We know that a person knows God when we see love, joy, peace, patience, kindness, goodness, faithfulness, and self-control overflowing in a person's life. In contrast, when a person's life is unholy, unrighteous, unloving, unfaithful, impatient, we recognize this person needs a deeper knowledge of God and a deeper relationship with Him. If it is not yet clear that Paul is praying for believers to have a knowledge of God that guides their attitudes and actions, then keep reading Ephesians. For when we finish reading Ephesians 4–6, we understand that Paul is praying for a spiritual knowledge of God that is ever transforming our behavior—conforming us to the image of God by the Spirit (1 Cor. 15:49).

Like Paul, the apostle John writes about deep, spiritual knowledge that transforms behavior.

> ¹*How great is the love the Father has lavished on us, that we should be called children of God! And that is what we are! The reason the world does not **know** us is that it did not **know** him.* ²*Dear friends, now we are children of God, and what we will be has not yet been made **known**. But we **know** that when he appears, we shall be like him, for we shall see him as he is.* ³*Everyone who has this hope in him purifies himself, just as he is pure.* ⁴*Everyone who sins breaks the law; in fact, sin is lawlessness.* ⁵*But you **know** that he appeared so that he might take away our sins. And in him is no sin.* ⁶*No one who lives in him keeps on sinning. No one who continues to sin has either seen him or **known** him* (1 John 3:1-6).

The more we know God, the more we appreciate, value, enjoy, and express who we are in Christ. The more we know God, the more He fills us. The more we know God, the more we resemble Him in our attitudes and actions.

*Sabio* says: "Godly character and actions are the fruit that grow from the root of knowing God well."

## B. We need to know the hope God has called us to have (Eph. 1:18).

Paul wants us to grasp the hope God gives us. Hope, in this context, is not an uncertain desire or dream. Rather, here in Ephesians 1:18, hope means the same as faith or trust. Our hope in God is an assurance—an anchor and confidence in the promises, provision, and faithfulness of God! Paul often presents this hope as the work of the Spirit in us—in spite of suffering and affliction. Paul, quoting Isaiah 64:4 said, *"No eye has seen, no ear has heard, no mind has conceived what God has prepared for those who love him"* (1 Cor. 2:9-10). We need the Holy Spirit to "open the eyes of our heart" so that we can begin to see the wonderful future that is ours "in Christ!"

> PAUL WANTS US TO GRASP THE HOPE GOD GIVES US.

A father took his son, and together they climbed a tall mountain. At the top, the dad said, "Son, come over here and look at this!" Standing high on the mountain, the boy saw the beauty of mountains far away, a lake, and a beautiful green valley. Likewise the Heavenly Father called the apostle John, saying, *"Come up here!"* And John saw the glory of God in heaven (Rev. 4:1)! In like manner, the Holy Spirit can show us the reality of our future hope.

Our hope includes a rich inheritance. What Jesus purchased for us through His death, burial, and resurrection is beyond our imagination. This is the second of five times that Paul uses the word *riches* in this letter (Eph. 1:7, 18; 2:7; 3:8, 16). In Romans Paul put it this way, *"He who did not spare his own Son, but gave him up for us all—how will he not also, along with him, graciously give us all things?"* (Rom. 8:32). Our hope and

**Q 58** How does knowing God affect our behavior (1 John 3:6)? Illustrate.

**Q 59** How does the hope of a believer differ from the hope of an unbeliever?

**Q 60** What is the greatest part of our inheritance?

**Q 61** What are some things that our hope includes?

inheritance include a new body, seeing Jesus face to face, enjoying fellowship that has no end, and living in the light of God's glory forever! God will wipe all tears from our eyes. He makes Himself, endless joy, and all the riches of heaven available to believers *in Christ*. As we noted in Ephesians 1:14, God Himself is the great treasure of our inheritance. And the Holy Spirit within us is the divine deposit of Himself that He has already given us. There is no one like God. And He has given Himself to us. There is no wealth that compares to having God as our God and Father. He is the Creator, Ruler, Sustainer, Owner, and Judge of the entire universe. We are rich beyond measure, because we are His children and He is our Father!

> <sup>21b</sup>*All things are yours,* <sup>22</sup>*whether Paul or Apollos or Cephas or the world or life or death or the present or the future—all are yours,* <sup>23</sup>*and you are of Christ, and Christ is of God* (1 Cor. 3:21b-23).

Paul wants us to have a deep, spiritual knowledge of our hope and inheritance. So let us encourage ourselves often with the hope God has given us. And let us live in harmony with the God who has adopted us into His family.

### C. We need to know God's great power (Eph. 1:18-23).

> <sup>18</sup>*I pray also that the eyes of your heart may be enlightened in order **that you may know** the hope to which he has called you, the riches of his glorious inheritance in the saints,* <sup>19</sup>*and **his incomparably great power for us who believe. That power is like the working of his mighty strength,** <sup>20</sup>**which he exerted in Christ when he raised him from the dead and seated him at his right hand in the heavenly realms,** <sup>21</sup>**far above all rule and authority, power and dominion, and every title that can be given, not only in the present age but also in the one to come.** <sup>22</sup>**And God placed all things under his feet and appointed him to be head over everything for the church,** <sup>23</sup>**which is his body, the fullness of him who fills everything in every way** (Eph. 1:18-23).*

Q 62 ⬎ What kind of power is available to us as Christians?

Besides praying for believers to know God Himself, and the hope He has given us, Paul prayed for believers to know God's power for us. Paul describes God's power as *going beyond greatness* (Greek: *hyperballon megathos*).[14] To grasp *beyond greatness*, imagine giving a ball to a great athlete and asking him to throw or kick the ball as far as possible. That would be *'ballon' greatness*. But if we put the ball in the hands of Almighty God and He threw it past the sun, that would be *'hyperballon' greatness—going beyond greatness*. God's power is beyond human comprehension—supernatural power in a heavenly realm. Yet Paul wants us to know it—through a spiritual revelation of God's Word and Spirit.

Q 63 ⬏ What are 5 ways God describes His power for us (Eph. 5:19)?

Besides saying that God's power on our behalf goes *beyond greatness*, Paul describes God's power with four other terms. He piles up one word after another to help us grasp the power we have on our side (Figure 1.25). In all of Paul's writing, Ephesians 1:19 has the most words to describe God's power.[15]

| Greek Words That Paul Uses to Describe God's Power | Meaning |
|---|---|
| *Hyperballon megathos* | Going beyond greatness |
| *Dunamis* | Dynamic power; explosive like dynamite |
| *Energeia* | Energy at work; erg (a measure of energy) |
| *Kratos* | A mighty force in action |
| *Ischus* | The strength of a strong arm, available when needed |

**Figure 1.25    Paul describes God's power for us five ways in one verse (Eph. 5:19).**

Q 64 ⬏ What does Paul say that the power he speaks about accomplished?

Q 65 ⬏ How does Paul illustrate the power he wants us to know?

To help us understand God's power, Paul uses a comparison. He says God's great power *for us* is **just like** the *might* of the *strength* of the *power* that God *worked—*

when He raised Jesus from the dead, and exalted Him to the Father's right hand in the heavenly realm,

> [21]***far above all*** *rule and authority, power and dominion, and every title that can be given, not only in the present age **but also** in the one to come.* [22]*And God placed **all things under his feet** and appointed him to be **head over everything** for the church,* [23]*which is his body, the fullness of him **who fills everything in every way*** (Eph. 1:21-23).

Paul described God's power with five terms (Figure 1.25). As you complete Figure 1.26, note that Paul also uses many terms to describe the degree to which God's power exalted Christ—such as *far above all*, *present* and *future*, and *head over everything*.

**Q 66**  Complete Figure 1.26 on the power God used to exalt Christ.

| Questions | Your Answers as Found in Ephesians 5:19b-23 |
|---|---|
| By His power, how far up did God exalt Christ? | |
| For how long did God exalt Christ? | |
| By His power, what did God place under Christ's feet? | |
| By His power, what did God exalt Christ to be head over for the Church? | |
| If Christ is the head and we are His body, where will we be exalted for eternity? | |

**Figure 1.26   Practice answering questions about God's power (Eph. 5:19b-23).**

Paul prays for believers to understand that the same power that exalted Christ as the head will one day exalt those who are members of His body, the Church.

Paul knew a lot about *power*. Before he became a follower of Christ, he received *power* from the Sanhedrin to imprison and even kill Christians. And on the road to Damascus, Paul encountered the *power* of Jesus, who spoke to him from the heavens. This *power* knocked stubborn Paul to his knees, and struck him blind, as it shone brighter than the sun at noon. This same *power* gave courage to Ananias to pray for Paul. And this *power* of Jesus healed Paul's blind eyes, and transformed his hard heart. Preaching the Christ he once persecuted, Paul saw the *power* of the gospel change the lives of hundreds of people. He saw the *power* of God heal the sick, open blind eyes, heal the lame, raise the dead, cast out demons, overcome demonic opposition through Elymas, and shake off a deadly serpent into the fire. As a traveling apostle, Paul experienced the *power* of the Sanhedrin and local Jewish leaders as they whipped him with 40 lashes less one, five different times; and beat him with rods three times. And Paul experienced the *power* of the Roman government, to beat, imprison, and finally behead him. Few men on earth have known as much about power as Paul. So God used him to assure us that whatever comes our way, the *power* of God that is working for us is FAR ABOVE any other powers in heaven or on earth. God's *power* at work on our behalf is *'hyperballon'* greater than any evil powers in this age or the one to come. Get the point? God is with us, so no one can spoil His eternal plans for us as we abide in Jesus Christ. So no matter what is happening to us or around us, let us rest in the power of God Almighty, our Father.

**Q 67**  What are some types of powers that Paul encountered?

**Q 68**  What is the point of Ephesians 1:18-23?

## PSALM 46:1-11

¹ GOD IS OUR REFUGE AND STRENGTH, AN EVER-PRESENT HELP IN TROUBLE.

² THEREFORE WE WILL NOT FEAR, THOUGH THE EARTH GIVE WAY
AND THE MOUNTAINS FALL INTO THE HEART OF THE SEA,

³ THOUGH ITS WATERS ROAR AND FOAM
AND THE MOUNTAINS QUAKE WITH THEIR SURGING. SELAH

⁴ THERE IS A RIVER WHOSE STREAMS MAKE GLAD THE CITY OF GOD,
THE HOLY PLACE WHERE THE MOST HIGH DWELLS.

⁵ GOD IS WITHIN HER, SHE WILL NOT FALL; GOD WILL HELP HER AT BREAK OF DAY.

⁶ NATIONS ARE IN UPROAR, KINGDOMS FALL; HE LIFTS HIS VOICE, THE EARTH MELTS.

⁷ THE LORD ALMIGHTY IS WITH US; THE GOD OF JACOB IS OUR FORTRESS. SELAH

⁸ COME AND SEE THE WORKS OF THE LORD,
THE DESOLATIONS HE HAS BROUGHT ON THE EARTH.

⁹ HE MAKES WARS CEASE TO THE ENDS OF THE EARTH;
HE BREAKS THE BOW AND SHATTERS THE SPEAR,

HE BURNS THE SHIELDS WITH FIRE.

¹⁰ "BE STILL, AND KNOW THAT I AM GOD;
I WILL BE EXALTED AMONG THE NATIONS, I WILL BE EXALTED IN THE EARTH."

¹¹ THE LORD ALMIGHTY IS WITH US; THE GOD OF JACOB IS OUR FORTRESS. SELAH

**Figure 1.27    Psalm 46 assures us that the Lord is with us in all His mighty power.**

---

**Lesson 5**

## The "Before and After" of Those "in Christ"—Part 1 (Eph. 2:1-10)

**Goal A:** *Explain 5 ways we were hopeless before we were in Christ (Eph. 2:1-3).*
**Goal B:** *Summarize and illustrate 3 aspects of salvation Christ provided (Eph. 2:4-10).*

**Q 69** *Complete Figure 1.28, summarizing life without Christ and with Him.*

In Ephesians 1:3-14 Paul praised God for all the blessings He has poured out on us in Christ. Then in Ephesians 1:15-23 Paul prays for believers to grow in three kinds of spiritual knowledge: knowing God, knowing the hope He has called us to, and knowing or experiencing His power working for us. Here, in Ephesians 2:1-10, Paul takes time to contrast our lives before Christ and in Christ.

| Ephesians 2:1-10 | Topics | Your Summaries on Aspects of Salvation | | |
|---|---|---|---|---|
| 2:1-3 | A. Past Problems: Before Christ | 1. | | |
| | | 2. | | |
| | | 3. | | |
| | | 4. | | |
| | | 5. | | |

**Figure 1:28    Practice summarizing life without Christ (Eph. 2:1-10).**

### A. Past problem: Paul mentions five sad characteristics of people without Christ (Eph. 2:1-3).

As you read Ephesians 2:1-3, note that Paul begins talking about *you* (Gentiles). Then he uses the word *us*, referring to Gentiles and Jews.

> ¹*As for you, you were dead in your transgressions and sins,* ²*in which you used to live* [walk] *when you followed the ways of this world and of the ruler of the kingdom of the air, the spirit who is now at work in those who are disobedient.* ³*All of us also lived among them at one time, gratifying the cravings of our sinful nature and following its desires and thoughts. Like the rest, we were by nature objects of wrath* (Eph. 2:1-3).

Let us look at each of the five, tragic characteristics of people without Christ.

**1. Without Christ, we were *dead* in our transgressions and sins, in which we used to *live* [Greek: *walk*].** ¹ "*As for you, you were dead in your transgressions and sins,* ²*in which you used to live* [walk]" (Eph. 2:1-2a). The word *dead* means "spiritually dead—separated from God, the source of spiritual life." In the Garden of Eden, God created Adam and Eve without sin. They walked with God and enjoyed a relationship of fellowship with Him. But God warned them that the day they disobeyed Him, they would *die*—in their spiritual relationship with Him (Gen. 2:17). And as God warned, the day they sinned He banished them from the Garden, separating them from His presence. Thus sin led to spiritual death—separation from God. Paul echoes this truth when he writes: "*The wages of sin is death*" (Rom. 3:23).

Those who live in sin are still alive physically. They are still breathing. But life without God is so empty that the Bible uses the word *death* to refer to living apart from the Heavenly Father.

The parable of the prodigal son tells of a son who chose to walk away from his father. He went to a distant country where he wasted his money on sinful pleasures of the world. Finally, a ray of light entered the dark mind of this wayward son. Feeding pigs, he was so hungry that he felt like eating some of their food. Then he realized how lifeless his existence had become. With a heart of repentance, he turned from his sins and began the journey back to his father. The older brother objected to the grace and joy the father showed to the son who came home. But the father replied, ³² "*We had to celebrate and be glad, because this brothers of yours was dead, and is alive again; he was lost and is found*" (Luke 15:32).

Scripture says that the person who lives in the pleasures of sin is *dead*, even while living (1 Tim. 5:6). Life apart from fellowship with God is as empty as death. The book of Revelation speaks of a time when God will raise the dead, judge them for their sins, and sentence them to eternity in the Lake of Fire. This final, lonely separation from God is called *the second death* (Rev 20:14-15). Thus, in Scripture *death* refers to separation from God for the years on earth; and *the second death* is separation from God after earth, forever. To avoid the *second spiritual death* of eternity, we must escape the *first spiritual death* of earth.

Spiritual death is the result of living in sin—also called transgressions, a synonym for sin (Eph. 2:1). Paul writes "*transgressions and sins*" to emphasize the problem. Without salvation through Christ, we were all *dead in sins*. Sin kills spiritual life. Sin is the lawless act of disobeying God and rebelling against His rule over our lives. God warned Cain that sin was crouching at the door like a wild animal, wanting to kill him (Gen. 4:7). Sin deceives us by making itself look attractive. But sin is the evil enemy of the soul. For the soul who sins will die—suffering separation from God (Ezek. 18:20).

**2. Without Christ, we followed the ways of the world.** ¹ "*As for you, you were dead in your transgressions and sins,* ²*in which you used to live* [walk] *when you followed the ways of this world*" (Eph. 2:1-2).

The world shapes the character and values of those without Christ. Scripture counsels us not to follow the ways of the world, but live as strangers on earth (1 Pet. 2:11). Paul reminds us that our time on earth is short, compared to eternity. What we buy

**Q 70** *What does it mean to be "dead" in sins?*

**Q 71** *In what sense was the son in Luke 15:32 "dead"?*

**Q 72** *How does the second death differ from being "dead in sins"?*

**Q 73** *If sin killed our relationship with God before we knew Christ, can sin kill our relationship after we have met Christ? Explain.*

**Q 74** *What are some examples of the ways of the world?*

we will not keep. And the pleasures of sin on earth will not last—they are only for a season (Heb. 11:25). So the wise *use* the things of earth, but do not *abuse* them (1 Cor. 7:30-31). Yet without Christ, we lack the wisdom and the strength to resist the ungodly temptations of the world. Those without Christ are slaves of the world's influence. They follow the crowd, and love what the world tells them to love. Like Esau, they live for the present and ignore the future.

John contrasts those who love the world and those who do God's will:

¹⁵*Do not love the world or anything in the world. If anyone loves the world, the love of the Father is not in him.* ¹⁶*For everything in the world—the cravings of sinful man, the lust of his eyes and the boasting of what he has and does—comes not from the Father but from the world.* ¹⁷*The world and its desires pass away, but the man who does the will of God lives forever* (1 John 2:15-17).

**3. Without Christ, we lived under the influence of Satan—the ruler of the kingdom of the air.** ¹*"As for you, you were dead in your transgressions and sins,* ²*in which you used to live* [walk] *when you followed the ways of this world and of the ruler of the kingdom of the air, the spirit who is now at work in those who are disobedient"* (Eph. 2:1-2).

Behind the world system is the "god of this world," Satan—who has blinded the spiritual sight of those without Christ (2 Cor. 4:3-4). Paul says that the devil traps those without Christ like hunters trap an animal. The devil takes them *"captive to do his will"* (2 Tim. 2:26). Paul prophesied concerning the Antichrist: ⁹*"The coming of the lawless one will be in accordance with the work of Satan displayed in all kinds of counterfeit miracles, signs and wonders,* ¹⁰*and in every sort of evil that **deceives those who are perishing**. They perish because they refused to love the truth and so be saved"* (2 Thess. 2:9-10).

Likewise, John writes: *"the whole world is under the influence of the evil one"* (1 John 5:19).

A visitor watched as a herd of pigs followed a man to the slaughter. The visitor knew that the building ahead was the place where they killed pigs. But he could not understand why the pigs were following the man, so he asked him. "The answer is easy," said the man leading the pigs to their death. Then he showed the visitor a small bag of beans, and said, "I just drop a few beans on the road as I walk along. The pigs have their minds on the taste of the beans. They give no thought to who is dropping them, or where they are going." Likewise the devil leads a multitude to destruction, giving them little pleasures of the world along the way. As James said, those living in sin are fattening themselves for the day of slaughter (James 5:5).

**4. Without Christ, we were guided by sinful desires of the flesh.** ³*"All of us also lived among them at one time, gratifying the cravings of our sinful nature and following its desires and thoughts"* (Eph. 2:3a). The flesh leads people in ways that are unrighteous. Paul describes the evil acts of the flesh. ¹⁹*"The acts of the sinful nature are obvious: sexual immorality, impurity and debauchery;* ²⁰*idolatry and witchcraft; hatred, discord, jealousy, fits of rage, selfish ambition, dissensions, factions* ²¹*and envy; drunkenness, orgies, and the like. I warn you, as I did before, that those who live like this will not inherit the kingdom of God"* (Gal. 5:19-21).

Many of the desires of the flesh are good, such as: hunger, thirst, the desire for food, shelter, rest, and sex. These desires are good as we fulfill them in God's plan. But the person without Christ often fulfills the desires of the flesh in ways that are ungodly—thinking only of self.

Those without Christ may claim to be free. But Paul says they are slaves of the world, the devil, and the flesh (Eph. 2:2-3). Crying over the fate of those without Christ, Paul wrote: ¹⁸*"For, as I have often told you before and now say again even with tears,*

**Q 75** Do followers of Christ love the world and its ways? Explain.

**Q 76** How does Satan influence those without Christ? Give examples.

**Q 77** How are those without Christ like pigs going be slaughtered?

**Q 78** Is it possible to be alive in Christ, but led by sinful desires of the flesh (Rom. 8:13; Eph. 2:1-3)? Explain.

**Q 79** When are desires of the flesh evil?

**Q 80** Are those led by the flesh free? Explain.

*many live as enemies of the cross of Christ.* [19] *Their destiny is destruction, their god is their stomach, and their glory is in their shame. Their mind is on earthly things.* [20] *But our citizenship is in heaven. And we eagerly await a Savior from there, the Lord Jesus Christ"* (Phil. 3:18-20).

**5. Without Christ, we were objects of God's wrath.** *"Like the rest, we were by nature objects of wrath"* (Eph. 2:3b).

It is true that God loves those without Christ. God loved sinners so much that He gave His only Son to save them. But each of us *must choose to accept God's love, or be under His anger.* Later in Ephesians, Paul explains that God's wrath comes on all who are disobedient by being immoral, impure, or greedy:

**Q 81** ⟍ *If God loves all, why are some "objects of God's wrath"?*

*[3] But among you there must not be even a hint of sexual immorality, or of any kind of impurity, or of greed, because these are improper for God's holy people. [4] Nor should there be obscenity, foolish talk or coarse joking, which are out of place, but rather thanksgiving. [5] For of this you can be sure: No immoral, impure or greedy person—such a man is an idolater—has any inheritance in the kingdom of Christ and of God. [6] Let no one deceive you with empty words, for because of such things God's wrath comes on those who are disobedient. [7] Therefore do not be partners with them* (Eph. 5:3-7).

**Q 82** ⟍ *What kind of things cause God's wrath to come on people?*

**Q 83** ⟍ Complete Figure 1.29 on reasons for the wrath of God.

| Bible | Your Summaries About What Causes People to Be Objects of God's Wrath |
|---|---|
| Eph. 2:3b | |
| Eph. 5:3-7 | |
| Rom. 1:18 | |
| Rom. 2:5-11 | |
| Rom. 11:22 | |

**Figure 1.29   Practice summarizing reasons why God is kind to some, but pours out wrath on others.**

Paul also wrote in Romans:

*[18] The wrath of God is being revealed from heaven against all the godlessness and wickedness of men who suppress the truth by their wickedness* (Rom. 1:18).

*[5] But because of your stubbornness and your unrepentant heart, you are storing up wrath against yourself for the day of God's wrath, when his righteous judgment will be revealed. [6] God "will give to each person according to what he has done." [7] To those who by persistence in doing good seek glory, honor and immortality, he will give eternal life. [8] But for those who are self-seeking and who reject the truth and follow evil, there will be wrath and anger. [9] There will be trouble and distress for every human being who does evil: first for the Jew, then for the Gentile; [10] but glory, honor and peace for everyone who does good: first for the Jew, then for the Gentile. [11] For God does not show favoritism* (Rom. 2:5-11).

*[22] Consider therefore the kindness and sternness of God: sternness to those who fell, but kindness to you, provided that you continue in his kindness. Otherwise, you also will be cut off* (Rom. 11:22).

We win or lose by the way we choose. In love, God offers salvation to each person. But He will not force anyone to choose heaven. We are targets for God's wrath, unless we repent and accept His forgiveness in Christ. This brings us to the solution God offers to those dead in sins and led away from Him by the world, the devil, and the flesh.

**Q 84** ⟍ *To whom does God offer salvation?*

**B. Present solution: God saved us (Eph. 2:4-10).**

Some of the most wonderful words in Scripture follow the terrible summary of the human condition in Ephesians 2:1-3! They are the words: [4] *"But because of his great love*

**Q 85** ⟍ *What is the great contrast between Ephesians 2:1-3 and Ephesians 2:4-10?*

*for us, God, who is rich in mercy, ⁵made us alive with Christ even when we were dead in transgressions—it is by grace you have been saved"* (Eph. 2:4-5)! The good news is that God stepped in when things were hopeless! He provided salvation for sinful, lost humanity through Jesus Christ. In these verses Paul proclaims that God offers salvation to all who will receive it!

⁴***But because of his great love for us, God,*** *who is rich in mercy,* ⁵***made us alive with Christ*** *even when we were dead in transgressions—it is by grace you have been saved.* ⁶*And* ***God raised us up with Christ*** *and* ***seated us with him*** *in the heavenly realms in Christ Jesus,* ⁷*in order that in the coming ages he might show the incomparable riches of his grace, expressed in his kindness to us in Christ Jesus.* ⁸*For it is by grace you have been saved, through faith—and this not from yourselves, it is the gift of God—* ⁹*not by works, so that no one can boast.* ¹⁰*For we are God's workmanship, created in Christ Jesus to do good works, which God prepared in advance for us to do* [to walk in] *(Eph. 2:4-10).*

Let us look at three aspects of the salvation God provided us in Christ.

**Q 86** ✎ *Complete Figure 1.30, summarizing life without Christ and with Him.*

| Ephesians 2:1-10 | Topics | Your Summaries on Aspects of Salvation |
|---|---|---|
| 2:4-10 | B. Present Blessings: In Christ | 1. |
| | | 2. |
| | | 3. |

**Figure 1.30    Practice summarizing blessings in Christ (Eph. 2:1-10).**

**1. God saved us from death, disobedience, and destruction by divine wrath.** *Paul uses three verbs to declare our salvation:* <u>made alive</u> *with,* <u>raised up</u> *with, and* <u>seated together with</u> (Figure 1.31). In Greek, each of these verbs begins with "Sun" (pronounced *soon*), which means "with" or "together with." Paul is emphasizing that all aspects of our salvation are in our union *with* Christ. Describing our salvation, Paul links us to what God has done in Christ at His resurrection, ascension, and enthronement (Figure 1.31). So with the salvation God provides, we share in Christ's victories.

| Ephesians | Exaltation of Christ | Greek Verb | Aspects of Salvation God Provided for Us *With Christ* |
|---|---|---|---|
| 2:5 | Resurrection | *Sunezoopoiesen* | We were dead in our sins, but God made us alive **with** Christ. Like the prodigal son, we were once dead in our relationship to the Father, but God made us alive in Christ. |
| 2:6 | Ascension | *Sunegeiren* | We were led by the world, the devil, and the flesh, but God raised us up ***together with*** Christ. |
| 2:6 | Enthronement | *Sunekathisen* | We were objects of wrath, and headed for judgment, but God seated us ***together with*** Christ in heaven in Christ. |

**Figure 1.31    In Ephesians 2:4-6, Paul emphasizes that through our union with Christ we share in His victories of the resurrection, the ascension, and the enthronement of Jesus Christ.**

**Q 87** ↗ *What difference did a little girl see in her daddy?*

Author, pastor, and former atheist Lee Strobel loves to testify of the difference God made in his life. His daughter was 5 years old when he began to follow Jesus. But during those 5 years *before* he met Christ, she knew a dad who was profane and angry. He came home angry one night and kicked a hole in the wall. Many times, his daughter hid in her room to stay away from her father. But 5 months after dad gave his life to Jesus Christ, that little girl said, "Mommy, I want God to do for me what he's done for Daddy." At age 5½ she had not studied the deep truths of the Bible. Yet she knew her dad used to be hard to live with, and God changed him into a wonderful father. So she decided that if that is what God does to people, then she wanted to be close to that God. Today, Pastor Lee testifies: "God changed my family. He changed my world. He changed my eternity."[16] In Jesus Christ, God resurrects us to new life. With Christ, God raises us to ascend above the sinful influences of the world, the devil, and the flesh. And He gives us a new position, even now and for the future—we are seated *"together with Jesus Christ in the heavenly realms."* So let us keep looking up—giving thanks and showing others what God has done for us *with* Christ!

**2. God saved us _through_ His love, mercy, and grace—not through our own good works.** We were dead in our sins, and under the influence of the world, the devil, and the flesh. We were unable to save ourselves. But still, God loved us. When we could not walk toward Him, He came to us with love and mercy. [4] *"**But because of his great love for us, God,** who is rich in mercy, [5] **made us alive with Christ even when we were dead in transgressions—it is by grace you have been saved"** (Eph. 2:4-5).

In the ages to come, God looks forward to displaying the incomparable riches of His grace in us. He delights to bless us. But let us always remember that we did not climb the ladder of our own good deeds to reach salvation. No! [8] *"For it is by grace you have been saved, through faith—and this not from yourselves, it is the gift of God—* [9] *not by works, so that no one can boast"* (Eph. 2:8-9).

At a conference on world religions, scholars from all over the world debated whether Christianity had any unique belief. Other religions had versions of the incarnation; and claimed victory over death. Then C. S. Lewis won the debate with one sentence; he said that Christianity is different from all other religions because we believe in salvation by God's grace, not our own good works. [17] Muslims seek salvation through the five pillars: faith in Allah (their name for God) and Mohamed (their prophet), prayers, alms, fasting, and a journey to Mecca. Hindus seek to escape the endless reincarnations and the wheel of Samsara through the threefold path of knowledge, work, or devotion (Figure 1.32).

**Q 88** *How is Christianity different from all other world religions?*

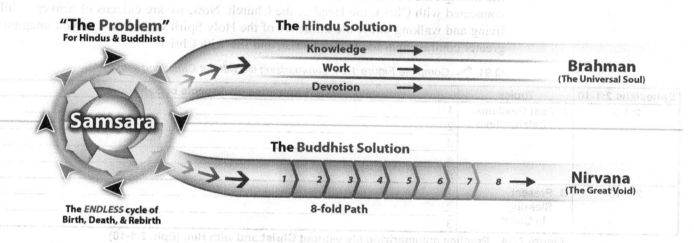

**Figure 1.32   Hindus and Buddhists agree on the quest for freedom, but seek solutions in different ways.**

Buddhists do not believe in a personal god, but they seek to escape reincarnation through the eight-fold path, and enter *Nirvana,* the great void. But true followers of Jesus do not hope to be saved, either by their own good deeds, by obeying all the rules, or by suffering in purgatory after death. We believe that salvation is the free gift of God, which we receive by grace through faith in Jesus Christ, who died to take away our sins, give us spiritual life, and deliver us from the penalty and power of sin. Salvation is by grace through faith, not by works, from beginning to end (Eph. 2:5, 7-9; Rom. 5:1-2; 1 Cor. 15:10; Gal. 3–5; 1 Pet. 5:12; 2 Pet. 3:18)!

**Figure 1.33 What is the main lesson in the parable of the Pharisee and the tax collector (Luke 18:9-14)?**

**Q 89** *In the parable of Luke 18:9-14, who would Jews, Muslims, Hindus, and Buddhists expect to be justified? Explain.*

**Q 90** ✎ *What is the relationship between salvation and good deeds? Give examples.*

### 3. God saved us to *"do good works"* (Eph. 2:10a).

*¹⁰For we are God's workmanship, created in Christ Jesus to do good works, which God prepared in advance for us to do* [to walk in] *(Eph. 2:10).*

We are not saved by works, but for works. We are saved by grace for **service**. Paul declares that we are God's *"workmanship"*—His grace-art. He created us for a reason. In Christ we have purpose and potential. God created us in His image to do good works in our world. In Ephesians 4–6, Paul gives many examples of the good works God calls us to do, such as living holy lives so we shine like stars in a dark world (Eph. 5:8-14). We are not saved by works, but our good works are the fruit that comes from the root of grace that brings our salvation. As James says, *"faith without works is dead"* (James 2:26). Righteous living and good deeds are the proof that we are alive in Christ. So put your faith to work, and let all around you see your faith in action! For this is one of the main reasons why God created you and me. He gives us the privilege to assist in reaching those who are still dead in their sins. Our godly living will help draw many to Christ, just as Pastor Strobel's new life in Christ drew his own daughter to the Savior.

**Summary.**    Everyone lives under the influence of various things. Addicts live under the influence of alcohol or other drugs. Addicts do not walk straight; they stagger and even fall. Without Christ we were spiritually dead, living and walking under the influence of the world, Satan, and the flesh (Eph. 2:1-3). Our walk was unrighteous—crooked rather than straight (Luke 3:5). We were objects of God's wrath. But God in His love, mercy, and grace saved us from being under the influence of the world, Satan, and the flesh. We moved from being objects of wrath to being highly favored children of God. He gave us life through the new birth. He resurrected and exalted us into a position in the heavens, connected with Christ, the Head of the Church. Now, we are citizens of heaven, while living and walking under the influence of the Holy Spirit within us. Can you imagine a greater contrast than life before Christ, and life with Christ?

**Q 91** ✎ *Complete Figure 1.34, summarizing life without Christ and with Him.*

| Ephesians 2:1-10 | Topics | Your Summaries on Aspects of Salvation |
|---|---|---|
| 2:1-3 | **A.** Past Problems: Before Christ | 1. |
| | | 2. |
| | | 3. |
| | | 4. |
| | | 5. |
| 2:4-10 | **B.** Present Blessings: In Christ | 1. |
| | | 2. |
| | | 3. |

**Figure 1.34    Practice summarizing life without Christ and with Him (Eph. 2:1-10).**

There is an English worship chorus that celebrates Ephesians 2:4-10—
https://www.youtube.com/watch?v=RrPLCcIZXGc (Chris Tomlin - How Can I Keep from Singing

**Q 92** ✎ *How many different gifts or ministries are possible in one church?*

| Some Ministries of Believers in a Church ||
|---|---|
| Community service | National Girls Ministries—a program in the Assemblies of God |
| Ministry to the poor (food, clothes) | Royal Rangers—boys program in the Assemblies of God |
| Home for abused women | College students (campus and church) |
| Crisis telephone line | Young adult ministry (younger) |
| Literacy—reading classes for the illiterate | Single adult ministry (older) |
| Skills (for jobs, marriage, society, and such) | Single mothers ministry (help and fellowship) |
| Prison ministry | Senior adult ministry |

Figure 1.35    Continued on following page

Continued from previous page

| Some Ministries of Believers in a Church | |
|---|---|
| Recovery Through Christ—addictions | Women's Ministry |
| Deaf culture ministry | Men's Ministry (includes Honor Bound—Men of Promise) |
| Soul winning—training and practice | Student ministries—evangelism and discipleship |
| Street evangelism—special events and gospel tracts | Youth Alive—secondary school program |
| Athletes ministry—outreach and discipleship | Youth discipleship |
| Adopt-an-Area—praying for and visiting every home | Youth Bible Quiz |
| Ministry to those with a handicap | Youth drama |
| Ministry to the terminally ill | Youth choir |
| Hospital visitation ministry | Speed the Light—youth missions fundraising |
| Comforting touch ministry (funerals, sickness, and such) | Youth leadership training |
| Counseling/marriage ministry | Master's Commission—1-2 year training program |
| Widows and orphans ministry | Adult choir |
| Foreign language ministry | Musical instruments ministry |
| Health ministry—basic health teachings and clinics | Worship team |
| Sidewalk Sunday School (Saturday outreach) | Evangelistic music—outreach team |
| Children's meeting or rally—for children outside the church | Drama—acting, costumes, and support |
| Camps for children and youth | Special events/productions—holiday and evangelistic |
| Sunday School for all ages | Illustrated sermons |
| Children's Church—for church children | Fine Arts—using art talents to bless others |
| Children's choir | Art and design for church needs |
| Junior Bible Quiz (children) | Helping hands ministry for church tasks |
| Weddings—coordinating | Small groups—home fellowships; Bible studies |
| Welcome center ministry | Prayer ministries (including prayer chain) |
| Communion—preparation and clean up | Follow-up ministries for visitors and converts |

**Figure 1.35   Some churches have as many as 200 different ministries that church members are doing![18]**

**Lesson 6**

## The "Before and After" of Those "in Christ"—Part 2 (Eph. 2:11-22)

**Goal C:** *Analyze these 3 relationships of Gentiles to Jews: included, united, made equal (Eph. 2:13-22).*

**Q 93** 🏹 *What is God's masterpiece—His greatest creation? Explain.*

**Q 94** 🏹 *What do the two halves of Ephesians 2 have in common? How do they differ (Figure 1.36)?*

**Overview.** Ephesians 2 contains two halves. The first half (Eph.2:1-10) reveals that God, by His love and grace, *saves* **individuals** (Gentiles and Jews) who were *separated from Him*, and transforms them into works of grace. The second half (Eph. 2:11-22), emphasizes that God *saves* and unites Jews and Gentiles into one spiritual community, His *masterpiece in Christ.[19]

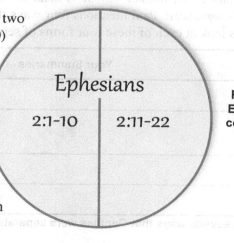

**Figure 1.36 Ephesians 2 contains two halves.**

Ephesians

2:1-10 | 2:11-22

**Q 95** *In Ephesians 2:11-22, in God's eyes, what 3 things happen at once when a Gentile receives Christ?*

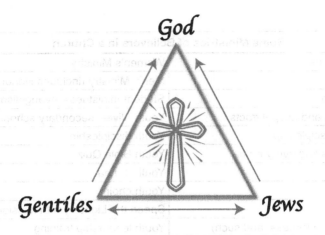

**Figure 1.37**
**In Ephesians 2:11-22, Paul reveals God's saving grace in two ways. He saves *individuals* who are *separated* from Him. And in Christ, He unites *Jews and Gentiles* who were *separated* from each other.**

**Q 96** *In Ephesians 2:11-22, what are 2 ways God reveals grace that saves?*

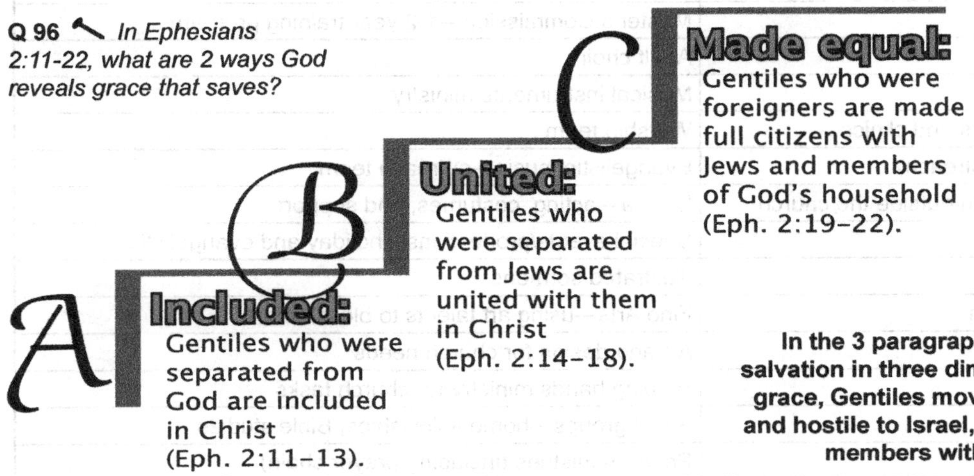

**Made equal:**
Gentiles who were foreigners are made full citizens with Jews and members of God's household (Eph. 2:19–22).

**United:**
Gentiles who were separated from Jews are united with them in Christ (Eph. 2:14–18).

**Included:**
Gentiles who were separated from God are included in Christ (Eph. 2:11–13).

There are three paragraphs in Ephesians 2:11-22. We will examine each of these paragraphs (A–C), noting the movement that occurs as God reconciles Gentiles and Jews to Himself and to each other (Figure 1.37).

**Figure 1.38**
**In the 3 paragraphs of Ephesians 2:11-22 we see salvation in three dimensions. In Christ, in a moment of grace, Gentiles move from being separated from God and hostile to Israel, to being fellow citizens and family members with Jews in God's household.**

**A. Included: Gentiles who were separated from God are included in Christ (Eph. 2:11-13).**

> [11] *Therefore, remember that formerly you who are Gentiles by birth and called "uncircumcised" by those who call themselves "the circumcision" (that done in the body by the hands of men)—* [12] *remember that at that time you were separate from Christ, excluded from citizenship in Israel and foreigners to the covenants of the promise, without hope and without God in the world.* [13] *But now in Christ Jesus you who once were far away have been brought near through the blood of Christ* (Eph. 2:11-13).

In Ephesians 2:1-2, the *key* phrase is *dead in sins*. But in Ephesians 2:11-12, the *key* thought is *separated*. Paul mentions four ways the Gentiles were separated, *before Christ*. Let us look at each of these four forms of separation, alienation, and exclusion.

**Q 97** *Complete Figure 1.38, explaining 4 ways Gentiles were separated before they received Christ.*

| Ways That Gentiles Were Separated Before Christ | Your Summaries |
|---|---|
| 1. **They were** *separate from Christ.* | |
| 2. **They were** *excluded from citizenship in Israel.* | |
| 3. **They were** *foreigners to the covenants.* | |
| 4. **They were** *without hope and without God.* | |

**Figure 1.39   Ephesians 2:12 mentions several ways that Gentiles were separated before they received Christ.**

***First***, Gentiles were *"separated from Christ."* In Ephesians 1:3-14, Paul lists eight blessings that come to us in Christ. Here, in Ephesians 2:12, the apostle reminds the Gentiles that *before salvation* they were separated from Christ and all of the blessings God pours out on His children.

It was never God's plan to bless only Jews. Rather, God chose Abraham and his children for the purpose of being a light to Gentiles—the nations of the earth. From the beginning, God loved all people. But the Jews failed to share the good news about God with the *Gentiles*—the ethnic groups and nations of earth. Instead, they became proud, self-righteous, and felt superior because of the privileges God gave them. The Jews looked down on Gentiles, and referred to them as *dogs*. Then the Jewish nation rebelled against God and lost the light God chose them to share. The disobedience of the Jews left the Gentiles in the dark, without the revelation of the prophets and the news of the Messiah. Yet at rare times, God sent a prophet such as Jonah with light to a Gentile nation.

Imagine a room full of food as a king and his family enjoy a great feast. But those outside the room are separated and left out. At the most, they might look through a window of the castle and long for the privileges of those close to the king. Likewise, before salvation, Gentiles were separated from Christ and the blessings He brings.

***Second***, Gentiles were *"excluded from citizenship in Israel."* God revealed Himself to the nation of Israel. He blessed them with protection, prosperity, and spiritual light. But under the old covenant, the main way to become an Israelite was through birth. So Gentiles were excluded from being citizens of Israel.

Being a citizen of a nation brings blessings and privileges. Today, many migrate from the problems of one nation, and seek to become citizens of another nation. But under the old covenant, few foreigners, such as Tamar, Rahab, Ruth, and Bathsheba, became citizens of Israel. And in many nations of the world today, it is very difficult to become a citizen of a nation in which you were not born.

***Third***, Gentiles were *"foreigners to the covenants of promise."* They were alienated from the great men, such as Abraham, Moses, and David. Therefore, they were foreigners to the promises and covenants that God gave. Gentiles were shut out from the spiritual promises about the Messiah.

In Romans 9, Paul reveals great sorrow for the Jews, his people. As a nation, Israel [the Jews] disobeyed God and fell short of all He planned for them. Still, Paul summarizes some of the blessings of being born a Jew:

*³For I could wish that I myself were cursed and cut off from Christ for the sake of my brothers, those of my own race, ⁴the people of Israel. Theirs is the adoption as sons; theirs the divine glory, the covenants, the receiving of the law, the temple worship and the promises. ⁵Theirs are the patriarchs, and from them is traced the human ancestry of Christ, who is God over all, forever praised! Amen* (Rom. 9:3-5).

***Fourth***, Gentiles were *"without hope and without God."* God is the source of hope. So those without God are without hope. We live in a fallen world with poverty, suffering, and sin. Without the God of hope, life is dark, troubled, empty, and hopeless (Rom. 15:13; 1 Cor. 15:14-19; 1 Thess. 4:5, 13).

Some put their hope in humanity, expecting governments or employers to solve the world's problems. But as the book of Job teaches:

*¹¹Can papyrus grow tall where there is no marsh? Can reeds thrive without water? ¹²While still growing and uncut, they wither more quickly than grass. ¹³Such is the destiny of all who forget God; so perishes the hope of the godless. ¹⁴What he trusts in is fragile; what he relies on is a spider's web. ¹⁵He leans on his web, but it gives way; he clings to it, but it does not hold* (Job 8:11-15).

**Q 98** Was it ever God's plan to bless Jews, but not Gentiles? Explain.

**Q 99** Before Christ, how were Gentiles like people looking at a feast through a window?

**Q 100** Under the old covenant, what was the main way to become a member of God's family?

**Q 101** Is it difficult for foreigners to become citizens of your nation? Explain.

**Q 102** Before Christ, what were some of the blessings God gave to Jews?

**Q 103** Was it ever God's plan to bless Jews, but not Gentiles? Explain.

**Q 104** Summarize the hopelessness of life without God. What is it like?

**Q 105** Without Christ, how are all of us like refugees, without a country?

**Q 106** What was the key to God bringing us near to Him?

**Q 107** What is the one reason why people remain separated from God?

**Q 108** How does Christ bring peace between tribes or groups who are separated? Illustrate.

As reeds must have water to live, people must depend on God to live and prosper.

Imagine being a refugee from another country. After surviving your journey to a foreign country, you are poor and without housing in a new land. No one is there to welcome you. You cannot speak the language. You have no friends. You are not a citizen and have no legal rights. You feel lonely, fearful, uncertain, and alienated. Without Christ, all of us are a lot like this spiritually.

Paul has reminded the Gentiles of the pit in which they once lived (Eph. 2:11-12). But in Ephesians 2:13, Paul moves from the problems of the past to the solution God provides in Christ. *"But now in Christ Jesus you who once were far away have been brought near through the blood of Christ"* (Eph. 2:13). It helps all of us to remember life before and after knowing Christ. For then, we are more thankful and live more worthy of the salvation and blessings God has given us. Notice that the key to our salvation is *"the blood of Christ"* (Eph. 2:13). It is not through our good works nor through the blood of animal sacrifices that we are able to overcome the separation between us, God, and His people. Only through the blood of Christ can we who were far away come close to God. Paul will explain this more in the next paragraph.

Many songs and hymns of the church emphasize that our hope is based on Christ alone. One great hymn states, "Nothing in my hand I bring; simply to your cross I cling."[20] Another famous hymn says, "Just as I am, without one plea—but that your blood was shed for me."[21] The one great theme of Christianity is that through Christ—not our good deeds—God offers sinners pardon, cleansing, adoption, and inheritance. No one remains separated from God because of sin. Rather, the one reason that some will be separated from God forever is that <u>they do not accept the family privileges God offers through the blood of Jesus Christ</u>. God's invitation to every sinner in the world is *" 'Come.'*[11] *As the Scripture says, 'Anyone who trusts in him will never be put to shame.'* [12] *For there is no difference between Jew and Gentile—the same Lord is Lord of all and richly blesses all who call on him,* [13] *for, 'Everyone who calls on the name of the Lord will be saved'* "* (Rom. 10:11-13). The greatest injustice in all the world is that some have not heard God's offer through Christ. How shall we stand before God with our heads up unless we do all we can to share God's invitation with those who are separated from His love?

## B. United: Gentiles who were separated from Jews are united with them in Christ (Eph. 2:14-18).

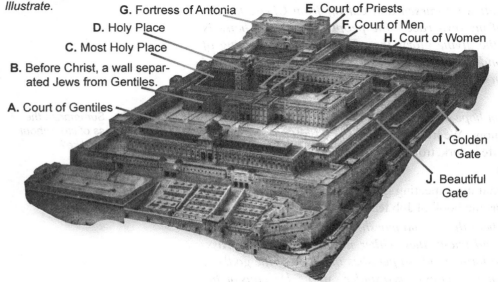

G. Fortress of Antonia
E. Court of Priests
D. Holy Place
F. Court of Men
C. Most Holy Place
H. Court of Women
B. Before Christ, a wall separated Jews from Gentiles.
A. Court of Gentiles
I. Golden Gate
J. Beautiful Gate

King Herod built the Jewish Temple on a raised platform in Jerusalem. This was the third temple built on Mount Moriah, following the temple of Solomon, and the temple rebuilt after the Exile. Herod tore down the temple built by the Jews who returned from the captivity in Babylon. And he built a huge new temple (35 acres) to win favor with the Jews. It took from 19 B.C. to A.D. 64 to complete the temple. Herod's temple had columns of white marble and gates of silver and gold. Only

**Figure 1.40   Model of Herod's Temple. The temple covered 35 acres (14 hectares).**[22]

Jews were allowed in the temple and the three courts on the top level. Five steps below the upper level was a barrier—a dividing wall that was 1.5 meters thick (Eph. 2:14). This wall prevented Gentiles from coming close to God, and warned of death to any violators. Paul himself was in danger of death because Jews thought he had taken a Gentile beyond the wall (Acts 21:27-32). Fourteen steps below the wall there was the court of the Gentiles that surrounded the temple. From this lower area, Gentiles could look up toward the temple and pray. Thus, the Jews treated Gentiles as inferior people on a lower level than God's chosen people. [23] The Romans destroyed the temple and the dividing wall in A.D. 70. Yet, through His death on the cross as the Lamb of God, Jesus had already destroyed the true barrier that the wall represented. For through Jesus Christ, all people have equal access into God's presence. Jesus replaced the priests and the sacrifices which the Law commanded under the old covenant. And the curtain of the Holy of Holies that separated God from humanity was torn apart from top to bottom at the moment our Savior died (Matt. 27:51).

With Ephesians 2:14, Paul begins to emphasize the horizontal dimension of salvation—peace between ethnic groups. He has stressed that Gentiles were separated from God *and from* God's people, the Jews. Now Paul emphasizes that salvation not only brought the Gentiles peace with God, but peace with Jews in Christ. Read this paragraph, and then we will examine the phrases that are in bold.

[14] *For **he himself is our peace**, who has made **the two one** and has destroyed **the barrier, the dividing wall of hostility**, [15] by **abolishing in his flesh the law with its commandments and regulations**. His purpose was to create in himself **one new man out of the two**, thus making peace, [16] and in this one body to **reconcile both of them to God** through the cross, by which he **put to death their hostility**. [17] He came and **preached peace to you who were far away** and peace to those who were near. [18] For through him **we both have access to the Father by one Spirit** (Eph. 2:14-18).*

There are several phrases in Ephesians 2:14-18 that are important for understanding Ephesians. So we will look closely at these phrases (Figure 1.41).

**Q 109** ✎ *Answer the questions in column two of Figure 1.41.*

| Key Phrases in Ephesians 2:14-18 | Explanations |
|---|---|
| *he himself is our peace* | Jesus is our peace—He is the harmony between those who were hostile. Has Jesus brought peace between you and a former enemy? Explain. _____ |
| *the two one* | Jesus makes Jews and Gentiles one—He unites those who follow Him. Which groups that you know has Christ united? |
| *the barrier, the dividing wall of hostility* | In the temple and its courts, where were Gentiles excluded (Figure 1.39)? _____ |
| | Gentile converts were not allowed in the Jewish temple, nor in the three courts nearby for Jewish priests, Jewish men, and Jewish women. A wall kept Gentiles out, with signs that warned "Trespassers will be EXECUTED" (Figure 1.39). This wall was a symbol of the barrier between Jews and Gentiles. Although Jesus did not destroy the wall itself, He destroyed the true barrier which included the laws about sacrifices, priests, and cleanliness—the laws that separated Jews from Gentiles. Did Jesus break down the physical wall that excluded Gentiles? Explain. |
| *abolishing in his flesh the law with its commandments and regulations* | Did Jesus abolish God's moral laws? Is there still law and order in God's kingdom? Explain _____ |
| | Verses throughout the New Testament teach that God requires us to respect and obey the moral laws of His kingdom (Matt. 5:17; 7:12; Rom. 3:31; 8:4; 13:8-10; James 2:8-9). We do not earn salvation by obeying God's laws, but obedience is the expression of our faith and love. What kind of laws, that separated Gentiles and Jews, did Jesus abolish? |
| | In contrast to the moral laws of God's kingdom, Jesus fulfilled and set aside ceremonial laws, such as those about abstaining from certain foods or offering animals sacrificed by priests (Col. 2:16-17; Heb. 9:11-28; 10:1-22). |

Figure 1.41

Continued on next page

Continued from previous page

| Key Phrases in Ephesians 2:14-18 | Explanations |
|---|---|
| *reconcile both of them to God* | By offering Himself as a sacrifice for all sins, Jesus brought in a new covenant that abolished the laws of cleanliness that separated Jews and Gentiles. How did Jesus reconcile Gentiles and Jews to God? _____ Now we are all clean through Christ, rather than through sacrifices in a temple by a priesthood. Both Jews and Gentiles can have peace with God through Christ. |
| *put to death their hostility* | By coming as the Lamb of God who takes away the sins of the world, Jesus did away with the laws about cleanliness and sacrifices that kept Jews and Gentiles apart. How did Jesus take away the hostility between Jews and Gentiles who believe in Him? _____ |
| *preached peace to you who were far away and peace to those who were near* | Jesus preached peace to Gentiles (who were separated and far away from God), and peace to Jews (who were near to God, but unable to obey the Law). Why did the Jews, who were near to God, need a way to make peace with Him? |
| *we both have access to the Father by one Spirit through Christ* | What does Ephesians 2:18 say about each member of the Trinity? _____ |
| | Note the roles of the Trinity in Ephesians 2:18. Through the blood of *Jesus*, Jews and Gentiles have access to the *Father* as the *Spirit* draws us, imparts spiritual life, empowers us to live holy lives, and fills us for service (Eph. 5:8-18). |

**Figure 1.41    Ephesians 2:14-18 mentions several ways Gentiles were separated before they received Christ.**

**Q 110** Did the temple God showed Solomon to build exclude Gentiles from God's presence (1 Kings 8:41-43)?

Jews, not God, sought to exclude Gentiles from God's presence. When Solomon dedicated the first temple, note the **lack of prejudice** against the Gentiles. Recall Solomon's prayer of dedication, about Gentiles:

[41] *"As for the foreigner who does not belong to your people Israel but has come from a distant land because of your name—* [42]*for men will hear of your great name and your mighty hand and your outstretched arm—when he comes and prays toward this temple,* [43]*then hear from heaven, your dwelling place, and do whatever the foreigner asks of you, so that all the peoples of the earth may know your name and fear you, as do your own people Israel, and may know that this house I have built bears your Name"* (1 Kings 8:41-43).

*Likewise,* after cleansing the temple, Jesus quoted Isaiah 56:7, saying, *"My house will be called a house of prayer for all nations"* (Mark 11:17). And John emphasizes that God loves *the whole world*, not just the Jews. Jesus came to be the door for Jews and Gentiles to come into God's presence. The Good Shepherd came to rescue *other sheep* that were not in the Jewish pen—and bring all the sheep together, so there would be one flock with one Shepherd (John 10:16). Jesus came to [51b] *"die for the Jewish nation,* [52]*and not only for that nation but also for the scattered children of God, to bring them together and make them one"* (John 11:51-52). From the beginning, before there were ever Gentiles and Jews, God's plan was to welcome all people into His family. Remember, even Abraham, the father of the Jews, was a Gentile! And God told him that through His seed (Christ), He would bless all the nations of the earth (Gen. 12:3; Gal. 3:8-9).

**Q 111** How can the nations of the earth be united in love? Explain.

**Application.** As long as there have been nations on the earth there have been feuds between various groups. Think of the things that divide people: national identity, sex, race, religion, politics, education, marriage, income, and opinions. But in Jesus Christ most of these differences fade away! Paul declared, *"There is neither Jew nor Greek, slave nor free, male nor female, for you are all one in Christ"* (Gal. 3:28).

Reconciliation is the major theme that unifies Ephesians 2. Reconciliation is the bringing together of two parties that are separated. *First,* Christ reconciles God and humans—bringing them together through the blood of Christ. *Second,* God reconciles Gentiles and Jews through Christ. In Ephesians 2:1-10, the emphasis was upon God reconciling individuals to Himself through Christ. Here, in Ephesians 2:11-22, the stress is on God reconciling groups of people *to each other* in Christ. We are united *in Christ!* Jesus brings together Jews and Gentiles who follow Him. He brings into being a new kind of identity—not just Jew or Gentile but "Christian!" The good news of this passage is that any group of people on earth can be reconciled to God and others *in Christ.* For those in Jesus Christ are all members of God's family! What an important message in a world torn apart by nationalism, racial prejudice, and sexual or financial strife!

### C. Made Equal: Gentiles who were foreigners are made full citizens and members of God's household (Eph. 2:19-22).

**Figure 1.42**   To show that believers in Christ are equal and united, Paul compares believers to stones that make a temple. He also compares Jesus Christ to the cornerstone, which aligns the temple; and the apostles and prophets of the new covenant to stones in the foundation of the temple (Eph. 2:20; 3:5; 4:11; 1 Cor. 12:28).

Some stones in Herod's temple were as big as a bus. The largest stone in Herod's temple was 44 feet by 11 feet by 16 feet and weighed about 500 tons. But most stones in Herod's temple were about 2.5 by 3.5 by 15 feet (about 28 tons).[24]

| Comparisons Paul Uses to Show That in Christ Believers Are United and Equal | Your Explanations |
|---|---|
| Citizens | |
| Family members | |
| Stones in a holy temple | |

**Figure 1.43**   Practice explaining three comparisons that show all believers in Christ are united and equal, sharing the love and blessings of God.

[19] *Consequently, you are no longer foreigners and aliens, but **fellow citizens with God's people** and **members of God's household**,* [20] *built on the foundation of the apostles and prophets, with Christ Jesus himself as the chief cornerstone.* [21] *In him the whole building is joined together and rises to become **a holy temple in the Lord.*** [22] *And in him you too are being built together to become a dwelling in which God lives by his Spirit* (Eph. 2:19-22).

Paul uses three comparisons to emphasize that believers are one in Christ—sharing His love and blessings. There is no favoritism with God. He loves all of His children the same (Figure 1.44). John adds that as we are united, the world recognizes that the Father loves believers even as He loved Jesus (John 17:23).

| Comparisons Paul Uses to Show That in Christ Believers Are United and Equal | Explanations |
|---|---|
| Citizens | As citizens in a city or nation are united, and share rights and privileges, all believers in Christ are one—with the same rights and privileges in God's kingdom. |
| Family members | As members of a family relate to one father, and love each other, members of God's family are all precious in His eyes, loving Him and one another. |
| Stones in a holy Temple | As stones in a temple are joined together to form a building, believers are joined together to be a temple for God to dwell in. (See 1 Pet. 2:9-10.) |

**Figure 1.44**   Paul uses three comparisons to show that all believers in Christ are united and equal, sharing the love and blessings of God.

**Q 112** ✎ *Do you think Jewish believers were shocked to learn that believers become the new temple of God? Explain.*

**Figure 1.45    Statue of Artemis (Diana) at Ephesus**

Gentile believers once worshiped in the temple of Artemis (Diana) in Ephesus. Likewise, Jewish believers worshiped in Herod's Temple in Jerusalem. Paul's point is stunning and revolutionary! The dwelling place of the living God is not made of stones and mortar, at Ephesus or in Jerusalem. Since the death and resurrection of Jesus Christ, God dwells in the midst of believers—Jews and Gentiles, *"being built together to become a* [spiritual] *dwelling in which God lives by His Spirit!"*

**Figure 1.46    Model of Herod's Temple in Jerusalem**

**Q 113** 🖎 *Does your church realize that all believers are equal in Christ, or is there pride, hostility, favoritism, and prejudice? Explain.*

**Application.** Ephesians 2:11-22 emphasizes the glorious standing of believers in Christ from every nation. These verses teach us that God has no favorites. There are no big people and little people in Christ. God loves all of His children. As this truth sinks into our hearts, it cleanses us of prejudice and favoritism. This passages helps us to not look down on others or ourselves—from the platform or the pew. No believers should feel superior or inferior. We are all special to God. He gave His Son for all of us. He adopted all of us into His family. He dwells among all of us. He gives us different gifts, but we are all members of the same body.

**Q 114** 🖎 *Complete Figure 1.47 as you fill in the column.*

| Reference | Your Analysis of Whether There Was Favoritism or Unity at the Time of an Event |
|---|---|
| Matt. 10:6 | At this stage of the Kingdom, Jews were favored over Gentiles. |
| Matt. 15:21-28 | |
| Luke 18:9-14 | |
| John 4:1-42 | |
| Acts 11:1-18 | |
| Acts 11:19-20 | |
| Eph. 2:11-22 | |
| James 2:1-13 | |
| Philem. 1:8-16 | |
| Rev. 7:9-10 | |

**Figure 1.47    Practice analyzing whether all believers were united, or if there was pride, prejudice, and favoritism.**

**Q 115** 🖎 *Complete Figure 1.48, summarizing aspects of salvation.*

| Ephesians 2:11-22 | Aspects of the Church | Your Summaries on Aspects of the Church |
|---|---|---|
| 2:11-13 | **A. Included:** Gentiles who were separated from God are included in Christ. | |
| 2:14-18 | **B. United:** Gentiles who were separated from Jews are united with them in Christ. | |
| 2:19-22 | **C. Made Equal:** Gentiles who were foreigners are made full citizens with Jews and members of God's household. | |

**Figure 1.48    Practice summarizing the progression of Gentiles into the family of God (Eph. 2:11-22).**

God loves the whole world! Jesus died for the sins of Jews and Gentiles! The peace He provides is both vertical and horizontal. Jesus brings us peace with God *above*, and peace with others *beside* us. So there is no place for racial, cultural, or sexual prejudice among followers of Jesus. In Christ, we can overcome our feelings of superiority or inferiority for any reason—such as physical, emotional, intellectual, social, national, educational, or financial. For as God's children, we are all members of His family. The ground is level at the foot of the cross. In Christ, let us *"accept one another, then, just as Christ accepted"* each of us (Rom. 15:7).

---

**Lesson 7**

## The "Mystery of Christ" (Eph. 3:1-13)

**Goal A:** *Explain the mystery in Ephesians 3:1-13.*
**Goal B:** *Summarize 3 ways "the mystery of Christ" includes Jews and Gentiles (Eph. 3:6).*
**Goal C:** *List 4 responsibilities we have in response to "the mystery of Christ."*
**Goal D:** *Explain 2 purposes of "the mystery of Christ."*

---

**Setting.** Ephesians 3:1 begins with the words *"For this reason."* The reason is *because* God has redeemed and united Jews and Gentiles as fellow citizens, family members, and His temple (Eph. 2:11-22). As Paul says *"for this reason,"* he is about to pray his second prayer for the Ephesians. He will go ahead with the prayer a little later, when he again says, *"for this reason"* in Ephesians 3:14. But as he is about to pray for all believers (Eph. 3:1), the Spirit guides Him to clarify his ministry to them—so they will grasp the full force of his prayer for them. As believers see Paul in four roles, we shout a loud amen to his prayer.

**In this lesson we will study Paul in four roles,** in relation to the great *mystery* God revealed to him and others. We will study Paul as a **prisoner**, a **steward**, a **servant**, and a **preacher** (A–D).

> **Q 116** ⌁ *What is the reason in Ephesians 3:1?*

> **Q 117** ⌁ *In Ephesians 3:1, as Paul is about to pray, what causes him to delay the prayer until Ephesians 3:14?*

### A. Prisoner Principle: In all circumstances, trust in God—the Creator and King of the universe.

Paul was a prisoner of Christ Jesus. He referred to himself as *a prisoner for the Lord*.

*¹For this reason I, Paul, **the prisoner** of Christ Jesus for the sake of you Gentiles—* (Eph. 3:1)

*¹³I ask you, therefore, not to be discouraged because of my sufferings for you, which are your glory* (Eph. 3:13).

*As **a prisoner** for the Lord, then ..."* (Eph. 4:1).

Paul wanted the believers in and around Ephesus to understand why he was in prison. He did not want them to lose their faith when they thought of his sufferings (Eph. 3:13). Although he was arrested on charges by the Jews, Paul did not consider himself a prisoner of the Jews. Although the Romans put him in prison, Paul did not consider himself a prisoner of the Romans. Although he had appealed to Caesar, he did not consider Caesar to be the highest ruler. Paul was in prison because of Jesus Christ whom he was serving (see Phil. 1:12-13)! Paul never saw himself as a mere *victim of circumstances*. Rather, this apostle recognized that Jesus is Lord—high above humans who affect our lives. Paul believed that God works out everything to conform to His own purpose (Eph. 1:11). So he avoided blaming people for his circumstances. Paul practiced believing that the steps of the righteous are ordered of the Lord (Ps. 37:23). He believed that all things work together for good, to those who are called of God (Rom. 8:28). Paul recognized that believers have human and spiritual enemies. And he reminded himself and others that we must live alert, be sober, and make wise decisions. But Paul knew whom he had believed, and was persuaded that God's hand would guide and protect him in his ministry to the Gentiles. This apostle believed that even when prison bars surrounded him, he was in the palm of God's hand. For the Father never forsakes His children, but as our Father, He provides, loves, and cares for us in all circumstances.

> **Q 118** ⌁ *Did Paul consider himself a victim of circumstances? Explain.*

**Q 119** ➚ *How was Paul like Joseph?*

**Q 120** ➘ *Do you blame others for trials you face, or claim verses like Ephesians 1:11, Psalms 37:23, and Romans 8:28? Explain.*

Joseph's brothers were jealous of him. They hated him because his father loved him so much. They mocked him because of the dreams God gave him at age 17. Then they threw him into a pit, and stripped him of the beautiful coat that Jacob made for him. Next, his own brothers sold him for 30 pieces of silver to some travelers going to Egypt. Even in Egypt, people continued to do wrong to Joseph. Potiphar's wife falsely accused him of sexual sins, so Potiphar put Joseph in prison. But even in the prison, God gave Joseph favor, and the warden put him in charge of almost everything (Gen. 39:23). Later, in the prison, God gave Joseph the interpretation to the cupbearer's dream. The interpretation came true, and Pharaoh restored the cupbearer from the prison to his position. Still, the cupbearer did not remember Joseph, but left him in prison for 2 more years. Finally, God gave Joseph the interpretation to Pharaoh's dream, and Pharaoh promoted Joseph to a top position in the kingdom. After more than 20 years of faith, faithfulness, and patience, Joseph's dreams came true. Through all these years, Joseph—like Paul—saw himself as a prisoner of God. He did not become bitter over Potiphar or his lying wife. Joseph did not blame the cupbearer for forgetting him. And he did not blame his brothers for hating him and selling him. Rather, [19] *"Joseph said to them, 'Don't be afraid. Am I in the place of God? [20] You intended to harm me, but God intended it for good to accomplish what is now being done, the saving of many lives'"* (Gen. 50:19-20).

**Q 121** ➚ *Why was Paul in prison in Rome?*

Paul wrote that he was *"a prisoner of Christ Jesus **for the sake of you Gentiles"*** (Eph. 3:1). In other words, prison was a part of what it cost Paul to love and serve the Gentiles. Paul was in a Roman prison because he was faithful to God's call to preach to the Gentiles. To understand that Paul was in prison for his Gentile ministry, we must review Acts 21–28.

| Acts 21 → | Acts 22 | Acts 23 | Acts 24 | Acts 25 | Acts 26 | Acts 27 | Acts 28 |
|---|---|---|---|---|---|---|---|
| **In Jerusalem** Jews accuse Paul for his ministry to Gentiles. | Jews riot as Paul mentions his Gentile ministry. | The Sanhedrin plots to kill Paul. | **In Caesarea** Governor Felix listens as Tertullus accuses Paul. | Governor Festus hears Paul's case after he has been in prison 2 years. | King Agrippa hears Paul's case. | Chained on a ship, Paul sails to Rome. | **In Rome,** Paul writes to Gentiles in Ephesus. |

**Figure 1.49    Acts 21–28 describe trials that led to Paul's imprisonment for the sake of his ministry to the Gentiles.**

**Q 122** ➘ *Complete Figure 1.50, summarizing trials that led to Paul's imprisonment for the Gentiles.*

The attitude of Paul the prisoner inspires us. He walked close to God, loved at any cost, and trusted God—as King of the world and the universe. We do not know where following Christ will lead us. Some of God's most spiritual children have spent time in cold, lonely, dingy prisons. Even today, thousands of believers are in prison for their faith. But we know God is faithful. We know that it is God's responsibility to guide us, and our responsibility to trust and obey Him—whatever the cost. And at the end of our brief time on earth, God will give us the glorious inheritance He has promised.

| Acts 21 → | Acts 22 | Acts 23 | Acts 24 | Acts 25 | Acts 26 | Acts 27 | Acts 28 |
|---|---|---|---|---|---|---|---|
| **In Jerusalem** | Jews | The Sanhedrin | **In Caesarea** | Governor Festus | King Agrippa | Chained on a ship, | **In Rome,** Paul writes to |

**Figure 1.50    Practice summarizing trials in Acts 21–28 that led to Paul's imprisonment for his ministry to Gentiles.**

### B. Steward Principle: As stewards of God's grace, we must all give an account at the end of our days.

Paul was a ***steward*** *of the grace of God*—the mystery God hid through the ages (Eph. 3:2-6).

[2]*Surely you have heard about **the administration** [stewardship] **of God's grace** that was given to me for you, [3]that is, the mystery made known to me by revelation, as I have already written briefly. [4]In reading this, then, you will be*

*able to understand my insight into **the mystery of Christ**, [5]**which was not made known to men in other generations** as it has now been revealed by the Spirit to God's holy apostles and prophets. [6]**This mystery is** that through the gospel the Gentiles are heirs together with Israel, members together of one body, and sharers together in the promise **in Christ Jesus*** (Eph. 3:2-6).

[8]*Although I am less than the least of all God's people, this grace was given me: to preach to the Gentiles the unsearchable riches of Christ, [9]and to make plain to everyone **the administration** [stewardship] **of this mystery**, which for ages past was kept hidden in God, who created all things* (Eph. 3:8-9).

Paul was a prisoner, but also a *steward*. The Greek word for stewardship is *oikonomian*—based on *oikos,* which means "house or household" (Eph. 3:2 and 3:9). An *oikonomos* is the chief steward, manager, or administrator of a house. Perhaps you have seen a brand of yogurt called *Oikos*. The sellers want their yogurt to be *in every house!* Also, the word *economics* comes from *oikonomika,* which deals with stewardship and managing. Paul was a steward over ministry to the *Gentiles*—the *nations* of the earth.

**Q 123** *What is a steward?*

Paul saw himself as a steward of God's grace (Eph. 3:2, 9). *Grace* (Greek: *charis*) is a free gift from God that comes to us in many forms. Grace comes to us in such forms as salvation, our bodies, our minds, abilities, our time, health, finances, opportunities, children, friends, and our spiritual gifts (*charis-mata*, Figure 1.51). All of these gifts of God's grace are free to us. As John writes, *"From the fullness of his grace we have all received one blessing after another"* (Greek: we have all received grace upon grace, John 1:16). **But these free gifts of grace come with responsibilities and accountability.** So Paul reminds us that we are all *stewards of God's grace* (Eph. 3:2, 9; 1 Pet. 4:10). At the end of our days, we must all stand before God and give account for the grace He has given us. A person who is put in charge as a manager **must** be faithful (1 Cor. 4:2). Faithfulness is the main characteristic of a steward.

**Q 124** *What are some forms in which grace comes to us?*

The parables of the talents, the minas, and the sheep and the goats remind us that God requires stewards to be faithful. And one day we will all give an account of how we managed the gifts of grace God entrusted to us (Matt. 25:14-46). Wise and faithful stewards manage God's grace with care. In contrast, those who call themselves followers of Christ, but are not good stewards of God's grace, are hypocrites, and deceived. These foolish stewards are like the man who hid his master's talent of grace in the dirt. When the master returned, the servant claimed to be responsible. But the master took the gift from him, and condemned the unworthy servant to outer darkness, where there will be weeping, wailing, and grinding of teeth (Matt. 25:28-30). It is a serious thing to despise God's grace and insult the Holy Spirit of grace (Heb. 10:29). So let us thank God for all of His gifts of grace. For *"to each of us grace has been given"* (Eph. 4:7). And as Paul urges, let us live worthy of the grace of God (Eph. 4–6).

**Q 125** *What are some responsibilities you have as a steward of God's grace?*

| Romans 12:6-8 | 1 Corinthians 12:8-11 | 1 Corinthians 12:27-31 | Ephesians 4:11-12 |
|---|---|---|---|
| Prophecy | Wisdom | Apostles | Apostles |
| Service | Knowledge | Prophets | Prophets |
| Teaching | Faith | Teachers | Evangelists |
| Encouragement | Healing | Workers of miracles | Pastors |
| Giving | Miracles | Those with gifts of healing | Teachers |
| Leadership | Prophecy | Those able to help others | |
| Mercy | Discernment | Those with gifts of administration | |
| | Tongues | Those speaking in tongues | |
| | Interpretation | Those who interpret tongues | |

**Figure 1.51    Paul lists several ministries, which are *gifts of God's grace, charis-mata* (Rom. 12:3, 6; 1 Cor 12:4, 9, 28).**

**Q 126** ⬉ *Complete Figure 1.52 on the mystery of God.*

**The mystery.**    Grace came to Paul in the form of the revelation of a *mystery*—a secret that God had hidden for centuries. Please read again Ephesians 3:2-6 above.

> *6This mystery is that through the gospel the Gentiles are heirs together with Israel, members together of one body, and sharers together in the promise in Christ Jesus* (Eph. 3:6).

| Questions | Your Answers |
|---|---|
| How long had God kept the mystery a secret? | |
| Why do you think God kept the mystery a secret? (1 Cor. 2:6-8) | |
| What is the mystery? | |
| Why was Paul in prison in Rome? | |
| What responsibility did Paul have to the Gentiles? | |

**Figure 1.52    Questions to answer related to the mystery (Eph. 3:2-9).**

This mystery is that through the gospel all the nations of the earth may share together in the promise of God in Christ Jesus (Figure 1.52; Eph. 3:6). All that God promises is available to all in Jesus. Those who receive and obey Jesus inherit all the promises of God. *"No matter how many promises God has made, they are 'Yes'* [available to all] *in Jesus"* (2 Cor. 1:20).

**Q 127** ⬉ *How did referring to the gospel as a "mystery" help Paul relate to the teachings of his day?*

**Q 128** ⬉ *How can you refer to the gospel in ways that will help you connect with today's hearers?*

There have always been mysteries on the earth. A writer of Proverbs said four things were mysterious to him. He did not understand: *"the way of an eagle in the sky, the way of a snake on a rock, the way of a ship on the high seas, and the way of a man with a maiden"* (Prov. 30:19). Likewise, the Greeks and Romans had *mystery religions*, such as Gnosticism, which we will study in Colossians. Followers of *mystery religions* thought that only a few could learn the spiritual secrets of the cosmos. And these few had to work hard to gain this spiritual knowledge. But in Ephesians 3:1-13 and Colossians 1:24–2:5, Paul uses the word *mystery* as a truth, once hidden, but now revealed. Paul writes about a mystery or truth made known by revelation. This mystery could not be uncovered by human effort. Rather, Paul wrote about a former mystery that became an *open secret*. Paul declared that God Himself had revealed the mystery *in Christ*. Now God wants the *mystery* proclaimed to *all nations* (Gentiles)—all peoples of the world!

**Q 129** ⬈ *What was the mystery that Paul preached?*

| Ephesians 2:5-6 | Ephesians 2:11-22 | Ephesians 3:6 |
|---|---|---|
| We were dead in our sins, but God made us alive **with** Christ. | We Gentiles who were separated from God are **included** in Christ. | We Gentiles are heirs **together with** Israel. |
| We were led by the world, the devil, and the flesh, but God raised us up **together with** Christ. | We Gentiles who were separated from Jews, are **united with** them in Christ. | Jews and Gentiles are **members together** of one body. |
| We were objects of wrath, and headed for judgment, but God seated us **together with** Christ in heaven. | We Gentiles who were foreigners are made full citizens **with** Jews and members of God's household. | Jews and Gentiles **share together** the promise in Christ Jesus. |

**Figure 1.53    In Ephesians 2–3, Paul emphasizes the union and equality of Jews and Gentiles in Christ Jesus.**

**Q 130** ⬈ *What type of attitude does a servant have toward others? Who is our example of serving?*

## C. Servant Principle: Believers should serve others with the gifts God has given and the Spirit's power.

Paul was a **servant** of Christ Jesus—by grace, through the power of God (Eph. 3:7).

*I became a **servant** of this gospel by the gift of God's grace given me through the working of his power* (Eph. 3:7).

When we think of a servant, we see a person who is humble, unselfish, and who cares for others rather than focusing on self. The disciples once schemed for positions of prestige and power. So Jesus contrasted being a servant or a lord:

> [25] *Jesus called them together and said, "You know that the rulers of the Gentiles **lord** it over them, and their high officials exercise authority over them.* [26] *Not so with you. Instead, whoever wants to become great among you must be your **servant**,* [27] *and **whoever wants to be first must be your slave**—* [28] *just as the Son of Man did not come to be served, but to serve, and to give his life as a ransom for many"* (Matt. 20:25-28).

The heart of serving is living to help others—as Jesus did.

Paul referred to himself as a servant—which was one of his favorite descriptions of himself (Rom. 1:1; Eph. 3:7; Phil. 1:1; Titus 1:1). But some have misunderstood this word. The Greek word for servant, *doulos,* means "one who waits on tables."[25] Paul, and all the other apostles, were servants, but they did not wait on tables. Recall the words of the apostles in Acts:

> [1] *In those days when the number of disciples was increasing, the Grecian Jews among them complained against the Hebraic Jews because their widows were being overlooked in the daily distribution of food.* [2] *So the Twelve gathered all the disciples together and said, **"It would not be right for us to neglect the ministry of the word of God in order to wait on tables.*** [3] *Brothers, choose seven men from among you who are known to be full of the Spirit and wisdom. We will turn this responsibility over to them* [4] *and will give our attention to prayer and the ministry of the word"* (Acts 6:1-4).

Being a servant means being humble and helping others. But being a servant does not mean living without focus, purpose, and priorities. The work of God's servants varies. The responsibilities of each servant differs. Paul teaches that each of us should serve **in the area of our gifts**. Those whom God calls to preach and teach should focus on these ministries, and allow other believers to perform other ministries.

> [3] *For by the grace given me I say to every one of you: Do not think of yourself more highly than you ought, but rather think of yourself with sober judgment, in accordance with the measure of faith God has given you.* [4] *Just as each of us has one body with many members, and these members do not all have the same function,* [5] *so in Christ we who are many form one body, and each member belongs to all the others.* [6] *We have different gifts, according to the grace given us. If a man's gift is prophesying, let him use it in proportion to his faith.* [7] *If it is serving, let him serve; if it is teaching, let him teach;* [8] *if it is encouraging, let him encourage; if it is contributing to the needs of others, let him give generously; if it is leadership, let him govern diligently; if it is showing mercy, let him do it cheerfully* (Rom. 12:3-8).

In Ephesians 3:8-13, we will see that Paul's focus was serving through preaching to all people the mystery of Christ. And note that Paul depended on **the power of God to serve** (Eph. 3:7)

Paul is a good example for us. He had many abilities, qualities, and connections. But he reminds us that the secret of spiritual ministry is spiritual power. Paul contrasted himself with those who trust in the flesh. Recall Paul's words.

> [4b] *If anyone else thinks he has reasons to put confidence in the flesh, I have more:* [5] *circumcised on the eighth day, of the people of Israel, of the tribe of Benjamin,*

**Q 131** Does being a servant mean saying yes to all opportunities to serve? Explain.

**Q 132** When doors of service open, how do we decide to say "yes" or "no"?

**Q 133** What is the source of your power to serve?

**Q 134** As you serve, do you depend on yourself or on God?

**Q 135** ✗ *Who was Paul's source of power to serve?*

**Q 136** ✎ *Who is your source of power for serving? As you serve, what do you depend on?*

**Q 137** ✎ *Do you see yourself as a servant? What are some ways God has gifted you to serve?*

**Q 138** ✎ *In what sense are all believers preachers, though few stand behind a pulpit?*

**Q 139** ✗ *Why did Paul make such a big deal about Jews and Gentiles?*

**Q 140** ✎ *What percentage of the earth is Gentile today?*

**Q 141** ✎ *In what sense is Abraham the father of all believers?*

*a Hebrew of Hebrews; in regard to the law, a Pharisee; ⁶as for zeal, persecuting the church; as for legalistic righteousness, faultless. ⁷But whatever was to my profit I now consider loss for the sake of Christ. ⁸What is more, I consider everything a loss compared to the surpassing greatness of knowing Christ Jesus my Lord, for whose sake I have lost all things. I consider them rubbish, that I may gain Christ... ¹⁰I want to know Christ and the power of his resurrection* (Phil. 3:4b-8, 10a).

Those who trust in themselves get the best that self has to offer. Those who trust in education, finances, and human abilities get the best these earthly resources offer. But as we trust in God and the power of His Spirit, we receive power from heaven to serve in a supernatural way, and bear spiritual fruit that will last for eternity.

The open doors to serve are many. But believers must choose those doors that are the best use of their time, resources, and gifts. ⁷ *"But to each one of us grace* [a spiritual gift] *has been given as Christ apportioned it. ⁸This is why it says: "When he ascended on high, he led captives in his train and gave gifts to men"* (Eph. 4:7-8).

## D. Preacher Principle: God's grace enables each member of the church to share the good news with others.

Paul was a preacher of the unsearchable riches of Christ Jesus—to the nations, the Gentiles (Eph. 3:8-13).

⁸*Although I am **less than the least** of all God's people, this grace was given me: **to preach to the Gentiles** the **unsearchable riches of Christ**, ⁹and to make plain to everyone the **administration of this mystery**, which for ages past was kept hidden in God, who created all things. ¹⁰His intent was that now, through the church, the **manifold wisdom of God should be made known** to the rulers and authorities in the heavenly realms, ¹¹according to his eternal purpose which he accomplished in Christ Jesus our Lord. ¹²In him and through faith in him we may approach God with freedom and confidence. ¹³I ask you, therefore, not to be discouraged because of my sufferings for you, which are your glory* (Eph. 3:8-13).

**Historical note:** As you read Ephesians 2–3, you may wonder why Paul makes such a big deal about the *Gentiles* being equal to Jews. Today, it seems strange that the Bible refers to some related to the small nation of Israel as *Jews*—but calls all the other ethnic groups of the world *Gentiles*! Today, the number of Jews on earth is only about 14 million. So 99.8 percent of the world's population is Gentile.[26] Why did biblical writers such as Paul give the few people from Israel a special title: *Jews*—yet refer to the masses of earth as Gentiles? Biblical history gives us the answer. After the Flood, spiritual light on earth was almost gone. So God revealed Himself to a Gentile named Abram, whose name became Abraham, which means *father of many nations*. Figure 1.54 shows that Abraham was the father of the Edomites, Ishmaelites, and Jews. God's plan was to use the Jews as a light to all the nations of earth. Israel disobeyed God and failed. Still, through Christ—the seed of Abraham—God fulfilled His plan to bless all the nations of earth (Gen. 12:3). Thus we Gentiles, who were once excluded from being Israelites, are now full heirs in the family of God. There was a time when the Jews were the stewards of the light God gave earth. Then Jesus Christ came as the light of God on earth. Over the past 2 millennia, the church has become mostly Gentiles. Thus John saw a vision of only 12,000 from each tribe of Israel (who represent the small number of Jews in the church); but he saw a multitude (the Gentiles) that no one could number from every tribe and nation (Rev. 7). So if the word *Gentile* seems strange to you in Ephesians 2–3, remember that in Paul's early ministry, 99.8 percent of God's people were Jewish. The main mission of Paul was to take the light of

Jesus to the nations. Today, this is God's Great Commission to all believers. We are His kingdom builders (Matt. 28:19-20).

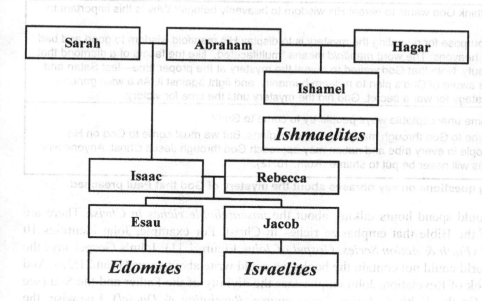

**Figure 1.54**
**Abraham has a physical family tree and a spiritual family tree.**[27] **Through Hagar, Abraham fathered the Ishmaelites. Through Sarah, Abraham became the father of the Edomites (via Esau), and the Israelites (via Jacob).**

**Paul explains that spiritually, there is a sense in which Abraham is the father of us all (Rom. 4:11-12; 16-18). As we live by the faith in God that Abraham lived by, we share the same *spiritual* DNA that Abraham had, and live as His children. So physically, Abraham was the father of few nations. But spiritually, Abraham is the father of many nations, who live by faith in Christ, the seed of Abraham. If we belong to Christ, we are Abraham's spiritual seed (Gal. 3:29).**

**Q 142** *What does a preacher proclaim?*

Paul was a *preacher*—a person who proclaimed the mystery God revealed to the apostles and prophets. Ephesians 3:8-13 explains much about the way Paul served as a preacher. Let us look at several key phrases in this rich passage.

**Q 143** *Answer the questions in Figure 1.55 on the mystery Paul preached.*

| Eph. 3 | Key phrase | Comments and Questions |
|---|---|---|
| 3:8 | Less than the least | Logic assures us that it is impossible to be greater than the greatest or less than the least. Yet Paul refers to himself as less than the least, because he once persecuted the Church. For the same reason he also calls himself the least of apostles, and the worst of sinners (1 Cor. 15:9; 1 Tim. 1:15).<br>**Q:** How do you see yourself—the least, middle, or greatest? |
| 3:8 | grace to preach to the Gentiles | **Q** To whom do the words *ethnos* and Gentiles refer?<br>**Q** How broad is the mystery that God revealed?<br>It is easy to miss the meaning of the Greek word (a form of *ethnos*) translated as Gentiles. *Ethnos* is a broad term for any group of people, a nation, tribe, or caste.[28] *Ta ethne* means ethnic groups or nations of people—the peoples of the world.[29] In the Great Commission, Jesus told the apostles to go and make disciples of *ta ethne* (all nations, and groups of people in them, Matt. 28:20). Paul affirms that God loves the Jews (see Rom. 9:1–11:32). But he explains *the mystery of God—*His plan that includes *all groups of people* in *all nations*—regardless of race, culture, age, sex, or status. Through Jesus Christ, God welcomes all the people of the world to be His children, to share His love and His kingdom. In Jesus Christ, there is no favoritism. God loves all who embrace and follow Jesus Christ as Savior and Lord.<br>**Q** Does your church preach to all ethnic groups, or exclude some? |
| 3:8 | unsearchable riches of Christ | The spiritual riches in Jesus Christ are too vast to search. They are deeper than the oceans and wider than the heavens. All the treasures of wisdom and knowledge are hidden in Christ (Col. 2:3). Jesus Christ ascended *to fill the whole universe* (Eph. 4:10). So to search the riches of Christ, one would have to search the whole universe—which is impossible for humans.<br>**Q:** What are some riches that are hidden in Christ? |
| 3:9 | administration of this mystery | Paul preached, making plain to all his ministry as a steward of the mystery of salvation for all people through Christ.<br>**Q:** What has God given you to administrate? |

Figure 1.55     Continued on next page

Continued from previous page

| Eph. 3 | Key phrase | Comments and Questions |
|---|---|---|
| 3:10 | *manifold wisdom of God should be made known to rulers and authorities in the heavenly realms* | **Q** Why do you think God wants to reveal His wisdom to heavenly beings? Why is this important to Him?<br>God's intent or purpose for revealing the mystery is to display His manifold wisdom to good and bad angels in the heavens. The word *manifold* means "multifaceted," like the facets of a diamond that reflect its beauty. Note that God waited to reveal the mystery at the proper time—lest Satan and his angels be aware of God's plan to redeem humanity, and fight against it. As a wise general keeps his strategy for war a secret, God hid the mystery until the time for victory. |
| 3:12 | *through faith in him we may approach God with freedom and confidence* | **Q:** What are some unacceptable ways people try to come to God?<br>People try to come to God through many ways and religions. But we must come to God on His terms. All people in every tribe and nation may approach God through Jesus Christ. Anyone who trusts in Jesus will never be put to shame (Rom. 10:12). |

**Figure 1.55**    Practice answering questions on key phrases about the mystery of God that Paul preached.

**Q 144** *What are your favorite riches in Christ?*

We could spend hours talking about the *unsearchable riches in Christ*. There are books of the Bible that emphasize riches in Christ. For example, John identifies 10 "I Am's" (*Faith & Action Series, Gospel of John*, Figure 1.11). John's Gospel says the whole world could not contain the books we could write about Jesus (John 21:25). And in the book of Revelation, John emphasizes the divinity of the Father and the Son (see Figure 6.4in the *Faith & Action Series* course, *Revelation & Daniel*). Likewise, the author of Hebrews gives seven comparisons to show the wealth in Jesus Christ. Paul emphasized that God the Son descended into a human body, but rose to fill the universe (Eph. 4:10). The most distant galaxies scientists can see today are 10 billion light-years away.[30] A light-year is the distance light travels in one year, at the speed of 186,000 miles per second. If a plane could travel at the speed of light, it could circle the earth seven times in 1 second. So try to imagine how vast the universe is—10 billion light years in every direction. And yet Jesus ascended to fill the universe. All the stars we see in the sky are just the lights on God's front porch! And God gives us the privilege of preaching the unsearchable riches of Christ. We cannot know all there is to know about Jesus. But we can share His riches that we have discovered at this season of our relationship with Him.

**Q 145** *Did common believers in Paul's day preach the good news to others? Explain.*

**Application.**   All believers are called to preach—which means to share the good news of Jesus Christ. As Jesus promised, we are His witnesses when we are filled with the Spirit (Acts 1:8). Few believers stand behind pulpits or get ministerial credentials. But as we are filled with the Spirit, we delight to tell others about Jesus.

**Q 146** *What is the key to being a preacher or witness for Jesus?*

[19]*Now those who had been scattered by the persecution in connection with Stephen traveled as far as Phoenicia, Cyprus and Antioch, telling the message only to Jews.* [20]*Some of them, however, men from Cyprus and Cyrene, went to Antioch and began to speak to Greeks also, telling them the good news about the Lord Jesus.* [21]*The Lord's hand was with them, and a great number of people believed and turned to the Lord* (Acts 11:19-21).

Jesus promised that as we are filled with the Spirit of grace, we become His witnesses—proclaiming the gospel where we live and to the ends of the earth (Acts 1:8). On the Day of Pentecost, 120 believers waited in an upper room to be filled with the Spirit. After these apostles and common believers were filled, they preached Jesus first in Jerusalem, their home town. Thousands came to Christ as believers shared the gospel through daily living and spiritual gifts. In time persecution arose in Jerusalem, driving everyone but the apostles out of Jerusalem (Acts 8:1). As a strong wind blows seeds, persecution blew the gospel seed in many directions. Luke writes [4] *"Those who had been scattered* **preached the word** *wherever they went"* (Acts 8:4). Note that it was common believers, filled with the Spirit, who preached the Word. Their changed lives and anointed testimonies were a powerful light in a dark world. Likewise today, common believers, filled with the Spirit, often lead family members, friends, and those around them to the Savior. True believers, filled with the Spirit, shine likes stars in the universe, among a crooked and sinful generation (Eph. 5:8-14; Phil. 2:15). Those who follow Jesus do not hide their light under a basket (Matt. 5:16). Rather, their lives and words preach Jesus everywhere they go. Wherever the Church is growing, much of the growth comes as common believers preach—not behind pulpits, but in daily life.

Some experts estimate that tens of thousands of people accept Jesus Christ each day in Northern Asia, where there may be 100 million believers.[31] Most of this growth is through preaching by common believers who are filled with the Spirit.

## Paul's Second Prayer for Believers (Eph. 3:14-21)

**Lesson 8**

**Goal A:** *Analyze the role of the Spirit in overcoming the flesh and the world, and how to live filled with the Spirit (Eph. 3:14-17a).*

**Goal B:** *Explain and illustrate the role of love in obeying the teachings of Jesus (Eph. 3:14-17a).*

**Goal C:** *Sketch and explain the relationship of Ephesians 1–3 and 4–6 to the doxology of Ephesians 3:20-21.*

**Introduction to Paul's prayer:** [14]*"For this reason I kneel before the Father,* [15]*from whom his whole family in heaven and on earth derives its name"* (Eph. 3:14-15).

The words *"for this reason"* introduced Paul's *first* prayer (Eph. 1:15). And we saw the words *"for this reason"* again in Ephesians 3:1 as Paul was about to begin his second prayer. But before sharing his prayer, Paul took time to explain his ministry to the Gentiles—as a prisoner, a steward, a servant, and a preacher (Eph. 3:1-13). (Scholars refer to a passage such as Ephesians 3:1-13 as an excursion or parenthesis—because a writer begins one thought, but pauses to explain something else.)[32] After Paul explains his ministry to the nations, he shares his prayer.

Paul's prayer begins with *"for this reason"* (Eph. 3:14). But what is the *reason* why Paul kneels to pray for believers on earth? *For this reason* looks back to all God has done (Eph. 1–3). God has blessed us in the heavenly realms with all spiritual blessings in Christ (Eph. 1:3-14). And in Christ, God has redeemed Jews and Gentiles, uniting them into one body, one family, and one temple (Eph. 2:1-22). Gentiles and Jews are joint heirs of God's promises. And through the Church, God displays His manifold wisdom to rulers and authorities in the heavenly realms. Through Jesus Christ we may approach God with freedom and confidence (Eph. 3:1-13). *For this reason,* this outpouring of blessings listed in Ephesians 1–3, Paul kneels to pray to the Father. Likewise, as Paul's prayer looks back to the blessings of Ephesians 1–3, his prayer looks forward to our responsibilities he lists in Ephesians 4–6. As the left and right sides of a mountain slope up to the top, Ephesians 1–3 and 4–6 slope up to Paul's prayer, the summit of Ephesians (Figure 1.61, page 68).

**Q 147** *For what reason does Paul kneel before the Father?*

**Q 148** *How are Ephesians 1–3 and Ephesians 4–6 like two sides of a mountain?*

All believers are members in the family of God. Some believers are already in heaven, so there is no need to pray for them (Eph. 1:15). They have finished the race. In contrast, many members in the family of God are still on earth, struggling to live by faith, finish the race, and inherit the promises of God. So Paul prayed two requests for believers. Let us look at each request, and the principle linked to the request.

## A. First Principle: Being filled with the Spirit is God's solution for overcoming the challenges of the world and the flesh.

**First Request:** [16]*I pray that out of his glorious riches he may **strengthen you with power through his Spirit in your inner being,*** [17]*so that Christ may **dwell** in your hearts through faith* (Eph. 3:16-17a).

**Q 149** ❦ *What types of challenges do all believers face?*

**The Challenges.**   Life on earth is a struggle between the powers of good and evil. Many are unaware that we are in a war. These are captives of the devil, who has captured them to do his will (2 Tim. 2:26). Others of us have been set free from sin. And yet the battles of earth continue for all believers. People may disagree with us, offend us, and do things that hurt us. We are tempted to withhold forgiveness. Our flesh encourages us to be proud and think only of ourselves. Even family members and friends may counsel us to walk paths that are unbiblical. But the paths of pride and unforgiveness lead to a root of bitterness, and the loss of salvation. So Paul urges us: [2] *"Be completely humble and gentle; be patient, bearing with one another in love.* [3] *Make every effort to keep the unity of the Spirit through the bond of peace"* (Eph. 4:2-3). But how is this possible when other believers are rude, hateful, and ugly to us?

**Q 150** ❦ *What types of temptations are normal for believers?*

Meanwhile, as we struggle with relationships, we face other temptations. False teachers offer all we want. They offer riches, prosperity, happiness, and success—without self-denial or a cross to carry. Thus Paul refers to the *"cunning and craftiness of men in their deceitful scheming"* (Eph. 4:14). But how can we avoid these teachings that seek to seduce us? Every day the world offers us its menu of attitudes, values, and pleasures. Opportunities of lust, greed, and sexual sins are as close as a book, a magazine, a televison, a computer, a phone, or a friend. Yet Paul warns:

> [3] *But among you there must not be even a hint of sexual immorality, or of any kind of impurity, or of greed, because these are improper for God's holy people.* [4] *Nor should there be obscenity, foolish talk or coarse joking, which are out of place, but rather thanksgiving.* [5] *For of this you can be sure: No immoral, impure or greedy person—such a man is an idolater—has any inheritance in the kingdom of Christ and of God.* [6] *Let no one deceive you with empty words, for because of such things God's wrath comes on those who are disobedient.* [7] *Therefore do not be partners with them* (Eph. 5:3-7).

**Q 151** ➚ *What happens to believers who are led by fleshly desires?*

**Q 152** ❦ *What is God's solution to the challenges and temptations we face?*

**The Solution.**   In our weakness, our flesh, and our fallen world, how is it possible to live a life of holiness and victory? Spiritual power is God's solution for overcoming the challenges of the world, the flesh, and the devil. As we are filled with the Spirit in our inner being, we discover that *"greater is he who is in us than he who is in the world"* (1 John 4:4). [13] *"If we are led by the flesh we will die spiritually and lose our inheritance. But if by the Spirit we put to death the misdeeds of the body, we will live,* [14] *because those who are led by the Spirit of God are sons of God"* (Rom. 8:13-14).

> SPIRITUAL VICTORY DEPENDS ON SPIRITUAL POWER.

So we see that spiritual victory depends on spiritual power. We use our mind and our will, but we depend on the power of God's Spirit in us for success. We realize that the secret to walking in victory is being filled with the Spirit, day by day.

**Q 153** ❦ *How can we live filled with the Spirit?*

**Application.**   How does this happen? Are we filled with the Spirit just because Paul prayed for us 2,000 years ago? No! God does not want us to go through life empty or half empty. But living full of the Spirit requires our cooperation—with God and with each other. We cooperate with God as we seek His presence day by day, and hour by hour. As we seek His presence through devotions, Bible study, prayer, and worship, the Holy Spirit fills our lives. And we cooperate with God as we submit to His presence—learning to hate what is wrong and love what is right (Rom. 12:9). The Spirit leads us to abstain from fleshly lusts that war against the soul (1 Pet. 2:11). Otherwise, the time we spend in God's presence can be nullified and canceled by the time we spend indulging the flesh. We cannot live filled with the Spirit if we spend an hour with God in the morning, and then indulge evil thoughts and entertainment later in the day.

To live filled with God, we must cooperate with God and also each other. Paul will emphasize that the answer to his prayer of Ephesians 3:14-21 depends on keeping the unity of the Spirit by getting along with each other (Eph. 4:1-6). Also, living strong in the Spirit depends upon using our spiritual gifts to help each other and speaking the truth in love (Eph. 4:7-16).

Living filled with the Spirit depends on enjoying and honoring God's presence throughout the day. Therefore Paul prays that Christ may *dwell* in our hearts (Eph. 3:17). *Dwell* emphasizes a residence or home—a place where someone abides—in contrast to a hotel, where a guest may stay for a night.

To welcome a special person to stay in our home, we make special preparations. We clean the home and take out the trash to make it free from unpleasant sights and smells. Likewise, let us be diligent to make our hearts a fitting home for Jesus, the Son of God, to dwell. We do not save ourselves by our own efforts. But as Paul says, let us live *worthy* of our calling. Jesus will feel *at home* in our hearts as we avoid evil thoughts, attitudes, and practices—and as we adorn our homes with holy and righteous choices that please God. Jesus is pleased to dwell in our hearts as we seek and honor His presence day by day.

I MET GOD IN THE MORNING,
WHEN THE DAY WAS AT ITS BEST,
AND HIS PRESENCE CAME LIKE SUNRISE,
LIKE GLORY IN MY BREAST;
ALL DAY LONG HIS PRESENCE LINGERED,
ALL DAY LONG HE STAYED WITH ME,
AND WE SAILED WITH PERFECT CALMNESS,
OVER A VERY TROUBLED SEA;
OTHER SHIPS WERE BLOWN AND BATTERED,
OTHER SHIPS WERE SORE DISTRESSED,
BUT THE WINDS THAT SEEMED TO DRIVE THEM,
BROUGHT TO ME A PEACE AND REST;
THEN I THOUGHT OF OTHER MORNINGS,
WITH A KEEN REMORSE OF MIND,
WHEN I TOO HAD LOOSED THE *MOORINGS,
WITH HIS PRESENCE LEFT BEHIND.
SO I THINK I KNOW THE SECRET,
LEARNED FROM MANY A TROUBLED WAY;
YOU MUST SEEK HIM IN THE MORNING,
IF YOU WANT HIM THROUGH THE DAY. [33]

Paul's first request in prayer is that God strengthen us in our inner being by His Spirit. His second request is closely related. In fact, as we study these two prayer requests, they tend to blend into one.

**Q 154** Is Paul's prayer all we need to live filled with the Spirit's power (Eph. 3:16-17)? Explain.

**Q 155** How is welcoming the Spirit in our lives like welcoming a guest in our home?

**Q 156** What is the secret to enjoying God's presence through the day?

**B. Second Principle: Being filled with the love of God empowers us to follow the teachings of Jesus.**

**Second Request:** *17b And I pray that you, being rooted and established in love, 18 may have power, together with all the saints, to grasp how wide and long and high and deep is the love of Christ, 19 and to know this love that surpasses knowledge—that you may be filled to the measure of all the fullness of God* (Eph. 3:17b-19).

**Q 157** ➤ *How is law both helpful, and unhelpful?*

**The Problem.** It is easy to write a list of laws and rules for pleasing God. But those who were under the laws of the Old Testament proved that it was impossible for humans to keep them. In Romans 7, Paul wrote his own testimony about life under the Law, before he knew Christ and was filled with God's love. Paul agreed that God's laws were righteous and good. He confessed that the Law points in the right direction. But it does not give us any power to help us *do* what is right. Law condemns us when we fall. But it never helps us stand up. Law points a finger up the hill. But it never lends a helping hand to climb the hill. Meanwhile, while law points up, the world and the flesh pull us downward toward sin.

Figure 1.56   In a game called "tug of war," each group tries to pull others a certain direction.

Figure 1.57   The struggle between law and flesh is unlike tug of war. Although the flesh pulls us toward sin, the Law only points toward righteousness.

**Q 158** ➤ *Complete Figure 1.58 on the love of Christ.*

| Love of Christ | Your Explanations of the Love of Christ |
|---|---|
| How wide? | |
| How long? | |
| How high? | |
| How deep? | |

Figure 1.58   Practice explaining the love of Christ.

**The Solution.** So what is the key to living a life worthy of our calling to be the family, the body, and the temple of God (Eph. 4:1)? Being filled with the love of God is the answer! The world today uses the word *love* in so many ways that *love* has lost much of its meaning. According to the world, *love* can refer to lust, sexual desire, or shallow friendship. The unbiblical love of the world may fade as fast as the dew, and be as undependable as the wind. Paul prays for believers *"to grasp how wide and long and high and deep is the love of Christ"* (Eph. 3:18).

- God's love is *wide* enough to reach the whole world—every tribe and nation on earth (Eph. 1:9, 10, 20). The life of Jesus shows that God loves even those who seem unlovable. Jesus loved Matthew, a national traitor. He loved tax collectors, prostitutes, and murderers. This means that God loves all of us. Here is the secret to and source of self-esteem. Since Jesus loves us and died for us, this gives us confidence that we are worth a great amount—regardless of what others may think.

- God's love is *long* enough to cover all eternity. God loved us in Christ *"before the creation of the world"* (Eph. 1:4). And *"in the coming ages he* [will] *show the incomparable riches of his grace, expressed in his kindness to us in Christ Jesus"* (Eph. 2:7). His love is long!

- God's love is *high* enough to make all of heaven rejoice when one sinner down on earth repents (Luke 15:7, 10). His love reaches from heaven to earth.

- God's love is so *deep* that it can reach even the worst of sinners. God's love reached and saved Paul, the worst of sinners, when he was persecuting believers, sending men and women to prison, and forcing them to blaspheme (1 Tim. 1:15-16). There is no sinner so low that God's love does not reach down to save him or her.

Paul prays for believers to know the love of Christ *"that surpasses knowledge"* (Eph. 3:19). Paul wants us to know God's love in a way that surpasses mere knowledge of the head. He prays for us to know God's love through experience—the experience of being *"filled to the measure of all the fullness of God"* (Eph. 3:19). In other words, Paul does not want us to be just half full of God's love. He wants us to receive the full measure of love that God delights to give His children. Paul wants us to live filled and overflowing with the love of God.

**Q 159** ⬈ *How is it possible to know Christ's love that surpasses knowledge?*

Look closely at the two requests of Paul in this prayer (Eph. 3:16-19). In his first request, Paul prays for God to strengthen us by the Spirit in our inner being—so that Jesus abides and feels at home in our hearts. In the second request, Paul prays for us to be filled with God's love. As we study these two requests, we see that they overlap and may blend into one. Paul teaches us that God pours His love into our hearts by the Holy Spirit (Rom. 5:5). Likewise, love is a fruit of the Spirit (Gal. 5:22). To be strengthened by the Spirit is to be filled with God's love, for God is love (1 John 4:8). Many have described the baptism in the Spirit as a baptism in pure love. When we are filled with God's love, we are strong in Spirit. As you complete Figure 1.58 recall that everything God calls us to do is possible when the Spirit fills us with God's love.

**Q 160** ✎ *Complete Figure 1.59 on the result of being filled with God's love.*

| Reference | Your Summaries on Biblical Love |
|---|---|
| Matt. 22:34-40 | |
| Rom. 13:8-10 | |

**Figure 1.59**   Practice analyzing what happens when the Spirit fills us with God's love. To be filled with God's love is to be filled with God, for God is love, and supernatural love is a manifestation of the Holy Spirit.

After Paul prays his two requests for believers, he closes his prayer with a *doxology—a word of praise to God. (The Greek word *doxa* means "glory" and *logos* means "word or message." So a *doxo-logy* is a message of praise.)

## C. The doxology is the peak of Ephesians (Eph. 3:20-21).

**Q 161** ⬈ *What is a "doxology"?*

**Q 162** ✎ *Complete Figure 1.60 on the doxology of Paul.*

| Questions to Answer on Paul's Doxology of Ephesians 3:20-21 |
|---|
| How is the doxology of Ephesians 3:20-21 like the summit of a mountain? |
| How does Ephesians 1–3 relate to the doxology? |
| How does Ephesians 4–6 relate to the doxology? |
| How is Ephesians 3:20-21 the key to living Ephesians 4–6? |

**Figure 1.60**   Practice answering questions on the doxology of Ephesians 3:20-21.

> [20] *Now* **to him** *who is able to do immeasurably more than all we ask or imagine, according to his power that is at work within us,* [21] **to him** *be glory in the church and in Christ Jesus throughout all generations, for ever and ever! Amen* (Eph. 3:20-21).

**Figure 1.61    The top of a mountain is its most glorious, inspiring point.**

The mountain peak of Ephesians is the doxology of 3:20-21. Ephesians 1–3 rises in praise for two reasons: for all the spiritual blessings God has poured out on us in Christ (Eph. 1:3-14), and for uniting Jews and Gentiles into one mature body in Christ.

Likewise, Ephesians 4–6 rises as the praise of our response, as we *live worthy* of all our Father has done for us in Christ. Ephesians 3:20-21 are the grandest verses of this letter. Let us look up to these verses as a mountain peak in the heavens. Let us praise and glorify God for raising us up more in Christ than we can ever ask or imagine. Likewise, as we seek to practice the 36 principles of Ephesians 4–6. Let us lift our eyes to the heavens, knowing that we can live in ways that please and glorify God, as we depend on the power of the Spirit at work in us (Eph. 3:20-21).

(On the final exam, we will ask you to draw and explain Figure 1.60, so be sure to learn this.)

Ephesians 3:20-21 is a praise wrapped around a promise. The promise is that God can do more than we ask or think, by His power at work in us. The praise is the result of what God does in the Church, as we pray and praise Him—led by the Spirit, filled with power and love.

Q 163 ✎ *Answer the questions in Figure 1.61 on Paul's doxology.*

| Eph. | Questions to Answer on the Doxology of Ephesians 3:20-21 |
|---|---|
| 3:20 | *To whom* does Paul direct praise? |
| | *Why* does God compare what God can do to our thoughts and prayers? |
| 3:20 | *How* is God able to do more than we pray or think? |
| 3:21 | *What* does Paul want God to receive? |
| 3:21 | *How* does God receive glory in the church? Illustrate. |
| | *Why* does Paul connect the church and Christ (Eph. 4:15)? |
| | *How* does Ephesians 3:21 relate to 3:10? |
| | Does God receive glory from a lukewarm, worldly church? Explain. |
| | *How* do the 36 principles of Ephesians 4–6 relate to God receiving glory? |
| 3:21 | *When* does Paul want God to receive glory in the church? |

**Figure 1.62    Practice analyzing the doxology of Ephesians 3:20-21.**

**Test Yourself:** Circle the letter by the *best* completion to each question or statement.

1. Which is a Prison Epistle?
   a) Romans
   b) Philippians
   c) James
   d) Titus

2. How many times does Paul write *"in Christ"*?
   a) 20
   b) 80
   c) 160
   d) 200

3. In Ephesians 1:4, why did God choose us?
   a) To be His children
   b) To inherit heaven
   c) To seal us with His Spirit
   d) To be holy and blameless

4. What seal shows God owns us?
   a) The Holy Spirit
   b) The new birth
   c) Our good deeds
   d) The Father's love

5. How does Paul illustrate God's power (Eph. 1:15-23)?
   a) The creation of earth
   b) The exaltation of Christ
   c) The judgment of evil
   d) The new creation

6. How do people without Christ live (Eph. 2:1-3)?
   a) Following truth where they find it
   b) In the light of conscience
   c) Without doing good deeds
   d) Under the influence of the world

7. In Christ, the relationship of Gentiles to Jews is
   a) united and made equal.
   b) separated, but equal.
   c) united as husband and wife.
   d) included, but submissive.

8. The mystery of Christ is about (Eph. 3:1-13)
   a) the Antichrist.
   b) Jews and Gentiles.
   c) the Rapture.
   d) the Resurrection.

9. Like Paul in Ephesians 3:2, we are stewards
   a) of time.
   b) of money.
   c) of grace.
   d) of opportunity.

10. We used a mountain to show
    a) the relationship of Ephesians 1–3 to Ephesians 4–6.
    b) the height of God's love.
    c) the beauty of creation.
    d) the climb to heaven.

**Essay Test Topics:** Write 50-100 words on each of these 18 goals you studied. Try to complete this test in 2 hours. On the final exam, we will combine some of these goals and ask you to write on a few of them. As you practice writing on each of these goals now, you are preparing well for the final test. (6.5 points each)

- List the Prison Epistles and explain their title.
- Summarize the background of the city of Ephesus and Ephesian believers.
- Explain the purposes and outline of Ephesians.
- Identify and explain the 5 key phrases in Ephesians 1:1-2.
- Clarify the roles of the Father, Son, and Spirit in providing salvation.
- Explain and illustrate blessings 1–4 that we have in Christ (Eph. 1:3-8).
- Explain and illustrate blessings 5–8 that we have in Christ (Eph. 1:9-14).
- Explain, illustrate, and apply 3 aspects of Paul's prayer for believers (Eph. 1:15-23).
- Explain 5 ways we were hopeless before we were in Christ (Eph. 2:1-3).
- Summarize and illustrate 3 aspects of salvation Christ provided (Eph. 2:4-10).
- Analyze these 3 relationships of Gentiles to Jews: included, united, made equal (Eph. 2:13-22).
- Explain the mystery in Ephesians 3:1-13.
- Summarize 3 ways the mystery of Christ includes Jews and Gentiles (Eph. 3:6).
- List 4 responsibilities we have in response to "the mystery of Christ."
- Explain 2 purposes of "the mystery of Christ."
- Analyze the role of the Spirit in overcoming the flesh and the world, and how to live filled with the Spirit (Eph. 3:14-17a).
- Explain and illustrate the role of love in obeying the teachings of Jesus (Eph. 3:14-17a).
- Sketch and explain the relationship of Ephesians 1–3 and 4–6 to the doxology of Ephesians 3:20-21.

# Chapter 2:
# Live Worthy of Your Calling: In the Church and in the World
## (Eph. 4:1–5:20)

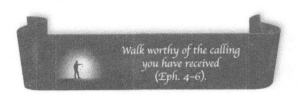

Walk worthy of the calling you have received (Eph. 4–6).

Figure 2.1   The banner over Ephesians 4–6

| Ephesians | Principles 1–16 for Living Worthy—in the Spirit and the Love of God (Eph. 4–6) |
|---|---|
| 4:2 | **1.** *Be completely humble and gentle; be patient, bearing with one another in love.* |
| 4:3 | **2.** *Make every effort to keep the unity of the Spirit through the bond of peace.* |
| 4:15 | **3.** Speak *the truth in love, so we will in all things grow up into him who is the Head, that is, Christ.* |
| 4:7, 16 | **4.** *Use the gifts God has given you; do your part to help the whole body grow, and be built up in love.* |
| 4:17-20 | **5.** *So I tell you this, and insist on it in the Lord, …you must no longer live* like those without Christ. |
| 4:22 | **6.** *Put off your old self, which is being corrupted by its deceitful desires;* |
| 4:23 | **7.** *Be made new in the attitude of your minds;* |
| 4:24 | **8.** *Put on the new self, created to be like God in true righteousness and holiness.* |
| 4:25 | **9.** *Put off falsehood and speak truthfully to his neighbor, for we are all members of one body.* |
| 4:26 | **10.** *"In your anger do not sin": Do not let the sun go down while you are still angry.* |
| 4:27 | **11.** *Do not give the devil a foothold.* |
| 4:28 | **12.** *He who has been stealing must steal no longer, but must work, doing something useful with his own hands, that he may have something to share with those in need.* |
| 4:29 | **13.** *Do not let any unwholesome talk come out of your mouths, but only what is helpful for building others up according to their needs, that it may benefit those who listen.* |
| 4:30 | **14.** *Do not grieve the Holy Spirit of God, with whom you were sealed for the day of redemption.* |
| 4:31 | **15.** *Get rid of all bitterness, rage and anger, brawling and slander, along with every form of malice.* |
| 4:32 | **16.** *Be kind and compassionate to one another, forgiving each other, just as in Christ God forgave you.* |

Figure 2.2   In Ephesians 4–6, Paul gives us 36 principles for living worthy—in the Spirit and the love of God. (See end of chapter for principles 17–24 and Figure 3.20 for principles 25–36).

**Q 1** ↖ *Why is it an error to emphasize Ephesians 1–3, apart from Ephesians 4–6?*

Ephesians 1–3 emphasizes our *riches* in Christ. Ephesians 4–6 focuses on our *responsibilities* in Christ. One teacher said we should focus on Ephesians 1–3, thinking *only* about what Christ has done for us. He told his listeners to ignore Ephesians 4–6. But there is no Ephesians 1–3 without 4–6! These sections of Ephesians are two parts of *one* letter.

**Q 2** ↗ *What banner can we put over Ephesians 4–6?*

The banner over Ephesians 4–6 is: *"Live a life worthy of the calling you have received"* (Eph. 4:1). God has *called* us out of darkness into the light, to be His people, His body, and His temple. He has *called* us to be His children, to imitate Him, to inherit His kingdom, and live with Him forever. Under the banner of *Live Worthy*, in the second half of Ephesians, Paul tells us what it means to *live worthy*. He gives us at least 36 principles for believers to practice. We will study these principles in lessons 9–16.

**Q 3** ↗ *What is the key to obeying the 36 commands of Ephesians 4–6?*

The 36 principles in Ephesians 4–6 are not a ladder we climb to heaven. We are saved by grace, not works. But we are saved by receiving and following Christ. The 36 principles show us what following Jesus looks like. God does not intend for us to live these principles in our own strength. So as we study these 36 principles for following Jesus, remember that Ephesians 3:20-21 is the glorious top of the mountain of Ephesians. In our own strength, we lack the power to please God. But *He* is able to do immeasurably more than all we can ask or imagine, by *"the power that is at work within us"* (Eph. 3:20; 5:18). As we walk in His Spirit and are filled with His love, we delight to keep His commandments, and they are not a burden to us (Rom. 8:4; 1 John 5:3).

## Lessons:

### Live Worthy in Your Relationships in the Church (Eph. 4:1-16)

**Goal A:** *Analyze the need to live worthy, and the roles of love and effort on the path of unity (Eph. 4:1-6).*
**Goal B:** *List at least 10 ways people serve as gifts in the church, and the result of this serving (Eph. 4:7-13).*
**Goal C:** *Explain why truth and love must walk together as we walk worthy (Eph. 4:13-16). Describe the result.*

### Live Worthy as Children of Light—Introduction to Lessons 11–13 (Eph. 4:17-24)

**Goal A:** *Contrast how we lived in the past, without Christ, and how Paul insists we must live now, in Christ (Eph. 2:1-3; 4:17-24; Col. 3:25).*
**Goal B:** *Contrast 3 truths about physical and spiritual walking.*
**Goal C:** *Contrast the reasons of the devil and the reasons of God for identifying sins.*

### Live Worthy as Children of Light—Part 1: Be Truthful and Loving (Eph. 4:25-32)

**Goal A:** *Explain why lying is so offensive to God, and give examples of being truthful.*
**Goal B:** *Identify 5 levels of anger we must practice controlling, and the fruit of the Spirit that replaces anger.*

### Live Worthy as Children of Light—Part 2: Work, Edify, and Be Moral (Eph. 4:25–5:17)

**Goal A:** *Give examples of people who have stolen, and illustrate why we must replace stealing with hard work.*
**Goal B:** *Give examples of unwholesome and healthy words. Contrast the effects of good and bad talking.*
**Goal C:** *Analyze the problem and destination of the sexual immoral. Contrast followers of Christ and followers of lust, on the topic of morality.*

### Live Worthy as Children of Light—Part 3: Be Filled with the Spirit (Eph. 5:18-20)

**Goal A:** *Give an example of the fruit from the tree of alcohol.*
**Goal B:** *Summarize 5 reasons why millions of believers do not drink alcohol.*
**Goal C:** *Explain how being filled with the Spirit brings assurance, victory over sin, and power for service.*
**Goal D:** *Summarize 5 keys to living filled with the Spirit.*

## Key Words

**worthy**—appropriate and fitting; our response to the salvation God gives us in Christ, by living in ways that please God, and show we are grateful to be members of His family

**grace gifts**—the talents, skills, and abilities God gives to each member of His family to serve and strengthen others

**debauchery**—shame; sin, fleshly indulgence; the opposite of self-control

**abstinence**—choosing to do without something, such as avoiding drinking alcohol

**filled with the Spirit**—the process of living full of God's Spirit. When we are born again, the presence of God's Spirit in us gives new life. But when the Spirit fills us as He did the 120 believers at Pentecost, He brings us power to serve, and to live a holy life. Being filled *once* with the Spirit is *not* enough. We need to live filled day by day (Eph. 5:18).

## Live Worthy in Your Relationships in the Church (Eph. 4:1-16)

**Lesson 9**

**Goal A:** *Analyze the need to live worthy, and the roles of love and effort on the path of unity (Eph. 4:1-6).*

**Goal B:** *List at least 10 ways people serve as gifts in the church, and the result of this serving (Eph. 4:7-13).*

**Goal C:** *Explain why truth and love must walk together as we walk worthy (Eph. 4:13-16). Describe the result.*

**Q 4** *When did a generation of Israelites lose their inheritance?*

**Q 5** *Is it possible to lose our inheritance of heaven after being delivered from sin? Explain.*

*Praise God for blessing us in the heavenly realms with every spiritual blessing in Christ (Eph. 1–3).*

**Figure 2.3    The banner over Ephesians 1–3**

**The need to live worthy.** The banner over Ephesians 1–3 is: *Praise God for blessing us in the heavenly realms with every spiritual blessing in Christ*. And the banner over Ephesians 4–6 is: *Walk worthy of the calling you have received*. We are called to be God's people, family, and temple. May we avoid the mistake that the nation of Israel made. God called them to be His people, and delivered them from bondage with a mighty hand. He drowned their enemies in the Red Sea. Moses led them forward to a land of promise. Yet most of them quit walking by faith, and died in the wilderness. They failed to walk worthy of their calling.

### Paul warns us to avoid Israel's mistakes.

¹*For I do not want you to be ignorant of the fact, brothers, that our forefathers were all under the cloud and that they all passed through the sea.* ²*They were all baptized into Moses in the cloud and in the sea.* ³*They all ate the same spiritual food* ⁴*and drank the same spiritual drink; for they drank from the spiritual rock that accompanied them, and that rock was Christ.* ⁵*Nevertheless, God was not pleased with most of them; their bodies were scattered over the desert.* ⁶**Now these things occurred as examples to keep us from setting our hearts on evil things as they did.** ⁷*Do not be idolaters, as some of them were; as it is written: "The people sat down to eat and drink and got up to indulge in pagan revelry."* ⁸*We should not commit sexual immorality, as some of them did—and in one day twenty-three thousand of them died.* ⁹*We should not test the Lord, as some of them did—and were killed by snakes.* ¹⁰*And do not grumble, as some of them did—and were killed by the destroying angel.* ¹¹**These things happened to them as examples and were written down as warnings for us, on whom the fulfillment of the ages has come.** ¹²*So, if you think you are standing firm, be careful that you don't fall!* (1 Cor. 10:1-12).

**Q 6** *Why did the Israelites who inherited Canaan lose it? Apply this to us?*

**Q 7** *Why is it important to obey the 36 commands of Ephesians 4–6?*

The younger generation inherited Canaan. But they did not learn the necessity of walking worthy of their calling. For as the blessings of God increased and the years passed, the hearts of the Israelites grew cold and disobedient. Like their ancestors, they failed to walk worthy of God. They exalted riches, pleasure, immorality, and idolatry above God. He sent prophets to call them back to Him. But they rejected and mocked God's messengers—stoning some and persecuting others. The Northern Kingdom of Israel was destroyed by Assyria in 722 B.C. This kingdom became known as "the lost ten tribes." They never regained their place or inheritance. By the year 586 B.C., the Southern Kingdom of Judah was conquered and enslaved. Today, more than 2,600 years later, there are only about 12 million Jews among earth's population of eight billion. Most of them have never met Jesus—the Messiah God promised, and the key to inheriting the eternal kingdom. Over the centuries, the Jews as a whole have failed to walk worthy of their calling. John assures us that a small remnant, represented by

12,000 from each tribe, will be saved. But over the millennia of mankind, Jewish history is a tragedy.

**Q 8** ↖ *Complete Figure 2.4 on warnings Paul gives so we will walk wisely.*

| Reference | Your Summaries |
|---|---|
| Eph. 5:5-6 | |
| 1 Cor. 6:9-10 | |
| Gal. 5:19-21 | |

**Figure 2.4   Practice summarizing Paul's warning to those who live in rebellion against God.**

Paul reminds believers that he is writing from prison, for the sake of the Gentiles (Eph. 4:1). He lets his readers know that he is doing his part. And he wants them to do their parts. Paul urged all believers to live worthy of our calling (Eph. 4:1). He wants us to be like the few believers in Sardis who had not soiled their clothes, but walked worthy of their calling (Rev. 3:4). Paul wants us to live worthy, live by faith, and inherit the Kingdom. The apostle warns that those who ignore biblical responsibilities, such as avoiding immorality and impurity, have no inheritance in heaven (Eph. 5:3-17). We are not saved by godly living. But living a life worthy of fellowship with God reveals that God is our Father (1 John 3:4-10). Will those who respond to God with contempt, rebellion, and disobedience inherit God's kingdom? Paul says "no" (Eph. 5:3-17; 1 Cor. 6:9-10; Gal. 5:19-21). We are not saved by living worthy. But living worthy, by the power of the Spirit and God's love, is the evidence and assurance that Christ lives in our hearts and our names are written in the book of life. So, as we study the 36 principles Paul gives for living worthy of our calling, let us commit ourselves anew to being disciples of Jesus—following in His footsteps, learning, growing, maturing in grace—and pleasing God. In this lesson we will focus on principles about relationships.

**Q 9** ↖ *Why is it important to practice obeying the 36 principles of Ephesians 4–6?*

## A. The Path: Live worthy by spreading love to protect unity in the church (Eph. 4:1-6).

| Ephesians | Principles to Practice as We Live Worthy in the Spirit and the Love of God (Eph. 4:1) |
|---|---|
| 4:2 | Be completely humble and gentle; be patient, bearing with one another in love. |
| 4:3 | Make every effort to keep the unity of the Spirit through the bond of peace. |
| 4:7, 16 | Use the gifts God has given you; do your part to help the whole body grow, and be built up in love |
| 4:15 | Speak *the truth in love*, so *we will in all things grow up into Christ, the Head* of His body. |

**Figure 2.5   Principles 1–4 to practice as we seek to live worthy, relating to one another.**

Paul places a great emphasis on relationships. For Christians, getting along with people must be a priority. In the final chapter of Colossians, Paul calls eight individuals and two groups of people by name (Figure 2.6), and in Philippians, Paul refers to the names of several brothers and sisters, and groups of saints.

**Q 10** ↗ *How many people does Paul call by name in Colossians and Philippians? Apply this to your ministry.*

| Colossians | Name of Person or Group | Description/Comment |
|---|---|---|
| 4:7 | Tychicus | A fellow worker |
| 4:9 | Onesimus | A faithful and dear brother from Colosse |
| 4:10 | Aristarchus | A fellow prisoner |
| 4:10-11 | Mark and Justus | The only Jews who were working with Paul; a comfort to him |
| 4:12 | Epaphras | A fellow worker from Colosse, and known for praying |
| 4:13, 16 | Believers | Believers in the churches at Laodicea and Hierapolis |

**Figure 2.6**   Continued on next page

Continued from previous page

| Colossians | Name of Person or Group | Description/Comment |
|---|---|---|
| 4:14 | Luke | The doctor |
| 4:14 | Demas | Who later forsook Paul |
| 4:15 | Nympha | A godly woman in Laodicea, in whose house the church met |
| 4:17 | Archipus | A worker in the Lord |
| 4:18 | Paul | An apostle in chains |
| **Philippians** | | |
| 1:1 | All the saints | In Christ Jesus in Philippi, together with the overseers and deacons |
| 2:19-24 | Timothy | *"I have no one else like him"* |
| 2:25; 4:18 | Epaphroditus | Who is one of you |
| 4:2-3 | Euodia and Syntyche | Women who worked with Paul |
| 4:3 | Clement | A fellow worker with Paul |
| 4:21 | All the saints | In Christ Jesus send greetings |
| 4:22 | Saints | In Caesar's household send greetings |

**Figure 2.6 People must be our most important priorities in life. In Colossians and Philippians, Paul calls more than 20 individuals and groups by name. *Relationships* were one of Paul's main priorities.**

Love is the key to healthy relationships. In his summit prayer of Ephesians 3:14-21, Paul emphasized our need to be filled with God's love. In Ephesians 4:1-2, Paul continues to emphasize *three* characteristics of love.

> [1] *As a prisoner for the Lord, then, I urge you to live a life worthy of the calling you have received.* [2] *Be completely* ***humble*** *and* ***gentle****; be* ***patient****, bearing with one another in* ***love*** (Eph. 4:1).

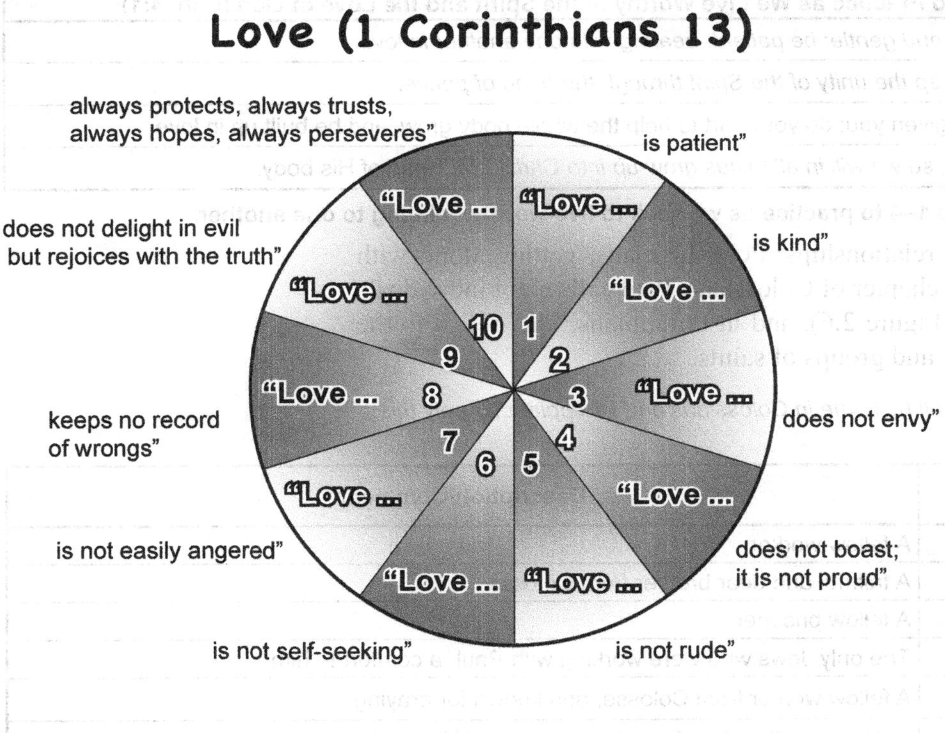
Love (1 Corinthians 13)
"Love ... is patient"
"Love ... is kind"
"Love ... does not envy"
"Love ... does not boast; it is not proud"
"Love ... is not rude"
"Love ... is not self-seeking"
"Love ... is not easily angered"
"Love ... keeps no record of wrongs"
"Love ... does not delight in evil but rejoices with the truth"
"Love ... always protects, always trusts, always hopes, always perseveres"
1
2
3
4
5
6
7
8
9
10

**Figure 2.7**
**Paul mentions at least ten characteristics of love.**

Love is humble, gentle, and patient—bearing with others in love. As we are filled with God's love, we can live worthy, getting along well with our brothers and sisters in the family of God. Let us look more closely at these four qualities of love Paul highlights.

**Q 12** *What truth does James 4:6 emphasize?*

**Q 13** *What are some things that humility reminds us of?*

**Be humble.** Humility is one of the most important characteristics of love. Love is not proud, but humble (1 Cor. 13). Humility is a vital attitude in our relationship with God and people. God resists the proud, but gives grace to the humble (James 4:6). Do we want grace? Then we must practice humility. God does not give grace to proud people—He resists them.

Seeking grace without humility is like fishing without a hook or a net. Grace is as distant as the heavens for those who are arrogant and stubborn. But grace is as near as the floor when we kneel in humility before God. May this mind of humility that was in Christ be in us. He dwelt in the form of God, but humbled Himself to serve us in flesh on earth. He humbled Himself and became obedient to death—even death on a despised, shameful cross (Phil. 2:1-8). When we are humble, we are imitating Jesus.

Notice that humility is the first characteristic of love that Paul mentions in Ephesians 4. Where the love of God is present, there is humility in our posture, humility in our words, and humility in our actions. Humility reminds us that God fills the universe (Eph. 4:10), but each of us can stand on one square foot of earth. Humility reminds us that God forgives our sins as we forgive those who sin against us. Humility teaches us that we will be judged by the same measure we judge others. Humility counsels that we all stumble in many ways. None of us is perfect. But God gives us grace, instead of what we deserve. Humility assures us that love covers a multitude of sins, including our own. Humility enables us to understand, rather than condemn; to encourage, instead of criticizing; to be silent, rather than gossip. It is easy to see why humility is the first characteristic of love that Paul mentions. Where humility is lacking, relationships sour. Be humble—it will help you get along with those who are as imperfect as you.

**Q 14** ✎ *What are some characteristics of those who lack humility?*

**Be gentle.** In tense times, gentleness preserves relationships. When conflicts arise and emotions heat up, gentleness guards the unity of the Spirit. [1]*A gentle answer turns away wrath, but a harsh word stirs up anger* (Prov. 15:1). Among young believers, Paul was as *gentle as a mother caring for her little children* (1 Thess. 2:7). Likewise Paul counseled Timothy and all of us that the Lord's servants must not quarrel, but be gentle and kind, not resentful (2 Tim. 2:24).

**Q 15** ✎ *Give an example of how gentleness preserves relationships.*

Jesus is our great example of gentleness, holding children in His lap; forgiving those that others would stone; as gentle as a lamb led to the slaughter. When they hurled insults at Him, He did not retaliate. When He suffered, He did not make threats (1 Pet. 2:23). Even with His back beaten raw, and His hands nailed to a cross, our Lord prayed kind words of forgiveness for His killers. Concerning the gentleness of Jesus, Matthew wrote:

> "[19]*He will not quarrel or cry out; no one will hear his voice in the streets.* [20]*A bruised reed he will not break, and a smoldering wick he will not snuff out, till he leads justice to victory.* [21]*In his name the nations will put their hope"* (Matt. 12:19-21).

***Sabio says:*** Where love is lacking in the church, the light of God is dim in the comunity.

Jesus is our Savior, our Shepherd, and our example. We are among those who trust Him. He is the most gentle person we know. He encourages us with tender words. He cheers us with His presence. And we welcome His discipline when we need it, for His love, mercy, and kindness know no bounds.

On the topic of walking worthy, Paul puts human relationships first on the list. Conflict and disagreements are a normal part of life. Still, we can be humble and gentle when tempers flare and emotions heat up. Two ladies in the church at Philippi forgot to be as gentle as mothers. So Paul pleaded with them (Euodia and Syntyche—whom some refer to as *Odious and Stinky), to agree with each other in the Lord (Phil. 4:2-3). For it is by *love*—that shows itself as humility, gentleness, and patience—that all people know we are Christ's disciples (John 15). But where love is lacking in the church, the light of God is dim in the community.

**Q 16** ✎ *Does the Spirit remind you to be humble and gentle in times of stress? Illustrate.*

**Be Patient.** *Love is patient* with people (1 Cor. 13:4). To be patient is to be tolerant, slow to anger—going the second mile to put up with people in difficult times. At times, we humans all can be rude, insensitive, selfish, forgetful, inefficient, unfruitful, clumsy, slow, or just plain mean! Love is not like a mirror that reflects the undesirable behavior of others. Love does not return insult for insult or evil for evil. Rather, love is like

**Q 17** ↗ *What promise does God give those who are patient and tolerant with others?*

**Q 18** ✎ *Are you known for being patient, or for having a short fuse? Explain.*

a sponge—it absorbs insults, harsh words, and offenses. *Love is patient* with people. Instead of striking back, it turns the other cheek.

Forms of explosives often have a fuse. Perhaps you have seen a firecracker that has a short fuse. Or you may have seen a stick of dynamite that has a longer fuse. People light the fuse with a match. The fuse gives them time to run away before the explosion. In contrast, those with love and patience have a long fuse. Hopefully, your nickname is not "short fuse." People with a short fuse become angry and explode quickly, harming others with harsh words or actions. Unlike a good deacon, a fleshly person lacks self-control. Those lacking patience may be violent and quarrelsome—not gentle (1 Tim. 3:2-3).

**Q 19** *What does a lack of patience reveal?*

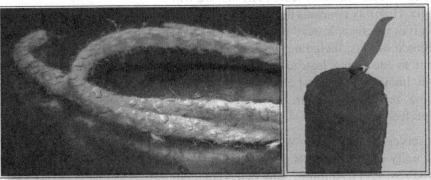

**Figure 2.8    Love has a long, wet fuse, not a short, dry fuse. It has a long temper, not a short one.**

**The Bible gives many examples of those without patience for others. There was a time as young apostles that James and John lacked humility, gentleness, and patience. They wanted to call down fire from heaven on the Samaritans who rejected Jesus. But the Master rebuked them and called them *sons of thunder* (Mark 3:17; Luke 9:54-55). Even those God calls to be ministers need to be filled with the Spirit and love. Likewise the unmerciful servant was impatient. His fellow pleaded, *"Have patience with me, and I will repay you. But he was unwilling"* (Matt. 18:29-30). A lack of patience reveals a lack of love. So when we need more patience, let us move a little closer to Jesus, the source of love and every virtue we need.**

A parallel passage in Colossians summarizes our need to be humble, gentle, and patient, bearing with one another in love:

> [12] *Therefore, as God's chosen people, holy and dearly loved, clothe yourselves with compassion, kindness, humility, gentleness and patience.* [13] *Bear with each other and forgive whatever grievances you may have against one another. Forgive as the Lord forgave you.* [14] *And over all these virtues put on love, which binds them all together in perfect unity* (Col. 3:12-14).

**Q 20** *Who is the best human example you know of humility, gentleness, patience, and tolerance?*

> ### BEAR WITH ONE ANOTHER—MAKE EVERY EFFORT TO GET ALONG WITH OTHER BELIEVERS.

[3] *Make every effort to keep the unity of the Spirit through the bond of peace.* [4] *There is one body and one Spirit—just as you were called to one hope when you were called—* [5] *one Lord, one faith, one baptism;* [6] *one God and Father of all, who is over all and through all and in all* (Eph. 4:3-6).

**Q 21** *How do we cooperate with the Spirit to protect unity?*

Paul stresses the role of the Spirit in creating and sustaining unity. Believers do not create unity. It exists because the Holy Spirit is at work in the body of Christ. Believers cannot create unity, but they can either destroy or protect it. The responsibility of believers is *to keep the unity of the Spirit*—to appreciate and nurture what the Holy Spirit creates.[1]

Paul instructs us to relate to other believers with humility, gentleness and patience—*at all times*. He does not want us to be nice, *only when* it is easy. Rather, Paul commands us to *make every effort* to keep the unity of the Spirit in the bond of peace. Here Paul pictures the peace that the Spirit brings as a bond that binds us together.

**Q 22** *Why does Paul mention 7 things that believers share? What are these?*

As believers, we may differ on many matters, such as culture, ethnicity, gender, age, social standing, education, temperament, and geography. Still, Paul mentions seven aspects that all believers have in common.

The idea of unity is profound and inspiring. We share one Spirit, one hope, one Lord, one faith, one baptism (in water), and one God and Father who is over all of us, in all of us, through all generations. But we confess that the unity of the church has been much less than God intended. As much as is possible, let us make every effort to work together for God's kingdom, in the unity the Holy Spirit can bring.

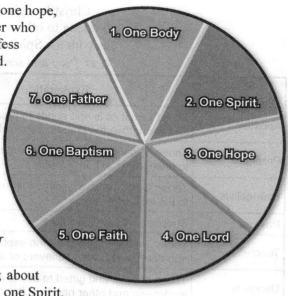

**Figure 2.9   Paul mentions seven aspects that unite all believers—seven things we share.**

## B. The Plan: Live worthy by using the grace (*charis*, gifts) God has given you to build up the body of Christ (Eph. 4:7-13).

**Q 23** ⟋ *What does Paul shift from and to in Ephesians 4:7?*

**Q 24** ⟍ *How do our gifts of grace help us live together in a worthy manner (Eph. 4:15-16)?*

A big shift takes place in Ephesians 4:7. Paul has been talking about unity in the body of Christ. He has emphasized that there is one body, one Spirit, one Hope, one Lord, one faith, one baptism in water; and one God and Father. But in 4:7, Paul shifts to the theme of diversity in unity. Even though we are united in one body, we each have *different* gifts of grace, so the body can grow and function well.

This passage is famous because it mentions apostles, prophets, evangelists, pastors, and teachers. We are thankful for all these ministries. But do not skip over the big point Paul makes in Ephesians 4:7 and again in 4:16. The point is: *"to each one of us grace has been given"* (Eph. 4:7). Paul is not referring to the *grace* we receive at conversion. Rather, in this passage, grace (Greek: *charis*), refers to the gifts of grace. See Romans 12:6-8 and 1 Corinthians 12:8-10, where Paul teaches about the *charismata*, the gifts of grace Christ has distributed among all the members of His body.[2]

**Q 25** ⟍ *Which gifts in the church are rare where you live? How can this change?*

[7]*But to each one of us grace has been given as Christ apportioned it.* [8]*This is why it says: "When he ascended on high, he led captives in his train and gave gifts to men."* [9]*(What does "he ascended" mean except that he also descended to the lower, earthly regions?* [10]*He who descended is the very one who ascended higher than all the heavens, in order to fill the whole universe)* (Eph. 4:7-10).

**Q 26** ⟍ *What gift has God given you to help believers live worthy? Are you using your gift? Explain.*

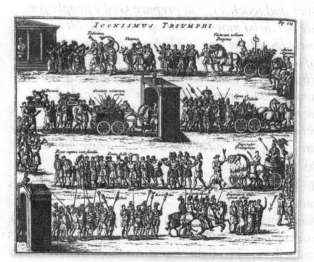

**Figure 2.10    Triumphal entry procession in Rome**

In Ephesians 4:8 Paul sees a parallel with Psalm 68:18. This Psalm probably first referred to King David, when he returned to Jerusalem and ascended to his throne after a conquest. In ancient times, it was common for a conquering king to lead a parade, called the *triumphal procession*. This parade celebrated a king's victory. The king or general would ride in a chariot pulled by a white horse. Psalm 68 mentions captives following behind the king, "in his train." King David was a man of war who won many victories and led many victory parades. In a much greater way, King Jesus conquered Satan, demons, and death. Then, He ascended to His throne in heaven. Colossians 2:15 pictures the scene of Jesus conquering at the Resurrection, and then leading Satan and his demons as captives. A king of Israel who conquered might share with soldiers or citizens the wealth he won in battle. In a similar way, Jesus won the victory for us, and then *gave gifts to men* (Eph. 4:8). Paul explains that each believer is a gift of grace to the church. As each part of the human body contributes something to the body, each member of the body of Christ helps the body of Christ in some manner. Thus, Paul says:

*"*[15]*speaking the truth in love, we will in all things grow up into him who is the Head, that is, Christ.* [16]*From him the whole body, joined and held together by every supporting ligament, grows and builds itself up in love, as each part does its work"* (Eph. 4:15-16).

Christ has given grace to every believer, so that each of us has ways we can be a blessing to others. Jesus is the One who saves us, then baptizes us in the Spirit and fills us with the Spirit day by day as we seek Him (Eph. 5:8; Matt. 3:11; Acts 2:4).

**Q 27** ⟋ *Fill in some examples in the third column of Figure 2.11.*

| Some Ministry Gifts | Explanations | Examples |
|---|---|---|
| Apostles | Those Christ calls and sends to preach the gospel and strengthen the church, especially in new areas | |
| Prophets | Those Christ gifts to speak supernatural messages to encourage, exhort, or edify | |
| Evangelists | Those God calls and anoints to proclaim the gospel to the lost | |
| Pastors | Shepherds over God's flock | |
| Teachers | Those, including pastors, who explain God's Word, and disciple and train believers of all ages | |
| Deacons | Those chosen and gifted to assist with the leadership and other needs of the church | |
| Administrators | Those who help manage finances, schedules, events, personnel, and policies of the church | |
| Helpers | Those who assist with any of the needs of the church or the community | Dorcas |
| Givers | Those who share their resources: finances, time, insights, energy, and such | |
| Others | See Figure 2.11 that follows | |

**Figure 2.11     The Bible mentions many types of ministries that are gifts in the body of Christ.**

**Q 28** ⟋ *What is the pastor's role as a leader of the church (Eph. 4:12)?*

The role of pastors and church leaders is *not* just to marry, bury, and preach sermons to believers who sit and observe ministry. God expects church leaders *"to prepare God's people for works of service"* (Eph. 4:12). Ministry in a local church and a community is not just for the pastor. Absolutely not! God wants the pastor to help each believer identify his or her gifts of service, equip them, and guide them to minister to others. Paul teaches that church leaders are like coaches—training and equipping others for action!

[11] *It was he who gave some to be apostles, some to be prophets, some to be evangelists, and some to be pastors and teachers,* [12] ***to prepare God's people for works of service,*** *so that the body of Christ may be built up* [13] *until we all reach unity in the faith and in the knowledge of the Son of God and become mature, attaining to the whole measure of the fullness of Christ.* [14] *Then we will no longer be infants, tossed back and forth by the waves, and blown here and there by every wind of teaching and by the cunning and craftiness of men in their deceitful scheming.* [15] *Instead, speaking the truth in love, we will in all things grow up into him who is the Head, that is, Christ.* [16] *From him the whole body, joined and held together* ***by every supporting ligament,*** *grows and builds itself up in love,* ***as each part does its work*** (Eph. 4:11-16).

**Q 29** ⟋ *What happens as believers use their gifts in the church (Eph. 4:14)? Give examples.*

As all believers use their gifts, the church expands, grows, and matures. Note Paul's special emphasis on growth in two areas:

- *"Then we will no longer be infants, tossed back and forth by the waves"* (Eph. 4:14a). These words may refer to the circumstances and trials of life that come to believers on the sea of life. Paul pictures believers in a light ship at sea. New believers may not expect the trials that come to God's people. But as we mature in Christ—through the teaching, training, counsel, and encouragement of other believers—we find that although trials continue, we have become rooted and steadfast in Christ.

- *"Blown here and there by every wind of teaching and by the cunning and craftiness of men in their deceitful scheming"* (Eph. 4:14b). Immature believers are like a ship that a strong wind blows in the wrong direction. But thanks be to God for giving the church the gifts of godly pastors, teachers, elders, and other mature believers. For as these mature believers use their gifts of grace, other believers mature and become strong in the faith.

## C. The Partnership: Live worthy by speaking truth in love.

God does not want believers to be tossed back and forth by circumstances—the waves of life. And He does not want us to be blown here and there by every wind of false teaching that comes from cunning and **crafty schemers**. Concerning crafty schemers, Peter writes:

> [18] *For they mouth empty, boastful words and, by appealing to the lustful desires of sinful human nature, they entice people who are just escaping from those who live in error.* [19] *They promise them freedom, while they themselves are slaves of depravity—for a man is a slave to whatever has mastered him* (2 Pet. 2:18-19).

To avoid being a victim of the waves and winds, Paul stresses *"speaking the truth in love"* (Eph. 4:15).

> [15] *Instead,* **speaking the truth in love**, *we will in all things grow up into him who is the Head, that is, Christ.* [16] *From him the whole body, joined and held together* **by every supporting ligament**, *grows and builds itself up in love,* **as each part does its work** (Eph. 4:15-16).

Truth and love must always walk together. In Ephesians 4:1-6, Paul emphasized that **love** reveals itself in our relationships, as we are humble, gentle, patient, and put up with each other. Love is the birthmark of heaven—the outward sign that we are God's children. Love is the identity card of a Christian. It verifies that Jesus Christ dwells in our hearts. All people know we are Christ's disciples as we love one another (John 13:35).

In Ephesians 4:15 Paul emphasizes that love is the vital companion of truth. We must speak the truth in love (Eph. 4:15). As a host opens the door to a guest, love opens the heart to truth.

Neither love nor truth should ever walk alone. Truth without love is as cold as ice, as hard as steel, and as sharp as a sword. Truth without love is as noisy as a clanging cymbal, as harsh as a hurricane, and as stern as a Pharisee's face. Truth without love is as empty as a dead church, and as lifeless as a corpse. So truth must always walk with love. Likewise love must always walk with truth. For the truth of the gospel is absolutely necessary for knowing God and reaching heaven. Many things draw people together. Citizens of a city or nation may feel brotherhood. Members of a team, a school, or a family feel close to each other. But truth is what connects the followers of Jesus Christ. For it is only as we believe the gospel and seek to obey the teachings of Christ that we are members of God's family. So let us always walk in love. But let us never fail to speak the truth in love. For love without truth is not truly Christian love, but mere emotion. Biblical love is not a soft, silent tolerance to immaturity, laziness, or evil. Biblical love is not spineless or cowardly. Agape love is a courageous decision and commitment to truth—as we seek to help, care for, encourage, and leave people better than when we met them. Thus, Paul stresses that when we speak the truth in love, believers grow and mature in Christ.

Paul envisions a church that grows to maturity, in the image of Christ, the head of the body. And God's apostle sees all believers as parts of the body, like ligaments that connect, support, and edify. The human body suffers when any part does not do its part. If one leg will not help walk, then the body must walk with a limp. The human body is healthy, strong, and mature as each member of the body does its part. Likewise, the body

**Q 30** ⟋ *What are some things that truth without love is like?*

**Q 31** ⟍ *What connects the followers of Jesus? Explain.*

**Q 32** ⟍ *What happens in the body of Christ when some belivers do not use their gifts?*

of Christ suffers when some of its members refuse to do their part. If givers will not give, the church is crippled by a lack of finances. If teachers will not teach, believers will continue to be tossed by waves and blown here and there by false teachings. But the body of Christ *"grows and builds itself up in love, **as each part does its work**"* (Eph. 4:16).

**Q 33** ⬉ *What are some gifts of grace that Christ has given in the church you attend?*

**Application.**   How has Christ equipped you to minister in His body? Figure 2.12 lists many ministries that should be in a church. Which of them are areas in which you can serve? Or perhaps God is speaking to you about a ministry that is not on this list. There are thousands of ways to help others. Be sure that you are a good steward of the grace God has given you to help others. Do not be like a sponge, that only comes to church to receive. Ask Jesus to help you be a blessing to those for whom He bled and died. Even the least part of a body is important.

**Q 34** ⬉ *How many different gifts or ministries are possible in one church?*

| Some Ministries of Believers in a Church | |
|---|---|
| Community service | National Girls Ministries—a program in the Assemblies of God |
| Ministry to the poor (food, clothes) | Royal Rangers—boys program in the Assemblies of God |
| Home for abused women | College students (campus and church) |
| Crisis telephone line | Young adult ministry (younger) |
| Literacy—reading classes for the illiterate | Single adult ministry (older) |
| Skills (for jobs, marriage, society, and such) | Single mothers ministry (help and fellowship) |
| Prison ministry | Senior adult ministry |
| Recovery through Christ—addictions | Women's Ministry |
| Deaf culture ministry | Men's Ministry (includes Honor Bound—Men of Promise) |
| Soul winning—training and practice | Student ministries—evangelism and discipleship |
| Street evangelism—special events and tracts | Youth Alive—secondary school program |
| Athletes ministry—outreach and discipleship | Youth discipleship |
| Adopt-an-Area—praying for and visiting every home | Youth Bible Quiz |
| Ministry to the handicapped | Youth drama |
| Ministry to the terminally ill | Youth choir |
| Hospital visitation ministry | Speed the Light—youth missions fund-raising |
| Comforting Touch ministry (funerals, sickness, and such) | Youth leadership training |
| Counseling/Marriage ministry | Master's Commission—1-2 year training program |
| Widows and orphans ministry | Adult choir |
| Foreign language ministry | Musical instruments ministry |
| Health ministry—basic health teachings and clinics | Worship team |
| Sidewalk Sunday School (Saturday outreach) | Evangelistic music—outreach team |
| Children's meeting or rally—for children outside the church | Drama—acting, costumes, and support |
| Camps for children and youth | Special events/productions—holiday and evangelistic |
| Sunday School for all ages | Illustrated sermons |
| Children's Church—for church children | Fine Arts—using art talents to bless others |
| Children's choir | Art and design for church needs |
| Junior Bible Quiz (children) | Helping Hands ministry for church tasks |
| Weddings—coordinating | Small groups—home fellowships; Bible studies |
| Welcome center ministry | Prayer ministries (including prayer chain) |
| Communion—prepare and clean up | Follow-up ministries for visitors and converts |

**Figure 2.12   Some churches have as many as 200 different ministries that church members are doing!**[3]

It is a joy to watch a child grow into a mature, productive adult. We parents like to show pictures of our children! We are proud of them. But we also rejoice to see them grow up and become mature, responsible adults. Likewise, our Father in heaven rejoices to see believers bearing fruit, maturing, and *growing in every way*—becoming the mature expression of Jesus in a dark world (Eph. 4:16)!

Jesus has a purpose for your life! You are important to Him. He cared enough to give His life to rescue you and redeem you from sin. Apart from Him, you will waste your life. With Him, your life counts! He wants to include you in what He is doing in the world through the Church. Will you commit yourself to Him and His purposes for your life? Will you take your gifts, develop them, and invest your best efforts to serve Him in and through the Church—the "body of Christ" on earth?

### Lesson 10 — Live Worthy as Children of Light—Introduction to Lessons 11–13 (Eph. 4:17-24)

**Goal A:** *Contrast how we lived in the past, without Christ, and how Paul insists we must live now, in Christ (Eph. 2:1-3; 4:17-24; Col. 3:25).*
**Goal B:** *Contrast 3 truths about physical and spiritual walking.*
**Goal C:** *Contrast the reasons of the devil and the reasons of God for identifying sins.*

**Overview:**   We must not live like sinners any longer—but like God, righteous and holy, as children being renewed in the image of our Creator (Eph. 4:17-24; Col. 3:10).

**Q 35** ↗ *In what sense are we created in God's image? How are we like Him?*

**The Past.**   In Ephesians 4:17–5:32, Paul contrasts the past with the present—in view of our future inheritance. He contrasts our lives *without* Christ, and how we must live now, *in* Christ. Recall what Paul wrote in Ephesians 2:

> [1] *As for **you, you were** dead in your transgressions and sins, [2] in which you **used to live** [walk] when **you followed** the ways of this world and of the ruler of the kingdom of the air, the spirit who is now at work in those who are disobedient. [3] All of **us** also **lived among them at one time**, **gratifying** the cravings of our sinful nature and **following** its desires and thoughts. **Like the rest, we were** by nature objects of wrath* (Eph. 2:1-3).

**Q 36** ✎ *Complete Figure 2.13, summarizing life before Christ and with Him (Review Lesson 4).*

| Ephesians 2:1-10 | Topics | Your Summaries on Aspects of Salvation |
|---|---|---|
| 2:1-3 | A. Past Problems: Before Christ | 1.<br>2.<br>3.<br>4.<br>5. |
| 2:4-10 | B. Present Blessings: In Christ | 1.<br>2.<br>3. |

**Figure 2.13   Practice summarizing life *without* Christ and *with* Him (Eph. 2:1-10).**

Before Christ, we were spiritually dead in our sins. We followed the ways of the world. We lived under the influence of Satan, and sinful desires of the flesh. And we were objects of God's wrath, rather than His love (Eph. 2:1-3).

**The Present.**   In Ephesians 4:17-19, Paul insists that we must no longer live as Gentiles (those without Christ). He is emphasizing that as *followers of Christ*, we must no longer live the way we used to live, *before* we received Christ as Savior and Lord. Paul writes about children of wrath, the world, and the flesh:

**Q 37** ✎ *Are those who live in sinful ways connected to God or separated? Explain.*

*17So I tell you this, and **insist on it** in the Lord, that you must no longer live as the Gentiles do, in the futility of their thinking. 18They are darkened in their understanding and **separated from the life of God** because of the ignorance that is in them due to the hardening of their hearts. 19Having lost all sensitivity, they have given themselves over to sensuality so as to indulge in every kind of impurity, with a continual lust for more* (Eph. 4:17-19).

Paul, in a solemn way, insists that those who have become Christians must not live like the unconverted live. In ways we **used** to live, the lost **continue** to live. Paul is writing mostly to Gentile believers. *Gentile* in Ephesians 4:17 is not used in a racial way, but refers to non-Christians—those who are not the people of God. Paul's readers faced the same challenge we faced today. We must leave our old way of life. We must no longer live as we lived before receiving Christ.

Paul reminds us that following Jesus requires a new lifestyle. God's apostle will not negotiate or bargain about what it means to be a child of God. He uses the strongest language possible: *"So **I tell you this, and insist on it** <u>in the Lord</u>, that **you must no longer live as the Gentiles do**, in the futility of their thinking"* (Eph. 4:17).

Paul paints a bold contrast between the way sinners live and the way followers of Jesus live.

*20You, however, did not come to know Christ that way. 21Surely you heard of him and were taught in him in accordance with the truth that is in Jesus. 22You were taught, with regard to your former way of life, to put off your old self, which is being corrupted by its deceitful desires; 23to be made new in the attitude of your minds; 24and to put on **the new self, created to be like God in true righteousness and holiness*** (Eph. 4:20-24).

*10...and have put on the **new self, which is being renewed in knowledge in the image of its Creator*** (Col. 3:10).

**Q 38** ↖ *Complete Figure 2.14 on the contrast between sinners and saints.*

| Reference | Your Summaries on |
|---|---|
| Eph. 4:20- 24 | |
| Col. 3:10 | |
| 2 Cor. 5:17 | |
| Eph. 2:10 | |

**Figure 2.14    Practice summarizing the ways we are like God as we follow Jesus.**

In another letter Paul wrote: *"If anyone is in Christ, he is a new creation; the old has gone, the new has come!"* (2 Cor. 5:17). We used to follow the ways of Satan and the world. But now, we follow Jesus. Earlier, Paul wrote that turning from sin and following Jesus is like being raised from death to life—to do good works God has planned for us.

*4But because of his great love for us, God, who is rich in mercy, 5**made us alive with Christ even when we were dead in transgressions**—it is by grace you have been saved. 6**And God raised us up with Christ** and seated us with him in the heavenly realms in Christ Jesus, 7in order that in the coming ages he might show the incomparable riches of his grace, expressed in his kindness to us in Christ Jesus. 8For it is by grace you have been saved, through faith—and this not from yourselves, it is the gift of God— 9not by works, so that no one can boast. 10**For we are God's workmanship, created in Christ Jesus to do good works, which God prepared in advance for us to do*** (Eph. 2:4-10).

**Q 39** ↖ *What difference does Jesus make in the way you live? Illustrate.*

When we come to Jesus with repentance and faith, He forgives our sins and saves us *from* our sins—our old way of living. Jesus gives us a new beginning. We begin to *walk worthy*, instead of living like we do not know God. This is what Paul is talking about in Ephesians 4. Christians are new and different people: Not different in terms of being weird or odd, but different because our lives are transformed by Jesus Christ. Followers of Christ have new values and behavior—it impacts the way they think, talk, live, and respond to the various issues of life. Following Jesus means that we *put on **the new self, created to be like God in true righteousness and holiness*** (Eph. 4:24). In our old ways, we were influenced by the devil (Eph. 2:1-3). But now we live as children being renewed in God's image, holy and righteous (Col. 3:10; Gen. 1:26). Our children share our nature and likeness. Because of this, they are able and desire to imitate us. Likewise, as God's children, let us imitate our Father, empowered by His DNA and His Spirit within us—as we are being renewed in the image of our Creator (Col. 3:10; Rom. 8:31; 2 Cor. 3:18).

John emphasizes that children behave like their father.

*[7] Dear children, do not let anyone lead you astray. He who does what is right is righteous, just as he is righteous. [8] He who does what is sinful is of the devil, because the devil has been sinning from the beginning. The reason the Son of God appeared was to destroy the devil's work.*

**Q 40** How can we recognize if God is a person's Father?

*[9] No one who is born of God will continue to sin, because God's seed remains in him; he cannot go on sinning, because he has been born of God. [10] This is how we know who the children of God are and who the children of the devil are: Anyone who does not do what is right is not a child of God; nor is anyone who does not love his brother* (1 John 3:7-10).

**Q 41** Complete Figure 2.15 about 6 old ways to put off (A–F) and 6 new ways to put on.

| | Take Off (Darkness and Lust) | Put On (Light and Love) |
|---|---|---|
| A. | | |
| B. | | |
| C. | | |
| D. | | |
| E. | | |
| F. | | |

**Figure 2.15** Practice summarizing six old ways to take off and six new ways to put on—like dirty and clean clothes.

| | Six Old Ways of the Flesh to Replace—With Six New Ways of the Spirit | | |
|---|---|---|---|
| **Eph.** | **Take Off (Darkness and Lust)** | **Put On (Light and Love)** | **Eph.** |
| 4:25 | A. *...put off falsehood* | [25] *...speak truthfully to his neighbor, for we are all members of one body* | 4:25 |
| 4:31 L e s s o n 11 | B. *Get rid of all bitterness, rage and anger, brawling and slander, along with every form of malice.* | **Self-control:** [26] *"In your anger do not sin": Do not let the sun go down while you are still angry, [27] and do not give the devil a foothold.* | 4:26-27 |
| | | **Kindness, Compassion, Forgiveness:** [32] *Be kind and compassionate to one another, forgiving each other, just as in Christ God forgave you.* | 4:32 |
| | | **Love:** [1] *Be imitators of God, therefore, as dearly loved children [2] and live a life of love, just as Christ loved us and gave himself up for us as a fragrant offering and sacrifice to God.* | 5:1-2 |

**Figure 2.16** Continued on next page

Continued from previous page

| Six Old Ways of the Flesh to Replace—With Six New Ways of the Spirit | | | |
|---|---|---|---|
| **Eph.** | **Take Off (Darkness and Lust)** | **Put On (Light and Love)** | **Eph.** |
| 4:28 | C. *He who has been stealing must steal no longer.* | **Healthy Words:** [28] *...**work**, doing something useful with his own hands, that he may have something to share with those in need.* | 4:28 |
| 4:29-30<br><br>5:4 | D. *Do not let any **unwholesome talk** come out of your mouths, [30] And **do not grieve the Holy Spirit** of God, with whom you were sealed for the day of redemption.*<br>*Nor should there be **obscenity, foolish talk or coarse joking,** which are out of place, but rather thanksgiving.* | **Healthy Words:**<br>[29] *...but only what is helpful for building others up **according to their needs,** that it may benefit those who listen.* | 4:29 |
| 5:3, 5-7<br><br>L<br>e<br>s<br>s<br>o<br>n<br><br>12 | E. *But among you there must not be even a hint of **sexual immorality**, or of any kind of **impurity**, or of **greed**, because these are improper for God's holy people.*<br>[5] *For of this you can be sure: No immoral, impure or greedy person—such a man is an idolater—has any inheritance in the kingdom of Christ and of God.*<br>[6] *Let no one deceive you with empty words, for because of such things God's wrath comes on those who are disobedient.*<br>[7] *Therefore do not be partners with them.* | **Light:**<br>[8] *For you were once darkness, but now you are light in the Lord. Live as children of light* [9] *(for the fruit of the light consists in all **goodness, righteousness and truth**)* [10] *and find out what pleases the Lord.*<br>[11] *Have nothing to do with the fruitless deeds of darkness, but rather expose them.* [12] *For it is shameful even to mention what the disobedient do in secret.* [13] *But everything exposed by the light becomes visible,* [14] *for it is light that makes everything visible. This is why it is said: "Wake up, O sleeper, rise from the dead, and Christ will shine on you."*<br>**Wisdom:**<br>[15] *Be very careful, then, how you live—not as unwise but as wise,* [16] *making the most of every opportunity, because the days are evil.* [17] *Therefore do not be foolish, but understand what the Lord's will is.* | 5:8-17 |
| 5:18a<br><br>L<br>e<br>s<br>s<br>o<br>n<br><br>13 | F. *Do not get **drunk** on wine, which leads to ***debauchery** (shame; sinful, fleshly indulgence; the opposite of self-control)* | **The Holy Spirit:**<br>[18b] *Instead, be filled with the Spirit.*<br>[19] *Speak to one another with psalms, hymns and spiritual songs. Sing and make music in your heart to the Lord,*<br>[20] *always giving thanks to God the Father for everything, in the name of our Lord Jesus Christ.* | 5:18b-20 |

**Figure 2.16   To Walk Worthy, we must replace six old ways of darkness with six new ways of light (Eph. 4:25–5:20).**

In Lessons 11–13, we will study six old ways of the flesh that Paul insists we replace with six new ways of the Spirit. But before we study the challenge of replacing old ways with new ways, let us consider the *process of learning to walk* in new ways, and *the motivation for learning to walk in new ways of the Spirit.*

**Walking.**   Ephesians 4:17 uses a form of the Greek verb *peripateo,* which means to *walk, live, or behave.* This is a favorite word of Paul in the second half of this letter (Eph. 4:1; 5:1, 8, 15). It is helpful to compare *spiritual walking* to *physical walking* in three ways.

Q 42 ✎ *Complete Figure 2.17 comparing physical and spiritual walking.*

| Walking: | Your Summaries on Walking |
|---|---|
| A process to learn | |
| Becomes normal | |
| A privilege to use or lose | |

**Figure 2.17   Practice comparing physical and spiritual walking in three ways.**

- *Walking* is something we must *learn* to do *after* we are born. A baby does not just appear, flop over, and start walking. Learning to walk is a **process**. A baby must learn to turn over, crawl, and stand up *before* it begins to walk. Step by step, and a few falls later, a baby is wobbling along. Likewise, Paul says that as we grow in Christ, *we will no longer be infants* (Eph. 4:14).

- What causes a baby to want to stand up and walk? Is it a desire that God places in a baby human? Or is walking something a young child imitates as it watches others walk? If a baby was raised among cows, would it move on its hands and feet, imitating cows? One thing is certain, we *learn* to walk spiritually, as we imitate good examples. Thus, Paul tells Timothy to be an example in speech, life, love, faith, and purity (1 Tim. 4:12). The spiritual walk of believers improves as mature believers set good examples and as young believers choose the best examples to follow. We are not perfect in this life, but our new self is *being renewed* in the image of our Creator (Col. 3:10).

- *Walking* becomes normal with practice. It is a complex activity. The best robots do not walk smoothly. Walking requires many muscles working together. It involves pushing with the bottom of the foot, then relaxing some muscles so the knee will bend, and then tightening muscles so the leg will straighten. Walking requires concentration, coordination, and timing—using both legs in sequence. But after a little practice, we walk without even thinking about it. Walking becomes a normal habit of life. Likewise, in the spiritual realm with growth and maturity, walking like God in holiness and righteousness (Eph. 4:20-24) becomes a habit for the children of God. For the word of God lights our path and the Holy Spirit guides our desires and steps. "²³*If the LORD delights in a man's way, he makes his steps firm;* ²⁴*though he stumble, he will not fall, for the LORD upholds him with his hand*" (Ps. 37:23-24).

- *Walking* is a privilege we must use or lose. If a person decides to go to bed for a month and then decides to walk again, he or she will find it difficult to walk. We must exercise our muscles to keep them in shape. Likewise, to stay spiritually fit, we need spiritual exercise—such as devotions, Bible study, prayer, worship, attending church, giving, witnessing, and right choices. Jesus taught the spiritual principle: use it or lose it (Matt. 13:10-15; 25:14-30).

Walking in the Spirit involves a struggle. We must daily choose to submit to God and honor him. Earlier, Paul wrote that we used to follow *"the ways of this world and of the ruler of the kingdom of the air, the spirit who is now at work in those who are disobedient"* (Eph. 2:2). Our struggles with the world, the flesh, and the devil do not disappear when we become God's children. (We will study more about our spiritual warfare in Ephesians 6:10-18). Paul warns us that day by day, we must put off our old self *which is being corrupted by its deceitful desires*—the desires of the flesh. The evil desires of the flesh continue to appear from time to time. For the desires of the flesh remain with us as long as we live in a body of flesh. As Paul wrote, *"the flesh wars*

Q 43 ✎ *Do our struggles with the flesh disappear when we are born again? Explain.*

*against the Spirit"* (Gal. 5:17). But Paul also wrote that grace teaches us to *"say 'No' to ungodliness and worldly passions, and to live self-controlled, upright and godly lives in this present age"*—as we wait for Jesus to return and bring the future age (Titus 2:12). Paul assures us that as we choose to walk in the power of God's Spirit, we will not fulfill the evil desires of the flesh (Gal. 5:16). As we choose the privilege of walking in the Spirit and practice it, the rude and loud voice of the flesh decreases to faint whispers; and we enjoy walking with God in unbroken, holy fellowship.

God's plan that we see in Eden was to walk in fellowship with humans. Enoch walked with God long before the days of the new covenant. And Jesus, who provides for us the new covenant, shows, teaches, and enables us to walk with God. So Paul urges us to walk in the light (Eph. 5:8-10). John assures us that as we walk in the light, we have fellowship with God and others, and the blood of Jesus Christ cleanses us from all sin (1 John 1:5-7). So let us enjoy and practice this blessed privilege of walking with God.

**The motivation for walking worthy of God's blessings.**   In Ephesians 4–6, Paul emphasizes that we must walk worthy of our relationship with God. Why does Paul identify six kinds of sins we must avoid (Eph. 4:17–5:20, Figure 2.14)? Why does Paul point out these sins? What is his motivation? Why does the Holy Spirit convict us when we sin?

The devil may accuse us when we sin, to discourage us. The enemy of our souls is called Satan—which means *Accuser*. He likes to remind us of our past sins. He likes to beat us down with our faults and failures. John sees a glorious day in the future when *"the accuser of the brothers is cast down"* (Rev. 12:9-11). Satan accuses us, as he accused Job to condemn him (Job 2:4-5). In contrast, God continues to cheer for us, even when we fall short. God was not pleased with Cain's offering (Gen. 4:5). But what was God's response when He talked with Cain? God encouraged Cain to try again. *"⁶Then the LORD said to Cain, 'Why are you angry? Why is your face downcast? ⁷If you do what is right, will you not be accepted? But if you do not do what is right, sin is crouching at your door; it desires to have you, but you must master it'"* (Gen. 4:6-7). God was still cheering for Cain after his first offering was not acceptable. God was more concerned about Cain's future than his past.

King David committed adultery and murder (2 Sam. 11). So God sent the prophet Nathan to confront the king about his sin. When David repented, God forgave him, and disciplined him to prevent the sin from happening again. David and his household reaped the results of his sin, for *the sword never departed from his house* (2 Sam. 12:10). Although God forgives, the seeds that we plant in sin may bring a harvest of pain. Still, our Father in heaven has always been the God of the second chance. He is and has always been slow to anger and quick to forgive (Exod. 34:6; Num. 14:18; Neh. 9:31; Ps. 86:5; 103:8; John 3:16).

Jesus showed mercy to the woman caught in adultery. He did not approve of her sin. But He offered her mercy and a new beginning. Picture this woman kneeling with her head down as Jesus said: ***"Woman, where are they*** [your accusers]***? Neither do I condemn you ... Go and leave your life of sin"*** (John 8:10-11). Likewise, Jesus offered living water to the immoral woman at the well who had five husbands, and was living with yet another (John 4). Jesus knows all of our sins and secrets, yet He still offers us a new relationship with Him. Satan accuses *to condemn*. But God points out our sins *so we will repent, turn from evil to Him, and receive His forgiveness and eternal blessings.*

**Application.**   When God talks to you and me about our weaknesses, faults, and sins, let us respond with humility. For we know that His purpose is to cleanse, forgive, restore, and bless us. God's motivation in insisting that we turn away from sin is so we can be obedient children who inherit what He wants to share with us.

**Q 44** ⭘ *Do you walk with God, submitting to the Word and the Spirit? Explain.*

**Q 45** ⭘ *Is God more concerned about your past or your future? Illustrate your answer.*

**Q 46** ⭘ *Why does Paul identify 6 types of sin we must avoid?*

**Q 47** ⭘ *Does God's forgiveness mean there will be no harvest for seeds of sin we plant? Illustrate.*

**Q 48** ⭘ *What helps us respond with humility, when the Spirit convicts us of sin?*

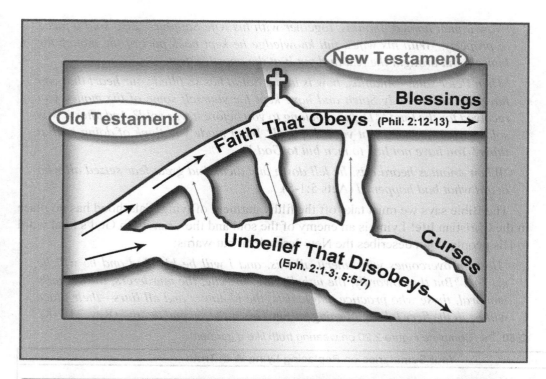

**Figure 2.18**
Two roads run through both the old covenant and the new covenant. God will bless those whose faith expresses itself in obedience to Him (Phil. 2:12-13). And He will curse those whose unbelief expresses itself in disobedience to Him (Eph. 2:1-3; 5:5-7; Rom. 2:6-11; 1 Cor. 6:9-11; Gal. 5:19-25).

## Lesson 11 — Live Worthy as Children of Light—Part 1: Be Truthful and Loving (Eph. 4:25-32)

**Goal A:** *Explain why lying is so offensive to God; and give examples of being truthful.*

**Goal B:** *Sketch 4 directions an angry person may turn; and the fruit of the Spirit that replaces anger.*

In Lessons 11 and 12, we will study six types of old ways to replace with six new ways of walking in the Spirit's power. Take a few minutes to study these six contrasts in behavior (Figure 2.14). And then we will examine each of them.

## A. Replace lying with truth (Eph. 4:25).

*Therefore each of you must put off **falsehood** and speak truthfully to his neighbor, for we are all members of one body (Eph. 4:25).*

Q 49 ✎ *Complete Figure 2.19 on the sin of lying.*

| Reference | Your Summaries on the Problem of Lying |
|-----------|----------------------------------------|
| Gen. 3:4 | |
| John 8:44 | |
| Acts 5:1-5 | |
| Rev. 21:7-8 | |
| Eph. 4:25 | |

**Figure 2.19  Practice summarizing verses about the problem of lying.**

**Take off lying.** The sin of lying is as old as Eden. In the Garden, Satan told the first lie. He said to Eve through the serpent, *"You will not surely die"* (Gen. 3:4). As a result of Adam and Eve's disobedience, sin and death entered the world (Rom. 5:12; 1 Cor. 15:21). So Jesus refers to Satan as a liar, and the father of lies (John 8:44).

Every day, people deny the truth, shade the truth, cheat, exaggerate, flatter, betray promises, tell half-truths, and deceive. Lying is a way of life for the world. And some studies show that attending church makes little difference in practicing falsehood.

Ananias and Sapphira lied and died.

*¹Now a man named Ananias, together with his wife Sapphira, also sold a piece of property. ²With his wife's full knowledge he kept back part of the money for himself, but brought the rest and put it at the apostles' feet.*

*³Then Peter said, "Ananias, how is it that Satan has so filled your heart that you have lied to the Holy Spirit and have kept for yourself some of the money you received for the land? ⁴Didn't it belong to you before it was sold? And after it was sold, wasn't the money at your disposal? What made you think of doing such a thing? You have not lied to men but to God."*

*⁵When Ananias heard this, he fell down and died. And great fear seized all who heard what had happened* (Acts 5:1-5).

The Bible says we must take off the filthy garment of lying. Falsehood has no place in the Christian life! Lying is an enemy of the soul and the Church. In God's final word to His people, John describes the New Jerusalem, but warns:

*⁷He who overcomes will inherit all this, and I will be his God and he will be my son. ⁸But the cowardly, the unbelieving, the vile, the murderers, the sexually immoral, those who practice magic arts, the idolaters and **all liars**—their place will be in the fiery lake of burning sulfur. This is the second death"* (Rev. 21:7-8).

**Q 50** ✎  Complete Figure 2.20 on wearing truth like a garment.

| Reference | Your Summaries on Replacing Lying With Truth |
|---|---|
| Titus 1:2 | |
| Eph. 4:15 | |
| Eph. 4:25 | |
| Eph. 6:15 | |
| Rom. 12:17 | |
| 2 Thess. 2:10 | |

**Figure 2.20    Practice summarizing verses about replacing lying with truth.**

**Put on truth.**    Is the Holy Spirit convicting you of lying to your spouse, your children, your neighbor, your church, your employer, or your government? Repent! Take off the filthy garment of lying. Put on the holy garment of truth. Tell the truth to your family, your neighbor, and your church (Eph. 4:25).

Truth is a characteristic of God and His people. God cannot lie (Titus 1:2; Num. 23:19). And Jesus referred to Himself as the way, the truth, and the life (John 14:6). Everyone on the side of truth listens to Jesus (John 18:37). And everyone on the side of Jesus speaks the truth (Eph. 4:25). Paul says, *"Each of you must put off falsehood and speak truthfully to His neighbor, **for we are all members of one body**"*—the body of Christ! (Eph. 4:25). Without truthfulness, family relationships break down. Remember Ananias and Sapphira. Their untruthfulness hurt the church. Lying pollutes and sins against the body of Christ. So say what you mean. Keep your word. Do what you say you will do. Let your "Yes" be "Yes," your "No" be "No" (Matt. 5:37; James 5:12). Let your "I do" be "I do" to your spouse; and let your "I will" be "I will" to your children. Keep your word! Being truthful means keeping your promises to God, your spouse, your children, and everyone else. Being truthful means being honest in private and in public. Be honest in the eyes of all you meet (Rom. 12:17). Speak the truth in love (Eph. 4:15). Buckle on truth like a belt around your waist (Eph. 6:14).

We have security and protection as we love and practice the truth. Paul warns that the Antichrist will lead people of the world astray *"because they refused to love the truth and be saved"* (2 Thess. 2:10). Under the old covenant and the new, God desires truth in the heart (Ps. 51:6). One of the Ten Commandments is that God's people must not bear false witness (Exod. 20:16). Lying links us with Satan, the Father of lies. So let us repent of falsehood and always ask the Spirit to help us be truthful.

## B. Replace anger with self-control, kindness, compassion, forgiveness, and love (Eph. 4:26-27, 32; 5:1-2).

Anger is a feeling of hostility. This emotion may range from annoyance to rage (Figure 2.21). Figure 2.21 shows five levels of anger. Like water in a pot, anger can range from warm to boiling.

**Q 51** ⬉ *Which of the five levels of anger do you struggle with?*

| Fahrenheit | Celsius | |
|---|---|---|
| 212 | 100 | **5.** Enraged—violent; out of control emotionally and mentally; an enraged person hardly knows what he or she is doing. |
| 194 | 90 | **4.** Furious—the angry person may yell, break things, or strike. |
| 176 | 80 | 3 Wrathful—showing a strong desire to avenge |
| 158 | 70 | **2.** Offended or threatened—feeling the need to correct a wrong |
| 122 | 60 | **1.** Irritated—feeling annoyed, frustrated or perturbed |

| Fahrenheit | Celsius |
|---|---|
| 212 | 100 |
| 194 | 90 |
| 176 | 80 |
| 158 | 70 |
| 122 | 60 |

**Figure 2.21    Five levels of anger, from warm to boiling**

Take off the garment of anger.

[26]*"In your anger do not sin"* [practice self-control]: *Do not let the sun go down while you are still angry,* [27]*and do not give the devil a foothold.* [31]*Get rid of all bitterness, rage and anger, brawling and slander, along with every form of malice* (Eph. 4:26-27, 31).

**Q 52** ⬈ *What are the characteristics of sinful anger?*

There is a place for righteous anger. Jesus was angry when He cleansed the temple. But in Ephesians, Paul is not talking about righteous anger or he would not tell us to get rid of it. The anger Paul writes about in Ephesians 4 has sinful characteristics such as harshness, bitterness, resentment, vengeance, rage, fury, or even violence. Whoever has this kind of anger is low on love and humility, but overflowing with pride. For when we get angry with another, we are setting ourselves up as the divine judge over another human. Jesus warned: *"...anyone who is angry with his brother will be subject to judgment"* (Matt. 5:22). God is the only Judge of mankind. So we must leave judgment, wrath, and vengeance to God (Rom. 12:17-21). [12]*There is only one Lawgiver and Judge, the one who is able to save and destroy. But you—who are you to judge your neighbor* [or anyone else]? (James 4:12).

We must recognize that anger is an enemy and a hindrance to the kingdom of God. We all struggle with anger at times. Anger is like an uninvited guest that rudely bursts into our home. It appears even when we do not choose to be angry. Anger is an emotion that can jump to its feet like a dog that suddenly awakens and begins to growl and bark. Although we do not choose to be angry, we must choose *not* to be angry. For God will surely hold us accountable for our anger and those we hurt with it.

**Q 53** ⬉ *Although Moses was a great leader, how did anger hinder him?*

Moses is a man God used in many ways. He led God's people out of slavery in Egypt. He molded them into a nation. He wrote the Pentateuch. Without a doubt, Moses is one of the greatest men who ever lived. And yet he struggled a lifetime with the problem of anger. At key moments in his life, Moses lost his temper and his ability to think clearly. The first outburst of his anger we read about is when he killed an Egyptian who was mistreating an Israelite (Exod. 2:11-12). His temper flared again and he shattered the Ten Commandments that God wrote (Exod. 32:19). And after leading the Israelites in the desert for 38 years, his anger boiled over and he struck the rock God told him to speak to (Num. 20:8-11). Moses was not known as a man with a short temper. He was not like the man who said, "I have only one nerve left, and you are close to getting on it!" But despite all his great deeds, anger caused him to die just short of his life's mission.[4]

Moses will rejoice if we learn from his anger. May he remind us to humble ourselves and depend on the Holy Spirit for the fruit of self-control. For *"man's anger does not bring about the righteous life that God desires"* (James 1:19): Not then, not now, not ever. So Paul commands believers: *"Get rid of all **bitterness, rage and anger, brawling** and **slander**, along with every form of **malice**"* (Eph. 4:31).

**Q 54** *Why is it foolish to muse on anger, as a hen broods on her eggs?*

**Q 55** *What are some ways to turn away from anger?*

When it comes to getting rid of anger, sooner is better than later. Spiritual, skillful believers overcome anger quickly—even seconds after it appears. Sometimes it may take us a few minutes to cool down. But we must never allow anger to brood like a hen on her nest of eggs; or boil over like a pot of water on a stove. The servant of the Lord must not quarrel, but be gentle to all (2 Tim. 2:24). We must learn to express our emotions in ways that are polite, and must avoid being rude. And in personal matters, all anger should cool down by sundown! For those who nurse anger through the night find that it grows into a giant they cannot control. As the Psalmist warned, *"As I mused, the fire burned"* (Ps. 39:3). *"The more I thought about it, the hotter I got, igniting a fire of words"* (Ps. 39:3 ESV). Musing on anger is like putting wood on a fire. Musing makes anger hotter. We can turn away from anger by changing our thoughts in ways such as: forgiving, understanding, quoting Scripture, saying a prayer, singing a chorus, or raising our hands to give thanks. Live love (See Eph. 4:1, 17; 5:8, 15).

**Figure 2.22**
**There are four directions an angry person may turn:**
1. Away from the problem,
2. Inward,
3. Toward others,
4. Toward the problem.

**Q 56** *Complete Figure 2.23 on the four directions an angry person may turn.*

| Directions | Your Summaries on Directions One May Turn With Anger |
|---|---|
| Away | |
| | |
| | |
| | |

**Figure 2.23    Practice explaining four directions we can turn with anger.**

**Q 57** *Do you suffer from any of these physical or psychological problems? Is it possible that you are in denial about being angry?*

**Q 58** *Are you likely to turn away or respond with hateful words when angered?*

**1. Angry people may turn away from the problem by leaving the room or situation.** This prevents an angry outburst. It gives one time to consider the cause. But walking away is not a permanent solution. Unresolved anger can lead to bitterness, sarcasm, and criticism. The angry person becomes self-centered, impatient, and rebellious; thereby creating tension in the family.

**2. Angry people may turn inward by denying the problem.** This is accompanied by physical problems such as headaches, ulcers, high blood pressure, or heart attacks. It may lead to psychological reactions such as anxiety, fear, tension, and depression.

**3. Angry people may direct anger toward others.** People may openly show anger to those who have offended them. Or, they may seek revenge by hiding hurtful words in stories that make everyone laugh. Some may direct their anger toward the innocent instead of the offender. These "get-even" actions are destructive. Paul reminds us that revenge is God's right, but not ours (Rom. 12:19).

**4. People may choose to face the cause of their anger.** First, they must admit they are angry. They must pray and try to understand what has caused the anger. They may need to view the situation from a different perspective. Then they should do whatever is best to accept or improve the situation—depending on the Spirit for the fruit of self-control, kindness, compassion, forgiveness, and love.

**To replace anger, put on self-control, kindness, compassion, forgiveness, and love.** *32 Be kind and compassionate to one another, forgiving each other, just as in Christ God forgave you* (Eph. 4:32).

> *1 Be imitators of God, therefore, as dearly loved children 2 and live a life of love, just as Christ loved us and gave himself up for us as a fragrant offering and sacrifice to God* (Eph. 5:1-2).

We do not lose our emotions when we begin to follow Jesus. And by effort alone, we cannot conquer the enemy of anger. But remember the mountain peak of Ephesians. Glory be to God, who *is able to do "immeasurably more than all we can ask or imagine, by His power that is at work within us"* (Eph. 3:20). As we cooperate with, seek, and depend on the Spirit, He produces the fruit of self-control in us.

Some anger is sinful, but some is not.[5] There is a time for righteous anger. Jesus became angry at the right things, such as hypocrisy, misuse of God's house, and caring more about rules than people. When we see injustice and unrighteousness, these should make us angry. It should stir us when someone dishonors God, profanes His Name, or ridicules biblical principles. Immorality, mistreating the poor, and abuse or neglect of women and children ought to heat our emotions. But we must beware lest our anger gets out of control, causing us to act in un-Christ-like ways. We must learn to express strong emotions in Christian ways. We must avoid knocking people down with our convictions or our words. We must *practice* the skill of being polite. We must harness and bridle anger, allowing the wisdom of the Holy Spirit to flow through us in ways that are skillful, gentle, kind, compassionate, and loving. Anger is a feeling we must learn to manage, with the Spirit's help.

**Q 59** ✎ *Why does God forbid us to seek revenge?*

**Q 60** ✎ *Have you been the innocent victim of a person who is angry with someone else? Illustrate.*

**Q 61** ✎ *Have you been guilty of taking your anger out on an innocent person? Explain.*

**Q 62** ✎ *When you are angry, are you aware of the specific cause? Explain.*

**Q 63** ✎ *How might the Spirit lead you to respond to righteous anger?*

---

## Live Worthy as Children of Light—Part 2: Work, Edify, and Be Moral (Eph. 4:25–5:17)

**Lesson 12**

**Goal A:** *Give examples of people who have stolen; and illustrate why we must replace stealing with hard work.*

**Goal B:** *Give examples of unwholesome and healthy words. Contrast the effects of good and bad talking.*

**Goal C:** *Analyze the problem and destination of the sexual immoral. Contrast followers of Christ and followers of lust, on the topic of morality.*

### C. Replace stealing with working (Eph. 4:28).

**Put off stealing (Eph. 4:28a).** *28 He who has been **stealing** must steal no longer* (Eph. 4:28).

Stealing is a common problem in the world. Students steal answers from others. Workers steal time, money, and merchandise from their employees. Shoppers steal from stores. Immoral people steal sex from those who do not belong to them. Church members steal from God by not paying tithes, or by not being good stewards (Mal. 3:8). So Paul emphasizes the eighth commandment from God: *"You shall not steal"* (Exod. 20:15).

Followers of Jesus must not steal. Stealing is selfish. It breaks the law of love that guides those in God's kingdom, exalting self above others (Rom. 12:8-10). Stealing puts people in bad company with sinners such as Achan and Judas.

**Q 64** ⬂ *Complete Figure 2.24 about replacing stealing with working.*

| Reference | Your Summaries on Stealing and Working |
|---|---|
| Exod. 20:15 | |
| Josh. 12:6 | |
| Rom. 12:8-10 | |
| 2 Thess. 3:10 | |
| Phil. 2:7 | |
| Eph. 4:28 | |

**Figure 2.24    Practice summarizing verses that guide us from stealing to working.**

**Q 65** ⬈ *What curse did Achan bring on his family through stealing?*

Achan was a man who reaped the curse of stealing (Josh. 7). He was selfish, thinking of himself and not the nation upon which he brought a curse. Like any thief, he did not care about others. He thought only of his own interests, not the interests of others (Phil 2:4). Joshua had told the Israelite soldiers to bring all the silver and gold into the treasury of the Lord. At the battle of Jericho, God gave a tremendous victory. But Achan, a soldier of Israel, saw a beautiful robe from Babylon, about five pounds of silver, and a pound of gold. In disobedience, he stole these and hid them in his tent. This one sin prevented the Lord from blessing the Israelites, and caused the deaths of 36 soldiers at the next battle. Soon, the Lord revealed the sin of Achan. As a result of this one sin of stealing, the Israelites stoned Achan, his wife, his son, and daughters, and even his cattle. Then they burned all the bodies with fire. Thus one man, the head of his house, brought the curse of death on a nation and his whole family. As a payment for his sin of stealing, he lost what he stole, his life, the lives of everyone in his family, and the lives of many of his fellow soldiers. Likewise today, those who steal prevent the blessings of God on a group, and bring a curse on themselves, their family, and many others. Be not deceived, God is not mocked. Those who sow seeds of thievery will reap a harvest of destruction. Stealing is bad business. Those who steal lose money. For stealing always costs people more than they steal.

**Q 66** ⬂ *What warning does Judas teach us about the sin of stealing?*

**Figure 2.25**
**Achan and Judas remind us that those who steal lose more than they gain. The foolish steal from a purse to buy a curse.**

Judas was a dishonest apostle. He had the bad habit of stealing money (John 12). At first, Judas stole only a coin or two. In those early days, there was only a little sin in Judas. His heart was a mixture of good and bad. But where sin is tolerated, it spreads like a cancer. If you give sin a centimeter, it will soon take a meter. Give the devil a small place in your heart, he will soon take over your whole life. So Paul warns us not to give the devil a foothold—not even a small way to attack us (Eph. 4:27). The sin of stealing opened the door to sin, and Satan himself entered into the heart of Judas (Luke 22:3; John 13:2, 27). In the end, Judas lost everything he stole plus more: his ministry, his life, his eternal inheritance, and his soul. Sin will take you further than you want to go; keep you longer than you want to stay; and charge you more than you want to pay.

**Q 67** ⬂ *Has working always been part of God's plan? Explain.*

**Put on working (Eph. 4:28b).** *28 He who has been stealing must steal no longer, **but must work, doing something useful with his own hands, that he may have something to share with those in need*** (Eph. 4:28).

Paul steers believers away from stealing what someone else has worked for with *their* hands. He guides us to work with our *own* hands. Lazy, unrighteous people watch others work, and then steal from them. In contrast, Christians are responsible, hard-working citizens (Acts 20:35; Col. 4:22-24; 1 Thess. 4:11-12; Titus 3:14). Followers of Jesus have a good work ethic. We remember the words of Paul to new believers in Thessalonica: *"10For even when we were with you, we gave you this rule: 'If a man will not work, he shall not eat'"* (2 Thess. 3:10).

Work has been a part of God's plan from the very beginning. *"The LORD God took the man and put him in the Garden of Eden to work it and take care of it"* (Gen. 2:15). And it has always been God's plan for us to work six days a week.

Without Christ, the goal of life is to get all you can so you can have more. Because of greed, some people steal. Paul teaches us that once we come to Christ, we should work hard to meet our needs and *"have something to share with those in need"* (Eph. 4:28). Following Jesus leads us from stealing to sharing![5]

**Q 68** *Besides ourselves, who can we help as we work?*

## D. Replace harmful speech with wholesome words (Eph. 4:29).

*29Do not let any unwholesome talk come out of your mouths, but only what is helpful for building others up according to their needs, that it may benefit those who listen. 30And do not grieve the Holy Spirit of God, with whom you were sealed for the day of redemption* (Eph. 4:29-30).

**Put off unwholesome speech (Eph. 29a).** Unwholesome words from a Christian are as out of place as mud on a wedding dress.

**Q 69** *What are some examples of unwholesome speech?*

*29aDo not let any unwholesome talk come out of your mouths* (Eph. 4:29a).

*4Nor should there be **obscenity, foolish talk** or **coarse joking**, which are **out of place**, but rather thanksgiving* (Eph. 5:4).

*12For it is shameful even to mention what the disobedient do in secret* (Eph. 5:12).

Watch your mouth! Keep it clean. The Greek word translated *unwholesome* points to rotting (Eph. 5:29a). Unwholesome speech includes swearing, coarseness, harshness, and obscenities—and even talking about sinful deeds or evil entertainment (Eph. 5:12). But unhealthy talk also includes gossip, slander, complaining, criticizing, grumbling, doubt, and words that discourage, damage, or drive a wedge between people. The negative words of the 10 spies lacked faith in God. These words of doubt spread like a plague and influenced an entire nation to miss the Promised Land (Num. 12). God listens to our conversations. So let us honor and respect God the Spirit who lives within us. Let us avoid grieving the Spirit with unwholesome talk (Eph. 4:30). Recall that Jesus said we will give an account for every idle word we speak (Matt. 12:36).

**Q 70** *Complete Figure 2.26 about replacing bad talk with good talk.*

| Reference | Your Summaries on Speech |
|---|---|
| **The Tongue** James 1:19 Prov. 29:20 | |
| **The Heart** Matt. 15:20-16 | |
| **The Mind** 2 Cor. 10:5 | |

**Figure 2.26** Practice summarizing verses relating speech to the tongue, heart, and mind.

*Bridle your tongue.* Be quick to listen and slow to speak (James 1:19). *"Do you see a man who speaks in haste? There is more hope for a fool than for him"* (Prov. 29:20). So let us talk less, and talk better.

*Check your heart.* What we say reveals the condition of our heart. For out of the heart the mouth speaks (Matt. 15:20-16). If our speech is unhealthy, our heart is unhealthy. Sweet and bitter water should not come out of the same fountain (James 3:2-12). If our words are unwholesome, we need Jesus to cleanse our hearts.

*Guide your mind.* Notice that Paul puts **obscenity, foolish talk,** and **coarse joking** beside immorality (Eph. 5:3-4). Dirty talk leads to dirty actions. **All sin begins in the mind.** Soaking the mind in evil thoughts prepares a person for sinning, like soaking charcoal in a fuel prepares it for burning. We avoid immorality by first avoiding the evil thoughts and speech that lead to it. Bring every thought into captivity—making it kneel at the feet of Christ your Lord (2 Cor. 10:5). Shepherd thoughts that go astray, and bring them back into the flock. Our thoughts are many, but mighty. They are like grains of sand—tiny alone, but together they can weigh a ton. If your thoughts are your enemies, they will drag you down to destruction. Let the Spirit and the Word guide your thoughts. Make your thoughts your friends, and they will escort you to heaven.

**Put on wholesome Words (Eph. 4:29).**     ²⁹*Do not let any unwholesome talk come out of your mouths, but only what is helpful for building others up according to their needs, that it may benefit those who listen* (Eph. 4:29).

**Q 71** Have people's words caused you to respect them less? Illustrate.

Paul urges us to watch our words. He commands us to replace vice with nice. Some people like to be the center of attention. They talk too much, hurting their testimony and wasting time. They will do anything to make others laugh. This type of behavior is immature and foolish. A wise person speaks wise words. An immature or foolish person speaks every thought he thinks—he chases every rabbit that runs out of a bush. In contrast, mature, wise people weigh their words. They study people, asking the questions: "What problem is my friend facing? What would the Spirit have me say to encourage this person?"

> PAUL URGES
> US TO WATCH
> OUR WORDS.

²⁷*A man of knowledge uses words with restraint, and a man of understanding is even-tempered.*

²⁸*Even a fool is thought wise if he keeps silent, and discerning if he holds his tongue* (Prov. 17:27-28).

**Q 72** Do you know a good example to follow, whose words always bless others? Explain.

So when we meet with others, let us follow Paul's advice and be praying the questions: "How can I edify you?" "How can my ears and my words make you a better person?" When we walk away from a person who has unwholesome words, we feel discouraged, or even dirty—like we need a bath. In contrast, let us be the type of people whom others walk away from, saying, "Wow, that person's words always lift me up and make me feel closer to Jesus."

*A word aptly spoken is like apples of gold in settings of silver* (Prov. 25:11).

Pastors, teachers, parents, and youth—obey God's Word! Let NO "*unwholesome talk come out of your mouth*" (Eph. 4:29a; 5:4). Let the devil's crowd be known for obscenity, foolish talk, and coarse joking. But let us, the people of God, be known for pure, edifying words. Then the Holy Spirit will be a happy resident within us, and those we talk to will be grateful for our godly friendship.

### E. Replace the darkness of sexual immorality with the light of holy living (Eph. 5:3-17).

**Q 73** Create an ending for this: Sex outside of marriage is as improper for a follower of Christ as ….

³*But among you there must not be even a hint of* **sexual immorality,** *or of any kind of* **impurity,** *or of* **greed,** *because these are* improper for God's holy people (Eph. 5:3).

**Q 74** How does God's plan for sex protect the dignity of all—parents, youth, and children?

**Take off the dark and dirty clothes of immorality.** Paul did NOT lower God's standard for holiness in an ungodly society. He did NOT say, "Some immorality is okay, now and then. I understand. Just try to be sexually pure *most* of the time. I am sure God will wink at a few immoral acts by believers." No! Paul knew God's standard for moral behavior is high and fixed, without compromise. So Paul said, "*But among you there* must **not be even a hint** *of sexual immorality, or of any kind of impurity"* (Eph. 5:3a). The low, degrading, sensual acts and topics of the pagan world are unacceptable among God's holy people. Some claim to know Christ, but their actions deny Him (Titus 1:16).

Likewise, Paul warns against *greed*—sexual desire out of control, lusting for more than God's will and plan. God's will includes a plan to fulfill all of our righteous desires. God has planned for us to fulfill our sexual desires within marriage. In this way, children are born into a safe home, where the father and mother care for them and lead them in the paths of righteousness. In contrast, the world treats sex as a love for self—without concern for the dignity of a spouse or the lives of children conceived in the womb.

Sadly, immorality has always been a problem in the church. In Corinth, Paul wrote for the church to discipline an immoral man (1 Cor. 5:1-5). Likewise, Thyatira was on God's radar. John commended them for some good things, but warned against tolerating sexual immorality in the church. John wrote:

**Q 75** *What warning does God give the sexually immoral (Rev. 2:19-23)?*

> [19]*I know your deeds, your love and faith, your service and perseverance, and that you are now doing more than you did at first.* [20]*Nevertheless, I have this against you:* **You tolerate that woman Jezebel, who calls herself a prophetess. By her teaching she misleads my servants into sexual immorality and the eating of food sacrificed to idols.** [21]*I have given her time to repent of her immorality, but she is unwilling.* [22]*So I will cast her on a bed of suffering, and I will make those who commit adultery with her suffer intensely, unless they repent of her ways.* [23]*I will strike her children dead. Then all the churches will know that I am he who searches hearts and minds, and I will repay each of you according to your deeds* (Rev. 2:19-23).

How should we respond to sexual sins in the church? God does not tolerate sexual immorality in the church, and we must share His values. He is loving and long-suffering, but He does not tolerate perversion in the church. This is His bride! As Paul wrote to the Corinthians, we must put out of the church those who live in immorality. We must commit the body of a sexually immoral person to Satan, so the spirit might be saved (1 Cor. 5:1-5). This is biblical love—taking a strong stand to save the soul of a church member living in immorality.

**Q 76** *How should the church respond to a member who commits a sexual sin?*

> [9]*I have written you in my letter not to associate with sexually immoral people—* [10]*not at all meaning the people of this world who are immoral, or the greedy and swindlers, or idolaters. In that case you would have to leave this world.* [11]*But now I am writing you that you must not associate with anyone who calls himself a brother but is sexually immoral or greedy, an idolater or a slanderer, a drunkard or a swindler. With such a man do not even eat* (1 Cor. 5:9-11).

Some teach that grace covers all of our past, present, and future sins—even as we live in sin. But the Bible promises *wrath*, not blessing, to those who turn away from Christ to follow immoral desires of the flesh.

> [5]*For of this* **you** *can be sure: No immoral, impure or greedy person—such a man is an idolater—has any inheritance in the kingdom of Christ and of God.* [6]*Let no one deceive* **you** *with empty words, for because of such things God's wrath comes on those who are disobedient.* [7]*Therefore do not be partners with* **them** (Eph. 5:5-7).

> AN INHERITANCE IS AHEAD FOR *YOU* AND ME, AS WE WALK IN THE LIGHT OF HOLINESS.

Note the contrast between *you* and *them.* An inheritance is ahead for *you* and me, as we walk in the light of holiness. But the wrath of God is coming on *them*—the immoral and disobedient. So let us not be partners with *them*—but keep a wide space of safety between us and them.

**Q 77** ↘ *Complete Figure 2.27 on warnings Paul gives about immorality and impurity.*

| Paul's Warnings | Your Summaries on Warnings Against Drunkenness |
|---|---|
| Gal. 5:19-21 | |
| Eph. 5:3-17 | |
| 1 Cor. 6:9-10 | |

**Figure 2.27**    Paul's many warnings about immorality, impurity, and greed show that these sins have been a danger to believers. God's apostle insists that followers of Jesus must turn away from darkness and walk in light.

### Put on the clean clothes of light, holiness, and righteousness (Eph. 5:8-14).

**Q 78** ↘ *Complete Figure 2.28, giving definitions, synonyms, and antonyms of the fruit of light.*

| Key Words | Your Definitions, Including Synonyms and Antonyms |
|---|---|
| Goodness | |
| Righteousness | |
| Truth | |

**Figure 2.28**    Practice defining and explaining the fruit of light: goodness, righteousness, and truth.

⁸*For you were **once** darkness, **but now** you are light in the Lord. Live as children of light* ⁹*(for the fruit of the light consists in all **goodness, righteousness and truth**)* ¹⁰*and **find out what pleases the Lord**.* ¹¹*Have nothing to do with the fruitless deeds of darkness, but rather expose them.* ¹²*For it is shameful even to mention what the disobedient do in secret.* ¹³*But everything exposed by the light becomes visible,* ¹⁴*for it is light that makes everything visible. This is why it is said: "Wake up, O sleeper, rise from the dead, and Christ will shine on you"* (Eph. 5:8-14).

¹⁵*Be very careful, then, how you live—not as unwise but as wise,* ¹⁶*making the most of every opportunity, because the days are evil.* ¹⁷*Therefore do not be foolish, but **understand what the Lord's will is*** (Eph. 5:15-17).

**Q 79** ↘ *Give some examples of how we can be careful and wise—making the most of every opportunity.*

Note that Paul emphasizes pleasing the Lord and knowing the Lord's will for the way we live (Eph. 5:10, 17). Some seem to think that the Lord's will is a *mystery*. Earlier in Ephesians, Paul wrote about the mystery of God—that in Jesus Christ our Father saves people from all tribes and unites them. But there is no *mystery* about God's will for how we must live. Paul plainly tells us to take off six dirty garments, and replace them with six godly garments. We have studied five of the sinful garments to replace. Now, we have come to the sixth type of clothing to replace in Paul's list about the will of God for us (Review Figure 2.15).

---

### Lesson 13

### Live Worthy as Children of Light—Part 3: Be *Filled With the Spirit (Eph. 5:18-20)

**Goal A:** *Give an example of the fruit from the tree of alcohol.*
**Goal B:** *Summarize 5 reasons why millions of believers do not drink alcohol.*
**Goal C:** *Explain how being filled with the Spirit brings assurance, victory over sin, and power for service.*
**Goal D:** *Summarize 5 keys to living filled with the Spirit.*

---

### F. The Problem: Take off the shameful garment of drunkenness (Eph. 5:18a).

*"Do not get **drunk** on wine, which leads to \*debauchery"* (shame; sinful, fleshly indulgence; the opposite of self-control) (Eph. 5:18a).

**Q 80**  *Complete Figure 2.29 on the shame that drunkenness leads to.*

| Reference | Your Summaries on Warnings Against Drunkenness |
|---|---|
| Gen. 9:20-27 | |
| Gen. 19:30-38 | |
| Prov. 23:29-35 | |
| Luke 15:13 | |

**Figure 2.29   Practice summarizing verses that warn against drunkenness.**

Drunkenness has always been a huge problem in the world. Scripture warns of the danger of drunkenness (Prov. 23:29-35). The Bible records that Noah's drunkenness led to the curse on his own grandson (Gen. 9:20-27). Lot's drunkenness led to incest with his own daughters—and the birth of the pagan nations of Moab and Edom (Gen. 19:30-38). In biblical times, even pagans considered drunkenness a disgrace. Alexander the Great, one of the most famous generals of the world, got drunk at a party and killed his best friend in a fight.

Christians leaders must beware of alcohol. Those who get drunk damage the church's reputation, and disqualify themselves from leadership. The *first* qualification Paul gives for pastors and deacons is: *"not given to drunkenness"* (1 Tim. 3:3, 8; Titus 1:7).

**Figure 2.30   Replica of Rembrandt's famous painting of Christ calming the storm. This famous painter, after the death of his wife, tried to drown his sorrows in alcohol, and he became one of the millions of slaves of alcohol. He died in a state of drunkenness at the young age of 36. Imagine the beautiful paintings that alcohol stole from the Church through the drunkenness of Rembrandt.**

*Sabio* **says:** "Alcohol is one of the greatest traps life has ever set for the feet of humanity!"

**Alcohol has ruined millions and millions of people.**

Some question whether drinking alcohol is acceptable for Christians. In this passage Paul warns believers to avoid drunkenness because it leads to a life of *debauchery*. The Greek word translated *debauchery* in Ephesians 5:18a is the same Greek word translated *wild living* in the story of the prodigal son. Jesus said he *"squandered his wealth in wild living"* (Luke 15:13). Here is a truth we can illustrate over and over: Drinking alcohol often leads to *living wild*—like the prodigal son who rebelled against his father.

We agree that Jesus and the apostles drank wine, in Israel, about 2,000 years ago. And if the wine of that day was not fermented at times, then the Scriptures would not warn us about drunkenness. In biblical times, wine was a part of many cultures. Water was often impure, and fresh juice did not stay fresh for long. But over the past 2,000 years, societies have purified water, and marketed over 200 new drinks, including 100 Coke products, various coffees, teas, and sodas, many juices, and a host of other beverages. So the question arises, "Would Jesus and the apostles drink wine if they were living on the earth *today*?" The answer to this question varies from nation to nation, and even within nations. Many national churches in Europe and elsewhere drink wine as a part of their culture. No doubt there are thousands of believers who drink wine without feeling any sense of guilt or condemnation. *We should love and respect believers everywhere. And as Paul says about matters of conscience, believers should not judge each other on disputable matters, outside of the main beliefs of the gospel* (Rom. 14:1-13).

Why do people drink alcohol? Answers vary. Some drink for social and cultural reasons. Others drink because they see ads showing beautiful people having fun. Those who make and sell alcohol spend billions of dollars guiding people to think that drinking is cool. Children and youth may try alcohol *because* they see adults and peers drinking

**Q 81** *Did Jesus and the apostles drink fermented wine?*

**Q 82** *What types of drinks are available today that were not present in the days of the apostles?*

**Q 83** *Where you live, what are some reasons why people drink alcohol?*

it. Many drink to forget their problems for a few hours. Alcohol is a drug that clouds and depresses the brain. So it offers a *quick fix*—a temporary relief, like hiding a problem under a blanket. Yet alcohol creates many *lasting* problems for each one it *briefly* covers.

While some national churches drink wine, other national churches, such as the Assemblies of God in the United States, have taken the position of *abstinence—not drinking alcohol. These believers do not look down on or condemn believers who drink wine. Still millions of believers worldwide give these reasons for refusing alcoholic drinks (Figure 2.31).

| Reasons | Reasons Why Millions of Believers Do Not Drink Alcohol |
|---------|--------------------------------------------------------|
| 1. | Some abstain from drinking as a protest to the suffering that results from alcoholic drinks. The US government estimated that the damage alcohol causes cost more than $2.23 billion each year.[6] Suffering that alcohol causes includes accidents, loss of health, violent crimes, spouse abuse, child abuse, loss of virginity, loss of jobs, loss of property by fire, and loss of reputation. Such terrible fruit guides many to turn from alcohol rather than toward it. |
| 2. | Many choose not to drink alcohol because it is not the *best* decision. Paul prayed for us *to discern what is best* (Phil. 1:10). Many agree that alcohol brings out the worst in us, not the best. |
| 3. | Others refuse to drink because of the worldliness, sin, and shame linked with liquor, beer, and wine. Drinking alcohol is one of the world's core values. Wherever sinners party, they drink alcohol. Those who make and sell alcoholic drinks use lust, sex, and worldly desires to seduce buyers. In contrast, the Bible guides believers to separate from the world, and not be guided by the lust of the flesh and the lust of the eyes (1 John 2:16) Is it the Spirit or the flesh that leads people to drink alcohol? |
| 4. | Multitudes avoid alcohol because it is a risk—a bridge to danger. It is a known fact that too much alcohol makes fools out of people. Why play with fire? The person who never drinks will never be drunk, and never be on the long list of alcoholics. Why take the risk? Scripture warns that wine is a mocker. So why take the risk of taking the first drink? <br><br> [29]*Who has woe? Who has sorrow? Who has strife? Who has complaints? Who has needless bruises? Who has bloodshot eyes?* [30]*Those who linger over wine, who go to sample bowls of mixed wine.* [31]*Do not gaze at wine when it is red, when it sparkles in the cup, when it goes down smoothly!* [32]*In the end it bites like a snake and poisons like a viper* (Prov. 23:29-32). <br><br> The risk of being bitten by a snake increases if you pick up the snake! Abstinence is a guaranteed cure for drunkenness. |
| 5. | A number of believers do not drink alcohol so they will not cause weaker believers to stumble. As sheep follow their shepherd, disciples follow their mentors, and children follow their parents. What parents may handle in moderation, their children often use in excess. What big brother steps over, little brother trips over. What big sister can master, enslaves little sister. The weak we have with us always. <br><br> [13]*...let us stop passing judgment on one another. Instead, make up your mind not to put any stumbling block or obstacle in our brother's way....* [20]*Do not destroy the work of God for the sake of food* [or anything else].... [21]*It is better not to eat meat or drink wine or to do anything else that will cause your brother to fall* (Rom. 14:13, 20-21). <br><br> If only **one person** is saved from harm or hell by refusing alcohol, it is worth the abstinence. |

Figure 2.31   Five reasons millions of believers abstain from alcoholic drinks

Q 84 ✎ *Complete Figure 2.32 on five reasons why millions abstain from drinking alcohol.*

| Reasons why | Your Brief Summaries on Why Millions Abstain From Alcoholic Drinks |
|-------------|-------------------------------------------------------------------|
| 1. | |
| 2. | |
| 3. | |
| 4. | |
| 5. | |

Figure 2.32   Practice summarizing five reasons why millions
do not drink alcohol for pleasure.

Q 85 ✎ *What is the difference between having the Spirit, and being filled with the Spirit? Explain.*

## B. The Need: Why we must live filled with the Spirit (Eph. 5:18-20).[7]

[18]*Do not get **drunk** on wine, which leads to **debauchery**. Instead, be filled with the Spirit.* [19]*Speak to one another with psalms, hymns and spiritual songs. Sing and*

*make music in your heart to the Lord,* [20] *always giving thanks to God the Father for everything, in the name of our Lord Jesus Christ* (Eph. 5:18-20).

Nothing can fill the Spirit's place—in a believer, or in the whole church. What fuel is to a vehicle, the Holy Spirit is to the Church. We shall sit powerless and defeated before our problems and foes until we live filled with the power of the Spirit.

Many believers suffer from forms of spiritual weakness that result from a lack of the Holy Spirit. All followers of Christ have a measure of the Spirit. Otherwise they would not be Christians at all. But spiritual weakness is present when the Spirit within is like a shallow creek—rather than a deep river of living water (John 7:38). Why should we be content with this? The Pentecostal fullness is within our reach.

**Do you lack assurance of salvation?** Do you doubt that you are forgiven, alive in Christ, a member of His family with an inheritance in heaven (Eph. 2:4-22)? Sometimes you are calm, feeling happy and content. But these joyful hours flee, and your rest is changed to the rough waters of a storm. You need a deeper source of peace, which comes from being anchored in the Word and filled with the Spirit. The Spirit gives His holy witness deep within that we are the children of God. He is the Spirit of adoption, whereby we cry, *"Abba, Father!"* (Rom. 8:17).

**Do you lack victory over sin?** Do you live unworthy of Christ in your relationships— quarreling and arguing with other believers (Eph. 4:1-6)? Are you an unworthy husband, wife, father, mother, child, employee, boss, or Christian soldier (Eph. 5:21–6:18)? Then you need the fruit that comes from being filled with the Spirit—the fruit of love, joy, peace, patience, kindness, goodness, faithfulness, gentleness, and self-control (Gal. 5:22-23). Do you struggle with lying, anger, stealing, unhealthy speech, sexual immorality, or drunkenness (Eph. 4:17–5:18)? This is no wonder if you neglect the Holy Spirit. He is the secret to overcoming the evil desires of the flesh. For as we live filled with the Spirit, we do not fulfill the lusts of the flesh (Gal. 5:17). When He fills the heart, the suggestions of temptation are quenched as sparks in a wave of the ocean. As darkness cannot remain in the presence of morning light, sinful desires disappear when the Spirit fills our mind and heart. Look up! Remember the mountain peak of Ephesians 3:20! God is able to do much more than we can ask or think *by the power at work in us.* So live filled with the Spirit and you will have all the power you need to be victorious over sin.

**Do you lack power for service?** Do you fail to do your part in building up the body of Christ (Eph. 4:7-16)? Do you come to church with empty hands and an empty heart? Do you lack concern for the salvation of others? When you speak, is there no power or passion in your words? Do the demons laugh at your attempts to exorcise them? You cannot expect it to be otherwise until you live in the power our Lord promised when He said: *"You will receive power when the Holy Spirit comes on you"* (Acts 1:8). When the first Christians were filled with the Holy Spirit, they spoke the Word of God with boldness—and witnessed with great power about the resurrection of the Lord Jesus.

We overcome spiritual weakness as we live filled with the Holy Spirit. His presence brings us joy, power, the presence of Jesus, and a rest in the will of God. So let us refuse to be satisfied with anything less than the full measure of the Holy Spirit within.

Being fully committed to the service of Christ is a great step forward. But even this is not enough. We need power to fulfill our spiritual commitments! So Jesus made possible a new era for the Church—an age of being filled with the Spirit of God.

Of course the Spirit was always in the world. It was the Holy Spirit of Pentecost who brooded over the chaos that Genesis 1 records. And it was the same Holy Spirit who spoke through prophets and holy men such as Moses, Isaiah, and Jeremiah. It was this Holy Spirit who gave courage and power to the heroes and saints of the Old Testament. The Day of Pentecost did *not* introduce a new Spirit into the world. But Pentecost began

**Q 86** ↗ Do all believers have a measure of the Spirit's presence? Explain.

**Q 87** ↖ How does the Spirit give us a deep assurance of salvation?

**Q 88** ↖ How does the promise of Ephesians 3:20 relate to victory over sin?

**Q 89** ↖ How did the first disciples receive power to serve?

**Q 90** ↖ Why do we need the blessing of Pentecost, day by day?

an era in which the weakest and lowliest saints could possess the Spirit in the same measure as mightiest saints of the Old Testament. Before that great Day of Pentecost His fullness was the privilege of only the few and the elite—such as Moses, Elijah, Isaiah, Ezekiel, and Daniel. But since that Day of Pentecost, God has poured out the fullness of the Spirit on common believers—plain men, women, and children; common thinkers and hidden workers; on hand-maids and servants; on all and any who are hungry and thirsty for God's fullness that He wants to share. So let us live filled with the Spirit!

**Q 91** *Does God still want to fill people with His Spirit today?*

Peter told the listening crowd that the fullness of the Spirit that came at Pentecost was not for them only, but for their children, and for us, who were far off—as many as God calls to be members of His family (Acts 2:39). Are you one of those whom God has called into His family? Then rejoice because the fullness of the Spirit is for you today, and each day! How tragic that many think the Almighty is like a bankrupt builder, who began the foundation of His Church with marble, but must finish it with common brick! Nonsense! God gives as much of the Spirit for us today as He gave on the day of Pentecost (Luke 11:13)!

Paul gives 36 commands about walking worthy, in response to all that God has done for us in Christ (Eph. 4–6; Figures 2.2, 2.36, and 3.20). "Be filled with the Spirit" is just one of Paul's 36 commands in Ephesians, but it makes all the others possible. For example, "Husbands, love your wives" is possible as husbands are filled with the Spirit. In other words, what God commands He enables through filling those who continually seek His Spirit. Be not faithless, but believe! Lay claim at once to the fullness of the Spirit God has promised us in this covenant. And give thanks that you live in this era of the Spirit.

### C. The Solution: How we can live filled with the Spirit (Eph. 5:18-20).[8]

Let us consider some key principles that guide us to cooperate with God and live filled with the Spirit.

**Q 92** *Does God give us the Spirit in relation to our hungering, asking, and desiring Him? Explain.*

**1. Stir up holy desire by considering what the fullness of the Spirit brings (Eph. 5:18).** We cannot expect to be filled with the Spirit if we are content to live without His fullness. Our Father will not entrust this priceless gift to the satisfied, the lukewarm, or the indifferent. Where the flame of desire burns low, we cannot expect to find the Holy Spirit's fullness.

It is not enough to have a fitful desire that flames up today, but cools down for weeks, months, and even years. We must have a steady purpose that can stand the test of waiting. Recall that on the Day of Pentecost, the 120 believers had been waiting for 10 days (Acts 1–2). Like these faithful seekers, we must persevere through the silence or apparent denial.

Yet the flame of our desire to be filled with the Spirit needs fuel. We must muse and meditate before that fire can burn. We must stir up the gift of the Spirit within us by a quiet consideration of all it means to be Spirit-filled.

**Q 93** *How can we stir up our desire to live filled with the Spirit?*

**Q 94** *What promise does God give us in Isaiah 44:3?*

Studying the book of Acts fuels our desire to live filled with the Spirit. In Acts, Luke emphasizes the power of the Spirit 53 times. The apostles and the early church followed the example of Jesus, who Himself depended on the Spirit (Luke 4:18-19). For even though Jesus was God in the flesh, and conceived by the Spirit in the womb, He depended on the anointing of the Spirit day by day (John 1:32-34; Luke 3:22; 4:1, 14, 18; Acts 10:38). It is a marvel to see what the fullness of the Spirit did for those who first received Him. Cowards became brave. Dull minds that had stumbled over simple truths, awoke to grasp the Lord's plan. Apostles who had competed for top positions of power were united to serve. Such power attended their words that crowds became house churches. Killers of Christ became His worshipers and friends. Plain disciples of Christ overcame councils of learned men. The power of the Spirit shook towns and nations. Fishermen, anointed by the Spirit, preached and thousands filled the net of the gospel. The power of God was so great that He healed the sick by the shadow and sweat rags of God's apostles. All these works of power came by the Spirit who filled the whole Church. And God does not change. His desire is to fill His people with His presence, so that we lack no spiritual gift as we wait for the coming of our Lord Jesus Christ (1 Cor. 1:7). May we not settle for weakness. Let us daily seek to be filled with the Spirit, to glorify God and see Him expand His kingdom in the hearts of humans.

Likewise, studying the promises of the Scripture fans into flame our desire to be filled with the Spirit. God has promised that rivers of living water will flow from us (John 7). He has promised that we need not be anxious about our words, because the Spirit will guide them (Luke 12:11). He has assured us that as we walk in the Spirit we will overcome sinful desires of the flesh (Rom. 8:9; Gal. 5:16). God has told us that the Spirit will bring all things to our remembrance (John 14:26); and He will teach us all things, as we abide in Him (1 John 2:27). God's Word assures us that the Spirit is transforming us into God's image, little by little (1 Cor. 3:18). As we meditate on these promises, we must glow with a desire for the Spirit, as a light bulb glows with electricity. And we know that God delights to give the Spirit to those who ask Him (Luke 11:13). He pours out the Spirit on those who are thirsty, like floods on the dry ground (Isa. 44:3).

**2. Seek the fullness of the Spirit with the right motive (Eph. 5:18).** If you want Him in order to realize a certain experience, or attract people to yourself, or to transform some difficulty into a stepping-stone, you are likely to miss Him. Focus on the one purpose of magnifying the Lord Jesus in your body, whether by life or death. Ask God to cleanse you of lesser motives, and cause this one pure desire to burn brightly within you.

*Q 95 What types of motives should cause us to seek the Spirit's fullness?*

God will do nothing to minister to our pride or selfishness. He will not give us the Holy Spirit to enable fame, name, comfort, position, or power. Seek the Spirit so you can exalt Jesus. God's one passion is the glory of the Lord Jesus. And the Spirit will fill only those who agree to lift up our Lord. *"Can two walk together except they be agreed?"* (Amos 3:3 KJV). Be like John the Baptist, who was filled with the Spirit from the womb, ever desiring that people should turn from you to Jesus. If your motives fall below this standard, trust in Him to enlighten and purify you. Offer Him your heart to examine and cleanse. Then it will not be long until the Lord, whom you seek, will suddenly fill your body as His temple.

**3. Sing in the Spirit with Scripture songs (Eph. 5:18b-20; Col. 3:16).** Paul connects being filled with the Spirit to singing Scripture. As we are filled, we overflow with songs of praise. And as we sing the truths of Scripture, the Spirit rises up within us. So Paul writes:

*Q 96 How does singing Scriptural songs increase the presence of the Spirit in us?*

> *"18b Be filled with the Spirit. 19 Speak to one another with psalms, hymns and spiritual songs. Sing and make music in your heart to the Lord, 20 always giving thanks to God the Father for everything, in the name of our Lord Jesus Christ"* (Eph. 5:18b-20).

God's people have long recognized the relationship of singing to His presence. Elisha wanted the Spirit to fill him, so he could prophesy. So he called for a musician (2 Kings 3:15). As we sing songs of praise to come into God's presence, His presence comes into us (Ps. 100:4). When an evil spirit troubled Saul, David played his harp and sang praises to God. As a result, the evil spirit left and the presence of the Lord came. There is a direct connection between singing spiritual songs and enjoying the Spirit's presence. As the musicians played, the Spirit of God filled Solomon's temple (2 Chron. 5:13-14).

We are studying the Prison Epistles. Paul and Silas were bleeding from a beating, and locked in prison at Philippi (Acts 16:25-34). As they sang songs at midnight, the presence of God filled them and the prison, shaking the chains loose from the prisoners, and opening the prison doors. Soon, the jailer and his household were saved, and began to follow Christ. Let us turn upward from doubt, discouragement, and suffering to singing songs of praise—enabling the Spirit to fill us and minister to us and others. *"16Let the word of Christ dwell in you richly as you teach and admonish one another with all wisdom, and as you sing psalms, hymns and spiritual songs with gratitude in your hearts to God"* (Col. 3:16). Do we desire to live filled with the Spirit? Then let us practice the habit of praising and thanking God with songs based on Scripture. For as we are filled with the Word and with thanksgiving, we will also live filled with the Spirit. Singing Scripture songs and being filled with the Spirit belong together, like honey in the comb. Through singing praises to God, we invite, celebrate, and increase the measure of the Spirit in us. Show me a person who growls and frowns his way through the day, and I will show you a person with little of the Spirit. God inhabits the praises of His people (Ps. 22:3). Look up, sing up, and you will be filled up.

Notice the balance between the Word and the Spirit. Paul emphasizes that the Word is the sword of the Spirit (Eph. 6:9). The Spirit and the Word always belong together. Some sincere people have erred by emphasizing the fullness of God's Spirit—while neglecting the study of God's Word. This is a grave mistake and the parent of many false teachings. For if we put aside the Word of God, we open ourselves up to many voices that speak within our hearts. Without the Word, we have no test, no standard of truth. So Paul emphasized that being filled with the Spirit results in singing Psalms or other songs based on Scripture (Eph. 5:19-20). And as the Word of Christ dwells in us richly, we sing *"psalms, hymns and spiritual songs"* (Col. 3:16). The Spirit and the Word must walk hand in hand.

 *Sabio* **says:** "Those who have only the Spirit without the Word get blown away by winds of false teaching; and those who have only the Word without the presence of the Spirit shrivel away from lack of love and joy, like the Pharisees." Those who worship God must worship Him in Spirit *and* in truth (John 4:23-24); and Scripture is God's standard of truth. There is no better way to commune with God than to walk in your room or in the open air, singing Scripture songs. As God walked with humans in Eden, He fills those who praise Him with Scripture songs.

**Q 97** ✎ *Complete Figure 2.33 on the relationship of the Spirit's presence to singing Scripture.*

| Reference | Your Summaries on the Relationship of the Spirit's Presence to Singing Scripture |
|---|---|
| 2 Kings 3:15 | |
| 2 Chron. 5:13-14 | |
| Ps. 22:3 | |
| Ps. 100:4 | |
| Acts 16:25-34 | |
| Eph. 5:18-20 | |
| Col. 3:16 | |

**Figure 2.33    Practice summarizing the relationship of the Spirit's presence to singing Scripture.**

**Q 98** ✎ *How does being sensitive to the Spirit increase His ministry through us? Illustrate.*

**4. Do not grieve the Spirit; honor Him at all times (Eph. 4:30).** The Holy Spirit is in us, but we must constantly yield to Him. As children grow and mature, we also learn to submit to the Spirit. He teaches us to recognize sinful desires of the flesh. As Paul writes, the Spirit of grace *"[12]teaches us to say 'No' to ungodliness and worldly passions, and to live self-controlled...godly lives in this present age, [13]while we wait for the blessed hope—the glorious appearing of our great God and Savior, Jesus Christ, [14]who gave himself for us to redeem us from all wickedness, and to purify for himself a people that are his very own, eager to do what is good"* (Titus 2:12-14; see also Eph. 2:10).

**Q 99** ✎ *What are some ways we can welcome and submit to the Spirit?*

Are we sensitive to the Spirit? Do we invite Him into our conversations? Are we conscious that He looks through our eyes, seeing what we see; and He listens through our ears, to what we hear? Do we honor Him with what we watch, what we say, what we think about, and what we do? Do we walk softly through the day, listening for His insights, His directions, His objections, and His approval? We have chosen Jesus as our substitute; but have we also chosen Him as our Lord, through His Spirit within? Can we say, like the apostle: *"I no longer live, but Christ lives in me"* (Gal. 2:20)? If so, this involves practice. For the Spirit to be strong in us, the self-life must die daily. For the Spirit to increase, the voice of the flesh must decrease. We must live alert, paying attention to the Spirit's voice. The daily filling of the Holy Spirit is only possible to those who obey Him in all things. We must be faithful to Him in small things. By the neglect of slight commands, the Spirit's presence fades in us. A lustful look, a careless word, a refusal to submit—any of these may grieve and quench Him. So let us count the cost of letting the Spirit guide us, as a rider guides a bicycle, or as a writer uses a pen. And let us not be afraid of what He may demand. He is the Spirit of love. And He loves us too much to cause grief without reason.

At times, Balaam had visions and prophecies by the Spirit. But when his heart hungered for money, he failed to recognize the voice of the Spirit telling him to turn away from greed (Num. 22:12). His flesh led him to desire more than God was offering him. Thus, he grieved and quenched the Spirit, and lost his connection with God. Samson enjoyed a great anointing of the Spirit. But he refused to honor his parents or the voice of the Spirit, who often rebuked him for his immorality. Judas Iscariot shared in the ministry of the apostles (Acts 1:17). But he refused to obey the warning of the Spirit, who surely objected to stealing from the money bag (John 12:6). In contrast, let us live filled with the Spirit, obeying Him in the little things. For as small sins lead to a life of destruction, small acts of obedience lead to a life of blessings. So let us practice giving the Spirit full sway in our lives, without resistance—yielding as a sailboat to the wind. The one who is faithful with a little will be faithful with a lot (Luke 16:10).

*Q 100* ↗ *What does Balaam teach us about the Spirit's presence?*

**5. Remember it is not enough to be filled only once.** Like the apostles, we must seek daily fillings by the Spirit. Those who were filled in Acts 2 were filled again in Acts 4. Scripture describes at least four different ways we receive the Spirit in our Christian experience.[9]

*Q 101* ↖ *How often do we need to be filled with the Spirit? Explain.*

*Q 102* ↖ *Complete Figure 2.34 on four different times we receive the Spirit throughout life.*

| Times | Your Summaries on Four Times We Receive the Spirit Throughout Life |
|---|---|
| At conversion | |
| At Pentecost | |
| At key times | |
| Day by day | |

**Figure 2.34  Practice summarizing times we receive the Spirit as we follow Jesus throughout life.**

*First,* we receive the Spirit of God at conversion, as He brings us spiritual life. Paul explains that when we first believe, we receive the Holy Spirit as a seal that we belong to God (Eph. 1:13-14).

*Second,* after conversion, the Spirit comes to empower us as witnesses and servants of God. Five places in Acts, we see those who are already believers receiving a new dimension of the Spirit as they are filled with the Spirit (Acts 2, 8, 9, 10, 19). Luke refers to this initial equipping for service as being *"clothed with power from on high"* (Luke 24:49); being *baptized* in *the Holy Spirit* (Acts 1:4-5; 11:16); and being *filled with the Holy Spirit* (Acts 2:4). Luke often records that believers spoke in tongues as the Spirit filled them to be witnesses to all ethnic groups (Acts 2:4; 10:46; 19:6). Today, there are more than 500 million Pentecostal and Charismatic believers who speak in tongues, and rejoice to see the Spirit manifest spiritual gifts in their lives (1 Cor. 1:7; 12:7-11). (For a lesson on how to be filled with the Spirit for the first time, see the *Faith & Action* book, *Acts of the Holy Spirit*, Lesson 11).

**Figure 2.35   Like Elijah under the juniper tree, there are times we need a fresh filling of the Spirit.**

*Third*, at key times of ministry or pressure in life, God fills believers with the Spirit, enabling them to speak words of wisdom, or perform other spiritual gifts. For example, God gave Peter a fresh filling of the Spirit, enabling him to speak with boldness to the Sanhedrin (Acts 4). God filled Stephen, a deacon, with the Spirit and wisdom that his enemies could not match (Acts 7:55).

*Fourth*, Paul commands us to live *"filled with the Spirit"* (Eph. 5:18). Here, Paul is urging us to be filled anew, day by day. His emphasis is not, *"Were* you filled with the Spirit in the past?" Rather, his point is, *"Are* you filled with the Spirit today?" Being filled with the Spirit is a recurring need. We need new food, new water, and new sleep each day for the body. Likewise, we need to be filled with new spiritual energy day by day. To live today well, we need a fresh filling of the Spirit. So as we look to our Father for our daily bread, let us also look to Him for our daily filling of the Spirit.

**Q 103**  ✎  *Are you hungry for more of the Spirit in your life? Take time to receive more of Him now and each day.*

At times we become aware of lacking the fullness of the Spirit. Like Elijah, we may become weary from service (1 Kings 19:5-18). Like Jesus, our ministry to others may sap our strength (Mark 6:31). New ministries and tasks may drain us of our spiritual strength. When we find ourselves lacking God's presence, let us go again to the same source for a refilling—a recharging with spiritual power, a re-anointing of the Spirit. Blessed is the person who never leaves the house in the morning without first being filled with the presence of God for the day.

| Principles 17–24 for Living Worthy—in the Spirit and the Love of God (Eph. 5:1-20) | |
|---|---|
| 5:1-2 | **17.** ¹*Be imitators of God, therefore, as dearly loved children* ²*and live a life of love, just as Christ loved us and gave himself up for us as a fragrant offering and sacrifice to God.* |
| 5:3-5 | **18.** ³*But among you there must not be even a hint of sexual immorality, or of any kind of impurity, or of greed, because these are improper for God's holy people.* ⁴*Nor should there be obscenity, foolish talk or coarse joking, which are out of place, but rather thanksgiving.* [**Explanation/restatement:** ⁵*For of this you can be sure: No immoral, impure or greedy person—such a man is an idolater—has any inheritance in the kingdom of Christ and of God.*] |
| 5:6-7 | **19.** ⁶*Let no one deceive you with empty words, for because of such things God's wrath comes on those who are disobedient.* ⁷*Therefore do not be partners with them.* |
| 5:8b-10 | **20.** ⁸ᵇ*Live as children of light;* ⁹*for the fruit of the light consists in all goodness, righteousness and truth)* ¹⁰*and find out what pleases the Lord.* |
| 5:11-12 | **21.** ¹¹*Have nothing to do with the fruitless deeds of darkness, but rather expose them.* [Explanation: ¹²*For it is shameful even to mention what the disobedient do in secret.*] |
| 5:15-17 | **22.** ¹⁵*Be very careful, then, how you live—not as unwise but as wise,* ¹⁶*making the most of every opportunity, because the days are evil.* ¹⁷*Therefore do not be foolish, but understand what the Lord's will is.* |
| 5:18 | **23.** ¹⁸*Do not get drunk on wine, which leads to debauchery. Instead, be filled with the Spirit.* |
| 5:19-20 | **24.** ¹⁹*Speak to one another with psalms, hymns and spiritual songs. Sing and make music in your heart to the Lord,* ²⁰*always giving thanks to God the Father for everything, in the name of our Lord Jesus Christ.* |

**Figure 2.36   In Ephesians 4–6 Paul gives at least 36 principles for living worthy—in the Spirit and the love of God. (See Figure 2.2 for principles 1–16 and Figure 3.20 for priciples 25–36.)**

**Test Yourself:** Circle the letter by the *best* completion to each question or statement.

1. The banner over Ephesians 4–6 is:
a) Alive in Christ
b) Jesus is Lord
c) Live worthy
d) Spiritual warfare

2. As believers share their gifts
a) the church has plenty of money.
b) the body grows and edifies itself.
c) believers learn to say, "Thank you."
d) our salvation is complete.

3. How are physical and spiritual walking alike?
a) Both are a process from birth.
b) Both are a privilege we cannot lose.
c) Both precede running.
d) Both become normal with practice.

4. Which is TRUE about sins?
a) Satan does not mention sins.
b) All believers sin throughout life.
c) God convicts of sins to help us.
d) God and Satan mention sins to condemn us.

5. Paul compares truth to
a) A belt
b) A helmet
c) A door
d) A destiny

6. Which leader struggled with anger?
a) Peter
b) Paul
c) Nehemiah
d) Moses

7. What does Paul say must replace stealing?
a) Sharing
b) Working
c) Self-control
d) Contentment

8. What does Paul say about the sexually immoral?
a) They have no spiritual inheritance.
b) They are saved by grace, but lose rewards.
c) They are saved, but are not saints.
d) Their sins are covered by grace.

9. Why do millions refuse to drink alcohol?
a) Scripture forbids it.
b) Paul did not drink it.
c) It is linked to sin and shame.
d) Only sinners drink alcohol.

10. A key to living filled with the Spirit is:
a) Memorize Scripture.
b) Beg God to fill you.
c) Claim the promise that you are filled.
d) Recall that one filling is not enough.

**Essay Test Topics:** Write 50-100 words on each of these 15 goals that you studied in this chapter. Try to complete this test in 1.5 hours. On the final exam, we will combine some of these goals and ask you to write on a few of them. As you practice writing on each of these goals now, you are preparing well for the final test (6 points each + 10 points free)

- Analyze the need to live worthy, and the roles of love and effort on the path of unity (Eph. 4:1-6).

- List at least 10 ways people serve as gifts in the church, and the result of this serving (Eph. 4:7-13).

- Explain why truth and love must walk together as we walk worthy (Eph. 4:13-16). Describe the result.

- Contrast how we lived in the past, without Christ, and how Paul insists we must live now, in Christ (Eph. 2:1-3; 4:17-24; Col. 3:25).

- Contrast 3 truths about physical and spiritual walking.

- Contrast the reasons of the devil and the reasons of God for identifying sins.

- Explain why lying is so offensive to God, and give examples of being truthful.

- Identify 5 levels of anger we must practice controlling and the fruit of the Spirit that replaces anger.

- Give examples of people that have stolen, and illustrate why we must replace stealing with hard work.

- Give examples of unwholesome and healthy words. Contrast the effects of good and bad talking.

- Analyze the problem and destination of the sexually immoral. Contrast followers of Christ and followers of lust, on the topic of morality.

- Give an example of the fruit from the tree of alcohol.

- Summarize 5 reasons why millions of believers do not drink alcohol.

- Explain how being filled with the Spirit brings assurance, victory over sin, and power for service.

- Summarize 5 keys to living filled with the Spirit.

# Unit 2:
# Exploring Ephesians and Colossians—Part 2

Ephesians 1–3, like the left side of a mountain, rises in praise for two reasons: *first*, for all the spiritual blessings God has poured out on us in Christ (Eph. 1:3-14); and *second*, for redeeming and uniting Jews and Gentiles into one body, one family, and one temple (Eph. 2–3).

Likewise **Ephesians 4–6** rises, like the right side of a mountain, as the praise of our response—as we *live worthy* of all our Father has done for us in Christ. We live worthy of God's blessings as we take off (like dirty clothes) six types of sins, and replace them with six virtues. God enables us to live worthy in society, in our homes, at work, and in spiritual warfare.

The top of a mountain is its most glorious, inspiring point. The peak of Ephesians is the doxology of **3:20-21**. These verses glorify God. They shout glory to God from the mountain top—because God *"is able to do immeasurably more than all we ask or imagine, according to his power that is at work within us"* (Eph. 3:20). As the peak of a mountain relates to both sides, Ephesians 3:20-21 relates to the two parts of Ephesians. By *His power* at work in us God has done all of Ephesians 1–3. He has poured out His blessings on us—redeeming and uniting Jews and Gentiles into one body (Eph. 1–3). And by the power of that same Spirit who works in us, God enables us to live worthy—causing us to rejoice as we obey the 36 commands of Ephesians 4–6. *By His power!* This is the key. So let us praise Him, and depend on the power of His Spirit for both sides of the mountain of salvation—for redemption and spiritual unity (Eph. 1–3), and for living worthy (Eph. 4–6). For *by His power* at work in us, He is able to do much more than we can ask or imagine.

As you study Unit 2, we will complete Ephesians. Then we will pay special attention to Paul's emphasis on our blessings *in Christ*. For the fullness of God is in Christ, in bodily form (Col. 1:19; 2:9). In Christ *"are hidden all the treasures of wisdom and knowledge"* (Col. 2:3). And Christ is the Supreme Creator and Reconciler of all things on earth and in heaven (Col. 1:15–23). Here are some goals we will help you reach:

## Chapter 3: Ephesians—Live Worthy of Your Calling, at Home and at War (Eph. 5:21–6:24)

- *Analyze responsibilities for each group in God's family.*
- *Summarize aspects of spiritual warfare in Ephesians 1–6, and explain the armor we need.*
- *Analyze praying in the Spirit, occasions for prayer, and types of prayer.*

## Chapter 4: Colossians, Powerful Doctrine About Our Supreme Savior (Col. 1–2)

- *Analyze the authorship, date, city, purposes, theme, and outline of Colossians.*
- *Summarize 6 errors of the Colossian heresy.*
- *Explain ways Christ is supreme as Creator and Reconciler (Col. 1:15-23). Apply these.*
- *Examine the cost, message, purpose, and power of spiritual ministry (Col. 1:24–2:5).*
- *Identify, illustrate, and apply 4 ways to overcome false teachings (Col. 2:6-23).*

# Chapter 3:
# Live Worthy of Your Calling: At Home, at Work, and at War
## (Eph. 5:21–6:24)

Figure 3.1  Live worthy at home, at work, and at war in spiritual battles.

---

## Lessons:

### Lesson 14: Live Worthy at Home: Wives and Husbands (Eph. 5:21-33; Col. 3:18-19)

**Goal A:** *Compare and contrast Paul's teachings on relationships in Ephesians and Colossians.*

**Goal B:** *Analyze the submission of a godly wife to her husband; and how she honors, respects, and admires him.*

**Goal C:** *Explain 5 ways a husband should love his wife as Christ loves the Church (Eph. 5:25-33).*

### Lesson 15: Live Worthy at Home and At Work: Children and Parents; Workers and Employers (Eph. 6:1-9; Col. 3:20–4:1)

**Goal A:** *Identify the groups in God's family that a pastor must shepherd.*

**Goal B:** *Analyze the problem, solution, and promise for children in God's family.*

**Goal C:** *State and illustrate 4 guidelines for parents to train children in God's family.*

**Goal D:** *State and illustrate 2 guidelines for employers and employees in God's family.*

### Lesson 16: Live Worthy at War: Soldiers and Enemies—Part 1 (Eph. 6:10-24)

**Goal A:** *Summarize aspects of our spiritual warfare in Ephesians 1–6.*

**Goal B:** *Explain the problem and the solution of standing firm against spiritual forces (Eph. 6:10-12).*

**Goal C:** *Analyze the need and the way to stand firm in the Lord against the devil's schemes (Eph. 6:10-14).*

### Lesson 17: Live Worthy at War: Soldiers and Enemies—Part 2 (Eph. 6:10-24)

**Goal D:** *List and explain the purposes of 6 pieces of spiritual armor in Ephesians 6:14-17.*

**Goal E:** *Explain and apply: praying in the Spirit, occasions for prayer, and types of prayer (Eph. 6:18-20).*

---

 **Key Words**

**submission**—the attitudes and actions of honoring a person in authority. Examples: children submit to the authority of their parents; all citizens submit to government leaders.

**spiritual warfare**—the process of standing firm in Christ to remain faithful to the gospel and to live worthy of our calling, as we face temptations of the world, evil desires of the flesh, and the influence of evil spirits

**armor of God**—the six pieces of armor that God provides for us (Eph. 6:14-17)

## Live Worthy at Home: Wives and Husbands (Eph. 5:21-33; Col. 3:18-19)

**Goal A:** *Compare and contrast Paul's teachings on relationships in Ephesians and Colossians.*

**Goal B:** *Analyze the submission of a godly wife to her husband; and how she honors, respects, and admires him.*

**Goal C:** *Explain 5 ways a husband should love his wife as Christ loves the Church (Eph. 5:25-33).*

Ephesians 5:21 begins the final section on relationships—in the home, at work, and at war (Eph. 5:21–6:24). Paul summarizes this section with the banner: *"²¹Submit to one another out of reverence for Christ"* (Eph. 5:21). Some have misunderstood the words: *Submit to one another.* Paul does not mean that husbands submit to wives; nor that parents submit to children; nor that masters submit to slaves; nor that Christ submits to the Church. Ephesians thunders on the truth that Christ is the Head of the Church, and that God the Father exalted Him far above all powers in heaven and in earth (Eph. 1:19-23). Likewise, Philippians emphasizes that every knee will bow and submit to Christ. Scripture does *not* teach that Christ will submit to those under His authority. Biblical *submission is to those God puts in authority *over* us. So Paul writes, *"²²Wives submit to your husband as to the Lord. ²³For the husband is the head of the wife as Christ is the head of the church..."* (Eph. 5:22-23). God's apostle understands submission to authority—in the home, at work, and at war. He gives four examples of submission, such as wives submitting to husbands, children submitting to parents, slaves submitting to masters, and the church submitting to Christ. The Bible teaches *mutual consideration*, but *not mutual submission*. Biblical submission is always to the authority that God places *above* us—whether in society, the home, or in heaven. All believers are equal in God's eyes. But there must be submission for there to be order in society.

**Q 1 ↗** *How many examples of Ephesians 5:21 does Paul give? Identify them.*

**Q 2 ↘** *Is submission to those over us or those under us? Explain.*

Submission is for all. Everyone on earth should practice submission. But we do not all submit to the same authorities. Wives submit to husbands. Husbands submit to Christ. Children submit to parents. Slaves submit to masters. Masters submit to Christ. All believers submit to Christ, and to government.

**Q 3 ↘** *Is submission only for wives, children, and slaves? Explain.*

The Bible does not teach mutual submission, such as children submitting to parents, and parents submitting to their children. This would create chaos. On the other hand, the Bible does teach *mutual consideration*. This means being sensitive to the needs of others. A big principle we will study in Philippians 2:4 is, *"Each of you should look not only to your own interests, but to the interests of others."* Likewise, Scripture teaches *mutual love*. Paul does *not* teach that a husband should *submit* to his wife, but he does teach that a husband should *love* his wife *as* he loves himself (Eph. 5:28). Likewise, in society, we believers are to love our neighbors as we love ourselves. This is *mutual love*, but *not mutual submission*. We submit to kings, but they do not submit to us. We submit to God, but He does not submit to us. Yet He loves us, and we love Him.

**Q 4 ↘** *What is the difference between mutual submission and mutual love? Which is biblical?*

> THE BIBLE TEACHES *MUTUAL CONSIDERATION.*

Ephesians and Colossians overlap on Paul's teachings. What Paul explains in Ephesians about relationships, he only summarizes in Colossians. Perhaps this is because churches shared Paul's letters, so he did not need to repeat every teaching. Therefore we will combine verses from Ephesians and Colossians, studying them together. Figure 3.2 Shows parallel passages on relationships in Ephesians and Colossians. Take a moment to compare passages in both columns, and then we will study Paul's teachings to God's family members.

**Q 5 ↗** *Why do we combine Paul's teachings on relationships, studying them together?*

**Q 6** ⟋ *Which letter has more details on relationships, Ephesians or Colossians?*

| | What Paul Explains on Relationships in Ephesians, He Only Summarizes in Colossians | | |
|---|---|---|---|
| | **Ephesians** | **Colossians** | |
| 5:22-24 5:33b | **Wives**, submit to your husbands as to the Lord. ²³For the husband is the head of the wife as Christ is the head of the church, his body, of which he is the Savior. ²⁴Now as the church submits to Christ, so also wives should submit to their husbands in everything…the wife must respect her husband. | **Wives**, submit to your husbands, as is fitting in the Lord. | 3:18 |
| 5:25-33 | **Husbands**, love your wives, just as Christ loved the church and gave himself up for her ²⁶to make her holy, cleansing her by the washing with water through the word, ²⁷and to present her to himself as a radiant church, without stain or wrinkle or any other blemish, but holy and blameless. ²⁸In this same way, husbands ought to love their wives as their own bodies. He who loves his wife loves himself. ²⁹After all, no one ever hated his own body, but he feeds and cares for it, just as Christ does the church— ³⁰for we are members of his body. ³¹"For this reason a man will leave his father and mother and be united to his wife, and the two will become one flesh." ³²This is a profound mystery—but I am talking about Christ and the church. ³³However, each one of you also must love his wife as he loves himself, and the wife must respect her husband. | **Husbands**, love your wives and do not be harsh with them. | 3:19 |
| 6:1-3 | **Children**, obey your parents in the Lord, for this is right. ²"Honor your father and mother"—which is the first commandment with a promise— ³"that it may go well with you and that you may enjoy long life on the earth." | **Children**, obey your parents in everything, for this pleases the Lord. | 3:20 |
| 6:4 | **Fathers**, do not exasperate your children; instead, bring them up in the training and instruction of the Lord. | **Fathers**, do not embitter your children, or they will become discouraged. | 3:21 |
| 6:5-8 | **Slaves**, obey your earthly masters with respect and fear, and with sincerity of heart, just as you would obey Christ. ⁶Obey them not only to win their favor when their eye is on you, but like slaves of Christ, doing the will of God from your heart. ⁷Serve wholeheartedly, as if you were serving the Lord, not men, ⁸because you know that the Lord will reward everyone for whatever good he does, whether he is slave or free. | **Slaves**, obey your earthly masters in everything; and do it, not only when their eye is on you and to win their favor, but with sincerity of heart and reverence for the Lord. ²³Whatever you do, work at it with all your heart, as working for the Lord, not for men, ²⁴since you know that you will receive an inheritance from the Lord as a reward. It is the Lord Christ you are serving. ²⁵Anyone who does wrong will be repaid for his wrong, and there is no favoritism. | 3:22-25 |
| 6:9 | And **masters**, treat your slaves in the same way. Do not threaten them, since you know that he who is both their Master and yours is in heaven, and there is no favoritism with him. | ²⁵Anyone who does wrong will be repaid for his wrong, and there is no favoritism. | |

**Figure 3.2**   In this course on the four Prison Epistles, sections in Ephesians 4–6 overlap Colossians 3–4. Rather than cover the same topics twice, we include the short sections of Colossians 3–4 in the lessons on Ephesians 4–6. For example, what Paul says to wives, we cover in Ephesians 5:22-24, including the one verse from Colossians 3:18. And what Paul says to husbands, we cover in the nine verses of Ephesians 5:25-33, including the one verse from Colossians 3:19.

## A. A loving wife submits to her husband (Eph. 5:22-24).

**Q 7** ⟋ *How do we know that a person who submits is not inferior?*

**Some err by thinking that** submission means being inferior—less than another. But the Bible uses the word *submit* in relation to order and purpose, not value. To *submit* means "to be under." Jesus submitted to the Father, but He is not inferior to the Father. As Philippians 2 says, Jesus is equal to the Father, though He submitted to Him (Phil. 2:6). In theology, we learn that the Father and Son are equal in every way. They have the same nature and power. For example, in the book of Revelation, we see that *all* worship the Father and the Lamb. Still, the Son submits to the Father for order and purpose.

Submission is necessary throughout society. Without submission, there can be no government, no schools, no armies, no businesses, and no families. Those who submit have a different role than those above them, but they are not inferior. Submission is an attitude of respect to one who leads.

**Scripture gives at least two examples of how a woman should submit to her husband.** *First,* a wife should submit to her husband as the Church submits to Christ. Because of how Jesus loves us, we as believers submit to Christ. We seek to honor, respect, please, obey, and follow Him as our leader. Likewise, a wife should submit to her husband.

> [22] *Wives, submit to your husbands as to the Lord.* [23] *For the husband is the head of the wife as Christ is the head of the church, his body, of which he is the Savior.* [24] *Now **as the church submits to Christ**, so also wives should submit to their husbands in everything* (Eph. 5:22-24).

Author and speaker Joyce Meyer wrote, "A woman's response to proper loving care and nurturing should be, then, to submit and adapt to her husband as the Church would do to the Lord."[1] Meyer emphasizes that a woman is to respect and reverence her husband. This does not mean that she never has an opinion or is afraid to say what she thinks. "Marriage is a partnership, but…someone has to make a final decision when two people don't agree. …The man is to love his wife as Christ loved the Church, and the woman is to submit to her husband and respect him. If both parties do their part, a glorious relationship will result."[2]

*Second,* a loving wife respects, honors, and admires her husband. **An important part of submission is showing respect. Just as a wife needs love, a husband needs respect. Think of how a wife would feel if her husband stopped loving her. That is how he feels when he thinks she does not respect him. Being respectful means several things:**

- A wife shows respect by not strongly disagreeing with her husband in front of the children or others.
- She shows respect by not discussing her husband's faults in public.
- She shows respect by doing things that please her husband.
- She shows respect by supporting her husband's choices and decisions.

When a wife respects her husband, it makes him stand tall like a man. It encourages him to be the husband and father God wants him to be. Respect inspires a man to be and do his best.

## B. A husband's relationship to his wife

How would you summarize the theme of Ephesians 5:25-33 in one word? Some seem to think these verses focus on control, headship, or authority. But the main topic of Ephesians 5:25-33 is *love* between a husband and wife.

God wants the wife to submit to her husband, as the Church submits to Christ. But why does the Church submit to Christ? Is it because He threatens us? Christ never whips or bullies His bride. We love Him because He first loved us. We love Him because He is kind, gracious, and gentle. Christ's love for the Church is the model for husbands. It is easy for a woman to submit to a husband who treats her as Jesus treats us.[3]

> [25] *Husbands, **love** your wives, just as Christ **loved** the church and gave himself up for her* [26] *to make her holy, cleansing her by the washing with water through the word,* [27] *and to present her to himself as a radiant church, without stain or wrinkle or any other blemish, but holy and blameless.* [28] *In this same way, husbands ought to **love** their wives as their own bodies. He who **loves** his wife **loves** himself.* [29] *After all, no one ever hated his own body, but he feeds and cares for it, just as Christ does the church—* [30] *for we are members of his body.* [31] *"For this reason a man will leave his father and mother and be united to his wife, and the two will*

**Q 8** What is the first way a wife should submit to her husband?

**Q 9** Does submission mean that a wise husband can ignore his wife's opinions? Explain.

**Q 10** What are ways that a wife can honor and respect her husband?

**Q 11** How does a wife's respect bring out the best in him?

**Q 12** What is the theme of Ephesians 5:25-33?

**Q 13** What causes the Church to submit to Christ? Apply this to the home.

*become one flesh."* ³²*This is a profound mystery—but I am talking about Christ and the church.* ³³*However, each one of you also must **love** his wife as he loves himself, and the wife must respect her husband* (Eph. 5:25-33).

In this lesson we will examine five ways in which a husband should love his wife as Christ loved the Church.

## C. Five ways a husband should love his wife

**1. A husband's love should sacrifice for his wife (Eph. 5:25).** Jesus *"gave himself up for"* the Church (Eph. 5:25). He loved so much that He died for His bride. *"*¹³*Greater love has no one than this, that he lay down his life for his friends"* (John 15:13). Jesus gave the greatest sacrifice—His life.

> FIVE WAYS A HUSBAND SHOULD LOVE HIS WIFE

Q 14 ➤ How does a husband follow the example of Christ's sacrifice?

*"*²⁵*Husbands, love your wives, just as Christ loved the church and gave himself up for her"* (Eph. 5:25). Husband, give yourself up to save your wife. Be willing to die to protect her. As Chrysostom said, be willing to be cut into pieces for her.⁴ Marriage is a privilege and a sacrifice.

Q 15 ✎ Husband, what are some sacrifices you make for your wife?

Some sacrifices are made through death. But the Bible also speaks of being a living sacrifice (Rom. 12:1). Few husbands are asked to die for their wives—but all are asked to live for them. Love that sacrifices requires dying to self. It means putting the needs of your wife above your own needs. Some husbands treat their wives like servants. But the Bible says a husband should love his wife as Christ loved the Church. This means that a husband should sacrifice some things to serve his wife. Husband, if you have desires for another woman, sacrifice them for your wife and marriage. Sacrifice some of your time to meet her needs. Sacrifice some of your will and seek what pleases her best.

Q 16 ➤ How can a husband make his wife better spiritually?

**2. A husband's love should make his wife better (Eph. 5:26-27).** A husband's love should make his wife better spiritually. Jesus' love for His bride led Him *"to make her holy, cleansing her..."* The love of Jesus made His bride purer. Wives need to see a pure husband—not one who is a slave to pornography, immorality, dishonesty, or other forms of sin (Eph. 5:26-27).

A husband should set a holy standard for the language in the home. No unholy words or coarse joking should ever come out of his mouth (Eph. 4:29). Rather, a husband should lead the wife in talking and thinking about godly things.

A love that drags a person down is false, worldly, and ungodly. Is your wife more beautiful in spirit because she has lived with you? A husband's love and devotion toward his wife should encourage her to grow in her spiritual life.

If a husband has a wife who is not a Christian, he is to live the Christian life in front of her. He should pray for her and do all he can to show the love of God to her. At times, some Christians feel that they can divorce a spouse because he or she is not a Christian. The Bible forbids this and tells us, *"*¹²*...If any brother has a wife who is not a believer and she is willing to live with him, he must not divorce her"* (1 Cor. 7:12).

Q 17 ✎ Husband, what can you do to help your wife improve mentally?

A husband's love should make his wife better mentally. How a husband does this will vary from country to country. In some countries, such as Bangladesh and Pakistan, up to 85 percent of the women cannot read. In Africa, about 50 percent of the women do not read. In such countries, a husband's love should lead him to help his wife learn to read. In countries where there is a higher standard of education, a husband's love might lead him to help his wife get a diploma, college degree, master's degree, or doctorate. Or it might at least guide him to buy various books for her to read or encourage her to buy books she chooses to read. In other situations, a husband might help his wife study and learn a skill, such as sewing, being a secretary, or nursing. A husband's love should make his wife better.

**3. A husband's love should care for and nourish his wife (Eph. 5:28-29).** A husband is the shepherd of his home. It is his job to care for the needs of each sheep in his little flock. Husband, where does your wife fit into your daily priorities? After your relationship with God, she is next. You are to care for your wife more than your job or ministry (Eph. 5:29). You are to love your wife as yourself.

Someone said, "If you treat your family like customers and your customers like family, things tend to work out pretty well." As a business leader, do you treat your customers better than you treat your family members? On the job, men find solutions, answers, and the right products for their customers. How much more should we assist our family members with their needs?

A man's role is not to rule over his wife. The Bible says that a husband should love his wife as Christ loves the Church. This means that as husbands, we must care for our wives as Jesus cares for the needs of the Church.

A missionary stood before a group of mature pastors and asked them, "How many of you obey Ephesians 5:28 and 33? That is, how many of you love your wife as you love yourself?" Most of the 50 pastors in the room were cautious. Only three raised their hands—and these three were younger pastors. The missionary continued, "I am a visitor in your country, and I do not know your ways well. So I want you to question these three men. They will come to the front and you will ask them questions. Afterward, you will be the jury to decide whether they love their wives as they love themselves."

So the three young pastors came forward and the elders began to ask questions. "After your wife raises the chicken, catches it, cleans it, and cooks it, who eats the first piece?" One of the three pastors immediately sat down without saying a word. Next, an elderly pastor asked, "Whose name is on the deed to your farm?" (This is important to a wife. If only her husband's name is on the deed to the family property, she will lose the property at his death.) Upon hearing this second question, a second pastor took a seat. Only one pastor was left for the third question: "Do you have a certificate of marriage that the government recognizes?" (This can be important at a husband's death.) It would have been interesting to hear more questions, but no more came, because the third young pastor sat down. May the Lord help each of us husbands to love our wives as we love ourselves. A husband and wife are one flesh in the Lord. May each husband discern that what he does to his wife he does to himself and to Christ within her (Eph. 5:28).

**4. A husband's love should unite him to his wife (Eph. 5:30-31).** Jesus is one with His Church. We are members of His body (Eph. 5:30). Nothing can separate us from the love of Christ (Rom. 8:35-39). Likewise, a husband and wife are one flesh (Eph. 5:31).

In cleaving to his wife, a husband does not reject his mother and father. He leaves the life of depending on his parents. He begins a new family with his wife. Indeed, he continues to love his parents, but his love is the mature love of an adult. His parents can count on him in hard times. They can depend on him as he depended on them as a child. But he does not allow any conflict with parents to harm his relationship with his wife. He cleaves to her, not allowing anything to separate them.

It is strange to see that some couples live together, sleep together, and raise children together, yet are emotional strangers to each other. Those involved in the seminars of *Marriage Encounter call such people "married singles." They are legally married, yet without the bond of deep love. In contrast, a husband's love should cause him to be close to his wife. He should seek to understand her feelings and emotions. Jesus cares about His bride. He knows the number of hairs on each head. He cares about the little things of life. Likewise, a husband should become very close to his wife.

How well do you know your wife? Do you know her favorite food? Would *she* rate your marriage as an A, B, C, D, or F? What part of her day does she like the most and the

**Q 18** ↖ *Husband, where does your wife think she is in your priorities? Ask her.*

**Q 19** ↖ *What are some needs that each wife has?*

**Q 20** ↖ *Husband, do you love your wife as you love yourself? Discuss this.*

**Q 21** ↖ *After marriage, how does a husband's love for his parents change?*

**Q 22** ↖ *Explain: "Sometimes a husband and wife live together, but are like strangers."*

**Q 23** ↖ *What are some things a husband should know about his wife?*

least? Is she your best friend? What does she like most about you? In which area would she like you to improve a little?

### 5. A husband's love should be faithful to his wife until death (Eph. 5:25-33).

Jesus was and is faithful to His bride, the Church. He came to die for us, and He was faithful. With His last words, He said, *"It is finished"* (John 19:30). He was faithful unto death.

**Q 24** ⤸ *What are some ways in which a husband must be faithful to his wife?*

Likewise, a husband's love causes him to be faithful to his wife. A loving husband guards his emotions. He refuses to love other women. In business or friendship, he is faithful to his wife with his words, actions, and private thoughts. The Bible says that each husband should love only one woman. [2] *"Each man should have his own wife, and each woman her own husband. [3] The husband should fulfill his marital duty to his wife, and likewise the wife to her husband"* (1 Cor. 7:2-3).

**Q 25** ⤢ *What is God's attitude toward an unfaithful husband?*

The prophet Malachi rebuked some husbands. He explained why God was angry with them.

[13] *Another thing you do: You flood the LORD's altar with tears. You weep and wail because he no longer pays attention to your offerings or accepts them with pleasure from your hands. [14] You ask, "Why?" It is because the LORD is acting as the witness between you and the wife of your youth, because you have broken faith with her, though she is your partner, the wife of your marriage covenant. [15] Has not the LORD made them one? In flesh and spirit they are his. And why one? Because he was seeking godly offspring. So guard yourself in your spirit, and do not break faith with the wife of your youth* (Mal. 2:13-15).

**Q 26** ⤸ *How should a husband respond to temptations about other women?*

A husband is to be totally committed to his wife—physically and emotionally. Even in his private thoughts, the Bible forbids a man to lust after a woman (Matt. 5:28). Paul teaches us to conquer every stray thought—to present it as a captive at the feet of Jesus (2 Cor. 10:5). Turn away from evil thoughts and sights. Resist the devil, and he will flee from you (James 4:7). It is not a sin to be tempted. But pray so that you will not enter into temptation (Matt. 26:41). The flesh is weak, but the Spirit is willing. Walk in the Spirit and you will not fulfill the lusts of the flesh (Gal. 5:16; Rom. 8:8-9). Do not turn an evil thought over and over in your mind, like a person tastes candy in his mouth. Reject evil thoughts. Love what is right and hate what is wrong (Rom. 12:9; Heb. 1:9). Husband or single man, do not gaze at prostitutes, pictures of beautiful women, or another man's wife. Be true to God and your wife with your thoughts. Then, God will honor you and bless your marriage. Say with Job, *"I made a covenant with my eyes not to look lustfully at a girl"* (Job 31:1).

**Q 27** ⤸ *Explain the proverb: "Drink all the water you want from your own well."*

Scripture condemns using pornography or becoming involved with another woman. God's plan is for a man to fulfill all of his sexual desires with his own wife.

[15] *Drink water from your own cistern, running water from your own well. [16] Should your springs overflow in the streets, your streams of water in the public squares? [17] Let them be yours alone, never to be shared with strangers. [18] May your fountain be blessed, and may you rejoice in the wife of your youth. [19] A loving doe, a graceful deer—may her breasts satisfy you always, may you ever be captivated by her love. [20] Why be captivated, my son, by an adulteress? Why embrace the bosom of another man's wife? [21] For a man's ways are in full view of the LORD, and he examines all his paths. [22] The evil deeds of a wicked man ensnare him; the cords of his sin hold him fast. [23] He will die for lack of discipline, led astray by his own great folly* (Prov. 5:15-23).

**Q 28** ⤢ *In which 2 cases does the Bible allow divorce?*

Divorce is like a disease that is spreading in much of the world. Most people who divorce do not follow the biblical reasons for divorce. Some say, "We do not love each other any more," or "We have grown apart." There are only two reasons why a couple could consider divorce. One is if a spouse commits adultery (Matt. 19:9). The other is if an unbelieving spouse deserts a believing spouse (1 Cor. 7:15-16). Scripture clearly instructs husbands: [11] *"A husband must not divorce his wife.... [27] Are you married? Do not seek a divorce"* (1 Cor. 7:11, 27).

Bonita was amazing! As a new Christian, she wanted her husband, a successful businessman in our community, to come to Christ. My wife and I encouraged her to let Jesus make her character beautiful. We urged her to submit in love to her husband, pray for him daily, and prepare herself for the opportunity God would give her. One evening in bed, Jerry spoke to her out of the darkness, "Honey, I want you to know that of all the people who call themselves a Christian, you are the best example I know!" She told him that it was all about Jesus in her life. A few days later Jerry prayed to receive Christ for himself. Many wives have lead their husbands to Jesus through godly submission.

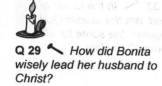

**Q 29** How did Bonita wisely lead her husband to Christ?

---

**Lesson 15**

## Live Worthy at Home and At Work: Children and Parents; Workers and Employers (Eph. 6:1-9; Col. 3:20–4:1)

**Goal A:** *Identify the groups in God's family that a pastor must shepherd.*
**Goal B:** *Analyze the problem, solution, and promise for children in God's family.*
**Goal C:** *State and illustrate 4 guidelines for parents to train children in God's family.*
**Goal D:** *State and illustrate 2 guidelines for employers and employees in God's family.*

| Symmetry of Ephesians ||
| Ephesians 1–3 | Ephesians 4–6 |
| --- | --- |
| Spiritual wealth in Christ | Spiritual walk in the Spirit |
| Heavenly position and privileges in Christ | Earthly life and duties in Christ |
| Behavior without Christ | Behavior with Christ |
| Work of Christ *for* us | Work of Christ *in* us |

**Figure 3.3   Symmetry in the two halves of Ephesians**

**Overview.** In Ephesians 1–3, Paul has written that we were dead in sins, and that our behavior was guided by the flesh, the world, and the spirit who is at work in the disobedient. But God, who is rich in mercy, redeemed us by the blood of His Son. In Christ, we have become members of God's family. Gentiles and Jews are equal heirs of God's kingdom. God has joined us together as one body, one temple, and one household. Together with all the saints, God has raised us up and given us a position in the heavenly realms, blessing us with every spiritual blessing in Christ. So in Ephesians 4–6, Paul emphasizes that our response to God must be to walk and live worthy of our calling. In Ephesians 4–5, Paul has written about the behavior of all believers. He has commanded that we walk in love, patience, humility, and kindness with each other—preserving the unity of the Spirit, who binds us together in peace. Paul has told us to *get rid of* six types of sins—lying, anger, stealing; immorality, unhealthy speech, and drunkenness. In contrast, the apostle urges us to put on six new ways of living. Living filled with the Spirit is the great key to replacing sinful ways with righteous ways. Living filled with the Spirit makes it possible to obey the 36 commands Paul gives in Ephesians 4–6.

**Q 30** How does Ephesians 4–6 relate to Ephesians 1–3?

**Groups.** Beginning with Ephesians 5:21, Paul writes to **specific groups in the church**. In letters to Timothy and Titus, Paul writes to groups such as: men, women, overseers and deacons, elders, and widows. The groups Paul writes to in Ephesians and Colossians are: **wives, husbands, children, fathers, slaves, and masters** (Eph. 5:21–6:9; Col. 3:18-25). Every church leader must recognize and care for *all the groups* of people in God's church.

**Q 31** To which 6 groups does Paul write in Ephesians and Colossians?

**Q 32** ⟋ *Which groups in the church must practice obedience and submission?*

**Q 33** ⟍ *In the family of God, are the morals God requires the same for all groups? Explain.*

*There is beautiful fairness of moral duty in God's household.* Obedience and submission are for everyone. Lowliness of position does not exclude a child from being obedient. The child is no less obedient than the parent. Neither does authority exclude adults from moral duty. The master is not less obedient than the slave. Rather, grace teaches all of us in God's household to do unto others as we would have them do unto us.[5] God's morals are the same for all family members, but they have different applications. The obedience of a child looks different than the obedience of a parent. But God requires obedience from both. Let us look at God's principles for living worthy of Christ in the home.

### A. As children obey and honor their parents, they position themselves to receive God's blessings (Eph. 6:1-3).

[1] ***Children, obey** your parents in the Lord, for this is right.* [2] *"**Honor** your father and mother"—which is the first commandment with a promise—* [3] *"that it may go well with you and that you may enjoy long life on the earth"* (Eph. 6:1-3).

**Q 34** ⟋ *What are 2 ways children submit to their parents?*

**Q 35** ⟋ *In Paul's day, how did adults treat children?*

**The Problem.** In Paul's day, children had a low status—duty without rights. The Greeks and Romans did not recognize a child as a person until the father chose to do so. Often, adults did not want children. So they mistreated, abused, raped, abandoned, or sold children as slaves to pay debts. Some parents abandoned a baby, or killed it, if it had any defects. The society of Paul's day was much like ours. There was little concern for children.

**Q 36** ⟍ *Where you live, do children obey and honor their parents? Explain.*

Today, many societies have created a culture of disaster in the home. Sexual and physical abuse of children are common. In some homes, and in public, some children are out of control—refusing to obey their parents. Unruly children break the rules, disobey their teachers, and dishonor their elders. Meanwhile, we see adults who do not know how to raise children. Today, there is a great need for biblical wisdom on family relationships.

*Children learn what they watch.*

*If children live with criticism, they learn to condemn and judge.*
*If children live with hostility, they learn to be angry and fight.*
*If children live with ridicule, they learn to be shy and withdrawn.*
*If children live with shame, they learn to feel guilty.*
*If children live with tolerance, they learn to be patient.*
*If children live with encouragement, they learn confidence.*
*If children live with praise, they learn to appreciate.*
*If children live with fairness, they learn justice.*
*If children live with security, they learn to have faith.*
*If children live with approval, they learn to like themselves.*
*If children live with acceptance and friendship, they learn to find life in the world.*[6]

**Figure 3.4    Children learn what they watch.**

**Q 37** ⟋ *Who must teach children to obey? Explain.*

**The Solution.** The Bible teaches that children are to obey and honor their parents. But obedience is not automatic for children. Children must learn to obey. And it is the duty of parents to teach their children to obey. God expects parents to teach children what is right and what is wrong. Parents must teach children good manners—how to be polite and considerate of others. Children must learn godly values, attitudes, and behavior. They learn the most from watching the examples of their parents. And they learn from watching other children in the home.

**Q 38** ⟍ *How could the dad have taught his child to obey?*

A pastor visited a family in the home. He was surprised to see the unruly behavior of a boy who was only 3 years old. The child came into the room and began throwing toys. When the father told the child to stop, the child threw a toy toward the dad. The embarrassed father said to the pastor, "This child behaves badly. I am not able to make him behave." The pastor was shocked. Here was a tall, strong dad who was allowing a small child to rule the home. The biggest problem in the home was not the child, but the dad who refused to teach the child to obey. *"The rod of correction imparts wisdom, but a child left to himself disgraces his mother* [and father]*"* (Prov. 29:15). So let us discipline our children when necessary. But as Luther said, let us keep an apple beside the rod, to reward the child when he does well. [7]

Children *learn to obey* as parents are consistent with rewards and discipline. When a child does what is right, a wise parent smiles and encourages the child for good behavior. And when a child does what is wrong, a wise parent discourages this unruly behavior, through a frown, a word of correction, and even a form of discipline, if necessary. (For a full treatment of how parents teach children to obey and mature, see the *Faith & Action* course: *Marriage & Family,* Chapters 9 and 10, on *How to Be An Effective Father or Mother.*)

**Q 39** *What do children learn if parents are not consistent?*

**Q 40** *How does Paul lift the status of children?*

Paul lifts the status of children. He recognizes that children have a place in the body of Christ—*in the Lord.* Imagine a house church where an elder read Paul's letter aloud to believers. The children listened as Paul read what Paul wrote for wives and husbands to do. Then the kids heard: *"Children obey your parents in the Lord, for this is right"* (Eph. 6:1). These words lifted the heads of the children. God's apostle put something in the letter for them! Children share the family's faith in God. Christianity is not just for adults. Children can know Jesus and follow His teachings. They participate in the faith as they learn the Bible in the home, and practice obeying and honoring their parents. Christianity is for the whole family. There are duties for the parents, and the children. When parents tell their child to do something, the child has a responsibility to obey, unless it is something unbiblical, immoral, or unethical. A child who learns to obey parents will learn to obey God and the rules of society. But a child who learns to disobey parents will disobey the rules of society and the rules of God.

Disobedience to parents is a symptom of a society that is decaying. Paul lists disobeying parents as a terrible result of rejecting God and a sign of God's judgment. Paul writes:

**Figure 3.5    Jesus rejoiced because the children worshiped Him (Matt. 21:1-16).**

[28]*Furthermore, since they did not think it worthwhile to retain the knowledge of God,* ***he gave them over to a depraved mind, to do what ought not to be done.*** [29]*They have become filled with every kind of wickedness, evil, greed and depravity. They are full of envy, murder, strife, deceit and malice. They are gossips,* [30]*slanderers, God-haters, insolent, arrogant and boastful; they invent ways of doing evil;* ***they disobey their parents*** (Rom. 1:28-30).

**Q 41** *What does disobedience to parents show about society? Explain.*

Disobedience to parents is a terrible sin. It is a form of rebellion and lawlessness. Paul says that disobeying parents is one of the sins we will see in the last days. The apostle warns:

**Q 42** *Is disobedience to parents a sin? Explain.*

[1]*But mark this: There will be terrible times in the last days.* [2]*People will be lovers of themselves, lovers of money, boastful, proud, abusive,* ***disobedient to their parents***, *ungrateful, unholy,* [3]*without love, unforgiving, slanderous, without self-control, brutal, not lovers of the good,* [4]*treacherous, rash, conceited, lovers of pleasure rather than lovers of God—* [5]*having a form of godliness but denying its power. Have nothing to do with them* (2 Tim. 3:1-5).

**Q 43** ➤ *What promise does God give children who obey parents?*

Small children who practice disobeying their parents grow up to be youth and adults who reject the wisdom and godly values of their parents. Disobedience to parents is a common characteristic of the last days we are living in.

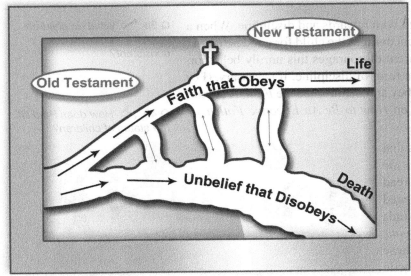

**Figure 3.6    Two roads run through both the old covenant and the new covenant. God will bless those whose faith expresses itself in obedience to Him, and He will curse those whose unbelief expresses itself in disobedience to Him (Deut. 28–30; Matt. 7:13-14, 21-27).**

**The Promise.**  As we teach children to obey, we guide them on the path of God's plan for success. Paul appeals to the fifth commandment (Exod. 20:12). He says it is the first commandment *with promise.* In other words, God attaches a promise to honoring father and mother. The promise is for a long, full life of blessing.

The wisdom of Proverbs teaches:

²⁰*My son, keep your father's commands and do not forsake your mother's teaching.* ²¹*Bind them upon your heart forever; fasten them around your neck.* ²²*When you walk, they will guide you; when you sleep, they will watch over you; when you awake, they will speak to you.* ²³*For these commands are a lamp, this teaching is a light, and the corrections of discipline are the way to life* (Prov. 6:20-23).

**Q 44** ➤ *How does allowing children to ask questions and discuss matters (with respect) strengthen them?*

Carissa was a toddler with a cheerful personality. She was joyful, filled with curiosity, and a little mischief. She liked to push the limits, to see how far her parents would let her go. But early in life—in family devotions, in Sunday school, and in church—she heard the gospel and opened her life to Jesus. Carissa was never one to accept what someone said just because they said it. But her mom and dad taught her to submit—to obey even when she did not fully understand or agree. She learned to obey them, and she learned to respect and obey other authorities as well. She was strong, and she could disagree with things that were wrong—but she knew when to submit. Over the years Carissa became a valuable, mature, responsible Christian leader.

### B. It is a duty of parents to lovingly train their children in God's ways (Eph. 6:4).

*Fathers, do not exasperate your children; instead, bring them up in the training and instruction of the Lord* (Eph. 6:4).

Paul did not need to emphasize the father's authority in the ancient world. A dad's power was absolute. But Paul cautions fathers to blend love with authority, and not rule their children with a hand that is too heavy. In Colossians Paul wrote: *"Fathers, do not embitter your children, or they will become discouraged"* (Col. 3:21). Consider four factors a parent must balance to raise a child well.

**Q 45** ➤ *Who is responsible for teaching God's ways to a child?*

**1. A parent must not neglect the duty of training and teaching a child God's ways.** God has given parents this responsibility. The church and the community may help train a child. But God gives to parents the primary duty of raising children. At the end of our days, every parent with children will give an account to God for their stewardship over those children. Moses gave God's law to parents:

⁶*These commandments that I give you today are to be upon your hearts.* ⁷*Impress them on your children. Talk about them when you sit at home and when you walk along the road, when you lie down and when you get up.* ⁸*Tie them as symbols on your hands and bind them on your foreheads.* ⁹*Write them on the doorframes of your houses and on your gates* (Deut. 6:6-9).

When Paul commands fathers to bring up children in the training and instruction of the Lord, he is echoing the words of God through Moses in Deuteronomy 6. The duty of raising a child in God's ways rests on the shoulders of parents. And our examples teach more than our words.

**2. Parents must remember that biblical principles remain the same, but customs change with each generation.** Most of the favorite church songs of the parents will not be the favorite songs of godly children. Moderation in dress will not look the same as moderation for their children. Clothing styles and hair styles change with each generation. Blessed are the parents who continue to emphasize biblical principles such as moderation, while realizing that moderation looks different through the eyes of each generation.

Q 46 ↖ *What does this mean: Biblical principles stay the same, but customs change? Illustrate.*

**3. Parents who exercise too much control insult their children and embitter them against the things of God.** As children grow and mature, wise parents loosen the reins. Some parents err by showing a lack of trust in their kids. It is true that children must earn trust and show themselves worthy of responsibility, little by little. But parents must let a child grow up. As children grow in the things of God, our confidence in them inspires them to grow even more.

Q 47 ↖ *What happens if parents use too much control on their children?*

One father was too strict with his daughter. He would not allow her to attend school functions for youth. She remained quiet and obedient up to the year she left home to attend university. After that, she never attended church again. At times, too much trust is a lesser error than too much control.[8]

**4. A Major role of parents is to encourage their children.** As we noted above, discipline is essential for all children. But encouragement is just as important. Encouragement brings out the best in all of us. Children learn how much God loves us as they see their parents cheering for them. One dad was known for criticizing. He told his son, "The things you do well, there is no need for me to mention. So I focus on emphasizing the things you need to improve." This father looked through sour eyes. Rather, let us be like the dad who gave 10 words of praise and encouragement for every one word of correction.

Q 48 ↖ *How can parents use encouragement to guide their children? Illustrate.*

Benjamin West told how he became a famous painter. One day when he was a boy, his mother left him to watch over his little sister, Sally. While mom was a way, the boy discovered some bottles of colored ink. So he decided to paint a picture of his sister. In the process, he spilled the colors of ink and made a big mess. But when mom returned, she did not scold him for the mess. Instead, she saw the picture and said, "Oh, you have painted a beautiful picture of Sally." Then she leaned down and kissed him. Years later the famous painter explained, "My mother's kiss made me a painter."[9] Many of us can testify that we have remembered all of our lives the encouraging words our parents spoke to us. As Paul put it, children must obey and honor their parents; and parents must encourage their children.

Q 49 ↗ *How did Benjamin's mother use encouragement to inspire him?*

Q 50 ↖ *Have you had a parent or family member who encouraged you?*

In a store a mother with two small children seemed to hate her children. She was frustrated and acted like both children were a bother to her. To please her, they would have had to stand still, say nothing, and show no interest in anything. Her words to them were cutting, her voice was harsh, and her language was vulgar. What a mom! I wonder if her children will grow up to love her and God?

Q 51 ↖ *If children learn to please parents, what will these children think about God?*

**C. Paul includes the groups of workers and employers in the family of God (Eph. 6:5-9; Col. 3:22-25; 4:1).**

Slaves and masters is Paul's final example of relationships between believers who are filled with the Spirit. We have studied the relationship between wives and husbands (Eph. 5:22-33), and the relationship between children and parents (Eph. 6:1-4). Submission to authority is a biblical principle for all believers (Eph. 5:18–6:9).

Q 52 ↖ *Is submission to authority a biblical principle for all believers? Explain.*

A Christian relationship in the home or at work reflects a biblical understanding of submission to authority.

Q 53 ↗ How many slaves were in the Roman kingdom of Paul's day?

Q 54 ↖ In Paul's day, how did people treat slaves?

Slaves were a central part of Roman culture. The Roman economy depended on slaves—which were about half of the Roman population. Some estimate that there were 60 million slaves in the Roman empire of Paul's day.[10] People became slaves in various ways: through birth, as punishment, by being captured in another land by a slave trader, by one's country being conquered, or by being sold by parents to pay for debt. The treatment of slaves varied. Some were treated cruelly. Others were treated with esteem and dignity. Many held positions of responsibility in the home and society. Many slaves and owners had become Christians in the first century and attended church together. In Christ, slaves and masters had equal value. Paul wrote: *"There is neither Jew nor Greek, slave nor free, male nor female, for you are all one in Christ Jesus"* (Gal. 3:28). And as we will study in the final lessons of this course, Paul urged Philemon, a master, to treat Onesimus, *"no longer as a slave, but better than a slave, as a dear brother"* (Philem. 16). But what were the duties of Christian slaves and Christian masters in a work relationship? Paul gives two principles about work relationships. These principles worked for slaves and masters, and they continue to work for employees and employers.

**Figure 3.7    Slaves were a central part of Roman culture.**

> *⁵Slaves, obey your earthly masters with respect and fear, and with sincerity of heart, just as you would obey Christ. ⁶Obey them not only to win their favor when their eye is on you, but like slaves of Christ, doing the will of God from your heart. ⁷Serve wholeheartedly, as if you were serving the Lord, not men, ⁸because you know that the Lord will reward everyone for whatever good he does, whether he is slave or free. ⁹And masters, treat your slaves in the same way. Do not threaten them, since you know that he who is both their Master and yours is in heaven, and there is no favoritism with him* (Eph. 6:5-9).

Q 55 ↗ Is God's plan for obedience and submission fair at all levels? Explain.

**1. Workers, obey those who are over you, paying the respect you owe in society.** Does this sound like what Paul has already said to other members of the family? Does it remind you of Paul's words, *"Wives submit to your husbands?"* Do Paul's words to workers remind you of: *"Children obey your parents in the Lord"*? As we said at the beginning of this lesson, the Bible requires submission and obedience to authority at every level in society. Paul insists that everyone must obey and submit to someone. Slaves obey masters. Children obey parents. Wives submit to husbands. Husbands obey and submit to Christ, and masters must submit to God—the Heavenly Master of all masters (Col. 4:1). No humans are exempt from some form of obedience and submission. God's moral duties are for all—great and small.

Q 56 ↖ What examples show that submission is for every level of society?

We see forms of obedience and respect at every level of our world. Among chickens there is a "pecking order." Small dogs submit to big dogs. Young children show respect to older children. All children should obey their parents. Students submit to teachers. Teachers submit to principals. Principals submit to superintendents. Superintendents submit to boards. And everyone bends the knee to God, sooner or later. Thus, Paul teaches us *"⁷Give everyone what you owe him: If you owe taxes, pay taxes; if revenue, then revenue; if respect, then respect; if honor, then honor"* (Rom. 13:7). The Bible teaches us to pay what we owe at every level of society. Followers of Jesus give to others the respect we owe—at home, at school, in church, in public, and at work. We recognize that submission to authority is a part of God's plan, throughout the universe. Anyone who is not under authority at some level is headed for trouble—unless He is sitting on God's throne!

**2. Workers and masters, live like God is watching, and He will judge us at the end of our days.**

Q 57 ✎ *How should God's judgment at the end of life affect workers and masters?*

²²*Slaves, obey your earthly masters in everything; and do it, not only when their eye is on you and to win their favor, but with sincerity of heart and reverence for the Lord.* ²³*Whatever you do, work at it with all your heart, as working for the Lord, not for men,* ²⁴*since you know that you will receive an inheritance from the Lord as a reward. It is the Lord Christ you are serving.* ²⁵*Anyone who does wrong will be repaid for his wrong, and there is no favoritism* (Col. 3:22-25).

¹*Masters, provide your slaves with what is right and fair, **because you know that you also have a Master in heaven*** (Col. 4:1).

Paul tells workers to work well, **because** the "Big Boss in the sky" is always watching. God's apostle warns against working to please only humans. Paul tells us to **work as though we are God's employees**, because we know that **the Lord will reward everyone for whatever good he does,** whether he is slave or free (Eph. 6:8). In contrast, he reminds us: *"Anyone who does wrong will be repaid for his wrong, and there is no favoritism"* (Col. 3:25).

Q 58 ✎ *How does Paul relate justice and injustice to God?*

> PAUL HAS A WAY OF RELATING EVERYTHING AND EVERYONE TO GOD.

*Paul has a way of relating everything and everyone to God.* Recall that earlier, Paul called himself a prisoner of Jesus Christ. It was the Jews and Romans who put Paul in jail. But Paul practices looking all the way to the top. He sees God as the judge and rewarder of all. When people were kind to Paul, he wrote things such as: *"**May the Lord show mercy** to the household of Onesiphorus, because he often refreshed me and was not ashamed of my chains"* (2 Tim. 1:16).

When humans mistreated Paul, his response was something like: *"Alexander the metalworker did me a great deal of harm. **The Lord will repay him** for what he has done"* (2 Tim. 4:14).

When enemies persecuted believers in Thessalonica, Paul assured them: *"*⁶***God is just: He will pay back trouble to those who trouble you*** ⁷***and give relief to you who are troubled, and to us as well.*** *This will happen when the Lord Jesus is revealed from heaven in blazing fire with his powerful angels"* (2 Thess. 1:6-7).

Paul counsels the lowest and the highest in society, slaves and masters, to live in ways that please God. For at the end of our days, the only thing that matters is what the One on the throne says about the way we lived. So let workers give a day's work for a day's pay. And let masters be fair and considerate. For a day is coming when the levels of earth will be behind us, and the rewards of eternity before us.

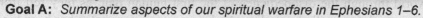

Lesson 16

**Live Worthy at War: Soldiers and Enemies—Part 1 (Eph. 6:10-24)**

**Goal A:** *Summarize aspects of our spiritual warfare in Ephesians 1–6.*

**Goal B:** *Explain the problem and the solution of standing firm against spiritual forces (Eph. 6:10-12).*

**Goal C:** *Analyze the need and the way to stand firm in the Lord against the devil's schemes (Eph. 6:10-14).*

**Setting.** As we study Ephesians 6:10-24, we must interpret it *as the end of Paul's letter*. These final verses about our conflict with Satan and demons are *not a new topic*. Paul has *already* referred to Satan— *"the ruler of the kingdom of the air, the spirit who is now at work in those who are disobedient"* (Eph. 2:2).

Q 59 ↗ *Does Paul wait until Ephesians 6 to introduce spiritual warfare? Explain.*

**Q 60** ➢ *Fill in the blanks in Figure 3.8, summarizing aspects of our \*spiritual warfare in Ephesians.*

| Ephesians | Your Summaries About Spiritual Warfare |
|---|---|
| 2:2 | |
| 2:1-3 | |
| 3:11 | |
| 4:1–6:9 | In our life on earth we are in the middle of a cosmic battle between God and Satan. We must put off six types of sin; and replace these with life in the Spirit. Likewise, we must let the Spirit lead us in healthy relationships in God's family. Otherwise, Satan will conquer us. |
| 5:18 | |
| 6:10-24 | |

**Figure 3.8    Practice identifying aspects of spiritual warfare in Ephesians, and keys to overcoming our spiritual enemy.**

**Q 61** ✎ *How does replacing six types of filthy clothes with clean clothes relate to spiritual warfare?*

Paul has *reminded us* that *before* we followed Christ, we followed the sinful desires of our flesh, the ways of the world, and the lures of the devil. We were dead in our sins, separated from God, and captives of Satan (Eph. 2:1-3). Paul has already written that *"now, through the church,"* God is revealing His manifold wisdom...to Satan and his demons—*"the rulers and authorities in the heavenly realms"* (Eph. 3:10). Already in Ephesians, Paul has made it clear that it is important for redeemed Jews and Gentiles to live worthy of God's blessings. Why? Because the Church is on display in the heavenly realms (Eph. 3:10). As we live as God's children of light, God is victorious—displaying us as those He has redeemed with the blood of Christ. As we live like the people of God, the temple of God, and the household of God, we fulfill His eternal purpose—the mystery He planned before the creation of the world. So Paul insists that we must live worthy of the salvation God freely provides for us by His grace. Paul commands us to take off the filthy clothes of lying, anger, stealing, immorality, unhealthy speech, and drunkenness. Instead of these dirty rags of the past, Paul commands us to put on truthfulness, self-control, love, and kindness. He urges us to work instead of stealing; and to speak wholesome words that edify instead of coarse talk, gossip, or slander. He guides us to be filled with the Spirit, always giving thanks, singing to ourselves and others with Scripture songs. He summarizes the right way to live as godly husbands, wives, children, fathers, mothers, workers, and employers.

**Q 62** ➢ *Whose captive are those who follow fleshly desires?*

**Q 63** ✎ *How do Paul's 36 commands for living worthy relate to spiritual warfare?*

Why, in Ephesians, does Paul give us 36 principles/commands on how all believers are to live worthy (Figure 2.2, 2.36, and 3.20)? Humans on earth live in the midst of a cosmic conflict between God and Satan. Sometime before Eden, the devil and lesser angels rebelled against God—and the Almighty cast them out of the highest heaven. In Eden, we see God creating humans, lower than the angels, but in His own image of holiness and righteousness (Eph. 4:24; Col. 3:10; Rom. 8:31; 2 Cor. 3:18). Yet in that first Garden on earth, Adam and Eve were in the battle between God and Satan. Satan lied through the serpent, and won a great victory over humans. Sin and death entered the world through the disobedience of the first human pair, as they fell from the high level on which God called us to live. And ever since Eden, Satan has been the temporary prince over earth. We find redemption—deliverance from sin and Satan—and victory in Christ alone, as we believe in Him—expressing our faith through obedience. Otherwise, all those outside of Christ remain prisoners of the flesh, the world, and the devil. As John explains, *"[19] We know that we are children of God, and that the whole world is under the control of the evil one. [20] We know also that the Son of God has come and has given us understanding, so that we may know him who is true. And we are in him who is true—even in his Son Jesus Christ"* (1 John 5:19-20).

Jesus has freed us from being under the control of the flesh, the world, and the devil. Yet the battle for the souls of humans continues. Throughout Ephesians, Paul has been writing about the conflict between God and Satan. Recall that we are studying the four letters Paul wrote from prison. He wrote as an *ambassador in chains* (Eph. 6:20). No doubt he often saw Roman soldiers and guards wearing their armor. So as Paul closes His letter, he uses the physical sight of a soldier in armor to illustrate the spiritual power and armor we need to win the war we are in.

**Q 64** ⤳ *What did the Spirit use to inspire Paul to write about the armor of God?*

## A. To stand firm against spiritual forces, we need the Lord's power and armor (Eph. 6:10-14).

*¹⁰Finally, **be strong in the Lord and in his mighty power.** ¹¹Put on the full armor **of God** so that you can **take your stand** against the devil's schemes. ¹²For our struggle is not against flesh and blood, but against the rulers, against the authorities, against the powers of this dark world and against the spiritual forces of evil in the heavenly realms. ¹³Therefore put on the full armor **of God**, so that when the day of evil comes, you may be able to **stand your ground**, and after you have done everything, **to stand.** ¹⁴**Stand firm then**, with the belt of truth buckled around your waist, with the breastplate of righteousness in place, ¹⁵and with your feet fitted with the readiness that comes from the gospel of peace.* (Eph. 6:10-15).

**Q 65** ⤳ *Why do humans need God's power and armor?*

**Problem:** Humans are no match for spiritual beings. Paul refers in four ways to the devil and demons: *rulers, authorities, powers of this dark world,* and *spiritual forces of evil in the heavenly realms* (Eph. 6:12). These terms are probably just descriptions rather than levels. Recall that Paul piles up descriptions throughout Ephesians, as in 3:20. The apostle's main point is that our enemies are powerful.

**Q 66** ⤳ *How many human warriors did one angel kill in one night?*

**Figure 3.9** In Ephesians 6 Paul uses the *physical* image of a strong Roman soldier in armor to illustrate the *spiritual* power and armor we need to win the war we are in. In this final passage, Paul emphasizes four principles to win spiritual warfare.

Natural beings, such as humans, are weak compared to supernatural beings. Take a few minutes to review Isaiah 36–37. Hezekiah was king of Judah. King Sennacherib of Assyria captured the strong cities of Judah, and marched to conquer Jerusalem. The king sent messengers to persuade King Hezekiah to surrender. The messengers mocked God and threatened to destroy Jerusalem. The godly King Hezekiah prayed and sent messengers, asking the Prophet Isaiah to pray. Isaiah prophesied that Sennacherib would not enter Jerusalem or shoot even one arrow in it. That night, God sent one angel, who killed 185,000 Assyrian warriors. The next day those who were still alive packed their bags and returned to Nineveh. So we dare not depend on ourselves in our battle against the devil and his demons.

The most powerful angels, who are much stronger than humans, respect the power of Satan. Jude wrote: *"⁹But even the archangel Michael, when he was disputing with the devil about the body of Moses, did not dare to bring a slanderous accusation against him, but said, 'The Lord rebuke you!'"* (Jude 1:9). Scripture teaches us that we need God's power to fight against supernatural enemies. We humans cannot break small string, but demons have the power to break chains (Mark 5:4). Are we so foolish that we would use human strength to fight against evil spirits? One demon-possessed man attacked seven sons of Sceva, and they all fled naked and wounded. Sending a person with only human strength to fight against Satan and his demons is worse than asking a duckling to chase off a pack of hungry wolves.

**Q 67** ⤳ *What are 2 examples that show demons are stronger than humans?*

**Solution:** Be strong in the Lord (Eph. 6:10-11). Throughout Ephesians, and all of his letters, Paul emphasizes that God's strength is the perfect solution for our weakness (2 Cor. 12:8-10). Thus Paul counsels us: *"¹⁰Be strong **in the Lord and in his mighty***

**Q 68** ⤳ *What is God's solution to our spiritual weakness? Illustrate.*

*power.* [11] *Put on the full \*armor of God so that you can take your stand against the devil's schemes"* (Eph. 6:10-11). The enemy of our souls has no fear of human power. But demons tremble at the name of Jesus. Evil spirits begged Jesus not to send them into the abyss—the fiery pit with no bottom (Luke 8:31).

**Q 69** ↖ *Complete Figure 3.10 that illustrates our need for the Lord's power.*

| Bible | Your Summaries About Our Need for the Lord's Power |
|---|---|
| Exod. 12:29-30 | |
| Exod. 14:23-28 | |
| Exod. 15:1-21 | |
| Judg. 15:14-15 | |
| 1 Sam. 17:45-47 | |
| 2 Chron. 20:15 | |
| Zech. 4:6 | |
| Luke 8:31 | |
| Rom. 8:5-9 | |
| Gal. 5:16 | |
| Eph. 5:18 | |
| Eph. 6:10-11 | |
| 1 John 4:4 | |

**Figure 3.10     Practice summarizing verses that show we need the Lord's power.**

**Q 70** ↖ *How do Isaiah 40:31 and Ephesians 5:18 encourage us in spiritual warfare?*

[28] *Do you not know? Have you not heard? The Lord is the everlasting God, the Creator of the ends of the earth. He will not grow tired or weary, and his understanding no one can fathom.* [29] *He gives strength to the weary and increases the power of the weak.* [30] *Even youths grow tired and weary, and young men stumble and fall;* [31] *but those who hope in the Lord will renew their strength. They will soar on wings like eagles; they will run and not grow weary, they will walk and not be faint* (Isa. 40:28-31).

Live filled with the Spirit and you will have all the power you need (Eph. 5:18). God is able to do more than we can ask or think, by His power at work in us (Eph. 3:20). And He delights to equip us for warfare with spiritual power and armor (which we will study in point C.).

### B. To stand firm against spiritual forces, we must stand firm in the Lord Jesus Christ (Eph. 6:1014).

**Q 71** ↗ *Do all who begin to follow Christ stand firm to the end? Illustrate.*

**Q 72** ↖ *If we do not wrestle with flesh and blood, why does Paul insist we conquer fleshly desires?*

**Problem:**     Some do not stand firm. It is amazing how much Paul emphasizes the *spiritual dimension* in our battle with *fleshly* desires and *spiritual* enemies. We do not wrestle against flesh and blood, *but* the devil and demons work through *fleshly desires* in this spiritual war we are in. So we must be strong *in the Lord* and *stand firm* in these final evil days. Paul warns that some believers will not stand firm. He warns that baby believers may be tossed back and forth on the waves of circumstances (Eph. 4:14). When trials and tragedies come, these infant believers may doubt the love of God. Paul warns that other believers will fail to stand against false teachings. These will be blown away *"...by the cunning and craftiness of men in their deceitful scheming"* (Eph. 4:14). So Paul urges us: *"...take your stand against the devil's schemes"* (Eph. 6:11).

**Q 73** ↗ *Why does Paul warn about being disqualified from the prize?*

Paul warns that we must be on guard so that no one will *disqualify* us from *the prize* of heaven (Col. 2:18). Paul made his own body his slave, rather than serving its lusts, so that after he had preached to others, he himself would *"not be disqualified for the prize"* (1 Cor. 9:27). *He* urges the Philippians to live without arguing, complaining, and fighting with each other, so that he *"did not run or labor for nothing"* among them (Phil. 2:16). Paul wants believers to stand firm in humility, and love—thinking of their own interests, but also the interests of other believers (Phil. 2:4). Grace belongs to those who *love the Lord with an undying love* (Eph. 6:24). But some forfeit the grace they receive because they do not *stand firm in the Lord.* Paul warns:

> [1] *The Spirit clearly says that in later times **some will abandon the faith** and follow deceiving spirits and things taught by demons.* [2] *Such teachings come through hypocritical liars, whose consciences have been seared as with a hot iron* (1 Tim. 4:1-2).

*Standing* firm in the faith does not sound very exciting. People can become weary of righteous living (Gal. 6:9). They can get tired of standing. They can be seduced to motion and action. We live in a shallow generation. People are eager for new clothes, new phones, new songs, new teachings, and new entertainment. Half of the population is even eager for a new spouse. One of the most difficult tasks for people of every generation is *standing firm.* So much of life is routine. Life serves us a steady diet of temptations, trials, suffering, and waiting. We wait year by year, and even a lifetime for the promise of His Second Coming. Even in the early years of the Church, false teachers mocked believers, saying, *"Where is the promise of his coming?"* (2 Pet. 3:4).

**Solution: Stand firm in the Lord.** As you read through Ephesians 6:10-14 again, notice that Paul emphasizes the word ***stand*** four times. We are to stand firm in the freedom and victory that Christ has won for us.

> [10] *Finally, be strong in the Lord and in his mighty power.* [11] *Put on the full armor of God so that you can **take your stand** against the devil's schemes.* [12] *For our struggle is not against flesh and blood, but against the rulers, against the authorities, against the powers of this dark world and against the spiritual forces of evil in the heavenly realms.* [13] *Therefore put on the full armor of God, so that when the day of evil comes, you may be able to **stand your ground**, and after you have done everything, **to stand**.* [14] ***Stand firm then**, with the belt of truth buckled around your waist, with the breastplate of righteousness in place,* [15] *and with your feet fitted with the readiness that comes from the gospel of peace.* (Eph. 6:10-15).

Paul commands us to be strong in the Lord, and patient. *Four times* this great apostle reminds us that we must keep standing firm in the Lord's power (Eph. 6:10-14). Using a parallel metaphor, he says we must be *rooted in love* (Eph. 3:17). We must keep on keeping on. Having done all to stand, we must stand, and keep standing! The battle belongs to the Lord. But we must stand firm in Him.

> [57] *Thanks be to God! He gives us the victory through our Lord Jesus Christ.* [58] ***Therefore, my dear brothers, stand firm. Let nothing move you.*** *Always give yourselves fully to the work of the Lord, because you know that your labor in the Lord is not in vain* (1 Cor. 15:57-58).

Much of our spiritual warfare involves standing—*standing firm, standing on the promises, standing steadfast and immovable* **in the word, in the Lord, and in the Spirit**. God fought for the Israelites to deliver them from the Egyptians—the most powerful army in the world at that time. Likewise, God fought the battle to deliver us from Satan, the ruler of this world. We were prisoners of Satan and sin, unable to free ourselves. *So God fought for us, sending His Son to defeat the devil and his army.* As Paul writes:

> [13] *When you were dead in your sins and in the uncircumcision of your sinful nature, God made you alive with Christ. He forgave us all our sins,* [14] *having canceled the written code, with its regulations, that was against us and that stood*

**Q 74** Did Paul think it was possible for believers at Philippi to lose their inheritance? Explain.

**Q 75** Did Paul believe that the love of some for Christ would become cold and die? Explain.

**Q 76** What warning does Paul give in 1 Timothy 4:1-2?

**Q 77** Do you know believers who grew weary of standing for Christ, and returned to sin?

**Q 78** How many times does Paul tell us to stand in Ephesians 6:10-17? Underline them.

*opposed to us; he took it away, nailing it to the cross.* ¹⁵***And having disarmed the powers and authorities, he made a public spectacle of them, triumphing over them by the cross*** (Col. 2:13-15).

**Q 79** ⬉ *In Ephesians 6:10-17, is Paul emphasizing offense or defense? Explain.*

In war, there is offense and defense. Some warfare requires the *offense* of moving forward, climbing over walls, conquering hills, and capturing cities. The *offense* of spiritual warfare is involved as missionaries expand the kingdom of God into new territories; and church members expand the kingdom of God into new neighborhoods, homes, and lives. We are on offense as we *shine as bright lights* in a dark world (Phil. 2:15). And Paul requests prayer for the *offense* of spiritual battles, as he fights the enemy in new places—even as an ambassador in chains (Eph. 6:19-20). But in Ephesians 6:10-18, most of Paul's emphasis is on *defense*—holding our position **in Christ, standing firm** in the faith.

**Q 80** ⬉ *How does our participation decide whether we are winners or losers?*

Jesus has *already* defeated and disarmed our spiritual enemies (Col. 2:13-15). He has *already* won the victory. We know that God wins the war against Satan. But who will rise to heaven, and who will be cast into hell? Some will be conquered, and some will overcome. We must stand our ground as we live in-between the first and second comings of Christ. At His **First** Coming, Jesus won the battle over sin, Satan, death, and the world. But Christ has not yet come the **Second** Time, to announce His eternal victory over His enemies. The biggest battle has been won, but the battle for souls continues. Half of the world has not even heard that Jesus died for them. There are thousands of martyrs for Christ every year. An eternal celebration is coming. *Even now* we have the down-payment of our salvation—the Holy Spirit within us (Eph. 1:13-14). And yet our full inheritance is ahead of us. The devil and his demons are not yet cast into the lake of fire (Rev. 20:10). We must be alert and watchful, *for Satan our enemy still prowls like a roaring lion, seeking whom he may devour* (1 Pet. 5:8). So we must keep standing firm (Eph. 6:10-14). For as Jesus promised, ***the one who stands firm*** and endures to the end *will be saved* (Matt. 24:13).

---

**Lesson 17**

## Live Worthy at War: Soldiers and Enemies—Part 2 (Eph. 6:10-24)

**Goal D:** *List and explain the purposes of 6 pieces of spiritual armor in Ephesians 6:14-17.*
**Goal E:** *Explain and apply: praying in the Spirit, occasions for prayer, and types of prayer (Eph. 6:18-20).*

---

### C. To stand firm, we must put on six pieces of armor God provides (Eph. 6:14-17).

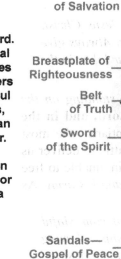

Helmet of Salvation
Shield of Faith
Breastplate of Righteousness
Belt of Truth
Sword of the Spirit
Sandals— Gospel of Peace

**Figure 3.11    Pretorian Guard. Paul compares the spiritual armor we need to six pieces of armor the Roman soldiers wore. Recall that when Paul wrote the Prison Epistles, he was chained to a Roman soldier wearing the armor. In Ephesians 6:14-17, Paul compares the Roman soldiers' armor to the armor we need as believers in a spiritual war.**

**Q 81** ⬈ *How often did Paul see a Roman soldier wearing armor?*

**Q 82** ⬈ *God provides the armor, but who chooses to wear it?*

The power and armor God provides *enable us* to stand firm. God gives us the power, but He expect us to use the power to stand. God provides the armor for our spiritual warfare. But He tells us two times to *"put on the full armor of God"* and wear it (Eph. 6:11, 13)!

**Q 83** ⬈ *How does modern warfare often differ from warfare in biblical times?*

In modern warfare, much of the fighting is with planes, missiles, and weapons that destroy enemies miles away. But in biblical times, soldiers fought close to each other—sometimes face to face, and hand to hand. Arrows and spears whizzed through the air. Chariots banged against each other. Swords clashed. Remember this as you read Paul's words about the need for armor in battle.

> [10] *Finally, be strong in the Lord and in his mighty power.* [11] ***Put on the full armor of God** so that you can **take your stand** against the devil's schemes.* [12] *For our struggle is not against flesh and blood, but against the rulers, against the authorities, against the powers of this dark world and against the spiritual forces of evil in the heavenly realms.* [13] *Therefore **put on the full armor of God**, so that when the day of evil comes, you may be able to stand your ground, and **after you have done everything, to stand.*** [14] *Stand firm then, with the **belt of truth buckled** around your waist, with the **breastplate of righteousness in place**,* [15] *and with **your feet fitted with the readiness that comes from the gospel of peace.*** [16] *In addition to all this, **take up the shield of faith**, with which you can extinguish all the flaming arrows of the evil one.* [17] ***Take the helmet of salvation** and **the sword of the Spirit**, which is the word of God* (Eph. 6:10-17).

**Q 84** ✎ *Fill in Figure 3.12 as you read the comments after the chart.*

| Armor | Your Explanations of Six Pieces of Armor We Must Put on to Stand Victoriously |
|---|---|
| 1. Belt of | |
| 2. Breastplate of | |
| 3. Sandals of the | |
| 4. Shield of | |
| 5. Helmet of | |
| 6. Sword of the Spirit | |

**Figure 3.12**  Practice explaining the six parts of armor we must wear to stand victoriously in spiritual warfare.

Paul presents the armor we need in two groups of three. Let us look briefly at each of these six pieces of armor that Roman soldiers wore (see Figure 3.11).

**1. Paul compares truth to a belt.** God provides the belt of truth, but we must buckle it in place. In Paul's day, the belt was an important piece of armor. The belt of leather kept the soldier's tunic or robe from moving around. The belt also held the sword in place when the soldier was not fighting.

**Q 85** ➚ *How does putting on the belt of truth relate to taking off falsehood (Eph. 4:25)?*

> IN SPIRITUAL WARFARE, TWO FORCES OPPOSE EACH OTHER—TRUTH AND FALSEHOOD.

Earlier, Paul urged believers to put off the old self and put on the new self. He emphasized six old ways of the flesh to replace with new ways of the Spirit (Figure 3.12). Falsehood was the first old way of living to replace with *truthful speech* (Eph. 4:25). And in this final section, *truth* is the first piece of armor Paul mentions (Eph. 6:14). Paul's emphasis on truth shows us it is very important. God is the author of truth, but Satan is the father of lies (John 8:44). **In spiritual warfare, two forces oppose each other—truth and falsehood**. The only winners in our spiritual battle are those who choose, embrace, and live truth.

Our relation to truth determines if we live or die spiritually. Jesus told Pilate that He came to earth to testify to the truth (John 18:37). Pilate mocked Jesus, asking: "What is

**Q 86** ✎ *From which 3 things does truth protect us?*

**Q 87** How could using truth have protected Adam and Eve?

truth?" Truth is the standard by which God will judge every person who lived on earth. Truth must be one of our greatest concerns. The armor of truth **protects us** from the *devil's schemes*, lies, and deception (Eph. 6:11). Because Adam and Eve did not use the armor of truth, Satan defeated them with a lie in Eden. And Paul warned that in these last days, the Antichrist will deceive those who refuse to love and live the truth. Paul warned:

> [9]*The coming of the lawless one will be in accordance with the work of Satan displayed in all kinds of **counterfeit** miracles, signs and wonders, [10]and in every sort of evil that **deceives** those who are perishing. They perish **because they refused to love the truth** and so be saved.*
>
> [11]*For this reason God sends them a powerful **delusion** so that **they will believe the lie** [12]and so that **all will be condemned who have not believed the truth but have delighted in wickedness*** (2 Thess. 2:9-12).

**Q 88** Paul contrasts truth with _____ (2 Thess. 2:9-12)? Apply this.

Notice that Paul contrasts truth with wickedness. Today, many claim to live the truth, but they practice wickedness—secret sins that God forbids. The Judge of mankind searches the hearts and minds (Rev. 2:23). He sees those who pretend to love the light of truth, but rebel against Him and live in darkness. God is no respecter of persons. Truth is His standard for judging everyone. On the day when God separates the sheep from the goats, He will condemn all who talked about truth, but lived in sin.

**Q 89** Do you allow truth to shine in every closet of your life, and set you free? Or are some areas off limits to God?

Submit to the truth and it will set you free (John 8:32). Whoever is a friend of truth is a friend of Jesus Himself (John 14:6). Treasure truth above all else. Keep it at any cost. Own it at any price. Embrace the truth as your closest friend. Allow truth to shine in every closet of your life. Be truthful in private and in public. Buckle on the belt of truth and wear it, or Satan will conquer you as his captive for eternity. If truth is not a part of your armor, you have no hope.

**Q 90** Do you examine yourself in the light of Scripture, or just ignore God's Word and pretend all is well? Explain.

> *Examine yourselves to see whether you are in the faith; test yourselves. Do you not realize that Christ Jesus is in you—unless, of course, you fail the test—the test of truth?* (2 Cor. 13:5).

We are as Christian as we are truthful—no less and no more.

**2. The breastplate of righteousness is the second piece of armor we need from God.** For centuries, soldiers have seen the need for a breastplate in battle. It protected the most vital organs, from the shoulders to the waist, and especially the heart. Even today, many policemen wear a bullet-proof vest—a plate under their shirt that prevents bullets from piercing the chest.

**Q 91** Why is the breastplate "vital"?

**Q 92** What caused the breastplate to shine like the lights of 50 cars coming? Apply this.

Figure 3.13   A breastplate was bronze or brass. It had two pieces of metal—one for the front and the other for the back. Brass rings on top of the shoulders often held the two parts of the breastplate together. This was the heaviest part of a Roman soldier's armor, weighing 40 lbs. (18kg) or more. Recall that Goliath's breastplate weighed about 125 pounds (57kg) (1 Sam. 17:5). A breastplate shone with boldness, and in bright sunlight its reflection could strike fear and hinder the enemy's vision. Imagine the sight of a hundred Roman soldiers facing the enemy, with the sun reflecting off their breastplates! To an enemy, this could look like the bright headlights of 50 cars coming at you! Likewise, as the righteousness of God shines through the church, may it cause the demons to tremble.

**Scripture refers to two aspects of righteousness:**

**Q 93** What are 2 kinds of righteousness that God provides? Describe each.

- *First,* we repent of our sinful ways, and turn from them to receive and follow Jesus in faith. At that moment, God gives us the *imputed righteousness of justification—the free gift of righteous standing and position (Rom. 3:21-22; 4:13).

**Q 94** Is our righteousness fixed and static, or does it grow? Explain.

- *Second,* at the same time God forgives and justifies us, He imparts His nature to us, as the Holy Spirit enters us. This *imparted righteousness is a result of the presence of God within us. So, Paul insists that we must put off our old ways and put on new ways, as we are being renewed in the image of God in true righteous and holy behavior (Eph. 4:22-24; 5:9; 6:14; Col. 3:10). Growing in righteous character and behavior is a process. Just as a child grows into an adult, we believers grow in the likeness of our Heavenly Father. We refer to this as progressive sanctification—growing in God's image, in the areas of holiness and righteousness.

**Figure 3.14 Growing in the likeness of our Father is a process that spans from regeneration to glorification. Romans 6–8 stresses the process of growing in the likeness of Christ. The imparted holiness of sanctification begins at regeneration, and reaches its highest level at glorification. In between the new birth and the new body, we perfect holiness—we increase in holy actions, holy attitudes, and holy character.**

**Some children of righteousness are babies in Christ, while others have grown to be more mature. Our glorious destiny is to become completely holy, like God the Son! Even now, the Spirit enables us to become more and more like our Savior (Rom. 8:29; 2 Cor. 3:18).[11]**

**24 *and to put on the new self, created to be like God in true righteousness and holiness* (Eph. 4:24)**
**10 *and have put on the new self, which is being renewed in knowledge in the image of its Creator* (Col. 3:10).**

God is the source of any and all righteousness that we have. All of the armor we are studying in Ephesians 6 comes from God (Eph. 6:11, 13). We depend on God for our righteous standing at justification, and we also daily depend on God to protect us *as we put on* the armor of righteous character and behavior. If a person is unrighteous, lacking integrity, or living as a hypocrite, this exposes a person to the spiritual attacks of the enemy. As anger can give the devil a foothold (Eph. 4:27), unrighteous behavior gives the devil an unprotected place to wound us. In contrast, submitting to God's Word and Spirit enables us to wear righteousness like a breastplate that covers and protects our hearts from the devil's deadly assaults.

**Q 95** *How does unrighteous behavior give the devil a place to wound us?*

**3. Like sandals on a soldier, believers need the gospel of peace on our feet.** Roman soldiers wore tough leather sandals that had cleats under the soles. These special shoes enabled a Roman soldier to stand firm and fight the enemy, even on slippery ground. Many athletes today wear shoes that have cleats or spikes that enable them to have good traction and footing, and prevent sliding.

**Q 96** *How did special sandals help a Roman soldier stand firm?*

**Q 97** *How does meditating on the gospel help us stand firm?*

**Figure 3.15 Roman soldiers wore tough leather sandals with cleats under the sole, and leather straps that added support. Likewise, having our feet fitted with the gospel of peace makes us ready for spiritual battle. For although we are at war with the enemy, we are at peace with God through Jesus Christ. This deep inner peace gives us confidence to stand firm against Satan's attacks, and not doubt God, or retreat in fear or despair. As Paul writes in another letter from prison, "...the peace of God, which transcends all understanding, will guard your hearts and your minds in Christ Jesus" (Phil. 4:7).[12]**

**4. The shield of faith is the fourth piece of divine armor we need to put on.** Paul is referring to a large shield that was 2.5 feet (.77 meters) wide, 4 feet (1.2 meters) tall, and weighed about 10 kilos (22 lbs). This shield was made from layers of wood, bronze, and ox hide. Roman soldiers often stood side by side, with their shields in front. This gave the army great protection. Before battle, the

**Q 98** *How big was the shield of a Roman soldier? How did it quench flaming arrows?*

**Figure 3.16 Roman soldiers stood side by side behind their large, heavy shields.**

soldiers soaked their shields in water. Then, when the enemy shot flaming arrows—the shield caught them and quenched the fire.

**Q 99** *From what kind of arrows does the shield of faith protect us? Illustrate.*

We cannot prevent our spiritual enemy from shooting at us. But as we hold up the shield of faith, it quenches the fiery arrows that Satan shoots at us. Faith is the victory that overcomes the world. Faith in God is focusing on our Father and trusting in His love, goodness, and faithfulness. Truly, faith is like a shield that deflects—and protects us from the lies, discouragement, and flaming missiles of hate the devil shoots at us.

**Q 100** *How does God save us from evil thoughts that come to our minds?*

**5. The helmet of salvation is the fifth piece of armor Paul mentions.** In warfare, the head and the heart are the most vital parts to protect. As the breastplate and shield protect the heart, the helmet protects the head. The believer's mind is a battlefield in spiritual warfare. Almost all of the temptations we face enter the mind through the eye. Likewise, all false teachings wage war on the battleground of the mind. We win or lose battles in our thoughts. (See Lesson 42, *Spiritual Thinking,* in the Faith & Action book: *First & Second Corinthians*).

**Figure 3.17   Roman helmet**

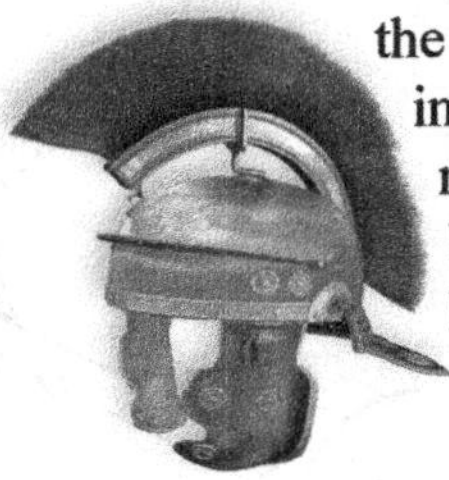

**Q 101** *What happens to minds that are not renewed, delivered, and protected by God?*

## God's Word Passes Through

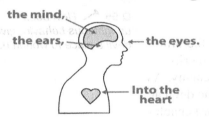

the mind,

the ears,

the eyes.

Into the heart

**Figure 3.18   God's Word enters the mind through reading with the eyes, hearing with the ears, and singing spiritual songs with our voices, and silently in our hearts. The mind and the heart work together to believe. So we must be careful what we think about. Paul guides us to think on things that are good, just, and pure (Phil. 4:8). And he tells us to let the Word of Christ dwell in us richly, as we sing to ourselves with spiritual songs (Col. 3:16).**

With the mind we meditate on assurance of salvation *now,* through our union with Christ. The promises of God's Word assure us that we are forgiven, delivered from Satan's bondage, adopted into God's family, and filled with His Spirit. Likewise, these promises of God assure us in our minds of *future* aspects of God's kingdom, such as the banishment of sin and death; the judgment of sinners, Satan, and demons; and our eternal inheritance with our Father in heaven. The helmet of salvation represents the renewal, deliverance, and protection of the mind in Christ.[13]

**Q 103** *How does the Spirit use the Word to help us defeat spiritual enemies? Give an example.*

**6. The sword of the Spirit (the Word of God), is the final piece of armor Paul mentions.** The Greek word for *sword* indicates a short sword, about a foot long, that soldiers used for fighting hand-to-hand. Note two things about the *sword, or Word of God:*

**Q 102** *How did Jesus use the sword of the Spirit to defeat Satan (Matt. 4)?*

- It is the sword *of the Spirit.* All Scripture comes *through* the Spirit of God. He inspired the writers of the Bible and carried them along, so that they wrote the words God intended us to have (2 Tim. 3:15-17; 2 Pet. 1:21). Likewise, the sword is *of the* Spirit, because we need Him to guide us in using the sword. We need the Spirit to remind us of God's promises. We need the Spirit to enlighten us, revealing the meaning of Scripture as we study to show ourselves approved of God. We need the Spirit to quicken verses of Scripture in our spiritual walk, and at times of ministry. The Bible is a spiritual book, and we must have the Spirit's help in using this sword. We need His hand on our hand, as we use the sword or the Word, to defeat God's enemies, who are also our enemies.

**Figure 3.19   Roman soldiers used a short sword or dagger, about 12-14 inches long, when fighting face to face, and hand to hand.**

- The sword or Word of God is the only piece of armor for offense, as well as defense. We need the Word of God to fight against our spiritual enemies and to overcome them. Recall that Jesus used the Word of God three times to overcome

Satan's temptations (Matt. 4). As the Spirit helps us use the Word of God, we can overcome the temptations of the world, the flesh, and the devil. The Word reminds us to be humble when the flesh wants to be arrogant. The Word encourages us to lift up our heads and hands when we are tempted to doubt or be discouraged. The Word reminds us to forgive when the enemy reminds us of those who have offended us. The Word guides us on the path of harmony to agree in the Lord when we face disagreements. The Word of God is the sword of the Spirit that we must wield to be victorious.

A preacher was attending a conference. An attractive prostitute came up to him and smiled. She asked if she could come to his room. At once, the Word of God came to him, *"Among you, there must not be even a hint of sexual immorality"* (Eph. 5:3). Embarrassed and annoyed, he said: "No!" He turned away from her, and she left as quickly as she came, but without her fake smile. His submission to the sword of the Spirit brought him instant victory over sin. The Word from the Spirit helped him win a battle in less than 5 seconds! That was one short battle!

**Q 104** ⟍ *How can a young person keep his or her way pure (Ps. 119:9)?*

### D. To stand firm, we must pray in the Spirit on all occasions (Eph. 6:18-19).

Prayer is not a piece of armor, but it connects us with our Commander, the Almighty God of heaven and earth.

**Q 105** ⟋ *How is prayer related to spiritual warfare?*

*18 And **pray in the Spirit** on all occasions with **all kinds of prayers and requests**. With this in mind, be alert and **always keep on praying** for all the saints. 19 **Pray also for me**, that whenever I open my mouth, words may be given me so that I will fearlessly make known the mystery of the gospel, 20 for which I am an ambassador in chains. **Pray that I may declare it fearlessly, as I should** (Eph. 6:18-20).*

### How to pray? Prayer in the Spirit is powerful (Eph. 6:18a).

Pentecostals and Charismatics enjoy being baptized in the Spirit (Acts 1:4-5; Mark 1:7-8), and being filled with the Spirit—as Paul, all the apostles, and early believers were filled (Acts 2:4; 9:17; Eph. 5:18). Living full of the Spirit is a great privilege of the New Testament. Those filled with the Spirit know that *praying in the Spirit* includes praying in tongues (1 Cor. 14:2, 14-15). But praying in the Spirit also includes being led and enabled by the Spirit as we pray in a language we have learned (see 1 Cor. 14:15).

**Q 106** ⟋ *What is "prayer in the Spirit"?*

There are many times that we believers do not know what to pray. For example, Paul prayed for God to remove his thorn, but this was not God's will (2 Cor. 12:7-9). When believers do not know what to pray, the Holy Spirit may pray *for* and *through* us with groans. These groans might be like those of the Israelites under bondage in Egypt (Acts 7:34). This groaning of the Spirit may include speaking in tongues (1 Cor. 14:2).[14] Or, the Spirit may be praying directly to God without our involvement.

On earth, we will never know all the times and all the ways the Spirit groans and prays for us. Nevertheless, it encourages us to know that the Spirit in us participates in our struggles. In our most difficult times, the Holy Spirit prays for us. *"And he who searches our hearts knows the mind of the Spirit, because the Spirit intercedes for the saints in accordance with God's will"* (Rom. 8:27). Likewise Jesus, at the Father's right hand, intercedes for us (Rom. 8:34). With this kind of help, we are going to make it!

### When to pray? Occasions for prayer are everywhere (Eph. 6:18b).

**Q 107** ⟍ *When should we pray? Give examples.*

Paul encourages believers to pray *"on all occasions."* He encourages us to be *"alert"* for opportunities to pray. Occasions to pray include the happy and unhappy times. James tells us to pray when we are suffering, and praise when we are cheerful (James 5:13). Prayer includes formal and informal opportunities. Paul wants us to pray when there is a problem, and when there is a victory. He wants us to pray with a group that meets, and also pray alone—silently on a bus or while taking a walk to meet with God. Praying on all occasions includes prayer for personal needs and the needs of others. We are to ask for help in trouble and temptation. God invites us to pray for guidance and direction. We should pray when we need to calm down and gain perspective. Prayer is the way to receive salvation; the baptism in the Holy Spirit; healing; or deliverance from a habit, demonic attack, or oppression. After we have sinned we should pray for forgiveness, cleansing, and restoration. It is proper to pray for renewal and revival. Let us pray on all occasions: at dawn, noon day, sunset, and in sleepless nights. Prayer is our great privilege—to talk with our Father, sharing all of our life, and the interests of His kingdom. Prayer should be as much a part of our day as breathing. One leader said that prayer has become such a part of his life, that he did not even lift a glass of water to his lips without prayer. John Wesley liked to ask those he met, "Do I meet you praying?" When and where have you met God this week? The best days of our lives are those we pray at least one hour.

**Q 108** ✎ *What kind of prayers should we pray? Give examples.*

**What kind of prayer? The types of prayers are many (Eph. 6:18c).**   Paul urges us to use *"all kinds of prayer."* A danger for Christians is to be content with just one kind of prayer—to get into a spiritual rut. The Bible describes types of prayer with words such as, *petitions, requests, supplication,* and *entreaty.* Since prayer is talking *with* God, praying includes listening—as we walk on God's earth and meditate on His goodness. We can pray Scripture, claiming the promises of God or reciting psalms that glorify Him. Our hearts can overflow with prayers of praise, worship, and adoration, just as Mary rejoiced in God, her Savior (Luke 1:46-55). Prayer included giving thanks, rejoicing, and magnifying God. Our prayers must include confession of sin and repentance, when these are fitting. Fasting is also a form of silent prayer. There is a time for loud, forceful prayer. But quiet prayers of wonder or submission are also important. Persistent, prevailing prayer always has power.

**Q 109** ✎ *Who are the saints? Does Paul say we should pray **to** the saints or **for** the saints (Eph. 6:18)? Explain.*

Near the end of Ephesians, Paul asks for intercessory prayer, which is prayer for others (Eph. 6:18-20). Paul requests prayer for all the saints, and for himself as a missionary.

> [18] *And pray in the Spirit on all occasions with all kinds of prayers and requests. With this in mind, be alert and **always keep on praying for all the saints.** [19] **Pray also for me**, that whenever I open my mouth, words may be given me so that I will fearlessly make known the mystery of the gospel, [20] for which I am an ambassador in chains. **Pray that I may declare it fearlessly, as I should*** (Eph. 6:18-20).

Notice that Paul requests prayer *for the saints*, not **to the saints.** The Bible refers to *saints* as God's *holy* people on earth. Recall that the word *saints*, Greek *hagios*, means "holy ones." In the Prison Epistles, Paul wrote to the *saints* in Ephesus, Colosse (including the saints who met in Philemon's home), and Philippi. In his letter to the *saints* in Ephesus (Eph. 1:1), he asks these *saints* to pray for *all the saints* (Eph. 6:18): in Ephesus, Colosse, Philippi, Rome, Corinth, Thessalonica, Laodicea, Galatia, Jerusalem, Syria, and everywhere.

**Q 110** ✎ *What example can you give showing that prayer changes people or circumstances?*

**Application.**   Prayer changes people and circumstances. Paul believed in the power of prayer as the Holy Spirit guides and anoints us to intercede for others! Parents must pray for their children. Church members must pray for their pastor and deacons. We must pray for suffering saints among the nations. God wants us to pray for missionaries, like Paul, to be fruitful and faithful (Eph. 6:19). All believers must pray for government leaders. Paul wrote: "[1] *I urge, then, first of all, that requests, prayers, intercession and thanksgiving be made for everyone—*[2] ***for kings and all those in authority,*** *that we may live peaceful and quiet lives in all godliness and holiness*" (1 Tim. 2:1-2). God tells us to pray and intercede for others. Intercession is part of our privilege and duty as followers of Jesus Christ. He prayed for His followers, and all of us who would believe because of those first disciples (John 17). And God invites and commissions <u>us</u> to pray for *all the saints.* We are brothers and sisters of the same family. May the Spirit teach us to love one another—to love enough to pray for each other.

Paul hopes to be released from prison in answer to prayers like those of Philemon (Philem. 22). But he does not ask the Ephesians to pray for his release. Rather, this *great heart*—the *apostle to the Gentiles*—asked them to pray that the Holy Spirit would give him the right words to testify for Christ without fear as *an ambassador in chains* (Eph. 6:19-20).

We do not know the difficult challenges our brothers and sisters in Christ are facing right now in communities around the world. Those who lead the church and guide nations need our prayers today! Believers facing suffering need our prayers. It is God's will that we pray for them (Eph. 6:18). Our unselfish, loving intercession helps our family members persevere and spread the gospel of God's kingdom in all nations.

Dr. Leroy Bartel, a professor at one university, opened each class with prayer for believers in a nation of the world. There was a prayer guide to lead faculty, staff, and students to pray for every nation, one by one, throughout the world. Participating in such praying every day helped form the heart of an intercessor in many lives. Dr. Bartel heard students pour out their hearts in prayer for people suffering with AIDS, for children lacking food, for nations at war, for believers facing persecution, and for those with no light of the gospel. Let us be intercessors and also teach others to intercede *for all the saints*. Paul's final request is as needed today as it was 2,000 years ago. Let us *pray, pray, pray* (Eph. 6:18-20).

**Conclusion.**

[21] *Tychicus, the dear brother and faithful servant in the Lord, will tell you everything, so that you also may know how I am and what I am doing.* [22] *I am sending him to you for this very purpose, that you may know how we are, and that he may encourage you.*

[23] *Peace to the brothers, and love with faith from God the Father and the Lord Jesus Christ.* [24] *Grace to all who love our Lord Jesus Christ **with an undying love*** (Eph. 6:21-24).

| Eph. | Principles 25–36 for Living Worthy—in the Spirit and the Love of God (Eph. 5:21– 6:19) |
|---|---|
| 5:21-22 | **25.** *Submit to one another out of reverence for Christ. Wives, submit to your husbands as to the Lord.* |
| 5:25, 28 | **26.** *Husbands, love your wives, just as Christ loved the church and gave himself up for her.* |
| | **27.** Husband, love your wife as you love your own body. |
| 5:31 | **28.** *For this reason a man will leave his father and mother and be united to his wife, and the two will become one flesh.* |
| 6:1-3 | **29.** *Children, obey your parents in the Lord, for this is right.* |
| | **30.** [2] *"Honor your father and mother"—which is the first commandment with a promise—* [3] *"that it may go well with you and that you may enjoy long life on the earth."* |
| 6:4 | **31.** *Fathers, do not exasperate your children; instead, bring them up in the training and instruction of the Lord.* |
| 6:5 | **32.** *Slaves, obey your earthly masters with respect and fear, and with sincerity of heart, just as you would obey Christ.* |
| 6:9 | **33.** *Masters, treat your slaves in the same way. Do not threaten them, since you know that he who is both their Master and yours is in heaven, and there is no favoritism with him.* |
| 6:10 | **34.** *Finally, be strong in the Lord and in his mighty power.* |
| 6:11-17 | **35.** *Put on the full armor of God so that you can take your stand against the devil's schemes.* |
| 6:18-19 | **36.** *Pray in the Spirit on all occasions with all kinds of prayers and requests.* |

**Figure 3.20** In Ephesians 4–6 Paul gives at least 36 principles for living worthy—in the Spirit and the love of God. (See Figure 2.1 for principles 1–16 and Figure 2.36 for principles 17–24.)

**Test Yourself:** Circle the letter by the *best* completion to each question or statement.

**1.** Which letter has the most words about relationships in God's family?
a) Ephesians
b) Colossians
c) Philemon
d) John

**2.** The word *submission* means:
a) "under in value."
b) "under in authority."
c) "under in ability."
d) "under in importance."

**3.** Ephesians 5 says a husband should love his wife
a) as he loves his children.
b) as he loves the Lord.
c) as the Father loves the Son.
d) as Christ loved the Church.

**4.** How many groups does Paul identify in the church?
a) 2
b) 3
c) 4
d) 5 or more

**5.** What causes children to become bitter?
a) Parents who control too little
b) Parents who earn too little money
c) Parents who control too much
d) Parents who lack education

**6.** What counsel does Paul give slaves and masters?
a) Bloom where you are planted.
b) Live as though God is watching.
c) Give honor to whom honor is due.
d) Owe no debt except to love.

**7.** Which chapter of Ephesians introduces spiritual warfare?
a) 2
b) 3
c) 5
d) 6

**8.** Which aspect of warfare does Paul emphasize?
a) Conquering
b) Standing
c) Attacking
d) Advancing

**9.** How many pieces of armor does Paul describe?
a) 2
b) 4
c) 6
d) 8

**10.** Pray *in the Spirit* means
a) "pray in tongues."
b) "pray mysteries."
c) "pray the Scriptures."
d) "pray led by the Spirit."

**Essay Test Topics:** Write 50-100 words on each of these 12 goals that you studied in this chapter. Try to complete this test in 1.5 hours. On the final exam, we will combine some of these goals and ask you to write on a few of them. As you practice writing on each of these goals now, you are preparing well for the final test. (8 points each + 4 points free)

- Compare and contrast Paul's teachings on relationships in Ephesians and Colossians.
- Analyze the submission of a godly wife to her husband; and how she honors, respects, and admires him.
- Explain 5 ways a husband should love his wife, as Christ loves the Church (Eph. 5:25-33).
- Identify the groups in God's family that a pastor must shepherd.
- Analyze the problem, solution, and promise for children in God's family
- State and illustrate 4 guidelines for parents to train children in God's family.
- State and illustrate 2 guidelines for employers and employees in God's family.
- Summarize aspects of our spiritual warfare in Ephesians 1–6.
- Explain the problem and the solution of standing firm against spiritual forces (Eph. 6:10-12).
- Analyze the need and the way to stand firm in the Lord against the devil's schemes (Eph. 6:10-14).
- List and explain the purposes of 6 pieces of spiritual armor in Ephesians 6:14-17.
- Explain and apply: praying in the Spirit, occasions for prayer, and types of prayer (Eph. 6:18-20).

# Chapter 4:
# Colossians: Powerful Doctrine About Our Supreme Savior
## (Col. 1–2)

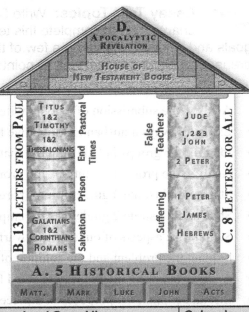

**Figure 4.1**
**The New Testament contains four letters that Paul wrote from prison: Ephesians, Colossians, Philippians, and Philemon.**

### Introduction

A key to success in life is: "Keep God first." It is easy for us to get priorities out of order. We can forget what is most important. For Christians, **Jesus must be number one—always Lord, highest, foremost, and first in our lives.** Believers in the ancient city of Colosse were in danger of forgetting that. So Paul wrote Colossians to remind believers that Jesus is supreme—above all.

| Statements Emphasizing That Jesus Christ Is Supreme—Lord Over All | Colossians |
|---|---|
| He is the image of the invisible God. | 1:15 |
| He is the Creator—the One through whom all things in heaven and earth were made. | 1:16 |
| He is the Sustainer—the One before all things, and who holds all things together. | 1:17 |
| He is the Head of the body, the Church. | 1:18 |
| He is Number One—the beginning and the firstborn from the dead, so that in everything He might have the supremacy. | 1:18 |
| He is the Reconciler—the One who changed us from being God's enemies into being God's children. | 1:21-22 |
| He is the mystery of God—in whom are hidden all the treasures of wisdom and knowledge. | 2:3 |
| He is the God-man—the One in whom the fullness of the Deity lives in bodily form. | 2:9 |
| He is the Head over every power and authority. | 2:10 |
| He is the Deliverer—the One who cancelled the ceremonial regulations of the Mosaic code that was against us. | 2:14 |

**Figure 4.2   In Colossians, Paul emphasizes that Jesus Christ is Divine—Lord over all.**

Paul is saying: "Keep Jesus first!" In this chapter we will study all the characteristics of Jesus listed above.

## Lessons:

### Understanding Colossians

**Goal A:** *Analyze the authorship, date, city, purposes, theme, and outline of Colossians.*
**Goal B:** *Compare and contrast Colossians and Ephesians.*
**Goal C:** *Summarize 3 reasons why Paul gave thanks for the Colossians (Col. 1:1-8).*

### Paul's Thanksgiving and Prayer (Col. 1:1-14)

**Goal A:** *Identify the 2 things Paul asked God to do for the Colossians.*
**Goal B:** *Explain 4 ways Paul wanted the Colossians to please God.*

### Jesus Christ Is Supreme (Col. 1:15-23)

**Goal A:** *Summarize 6 errors of the Colossian heresy.*
**Goal B:** *Explain 4 ways Christ is Supreme as Creator (Col. 1:15-17).*
**Goal C:** *Analyze 4 ways Christ is Supreme as Reconciler (Col. 1:18-23). Apply these.*

### Following Jesus to Serve Others (Col. 1:24–2:5)

**Goal:** *Examine the cost, message, purpose, and power of spiritual ministry (Col. 1:24–2:5).*

### Four Keys to Making Heaven Our Home (Col. 2:6–3:4)

**Goal:** *Identify, illustrate, and apply 4 ways to overcome false teachings (Col. 2:6-23).*

**Prison Epistles**—the letters Paul wrote from prison: Ephesians, Colossians, Philippians, and Philemon

**Colosse**—the city in the old province of Asia (modern Turkey) where the Colossians lived

**Colossian heresy**—the false teaching at Colosse that was pulling Jesus down and lifting humans up

**Christology**—the study of Christ; beliefs about who Jesus Christ is

**firstborn**—first in order, importance, or position. As God, Christ is the firstborn over the creation He created; also, He is the firstborn from the dead—the first to permanently rise from and conquer death.

**Supreme**—at the top, above all others; number one. Christ is Supreme as Creator, far above all that has been created; and He is Supreme as Reconciler—the One who through His sacrifice brought God and humans together in peace.

**syncretism**—mixing good and bad beliefs of different religions into one

**Gnosticism**—a false teaching based on secret knowledge that some claimed was needed for salvation

---

**Lesson 18**

## Understanding Colossians

**Goal A:** *Analyze the authorship, date, city, purposes, theme, and outline of Colossians.*
**Goal B:** *Compare and contrast Colossians and Ephesians.*
**Goal C:** *Summarize 3 reasons why Paul gave thanks for the Colossians (Col. 1:1-8).*

### A. The background and setting of Colossians

**Author and date.** We are studying the four letters that Paul wrote from prison: Ephesians, Colossians, Philippians, and Philemon. Each of these four letters begins with Paul's name, showing that he is the author. Also, all four of these letters refer to Paul's chains or bonds (Col. 1:24; Eph. 3:1; 4:1; 6:20; Phil. 1:1-13; Philem. 1, 9-10). Most scholars believe that Paul wrote these letters from Rome. He probably wrote the four prison epistles about A.D. 60–61. His time in prison was difficult, but fruitful. In Rome, Paul was chained to a Roman soldier. He lived in a house he rented for 2 years, where he received visitors (Acts 28:30-31). This enabled him to hear reports from churches. As a result, he wrote letters to encourage, solve problems, teach, and guide believers. His ministry of prayer and evangelism continued in spite of his chains (Col. 1:3-14; Eph. 1:15-23; Phil. 1:3-6, 12-18; Philem. 4-6).

**Q 1** ⤳ *When did Paul write Colossians? Where was he?*

**Q 2** ⤳ *What was the population and location of Colosse?*

We have reviewed the authorship, date, and setting of the Prison Epistles. Now let us consider several key things about Paul's letter to the Colossians.

**The city of Colosse.** Both Ephesus and Colosse were cities in the old Roman province of Asia (modern Turkey). But unlike Ephesus, Colosse was a small city. It was located on the banks of the Lycus River—about 100 miles east of Ephesus. Cities nearby were Laodicea and Hierapolis.

**Q 3** ⤳ *Who started the church at Colosse? When?*

**The church at Colosse.** The church in Colosse probably began during the revival at Ephesus. Recall that Paul stayed in Ephesus 3 years. During this mighty work of the Holy Spirit, all of Asia heard the Word (Acts 18–19). Epaphras was from Colosse and planted the church there (Col. 1:7).

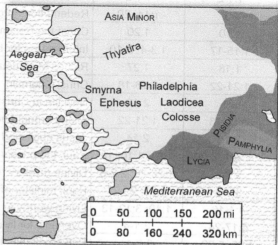

**Figure 4.3  Colosse was on the main business road between Rome and the East. Many people traveled the main road from Rome eastward. And some of these travelers brought false teaching to Colosse.**

The church at Colosse was mostly Gentiles, but had some Jewish influence.[1] Believers in Colosse were once far from God and were His *"enemies"* (Col. 1:21). In the past they were slaves of sexual sins, evil desires, lust, and greed (Col. 3:5-9). Before these people found Christ, they were dead in their sins—ruled by Satan and evil desires (Col. 2:13-15). Then, they believed in Christ. He freed and changed them by His power. When Paul wrote to the Colossian believers, they were growing as disciples—learning to follow Christ and to be like Him (Col. 2:6-7; 3:10).

The Colossian believers faced big challenges, but the church there was made up of godly people. Epaphras described them to Paul as people with faith, love, and hope. They had a good reputation, were evangelistic, firm in their faith, and orderly in their church life (Col. 1:1-8; 2:5). Although they needed some teaching, believers at Colosse deserved much praise.

Likewise today, there are no perfect churches. There are always areas in which every church needs to mature and improve. But the world is a better place because of the churches in it. We should seek to do better, but encourage ourselves for the things we are doing right.

## B. The relationship of Colossians to Ephesians

**Q 4** ➶ *Contrast the way Colossians and Ephesians refer to Christ and the Church.*

**Q 5** ➶ *What are 3 topics in both Colossians and Ephesians?*

Colossians is much like the letter to the Ephesians. But these two letters differ in the way they describe Christ and the Church. **Ephesians** emphasizes the Church, *His body* (Eph. 1:22-23). **Colossians** emphasizes Christ, the *"head of the body"* (Col. 1:18).

We may note three topics common to Colossians and Ephesians.

- Both letters teach about the relationship between Christ and His Church.
- Both letters describe the *"old man"* and the *"new man"* (Eph. 4:25–5:20; Col. 3:9-10).
- Both letters give instructions for the members of God's family (Eph. 5:22–6:9; Col. 3:18–4:1).

Though these letters are alike, they are also different. Ephesians emphasizes the nature of the Church and relationships in it. Colossians emphasizes the supremacy of Christ. Figure 4.4 summarizes similar verses in Colossians and Ephesians.

| Ephesians | Colossians | Topics |
|---|---|---|
| 1:1-2 | 1:1-2 | Introduction |
| 1:7 | 1:14, 20 | Redemption, forgiveness |
| 1:10 | 1:20 | Christ the Reconciler and Ruler over all |
| 1:15-17 | 1:3-4, 9-10 | Intercession for the readers |
| 1:18 | 1:27 | Riches of glorious inheritance |
| 1:21-22 | 1:16-18 | Christ's domain |
| 2:5 | 2:13 | New life in Christ |
| 2:12-13 | 1:21-22 | Aliens brought near |
| 2:15 | 2:14 | Jesus abolished the laws about priests, sacrifices, and outward purification |
| 3:1; 4:1; 6:20 | 1:24; 4:10, 18 | Paul, the prisoner |
| 3:2-3 | 1:25-26; 2:2-3 | Divine mystery revealed to Paul |
| 3:7-9 | 1:23, 25,27 | Paul, minister of the mystery—the gospel of Christ for all people |
| 4:1-16 | 1:10; 3:12-13 | Living worthy in all humility, meekness, patience, love, and unity |
| 4:17-24 | 3:1-4 | Overview for living a new way of life |
| 4:25–5:20 | 3:5-11 | Putting off the old self: lying, anger, stealing, impure speech, immorality |
| 4:25-5:20 | 3:12- 17; 4:2–6 | Putting on the new self, being renewed in God's image: truthfulness, self-control, kindness, compassion, patience, work, wholesome speech, love, forgiveness |
| 5:18-20 | 3:16-17 | Being filled with the Spirit and the Word—singing and giving thanks to God |
| 5:21-6:9 | 3:18-4:1 | Rules for relationships in God's family: husbands, wives, children, parents, slaves, masters |

Figure 4.4     Continued on next page

Continued from previous page

| 6:18-20 | 4:2-3 | Praying at all times |
| 6:21-22 | 4:7-8 | Receiving God's messengers (Tychicus) |

**Figure 4.4   Topics in Ephesians and Colossians**

## C. The purposes of Colossians

Paul received news about the Colossians from Epaphras (Col. 1:8). He wrote to them for two reasons.

**Q 6** ↖ *Summarize the 2 purposes of Colossians.*

- **Colossians emphasizes what to believe (Col. 1–2).** *First*, Paul wrote to correct false teachings about Christ (See Figure 4.5, on the Colossian Heresy). These dangerous teachings were pulling down Christ and lifting up rules and false religious experiences. Colossians emphasizes that Jesus Christ is Supreme—above all—our Creator, Savior, Redeemer, and Head of the Church. We must never follow any teaching that exalts experience or knowledge above Jesus.

- **Colossians emphasizes how to live (Col. 3–4).** *Second*, Paul wrote to emphasize the new life we must live in Christ. God's will is for us to take off the dirty clothes of our old, sinful ways—and put on the clean clothes of our new life in Christ (Col. 3:1-17). Likewise, God's will is for us to relate well to others in the home and at work (Col. 3:18–4:6).

Colossians reminds us *to believe* **in** Christ *above all*, and *to live* **for** Him *below*.

| Characteristics of the Colossian Heresy |
| --- |
| 1.  Salvation by _____ (Legalism) |
| 2.  Salvation by _____ (Asceticism) |
| 3.  Worshiping _____ |
| 4.  Lowering _____ |
| 5.  Salvation by _____ (A form of Gnosticism) |
| 6.  Salvation by _____ (Philosophy) |

**Figure 4.5   Practice identifying six aspects of the Colossian heresy.**

**Q 7** ↖ *Fill in the blanks in Figure 4.5 (If necessary, refer to Figure 4.16).*

## D. The theme of Colossians

To correct the false teachings at Colosse, Paul proclaims that <u>Jesus is above all—and is all we need</u>. The message of Colossians is: In the Christian experience, all there can be and all we need are in Christ.

**Q 8** ↗ *What does Paul emphasize to correct the Colossian Heresy?*

- We do not need Christ *and* a long list of rules that save us (legalism).

- We do not need Christ *and* denial of our body's needs—such as food, water, sleep, and shelter (asceticism).

- We do not need to approach God through angels, priests, or saints (using intermediaries).

- We do not need Christ *and* secret knowledge through spiritual experiences (Gnosticism).

- We do not need to understand Christ *and* worldly wisdom (philosophy).

Christ is enough! Christ is the answer! Christ is sufficient! Christ is supreme! Paul's message to the Colossians and to us is that the believers can find all they need in Christ!

*[15] He is the image of the invisible God, the firstborn over all creation. [16] For by him all things were created: things in heaven and on earth, visible and invisible, whether thrones or powers or rulers or authorities; all things were created by him and for him. [17] He is before all things, and in him all things hold together. [18] And he is the head of the body, the church; he is the beginning and the firstborn from among the dead, so that in everything he might have the supremacy* (Col. 1:15-18).

Jesus is above all, and He is all we need. This was Paul's answer to the false teachings at Colosse in the first century. And this must be the Church's message today! The *compass and the North Star help guide ships in the right direction. Likewise, Jesus Christ must be the center of our attention. We must lift up Jesus. He will keep us on track. He is our answer to error. He is the hope of the world and our key to victory! The key verse of Colossians is 1:18.

### E. Outline of Colossians

It is helpful to divide Colossians into two parts (Figure 4.6). Paul often followed a pattern in his letters. He wrote about doctrine first. That is, he wrote about the theological basis of our salvation. Then, in the second part of his letters, Paul liked to answer the question, "Now what?" Thus, in the second part of his letters, Paul applied theology to daily living. All good teaching connects the *what* with the *now what?* All good teaching and preaching applies theology and doctrine to daily living. Colossians is an example of how Paul talked about theology first and then applied it.

**Q 9** ➤ *Which chapters go with each of the two parts of Colossians?*

| Col. | Theme |
|------|-------|
| 1–2 | Powerful Doctrine: Our Supreme Savior |
| 3–4 | Practical Teaching: Guidelines for Holy Living |

**Figure 4.6**
**Colossians has a doctrinal part and a practical part.**

| Theme | Colossians |
|-------|-----------|
| **Introduction** | **1:1-14** |
| Greeting | 1:1-2 |
| Thanksgiving | 1:3-8 |
| Paul's prayer for believers | 1:9-14 |
| **A. Powerful Doctrine: Our *Supreme Savior** | **1:15–2:23** |
| The supremacy of Christ | 1:15-23 |
| Paul's work for the Church | 1:24–2:7 |
| Warnings against false teachers | 2:8-23 |
| **B. Practical Teaching: Guidelines for Holy Living** | **3:1–4:6** |
| The old self and the new self | 3:1-17 |
| Rules for the family of God | 3:18–4:1 |
| More teachings | 4:2-6 |
| Conclusion | 4:7-18 |

**Figure 4.7    Outline of Colossians**

### F. Paul's greeting and thanksgiving for the Colossians (Col. 1:1-8)

**Paul's greeting (Col. 1:1-2).**    Paul identifies himself as the author, and reminds his readers that he is an apostle of Christ. Also, he refers to Timothy, the pastor at Ephesus, as a brother (Col. 1:1). Then Paul turns from himself and Timothy to his readers (Col. 1:2). He draws attention to their life *in Christ*. Through the Savior, they have become holy and faithful.

**Q 10** ➤ *In which 2 places do you live?*

With the words *"in Christ"* and *"at Colosse"* Paul draws attention to *two places. At Colosse* reveals their physical location. *In Christ* describes their spiritual location. God called these believers to live the Christian life in two places at once! They lived in a Gentile city, where sinners surrounded them. But they daily drew life and power from Christ, their spiritual address.[2]

*In Christ,* all believers have *"grace and peace...from God our Father"* (Col. 1:2). Grace reminds us that we do not deserve the favor God has given us. Peace echoes the Hebrew greeting, *shalom*—a peace from God that includes wholeness and health.[3] *Grace* and *peace* remind us of the blessings we have *in Christ*. Outside of Christ, we were separated from God, and objects of His

**Figure 4.8**
**Paul probably wrote to the Colossians as a prisoner in Rome, the center of the Roman Empire. Rome was famous for its great buildings like the Colosseum, an outdoor stadium where Romans watched wild beasts kill believers.**

wrath. It is interesting that Paul opens his letter to the Ephesians with the greeting: *"Grace and peace to you from God our Father and the Lord Jesus Christ"* (Eph. 1:2). And Paul closes Ephesians with the words: *"Grace to all who love our Lord Jesus Christ with an undying love"* (Eph. 6:24). In Ephesians, Colossians, and all of his letters, Paul emphasizes that *grace* and *peace* we do not deserve are available to us as we abide in and submit to Jesus Christ as our Lord.

**Paul's thanksgiving (Col. 1:3-8).** Paul thanked God for the Colossians for three reasons.

**Reason 1: The gospel transforms lives—It produces faith, hope, and love (Col. 1:4-6a).**

Paul gives thanks that the gospel produces a famous trio of Christian virtues: *faith, hope,* and *love.* (Compare Rom. 5:1-5; 1 Cor. 13:13; Gal. 5:5-6; Eph. 1:15-18; 4:2-5; 1 Thess. 1:3; 5:8; Heb. 6:8-12; 10:22-24). Let us look more closely at these three important words.

**Faith** does not focus only on what you know—it focuses on Whom you know! Our faith is centered on Jesus Christ. He is the theme of Colossians and the focus of our faith. A person can know a lot and not have saving faith. James 2:19 explains that even demons believe that there is one God, and they tremble. Demons may know truth, but they are not saved. Knowing truth is not enough, and general faith is not enough. To be saved, a person must have *"faith in Christ Jesus"* (Col. 1:4). That is the kind of faith Colossian believers had, and it changed their lives. Those who have saving faith obey the teachings of Christ and the leading of His Spirit.

**Love** for all the saints is a result of receiving the gospel (Col. 1:4-5). Love is the greatest and highest Christian virtue or quality (1 Cor. 13). In Colossians 1:8, Paul explains that Christian love is love in the Spirit. In other words, the Holy Spirit is the source of our love. Galatians 5:22 mentions love as the firstfruit of the Spirit. In Colosse, false teachers called attention away from Christ—to themselves and their spiritual experiences. Paul said they had lost their connection with Christ, the Head (Col. 2:19). In contrast, the love that the Spirit produces exalts Christ, and this love from the Spirit seeks to strengthen and edify other saints.

**Hope** comes to us with faith and love. In Scripture, hope is not just a wish; it is a confidence, a trust—an expectation based on Jesus Christ. *"We have this hope as an anchor for the soul, firm and secure..."* (Heb. 6:19).

In the Bible, there are times when faith and hope refer to the same thing. Both can be a trust and confidence in God. At other times, hope is the result of faith. Because we have faith in God, we have the hope of Christ's return, and heaven. Paul states that our hope—the thing we expect—is already *stored up* for us *in heaven* (Col. 1:5).

Figure 4.9  As an anchor holds a boat during a storm, hope holds us steady during trials.

Those without God are without hope in the world (Eph. 2:12). People without hope are empty. They search to fill their lives with a reason to live. Those who are hopeless may then turn to alcohol or other drugs, crime, sexual sins, long hours of work, or pleasure. Some without hope commit suicide. But the gospel brings a message of hope beyond this life. People today often want to get something now and pay for it later. Christians are willing to pay now and receive it later. Paul said, *"I consider that our present sufferings are not worth comparing with the glory that will be revealed in us"* (Rom. 8:18). Missionary Jim Elliot put it this way, "He is no fool who gives what he cannot keep to keep what he cannot lose." Paul recognized the power of hope to inspire faith and love. The gospel brings hope!

**Q 11** ↖ *Which 3 things does the gospel bring to all who accept it?*

**Q 12** ↖ *How does saving faith differ from a belief in God?*

**Q 13** ↗ *What is a virtue?*

**Q 14** ↖ *How does love for the saints express itself?*

**Q 15** ↖ *How are faith and hope alike, yet different?*

**Q 16** Give an example of someone whose life has been changed by the gospel.

**Q 17** Summarize the gospel's effect on society, in spite of persecution.

Ram was known for bad language, drunkenness, and fighting. He wanted to be a part of every fight he saw. Ram had one defeat after another, including financial failures. Finally, he reached the end of himself. Someone shared the gospel with him, a message of forgiveness and hope through Christ. A great change began in his life. As his pastor, I saw Ram become a kind, tender husband and father. He developed a deep love for Jesus and a passion to reach the lost. Ram's story reminds me that the gospel changes lives. Into a life filled with sorrow, despair, anger, and hate, the gospel brings faith, hope, and love!

### Reason 2: You can put believers in prison, but the gospel still changes the world (Col. 1:6b)

Paul was in chains, but the gospel was free. The apostle Paul knew the gospel was like a seed that rooted and grew wherever it was planted. The Colossian church was proof. People heard the gospel and received its message. The result: people in Colosse were changed. They had received Christ as Savior, and God forgave their past sins. They discovered peace with God. They were learning to leave their old, sinful ways and to live holy lives. They were learning to avoid sexual sins, anger, slander, and revenge. In place of these evil actions, they were learning to be kind, patient, forgiving, tolerant, and holy. All of these changes began when they received the gospel of Jesus Christ. Paul rejoiced that the gospel was producing fruit in people, cities, and nations.

**Figure 4.10    You can chain a believer, but not the gospel**

### Reason 3: Faithful people share the gospel (Col. 1:7-8).

Paul gave thanks for Epaphras—the one who first brought the gospel to Colosse (Col. 1:7-8). Epaphras may have been a convert during Paul's ministry in Ephesus (Acts 19). He had lived in Colosse (Eph. 4:12-13). Some think he also planted churches in the cities of Laodicea and Hierapolis. Philemon 23 states that he became a prisoner with Paul. In Colossians 1:7-8, Paul honors Epaphras—calling him a *dear fellow-servant* and *faithful minister of Christ.*

**Q 18** In what way is Epaphras an encouraging example to all believers?

> GOD USES PEOPLE TO SPREAD THE GOSPEL.

God uses people to spread the gospel. Epaphras was a hometown man whom God used in Colosse. The gospel message is from heaven, but angels do not spread it. Nor does God preach the gospel with a voice that thunders from the crowds. Plain people tell this great message from God. Common people, who struggle with fears and faults, share the good news about Jesus Christ. Likewise, God uses imperfect churches. Some of these churches are torn by division and false doctrine. Still, God uses plain people and churches to tell His message to a community. The New Testament is filled with examples—Colosse, Corinth, Galatia, and others. May each of us remember that God wants to use us like He did Epaphras, a plain man who took the gospel to Colosse. God wants you and me to be remembered as His faithful messengers—plain people who told someone about Jesus.

**Q 19** What principle does the story about Edward Kimball illustrate?

Edward Kimball sold shoes and taught a Sunday School class. He was faithful to teach God's Word. He loved boys and spent hours of his free time visiting orphans in the poor parts of his city. One day Kimball placed his hand on the shoulder of a young man named D. L. Moody, and led him to Christ. Later, Moody became a preacher and led another young man, F. B. Meyer, to Christ. Meyer became a famous preacher. He won young J. W. Chapman to the Lord, and he became a fruitful preacher of the gospel. Chapman was the preacher who brought the message of Christ to Billy Sunday, who became an evangelist. Sunday led thousands to Christ, including Mordecai Ham. Ham shared the gospel with a man named Billy Graham, who responded to the gospel. And much of the world has heard the gospel through the preaching of Billy Graham. Person to person this message of the gospel spreads and grows. Be one of those who faithfully share it with others![4]

## Lesson 19 — Paul's Thanksgiving and Prayer (Col. 1:9-14)

**Goal A:** *Identify the 2 things Paul asked God to do for the Colossians.*
**Goal B:** *Explain 4 ways Paul wanted the Colossians to please God.*

[9]*For this reason, since the day we heard about you, we have not stopped praying for you...* (Col. 1:9).

In Colossians 1:9, the words *for this reason* refer back to the good report Paul received from Epaphras (Col. 1:3-8). *After* hearing about new believers, Paul *prayed* for them. Godly leaders care about the spiritual health of believers everywhere. How should we pray for other believers? **Paul's prayer is a model for us.** He prayed often and he prayed with great concern. Let us study two principles in Paul's prayer for the Colossians.

**Q 20** *Why did Paul keep praying for the Colossians (Col. 1:9)?*

### A. We should pray for believers to KNOW God's will (Col. 1:9).

*For this reason, since the day we heard about you, we have not stopped praying for you and **asking God to fill you with the knowledge of his will** through all spiritual wisdom and understanding* (Col. 1:9).

False teachers at Colosse claimed that they had secret knowledge about salvation. Paul emphasized to the Colossians that they were *already* saved. Now that they were saved, Paul wanted the Colossians to be filled *"with the knowledge of his will"* (Col. 1:9b). Colossians is a book about knowing the will of God. Look again at the outline of Colossians (Figure 4.7). Looking at the whole letter to the Colossians, we see that God's *general* will includes four things.

**Q 21** *What are 4 things that Colossians shows to be the general will of God?*

**Q 22** *What is the difference between the general and specific will of God? Explain.*

| Colossians | God's Will for All Believers |
|---|---|
| 1:15–2:7 | It is God's will for us to exalt Christ above self and all others. |
| 2:8-23 | It is God's will for us to reject false teachers and their teachings. |
| 3:1-17 | It is God's will for us to take off the dirty clothes of the flesh, and put on the new clothes of the Spirit. |
| 3:18–4:6 | It is God's will for us to relate well to others at home, at work, and in society. |

**Figure 4.11 Colossians emphasizes four aspects of God's will for all believers.**

Paul introduces the will of God in his prayer of Colossians 1:9. He will help answer his own prayer by explaining to the Colossians how to fulfill the will of God.

**Application.** Sincere Christians sometimes gaze into the future, straining to see God's will. But the will of God is not hard to find. To find God's will, we do not need to climb a mountain or cross the sea. Each of us finds the will of God as we exalt, obey, and follow Jesus. His Spirit leads us to live holy lives. He guides us to be kind and courteous to others. As we do these plain things that are His *general* will, it is easy for Him to guide us in *specific* ways. *Sabio* says: "God's will is not for us to *see* mysteries that are far away, but to *do* the good that is close at hand."

**Q 23** *What is the key to knowing the specific will of God?*

Professor Kessler and his wife were teachers with a powerful influence at a Bible school. Several students lived nearby. Many mornings, when the students woke up, they heard the voices of the Kesslers praying. They asked God to help students know and fulfill God's will for their lives. These teachers not only talked about prayer—they prayed!

**Q 24** *How long has it been since you prayed for another believer to know God's will? Explain.*

### B. We should pray that believers DO God's will (Col. 1:10-14).

Paul prayed for believers to know God's will—**so they would do it!** Knowing is a step in the right direction, but it is not far enough. As Jesus said, *"Now that you know these things, you will be blessed **if you do them**"* (John 13:17). Socrates taught: "Know yourself." But Jesus taught: "Behave yourself!"

**Q 25** ⬉ *Why did Paul want believers to know God's will?*

**Q 26** ⬉ *Explain: Christianity is not just an **intersection**—it is a **way** of life.*

**Q 27** ⬉ *Complete Figure 4.13 on living to please God*

<sup>9</sup>*For this reason, since the day we heard about you, we have not stopped praying for you and asking God to fill you with the knowledge of his will through all spiritual wisdom and understanding.* <sup>10</sup>*And we pray this **in order that you may live a life worthy of the Lord and may please him in every way**...* (Col. 1:9-10a).

**Figure 4.12**
**Hundreds of people walked on the Egnatian Way that began in Rome and passed through Colosse. Likewise, millions of people walk with Jesus, the Way to heaven.**

Paul wrote often about walking and living for Jesus (Figure 4.13). He taught believers in many places that they should live to please God. All of the verses in Figure 4.13 use a form of the Greek verb *peripateo—to walk around*. Christianity is not just an *intersection* where we meet Jesus—it is a *way* of life to walk.

| Bible | Verses in the Prison Epistles About Living to Please God |
|---|---|
| Eph. 2:10 | |
| Eph. 4:1 | |
| Eph. 5:2 | |
| Eph. 5:15 | |
| Col. 2:6 | |
| Col. 3:1-3 | |
| Col. 3:7 | |
| Phil. 3:17 | |

**Figure 4.13    Practice summarizing verses in the Prison Epistles about living to please God.**

As true followers of Christ, we desire to honor and please God in every part of our lives. Trials and temptations come to all of us. Whatever comes, we seek to honor Christ. Paul's advice to slaves is good for all of us:

<sup>23</sup>***Whatever you do**, work at it with all your heart, as working for the Lord, not for men,* <sup>24</sup>*since you know that you will receive an inheritance from the Lord as a reward. It is the Lord Christ you are serving.* <sup>25</sup>*Anyone who does wrong will be repaid for his wrong, and there is no favoritism* (Col. 3:23-25).

Paul was a good model for believers. He lived to exalt Christ in his body *"whether by life or by death"* (Phil. 1:20). Believers face all kinds of pressures and temptations. So let us pray that God will empower them to honor and glorify Him. In Colossians 1:10b-14, Paul prays for believers to please the Lord in **four specific ways**.

**Q 28** ⬉ *What are some of God's favorite fruits?*

**1. Let us please God by bearing fruit (Col. 1:10b).**

*And we pray this in order that you may live a life worthy of the Lord and may please him in every way: **bearing fruit in every good work**, ...* (Col. 1:10).

In Greek, *bearing fruit* is in the present tense. This emphasizes that God wants us to bear fruit at all times.

It is helpful to think of inner fruit and outer fruit—what we are and what we do.

**Q 29** ⬉ *Explain the difference between a believer's inner and outer fruit.*

*Inner fruit* is what we allow God to make us on the inside. God wants us to bear the fruit of character that is like Christ. Paul wrote to the Galatians about bearing inner fruit.

²²*But the fruit of the Spirit is love, joy, peace, patience, kindness, goodness, faithfulness,* ²³*gentleness and self-control. Against such things there is no law* (Gal. 5:22-23).

By the Spirit, we can bear wonderful inner fruit in our lives. Think about how much we like fruit such as bananas, apples, oranges, mangoes, pineapples, dates, and grapes. Fruit pleases us! Likewise, we please God when we bear the fruit of Galatians 5:22-23. Whenever you eat a piece of fruit, give thanks for it. Then pray that God will enable **you and others to bear fruit that pleases Him**. For whatever *inner fruit* we have soon shows through on the outside.

**Q 30** ↖ *Which 7 inner fruits or qualities does Peter say we must add (2 Pet. 1:5-7)? Why (2 Pet. 1:8)?*

*Outer fruit* refers to the good deeds we do for God and others. Paul often reminds us that the fruit of our good works pleases God.

**Q 31** ↖ *Complete Figure 4.14 on the fruit of good works that pleases God.*

| Reference | Verses About the Fruit of Good Works That Pleases God |
|---|---|
| Eph. 2:10 | |
| Titus 1:16 | |
| Titus 2:7 | |
| Titus 2:14 | |
| Titus 3:8 | |

Figure 4.14   God expects believers to produce fruit.

Bearing good fruit is part of walking worthy and pleasing God. Good fruit glorifies God, and attracts the lost to become members of our Father's family.

**Q 32** ↗ *What is the key to bearing fruit to please God?*

No branch can bear fruit alone (John 15:4). But as we abide in Christ, the Holy Spirit bears fruit through us (Gal. 5:22-23). Fruit trees produce fruit because of their character—they are fruit trees! Likewise, true Christians bear fruit because we are the children of God. In our world there are many spiritual enemies. Among these enemies are the cares of the world, the love of money, the lust of the flesh and the eyes, and the love of the world. Spiritual enemies cause people to be barren—to bear no fruit. Pray today that Christians around the world will respond to the Father—the One who trims the vine to get *fruit, more fruit, and much fruit* (John 15:1-5).

Figure 4.15   God desires fruit, more fruit, and much fruit.

## 2. Let us please God by growing in knowledge (Col. 1:10).

Paul was not satisfied with new birth alone. He knew that healthy children must grow in knowledge two ways. We grow in knowledge as we learn **about God**—understanding His qualities or attributes. God is Spirit, infinite, eternal, and sovereign. He is unchangeable in His being, wisdom, power, holiness, righteousness, sinlessness, love, goodness, grace, truth, faithfulness, justice, and wrath.[5] Much of Colossians emphasizes knowledge about Christ—the Supreme Lord over all (Review Figure 4.2).

**Q 33** ↖ *Explain: Paul was not satisfied with new birth alone.*

We also grow in knowledge as we get to *know* God better. This is not just head knowledge about God, but personal, heart knowledge—a relationship **with God**. We should grow in our relationship with the Lord day by day! In the physical, children who stop growing have a big problem. Polio or other diseases cause some children to stop growing. Often, those who stop growing die. Likewise, a lack of spiritual growth is a sign of disease or danger. In Ephesians, Paul emphasized growing up into the full measure of Christ (Eph. 1:17-23; 3:14-19; 4:11-16). And in Colossians, Paul emphasized growing in knowledge *about* God, and *with* God (Col. 1:10). Elsewhere, Scripture contrasts growing in grace with falling from grace (2 Pet. 1:5-11; 3:17-18). So let us seek to grow

**Q 34** ↖ *How does knowing God better go beyond mere head knowledge?*

in knowing God—in His likeness of holiness and righteousness (Eph. 4:24); in being renewed in knowledge in the image of our Creator (Col. 3:10; Rom. 8:31; 2 Cor. 3:18); and in our relationship with Him as our Father. The great promise of the Bible is God giving Himself to His people—to be their God and transform them into His likeness, as His children. Let us revel in this privilege. For knowing God is our greatest inheritance.

> LET US SAY WITH PAUL:     *"I CONSIDER EVERYTHING A LOSS COMPARED TO THE SURPASSING GREATNESS OF KNOWING CHRIST JESUS MY LORD, FOR WHOSE SAKE I HAVE LOST ALL THINGS."*

Let us say with Paul:

*⁷But whatever was to my profit I now consider loss for the sake of Christ. ⁸What is more, **I consider everything a loss compared to the surpassing greatness of knowing Christ Jesus my Lord,** for whose sake I have lost all things. I consider them rubbish, that I may gain Christ ⁹and be found in him, not having a righteousness of my own that comes from the law, but that which is through faith in Christ—the righteousness that comes from God and is by faith. ¹⁰**I want to know Christ** and the power of his resurrection and the fellowship of sharing in his sufferings, becoming like him in his death, ¹¹and so, somehow, to attain to the resurrection from the dead* (Phil. 3:7-11).

**Q 35** *Do believers in your country need your prayers for strength? Explain.*

### 3. Let us please God by growing stronger in endurance and patience (Col. 1:11).

*" ¹¹Being strengthened with all power according to his glorious might **so that** you may have great endurance and patience"* (Col. 1:11). Growing strong in endurance and patience is not a luxury, but a necessity. Only those who endure to the end will be saved (Matt. 24:14). We are in the middle of a war for our souls. Paul ends Ephesians with a blessing of grace and peace *for those who do not give up*—but continue to love Christ with an undying love (Eph. 6:24). Early in his letter to the Colossians, Paul reminds believers that we are saved—reconciled to God through Christ: *" ²³if you continue in your faith, established and firm, not moved from the hope held out in the gospel"* (Col. 1:23). Paul warns of the danger of being in the body of Christ, and then being separated. The apostle warns that such a person *has lost connection with the Head* (Col. 2:19). Some teach "once saved, always saved." But we cannot lose a connection we never had! So it is important to grow stronger, not weaker; and go forward, not backward. Paul warns that many Israelites lost their inheritance through unbelief, sexual sins, and grumbling. He warns us to be careful so we do not fall (1 Cor. 10:1-12). Likewise, Jude warns that God delivered the Israelites from bondage, and later destroyed them because of their unbelief that expressed itself as disobedience. And God did not spare the angels who sinned, but has bound them in chains where they await everlasting judgment (Jude 1:3-6). Endurance in the faith is essential. Paul prays with fervor and writes with passion so believers will become stronger, and endure to the end. False teachers at Colosse were trying to lead believers to be disqualified from the prize, like a runner disqualified from a race (Col. 2:16-19). So Paul prayed that believers would be *"strengthened with all power according to his glorious might **so that** they and we may have great endurance and patience"* (Col. 1:11).

> THIS YEAR, THERE WILL BE **160,000** BELIEVERS WHO DIE FOR THEIR FAITH.⁶

Colossians 2 reveals that these believers were under attack by criticism and seduction. In their past, they were in the kingdom of darkness (Col. 1:13). Jesus had rescued them. But the devil seeks to bring people back into his kingdom. Believers are free, but we are in a spiritual warfare (Eph. 6:10-18). Like the Colossians, we must depend on God's power to stand *with great endurance and patience!*

Christians in many parts of the world face great pressure and persecution. This year, there will be 160,000 believers who die for their faith.[7] Temptations, testing, and trials of all kinds come from many sources. Our great enemy, Satan, fights against us. He uses all of his forces and resources to discourage the disciples of Jesus. The devil wants to make Christians weak and put out their light in the world. He goes about as a roaring lion seeking to devour laymen and leaders (1 Pet. 5:8). We must pray that Christians everywhere are *"strengthened with all power so that they may have great endurance and patience"* (Col. 1:11).

**Q 36** ↖ *Where in the world do believers need our prayers the most? Explain.*

### 4. Let us please God by showing we are thankful (Col. 1:12-14).

*12Giving thanks to the Father, who has **qualified you** to share in the inheritance of the saints in the kingdom of light. 13For he has **rescued us** from the dominion of darkness, and **brought us** into the kingdom of the Son he loves, 14in whom we have **redemption**, the **forgiveness** of sins* (Col. 1:12-14).

**Q 37** ↗ *What are some reasons Paul gave for giving thanks?*

False teachers at Colosse wanted to disqualify believers by leading them away from Christ and the gospel. Paul lists the blessings God gives to believers.

♥ The Father has *qualified us* to share in the inheritance of the saints.

♥ He has *rescued us from* the kingdom of darkness, to the kingdom of light.

♥ He has *brought us into* the kingdom of the Son he loves.

♥ He has *redeemed us*—bought us with a price.

♥ He has *forgiven* our sins.

These are enough reasons for the Colossians and for us to give thanks!

We parents do much for our children, and we do not like to hear them grumble and complain. In contrast, it pleases us when our children say "thank you" for the sacrifices we make. Likewise, it pleases our Heavenly Father when we give thanks. So let us thank Him, and pray with Paul that other believers will give thanks. *" 6So then, just as you received Christ Jesus as Lord, continue to live in him, 7rooted and built up in him, strengthened in the faith as you were taught, and **overflowing with thankfulness**"* (Col. 2:6-7).

**Conclusion:**   Colossians 1:9-14 gives us a pattern to pray for others. It teaches us how to intercede for those we know and those we have never met—missionaries, pastors, evangelists, and other believers all over the world. There are sincere, faithful servants of the Lord facing great trials today—trials greater than we can imagine. Using Paul's prayer as a guide, we should pray for believers, so that …

**Q 38** ↖ *Summarize 4 ways that all believers should please God.*

• They fully understand God's will for their lives (Col. 1:9b).

• They honor and please the Lord in four ways (Col. 1:10):

  • bearing good fruit (Col. 1:10b);

  • growing to know God better (Col. 1:10c);

  • strengthened to stand firm under pressure (Col. 1:11);

  • overflowing with thanks (Col. 1:12-14).

---

### Lesson 20 — Jesus Christ Is Supreme (Col. 1:15-23)

**Goal A:** *Summarize 6 errors of the Colossian heresy.*
**Goal B:** *Explain 4 ways Christ is Supreme as Creator (Col. 1:15-17).*
**Goal C:** *Analyze 4 ways Christ is Supreme as Reconciler (Col. 1:18-23). Apply these.*

In Colossians 1:15–2:23, Paul emphasizes that Jesus Christ is Supreme. Paul wrote to the Colossians several teachings about Jesus Christ that we do not find in his other letters. Why did the Holy Spirit lead Paul to emphasize these truths about Christ to the Colossians? Which false teachings was Paul trying to refute? To identify the false teachings at Colosse, we must look behind the statements Paul wrote the Colossians about Jesus. So let us take a few minutes to analyze the Colossian heresy.

**Q 39** ↖ *Why do you think Paul emphasized that Jesus is Supreme?*

**Q 40** ⬉ *Summarize 6 errors of the Colossian heresy.*

**The Problem: The \*Colossian heresy.** The false teachings at Colosse were an example of \*syncretism—mixing good and bad beliefs. Mixing truth with error is the most dangerous kind of teaching. If a food is completely spoiled, it will smell bad and people will not eat it. Likewise, when a teaching is all bad, people avoid it. But a little poison mixed into good food will kill people. And false teachings mixed with truth lead many astray. Figure 4.16 summarizes the main false teachings that some call *the \*Colossian heresy.* Please study the six characteristics of false teachings at Colosse. Then you will fully appreciate the way Paul exalts Jesus Christ above the false teachings.

**Q 41** ⬉ *Which parts of the Colossian heresy are a problem today? Explain.*

| Characteristic | Explanation | Colossians |
|---|---|---|
| 1. Salvation by **RULES** (Legalism) | These strict rules were about salvation through diet, religious feasts, and circumcision. These rules had deep roots in Jewish traditions.<br>*Therefore do not let anyone judge you by what you eat or drink, or with regard to a religious festival, a New Moon celebration or a Sabbath day* (Col. 2:16). | 2:4, 8, 11, 16-17, 20; 3:11 |
| 2. Salvation by **SELF-DENIAL** (Asceticism) | Christ taught us to deny ourselves in some areas. But the false teachers at Colosse denied the body in ways that had no spiritual value. They treated the body harshly, denying its needs with rules such as *"Do not handle! Do not taste! Do not touch!"* | 2:20-21, 23 |
| 3. Worshiping **ANGELS** | Some taught that we should approach God through angels, rather than Jesus. These false teachers, like some today, taught that God is too far above us or too harsh to approach directly. | 2:18-19 |
| 4. Lowering **CHRIST** | The false teachers pulled Jesus down. In His place they put themselves, angels, and human rules. This is the main reason Paul emphasized the theme of Colossians—*Jesus is above all.* Review the Introduction that opens this chapter. | 1:15-20; 2:2-3, 9 |
| 5. Salvation by **SECRET KNOWLEDGE** (A form of Gnosticism) | Some of these false teachers were *Gnostics,* based on the Greek word that means "knowledge." Teachers of \*Gnosticism claimed they had *secret knowledge* needed for salvation. In contrast, Paul emphasized that Jesus is ALL we need for salvation. For in Christ *"are hidden all the* (secret) *treasures of wisdom and knowledge."* | 2:2-4, 18 |
| 6. Salvation by **HUMAN WISDOM** (Philosophy) | Paul warns the Colossian believers not to be *"deceived by fine-sounding arguments"* or taken *"captive through hollow and deceptive philosophy."* The Greek word *philosophy* means "love of wisdom." Paul contrasts human and divine wisdom. He says the false wisdom and teachings at Colosse *"are based on human commands and teaching!"* But in Christ *"are hidden all the treasures of **wisdom and knowledge."*** | 2:3-8, 22 |

**Figure 4.16    Main characteristics of the Colossian heresy**

The Colossian heresy was a mixture of false teachings, including extreme Jewish legalism; and an early form of Gnosticism that claimed secret knowledge from religious experiences. Figure 4.16 compares the six main teachings of the Gnostics with verses in Colossians.

**Q 42** ⬉ *Concerning the Colossian heresy, answer the questions in the middle column of Figure 4.17.*

| Characteristic | Questions to Answer | Reference |
|---|---|---|
| 1. Salvation by **RULES** (Legalism) | What is the role of obeying God's commands or rules? | Eph. 2:1-3; 4:17–5:20; Col. 1:10, 21 |
| 2. Salvation by **SELF-DENIAL** (Asceticism) | What did Paul mean when he said, *"I make my body my slave?"* | 1 Cor. 9:24–10:8 |
| 3. Worshiping **ANGELS** | Why is it wrong to worship angels, or pray to priests and saints? | Col. 2:18-19 |
| 4. Lowering **CHRIST** | How do teachings such as purgatory or salvation through our good deeds pull down Christ? | Col. 1:15-20; 2:2-3, 9 |

Figure 4.17    Continued on next page

Continued from previous page

| 5. Salvation by **SECRET KNOWLEDGE** (A form of Gnosticism) | What is the role of spiritual knowledge in Christianity? | Eph. 1:17-19; Col. 1:9-10 |
|---|---|---|
| 6. Salvation by **HUMAN WISDOM** (Philosophy) | Is it possible to follow Christ and appreciate some human wisdom? Explain a biblical attitude toward human wisdom. | Col. 2:3-8, 22; 1 Cor. 1:20-25 |

**Figure 4.17    Practice answering questions about the Colossian heresy—the false teachings at Colosse.**

In ancient times, sailors sailed across seas at night by focusing on key stars in the heavens. Otherwise, a ship and all the people on it could be lost. In Colossians 1:15-23 Paul emphasizes that we must fix our eyes on Jesus Christ, and who He is, so that we will safely reach heaven. Paul was concerned about the spiritual safety of believers at Colosse. They were in danger of being deceived and led astray.

We have looked at six aspects of the false teaching at Colosse. Now we are ready to appreciate what Paul says about Jesus to refute the false teachings. Colossians 1:15-20 may be part of an old hymn that believers sang when Paul was an apostle. We will study these verses in two parts: A. Jesus Christ is Supreme as Creator (Col. 1:15-17); and B. Jesus Christ is Supreme as Reconciler (Col. 1:18-23).

**Q 43** *What are the 2 parts of "Christ is Supreme" (Col. 1:15-20)?*

## A. Jesus Christ is Supreme as Creator (Col. 1:15-17).

*15 He is the image of the invisible God, the firstborn over all creation. 16 For by him all things were created: things in heaven and on earth, visible and invisible, whether thrones or powers or rulers or authorities; all things were created by him and for him. 17 He is before all things, and in him all things hold together* (Col. 1:15-17).

In Colossians 1:15-17 Paul emphasizes that Jesus Christ is the Creator of all things. As the Creator, Paul mentions several truths about Christ.

### 1. Christ is the image of the invisible God (Col. 1:15).

Paul is saying that Jesus Christ is the visible image of the God who created heaven and earth (Gen. 1:1). False teachers were saying that Jesus was only a man. So Paul emphasizes that Jesus is the God-man, the eternal Son of God who became flesh and lived among us. This truth is so important that Paul emphasizes it three times in Colossians. After Colossians 1:15 Paul writes: *"For God was pleased to have all his fullness dwell in him."* (Col. 1:19) Again Paul wrote: *"For in Christ all the fullness of the Deity lives in bodily form"* (Col. 2:9). *This threefold emphasis of the deity of Christ shows us that false teachers in Colosse were trying to pull Christ down from the throne of God upon which He sits.*

**Q 44** *What is Paul's point in Colossians 1:15 and 2:9? What were the false teachers saying about Christ?*

In another letter from prison, Paul again emphasizes that Jesus Christ was God in the flesh. Paul writes:

*5 Your attitude should be the same as that of Christ Jesus: 6 **Who, being in very nature God,** did not consider equality with God something to be grasped, 7 but made himself nothing, **taking the very nature of a servant, being made in human likeness.** 8 And being found in appearance as a man, he humbled himself and became obedient to death—even death on a cross! 9 Therefore God exalted him to the highest place and gave him the name that is above every name, 10 that at the name of Jesus every knee should bow, in heaven and on earth and under the earth, 11 and every tongue confess that Jesus Christ is Lord, to the glory of God the Father* (Phil. 2:5-11).

Paul makes it very clear that as the Creator of the universe, Jesus Christ was God in human flesh. Perhaps the apostle John was correcting the same type of false teachings that Paul faced at Colosse. John wrote:

*¹In the beginning was the Word, and the Word was with God, and the Word was God. ²He was with God in the beginning. ³Through him all things were made; without him nothing was made that has been made* (John 1:1-3).

*¹⁴The Word became flesh and made his dwelling among us* (John 1:14).

Jesus Christ, the Creator of all, is the image of the invisible God. We cannot see God, for He is Spirit. And as Spirit, like the wind, God is invisible (Col. 1:15; 1 Tim. 1:17). But God wanted us to know Him in a personal way. So He sent His Son, Jesus Christ, to show us exactly what God the Father is like. And even more important, God sent His Son to reconcile us through His death on the cross.

**Q 45** ✎ *Complete Figure 4.18 on verses stating that Jesus shows us what the Father is like.*

| Reference | Your Summaries of Verses Stating That Jesus Reveals the Father to Us |
|---|---|
| John 1:18 | |
| John 14:9 | |
| Col. 1:15 | |
| Col. 1:19 | |
| Col. 2:9 | |
| 2 Cor. 4:4 | |

**Figure 4.18    Practice summarizing verses that show us Jesus Christ reveals God the Father to us.**

**Q 46** ➚ *If Christ is eternal, why is He called the firstborn?*

**Q 47** ✎ *Besides comparing Christ as the firstborn, what other metaphors does Paul use?*

### 2. Christ is *firstborn over all creation (Col. 1:15).

The *firstborn* son had a special place of honor—especially in a Jewish family. The firstborn son received a unique blessing from his father. Recall that Jacob coveted this blessing so much that he bought it from his older brother Esau with a bowl of soup; and then Jacob conspired with his mother, Rebekah, to deceive his father, Isaac, into giving the blessing to the second born son (Gen. 27:1–28:9). Paul uses figurative language, comparing Jesus to the firstborn son over all creation. The members of the Trinity were never born. The Father, Son, and Spirit are eternal. Christ is before all things (Col. 1:17; John 1:1-2; 8:58). Paul uses this metaphor of *Jesus as firstborn over all creation* to show that Jesus is exalted above all creation—as a firstborn human son was higher than other sons. Paul's writing contains many metaphors, such as calling Jesus "the firstborn" and "the head of the body"; and comparing believers to "a bride," apostles to "a foundation," believers to "a stone temple," and Christ to "a cornerstone" (Col. 1:15, 18; Eph. 2:20-21). Twice, Paul emphasizes that Christ is God in flesh. (Col. 1:15; 2:9). And as the firstborn son, Christ has a higher place than other sons. Jesus has a place above all others *because* He created everything (Col. 1:16). Let us recognize that Scripture often uses figurative language to describe God in human terms to which we can understand and relate. And let us discern that Paul compares Christ to a firstborn son, *not* because Christ was born *before* the rest of creation, but to show that He is above all others.

**Q 48** ✎ *Do you treat Jesus Christ with the respect He deserves as God above all creation? Explain.*

**Q 49** ➚ *Into which two groups can we put all things? Which one is Christ in?*

### 3. Christ is the Creator of all that has been created (Col. 1:15-17).

*¹⁵He is the image of the invisible God, the firstborn over all creation. ¹⁶For by him all things were created: things in heaven and on earth, visible and invisible, whether thrones or powers or rulers or authorities; all things were created by him and for him. ¹⁷He is before all things...* (Col. 1:15-17).

False teachers at Colosse were exalting themselves and angels. But Paul emphasizes that Christ is the Creator of all things—including humans and angels. The Father, Son, and Spirit worked together to create everything that has been created.

Paul proclaims that Christ is over all creation, and that all things came by Him and are for Him (Col. 1:15-16). This reminds us of Paul's glorious statement in Romans, where he says about God: *"For from him and through him and to him are all things"* (Rom. 11:36). The writings of Paul remind us to send our praise all the way to the top, to God, the source and sustainer of all creation.

**The Creator**

God the Father, Son, and Holy Spirit

**The Created**

Angels, humans, and all other created things

B. Actions (Doing)

C. Condition (Being)

The **HOLINESS** of God

**A. Position**

Figure 4.20 There are three aspects or sides of God's holiness. God is holy in position, in actions, and in condition (essence).

**Figure 4.19** Paul and other biblical writers divide everything that exists into two groups: the Creator and the created (Gen. 1:1; John 1:1-3; Col. 1:15-17; Acts 17:24-31; Rom. 1:25).

**Q 50** *In what way do some false teachers attack the holiness of Christ?*

**Q 51** *What do we mean, saying: "God is holy in His position"?*

False teachers attack the holiness of Jesus Christ. God is holy in three ways: in His position, actions, and being. Like the Father and the Spirit, God the Son is holy in His position. Holy is the opposite of common. We say that God is holy in position because He is high above all else. He is holy because there is none like Him. In His position, God is holy—divine, supreme, exalted, glorious above all of creation. God's holiness is His might that makes people tremble and nations dread (Exod. 15:11-18; 1 Sam. 6:20; Ps. 68:35; Rev. 6:15-17). In His position above all, God is holy, for He alone is God (Rev. 15:4)! Anyone who tries to put Jesus Christ in the circle of created things is insulting and attacking the holiness of God. He is the Creator of all things.

**4. Christ is the Sustainer of all things (Col. 1:17).**

He is before all things, and in Him *"all things hold together"* (Col. 1:15-17). Paul has been emphasizing that Jesus is Supreme as Creator (Col. 1:15-17). This is a great thought, but it looks far into the past. God did not just create the universe and then abandon it. He is not like a person who made a computer or a phone, and then did not provide any service. So as Paul is leaving the thought that Christ created all, he adds a thought that makes Jesus Christ personal and present. Christ is the Sustainer of all things. Christ is the One who holds all things together. Without His power, love, and care, everything would fall apart! Give thanks to the Lord for His love, care, and faithfulness. We are weak, but He is strong. Because of Jesus Christ, evil nations do not conquer the earth. Because of God's goodness and power, the forces of evil do not destroy the righteous. Because of Christ, the sun comes up every morning and the waves of the sea do not cover the land. Because Christ rules over the universe, we can face today and tomorrow with confidence. His presence sustains us. Because Christ empowers and protects His people, we can endure and reign with Him.

The psalmist glorifies God for taking care of His creation.

**Q 52** *How does Christ's role as Sustainer relate to His role as Creator?*

**Q 53** *What are some things Christ does as Sustainer of Creation?*

¹⁵*The eyes of all look to you, and you give them their food at the proper time.* ¹⁶*You open your hand and satisfy the desires of every living thing.* ¹⁷*The LORD is righteous in all his ways and loving toward all he has made.* ¹⁸*The LORD is near to all who call on him, to all who call on him in truth.* ¹⁹*He fulfills the desires of those who fear him; he hears their cry and saves them.* ²⁰*The LORD watches over all who love him, but all the wicked he will destroy* (Ps. 145:15-20).

**Q 54** *Why does Psalm 145 glorify God? What does He do?*

**B. Jesus Christ is Supreme as Reconciler (Col. 1:18-23).**

We have divided this lesson into two parts. In Part A, we stressed that Jesus Christ is Supreme as Creator (Col. 1:15-17). Here in Part B, our theme is that Christ is Supreme

**Q 55** *How does the theme of Colossians 1:18-20 difffer from Colossians 1:15-17?*

as Reconciler—the One who made peace between God and His creation. Christ's cosmic role in creation is now matched with His cosmic role in reconciliation.

> [18] *And he is the head of the body, the church; he is the beginning and the firstborn from among the dead, so that in everything he might have the supremacy.* [19] *For God was pleased to have all his fullness dwell in him,* [20] **and through him to reconcile to himself all things, whether things on earth or things in heaven, by making peace through his blood, shed on the cross** (Col. 1:18-20).

As we read Colossians 1:18-20, we see a great shift in the truth about Christ. The emphasis has changed from His role in creation, to His role in reconciliation. As in Part A, Paul makes several statements about Christ using the poetry of an ancient hymn. Scholars have suggested various *chiasms—a Greek word used to describe forms of parallel thoughts. Let us look at some parallel statements between Christ as Creator and Reconciler (Figure 4.21).

| Col. | Christ, Supreme as Creator | Christ, Supreme as Reconciler | Col. |
|------|---------------------------|-------------------------------|------|
| 1:15 | He is the image of the invisible God. | He is the Head of the body, the (visible and invisible) Church. | 1:18 |
| 1:15 | He is the Firstborn over all creation. | He is the Firstborn from among the dead. | 1:18 |
| 1:16 | He is the Creator of all things in heaven and on earth. | He is the Reconciler of all things on earth and in heaven. | 1:20 |
| 1:17 | He is before all things. | He is the beginning. | 1:18 |

**Figure 4.21    Paul uses an old hymn to show Christ is Supreme as Creator and Reconciler (Col. 1:15-20).**

### 1. Christ is the Head of the body, the Church—the group of those He reconciles to God.

As Christ is the divine image of the invisible God—Christ is also the Head of the visible and invisible Church. These parallel statements emphasize the supremacy of Christ over creation and over the Church. There are millions of visible members of Christ's Church on earth; and there is a multitude that no man can number of invisible members of Christ's Church who have died and are in God's presence in heaven. Jesus Christ is the Head over all members of His body as He is God over all creation.

### 2. Christ is the firstborn from among the dead.

Jesus Christ is the firstborn from among the dead in three ways: He is the first to rise from the dead with a spiritual body, He is the first to rise from the dead permanently, and He is first because of His high position as God over all who rise from the dead. As Christ is the Divine Firstborn over all creation, He is the Divine Firstborn over all who rise from the dead. Note that many will rise from death when they hear His voice and come forth from the grave—either to receive rewards or to be judged (John 5).

### 3. Christ is the Reconciler of all things in heaven and on earth.

It is easy to understand that Jesus reconciled humans on earth who receive the gospel, turn from their sins, receive forgiveness, find peace with God, and follow Jesus. God sent His Son to redeem and reconcile people on earth. But in what sense did Christ reconcile to the Father things in heaven? Some have suggested that the loyal angels in heaven are offended when humans on earth disobey and disrespect the God they love and serve. This is probably true. People on earth become enemies of those who show disrespect to leaders they love. Loyal angels obey and worship God. How do we think they feel toward mere humans who disobey and rebel against the God of the universe? It is likely that they share the feelings of God, who is angry with the disobedient. When Adam fell, a curse came upon all creation. The ground began to bring forth thorns, the woman began to have pain in childbirth, and the serpent began to crawl on its belly. Paul says that all of creation groans and awaits the day when Christ returns and the Church is liberated from the bondage of earth (Rom. 8:18-25). When Christ came the first time, to

**Q 56** *How is Christ supreme in relation to those He reconciles?*

**Q 57** *In which 3 ways is Jesus Christ the firstborn from among the dead?*

**Q 58** *How did Christ reconcile humans on earth to God?*

**Q 59** *What do you think God reconciled to Himself in heaven? Explain.*

reconcile men, the angels sang *"Peace on earth, and good will toward those on whom God's favor rests"* (Luke 2:14). When Christ comes the final time, He will restore peace to all of creation. Truly, Jesus Christ brings peace of cosmic proportions. The angels sing when one sinner on earth makes peace with God (Luke 15). He brings peace in heaven between the loyal angels and humans who become loyal to God. He is the One who brings peace and harmony back into creation. He brings peace between God and humans who have been separated from Him through their evil behavior (Col. 1:21). Christ is the Reconciler of all things in heaven and on earth—through the blood He shed for us on the cross, God's altar for reconciliation (Col. 1:20). As Christ created all things in heaven and earth, He also reconciles all things on earth and in heaven for those who accept God's offer and God's terms.

## 4. Christ is the beginning of the New Creation.

Christ is the *source* of the first creation (Col. 1:16). Likewise, as the One who begins the whole process of reconciling heaven and earth, as He was before the creation, He is also before any who are redeemed. He is the *beginning* of the New Creation—the Church (Col. 1:18). Jesus supplied the blood to redeem the first person who was reconciled, and all thereafter. He is the firstborn over creation and the firstborn from among the dead, after reconciling heaven and earth through His sacrifice.

*Q 60* In what sense is Christ the supreme beginning of the new creation?

It is amazing to study the way the Spirit guides Paul to use an old hymn of the Church—showing that Christ is the Creator and Reconciler of the universe. Christ is Supreme! Surely these teachings helped the first readers to overcome the false teachers who were trying to dethrone Christ at Colosse. And 2,000 years later, the Word of God through His apostle continues to strengthen our faith, and lift our hearts in worship to exalt the Son of God—who with the Father created and reconciled us.

## Application (Col. 1:21-23)

*21 Once you were alienated from God and were enemies in your minds **because of your evil behavior.** 22 But now he has reconciled you by Christ's physical body through death to present you holy in his sight, without blemish and free from accusation—23 if you continue in your faith, established and firm, not moved from the hope held out in the gospel. This is the gospel that you heard and that has been proclaimed to every creature under heaven, and of which I, Paul, have become a servant* (Col. 1:21-23).

*Q 61* Complete Figure 4.22 summarizing 3 principles in Colossians 1:21-23.

Paul moves from summarizing great truths about Christ as Creator and Reconciler, to his readers. He applies three truths to believers of every generation.

| Colossians | Your Summaries of Principles in Colossians 1 |
|---|---|
| 1:21 | |
| 1:22 | |
| 1:23 | |

Figure 4.22   Practice summarizing three truths in Colossians 1:21-23).

- Evil behavior offends God, and puts us in the camp with His enemies (Col. 1:21).
- Jesus Christ paid the price for us to be forgiven, made holy, and reconciled to God (Col. 1:22).
- We are at peace with God *if* we continue to live by faith, living in a close relationship with Jesus Christ, and *not* moved away from the hope God holds out to us through the gospel. We are not saved by our works. But our surrender to God and cooperation with the Word and the Spirit enable us to receive the salvation God freely offers through Christ, by His love and grace. Paul does *not* say that once we begin to follow Jesus we are saved no matter how we live. He warns of those who once knew Christ, but have *"lost connection with the head"* (Col. 2:19). But he assures us that we are certain of salvation as we continue in

our faith. So let us put down deep roots and remain steadfast. Let us grow in grace, showing our thankfulness for God's blessings by living worthy of Christ— the Supreme Creator and Reconciler of all in heaven and on earth.

**Q 62** *How was the Sitka chief like Christ?*

In Alaska in the late 1800s two tribes fought: the Sitka and the Thlinkit. These tribes were at war all summer. As a result, the Sitkas were unable to prepare for winter. The war prevented them from catching salmon from the rivers, and picking berries in the fields. So one day, the Sitka chief went to talk with the chief of the Thlinkit tribe. The chief of the Sitka appealed, "If this war continues, most of my people will die from hunger. We have fought long enough; let us make peace." The Thlinkit chief replied, "It is easy for you to say we should stop fighting; for your warriors have killed ten more of my tribe than we have killed of yours. Give us ten men who will die to balance the blood. Then we will make peace and go home." The Sitka chief answered, "You know my rank. I am worth much more than 10 common men. Kill me and let us make peace." The Thlinkit chief accepted the offer, and his warriors shot the Sitka chief to death in public. The chief gave himself as a sacrifice for his people, and he himself brought peace. Years later, missionaries brought the message of peace through Christ to the Sitka and Thlinkit tribes. They understood at once and accepted peace with God.[8]

The big theme in Colossians 1:15-23 is that Christ is the Supreme Creator and Reconciler of all in the universe. False teachers at Colosse sought to pull Jesus down, making Him one of many mediators between God and man. But in our journey from earth to heaven, we must exalt Christ as Lord of our lives and Lord of all. Let us be sure that our behavior and our beliefs proclaim Christ as God the Son over all.

**Q 63** *Complete Figure 4.23 comparing Christ as Creator and Reconciler.*

| Col. | Christ, Supreme as _____ | Christ, Supreme as _____ | Col. |
|---|---|---|---|
| 1:15 | He is the _____ of the invisible God. | He is the _____ of the body, the (visible and invisible) Church. | 1:18 |
| 1:15 | He is the Firstborn over all _____. | He is the Firstborn from among _____. | 1:18 |
| 1:16 | He is the _____ of all things in heaven and on earth. | He is the _____ of all things on earth and in heaven. | 1:20 |
| 1:17 | He is _____ all things. | He is the _____. | 1:18 |

**Figure 4.23   Paul uses an old hymn to show Christ is Supreme as Creator and Reconciler (Col. 1:15-20).**

**Lesson 21**

## Following Jesus to Serve Others (Col. 1:24–2:5)
**Goal:** *Examine the cost, message, purpose, and power of spiritual ministry (Col. 1:24–2:5).*

**Q 64** *How can studying Paul's ministry help us?*

Studying a letter from a spiritual leader such as Paul inspires and instructs us. As we examine Colossians 1:24–2:5, Paul explains aspects of his ministry. Although our ministry may be on a lower level, God calls all of us to serve others. Paul is a good servant for us to learn from. In this passage we see **four factors** of serving that Paul weaves together—the cost, the message, the purpose, and the power. Let us enjoy looking at each of these with open hearts in God's presence.

### A. The Cost: Jesus paid the full price for our salvation, but following Him costs us much (Col. 1:24-25, 29; 2:1).

*24 Now I rejoice in what was suffered for you, and I fill up in my flesh what is still lacking in regard to Christ's afflictions, for the sake of his body, which is the church. 25 I have become its servant by the commission God gave me to present to you the word of God in its fullness... 29 To this end I labor, struggling with all his energy, which so powerfully works in me. 1 I want you to know how much I am struggling for you and for those at Laodicea, and for all who have not met me personally* (Col. 1:24-25, 29; 2:1).

We are saved by grace, not by our own works (Eph. 2:8-9). Jesus Christ alone is the One who reconciles us to God. He paid the full price for us to be forgiven, redeemed, and members of God's family. No sacrifice, in this life or after it, can ever add to the cost of our salvation. Jesus paid it all. This is the clear teaching of the Prison Epistles, the Gospels, and all of Scripture. Jesus is the author and the finisher of our faith (Heb. 12:2).

**Q 65** *Do our good deeds or suffering help save us? Explain.*

Yet, although salvation is the free gift of God (Rom. 6:23), we greatly err if we think it is possible to follow Jesus at no cost. For the cost of following Jesus is great. It was Jesus Himself who said we must count the cost and decide if we want to follow Him. Recall the words of Jesus to the crowds who were starting to follow Him:

**Q 66** *If salvation is a free gift, why did Jesus say we must count the cost?*

> [25] **Large crowds were traveling with Jesus, and turning to them he said:** [26] *"If anyone comes to me and does not hate his father and mother, his wife and children, his brothers and sisters—yes, even his own life—he cannot be my disciple.* [27] *And* **anyone who does not carry his cross and follow me cannot be my disciple.** [28] *"Suppose one of you wants to build a tower. Will he not first sit down and estimate* **the cost** *to see if he has enough money to complete it?* [29] *For if he lays the foundation and is not able to finish it, everyone who sees it will ridicule him,* [30] *saying, 'This fellow began to build and was not able to finish.'* [31] *"Or suppose a king is about to go to war against another king. Will he not* **first sit down and consider** *whether he is able with ten thousand men to oppose the one coming against him with twenty thousand?* [32] *If he is not able, he will send a delegation while the other is still a long way off and will ask for terms of peace.* [33] ***In the same way, any of you who does not give up everything he has cannot be my disciple"*** (Luke 14:25-33).

The price Jesus paid for our salvation was full and expensive. Likewise, following Jesus is costly. There are many things we must give up as we deny ourselves to follow and serve Jesus Christ. Some pay more than others to follow Jesus. The call of God on Paul's life cost Him more than God asks most to pay. To fulfill God's call for being an apostle to the Gentiles, Paul had to work harder than others, spend more time in prison, be beaten more severely, and face death time after time. Take a couple of minutes to review his lifetime of suffering (2 Cor. 11:23-29). He often labored lacking sleep, food, encouragement, adequate clothes, and shelter. He suffered rejection, persecution, and beatings in almost every city where he preached the gospel. And in this course, we are studying the four letters he wrote while chained in prison. These letters teach us that following Jesus costs us energy, hard work, and struggles. Yet for Paul, Jesus was truly the "pearl of great price" for which he paid all. From prison, Paul wrote to the Philippians:

**Q 67** *What did following Jesus cost Paul?*

> [7] *But whatever was to my* **profit** *I now consider* **loss** *for the sake of Christ.* [8] *What is more,* **I consider everything a loss compared to the surpassing greatness of knowing Christ Jesus my Lord, for whose sake I have lost all things.** *I consider them rubbish, that I may gain Christ* (Phil. 3:7-8).

**Figure 4.24   The price Jesus paid for our salvation was full and expensive.**

**Application.**   Beware of those who offer cheap grace. Following Jesus is not an invitation to riches, popularity, comfort, or a place of prestige in a parade (1 Cor. 4:8-13). There is no gospel from God whose message is only for people to enjoy and keep for themselves. The true gospel teaches that following Jesus is expensive. Every follower of Jesus must make some sacrifices. Followers of Christ must deny self and practice loving and serving others. To follow Jesus, we **must** share with others in need. We **must** share our love, time, money, energy—and our Savior whom we have discovered! And sharing

**Q 68** *How does the true gospel differ from the cheap grace some offer?*

with others costs us something. At Colosse, following Jesus meant being rejected by an academic group of people who claimed that the gospel was not enough for salvation. These Gnostic teachers claimed they had *secret knowledge* necessary for salvation. Likewise today, some who follow the basic teachings of Jesus will be excluded from certain *intellectual* groups. Other followers of Jesus will suffer physical, emotional, mental, social, and economic trials (See Heb. 10:32-34).

**Q 69**    *Complete Figure 4.25 on what it may cost you and others to follow Jesus.*

| Topic | Your Explanations and Examples of What It Costs to Follow Jesus |
|---|---|
| Desires | |
| Time | |
| Study | |
| Energy | |
| Money | |
| Acceptance | |
| Suffering | |
| Other | |

**Figure 4.25    Practice explaining some of the costs of following Jesus.**

False teachers at Colosse taught that salvation was through self-denial—*the harsh treatment of the body* (Col. 2:23). Paul said there is no value in this type of self-denial. In contrast, the Bible teaches us to deny ourselves two coats, *when* another brother has none (Matt. 3:11). And Scripture teaches us to deny ourselves keeping extra food and clothing, when a brother or sister is hungry and cold (Matt. 25:31-46; 1 John 3:17). Jesus teaches us to deny ourselves some of our desires so that we can help make disciples in all nations (Matt. 28:19-20).

**Q 70**    *Are you carrying a cross, or do you just sing about it and wear it? What is your cross? What is following Jesus costing you?*

A central symbol of Christianity is the cross. Jesus died on His cross, and He insists that all of His followers must carry one. Following Jesus is wise, joyful, and rewarding, but costly. The gospel spreads, disciples increase, and believers mature as each follower of Jesus pays a portion of the price.

## B. The Message: Jesus Christ is the center of the gospel we share with others (Col. 1:25-27).

*24 Now I rejoice in what was suffered for you, and I fill up in my flesh what is still lacking in regard to Christ's afflictions, for the sake of his body, which is the church. 25 I have become its servant by the commission God gave me to present to you **the word of God in its fullness** 26 the mystery that has been kept hidden for ages and generations, but is now disclosed to the saints. 27 To them God has chosen to make known among the Gentiles the glorious riches of **this mystery, which is Christ in you, the hope of glory**. 28 **We proclaim him**, admonishing and teaching everyone with all wisdom, so that we may present everyone perfect in Christ* (Col. 1:24-28).

**Q 71**    *How did the mystery Paul preached differ from the mystery of the false teachers?*

False teachers at Colosse taught that God had shared a mystery with them. They claimed to be among the special *few* to whom God gave *secret knowledge*. Paul agreed that God had revealed a *mystery*. He wrote that God had hidden this *mystery—for ages and generations* (Col. 1:26; Eph. 3:4-6). But now God has revealed His mystery—not to a few, but to the saints (all believers). This mystery is Christ in us—our hope of glory (Col. 1:27). A big part of the mystery was that God had always planned through Christ to make the Gentiles full and equal heirs of salvation with the Jews (Col. 1:27; Eph. 2:11-22). Jesus Christ is the message we share. *"We proclaim him ..."* (Col. 1:28). Jesus is God's message to us. And in Him are *hidden* all the treasures of wisdom and knowledge (Col. 2:3). So we do not need the *secret* knowledge that false teachers advertise.

Paul writes many statements in Colossians emphasizing that Jesus Christ is the message we preach.

Q 72 ✎ *Complete Figure 4.26 on Jesus, the message we preach.*

| Colossians | Statements in Colossians Emphasizing That Jesus Christ Is Our Supreme Message |
|---|---|
| 1:15. | He is the _____ of the invisible God. |
| 1:16 | He is the _____—the One through whom all things in heaven and earth were made. |
| 1:17 | He is the _____—the One before all things, and who holds all things together. |
| 1:18 | He is the _____ of the body, the Church. |
| 1:18 | He is Number One—the _____ and the _____ from the dead, so that in everything He might have the _____. |
| 1:21-22 | He is the _____—the One who changed us from being God's enemies into being God's children. |
| 1:28 | He is the One we _____. |
| 2:3 | He is the _____ of God—in whom are hidden all the treasures of wisdom and knowledge. |
| 2:9 | He is the _____—the One in whom the fullness of the Deity lives in bodily form. |
| 2:10 | He is the _____ over every power and authority. |
| 2:14 | He is the _____—the One who cancelled the ceremonial regulations of the Mosaic code that was against us. |
| 2:16-17 | He is the _____ of the shadows, like feasts and Sabbath days, that predicted Him. |
| 2:20–3:1 | He is the One we belong to and the One in whom we are _____, above the basic principles and desires of the world. |
| 3:2 | He is the One in whom our life is secretly _____. |

**Figure 4.26   Practice explaining that Jesus is our Supreme message.**

We have looked at statements in Colossians where Paul emphasizes that Jesus Christ is our message. In *Hermeneutics 1* (see *Faith & Action Series—Hermeneutics 1: General Principles for Interpreting Scripture*), we studied that it is good to study the theme of an author in the book you are interpreting. So we began in Colossians, studying Paul's theme that Jesus is the supreme message we preach (Figure 4.21). Now we move to a broader literary context. In *Hermeneutics 1*, we called this Circle 4, studying the same author in different books. In all of his letters, Paul emphasizes that Jesus Christ is the message we preach.

Q 73 ↗ *In Hermeneutics 1, how do the literary contexts of circles 1 and 4 differ? Give an example.*

Circles of *literary context (Note that circles 4, 5, and 6 are *parallel passages.)

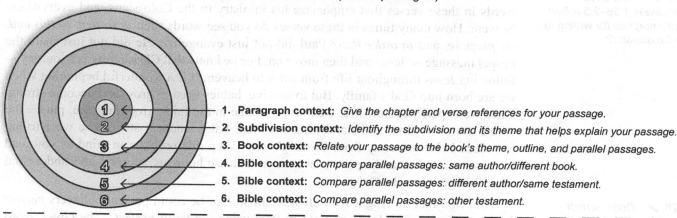

1. **Paragraph context:** *Give the chapter and verse references for your passage.*
2. **Subdivision context:** *Identify the subdivision and its theme that helps explain your passage.*
3. **Book context:** *Relate your passage to the book's theme, outline, and parallel passages.*
4. **Bible context:** *Compare parallel passages: same author/different book.*
5. **Bible context:** *Compare parallel passages: different author/same testament.*
6. **Bible context:** *Compare parallel passages: other testament.*

**Figure 4.27   In *Hermeneutics 1*, we studied Circles of Literary context.**

Q 74 ✎ *Complete Figure 4.28 on Jesus, the message we preach.*

| Reference | Your Summaries of Paul's Emphasis on Jesus, Our Message—In His Other Letters |
|---|---|
| Rom. 10:11-13 | |
| 1 Cor. 1:20-25 | |
| 1 Cor. 2:2 | |
| 1 Cor. 2:7 | |

Figure 4.28        Continued on following page

Continued from previous page

| Reference | Your Summaries of Paul's Emphasis on Jesus, Our Message—In His Other Letters |
|---|---|
| 2 Cor. 4:5-6 | |
| 2 Cor. 5:17-19 | |
| Gal. 5:4 | |
| Gal. 6:14 | |
| Eph. 2:11-13 | |
| Phil. 1:18 | |
| 1 Tim. 1:15 | |
| 1 Tim. 2:5-6 | |

**Figure 4.28    Practice summarizing some verses in Paul's other letters that emphasize Jesus, our message.**

**Q 75** ✎ *Where you live, what do false teachers add to, subtract from, or substitute for the message of Jesus Christ?*

**Q 76** ➤ *What purpose did Paul have for all who received the message of Christ?*

## C. The Purpose: We must encourage and teach to make disciples who are mature in Christ (Col. 1:28–2:5; Matt. 28:19-20).

Paul's *message* was Jesus Christ, who died to reconcile us to God; and who rose as Head over every power in heaven and earth, and Head of the Church. This was Paul's message. And for those who received the message, Paul was committed to a **purpose—making mature disciples**.

²⁸*We proclaim him, admonishing and teaching everyone with all wisdom, **so that** we may present everyone perfect in Christ.* ²⁹***To this end I labor**, struggling with all his energy, which so powerfully works in me.*

¹*I want you to know how much I am struggling for you and for those at Laodicea, and for all who have not met me personally.* ²***My purpose is** that they may be encouraged in heart and united in love, **so that** they may have the full riches of complete understanding, **in order that** they may know the mystery of God, namely, Christ,* ³*in whom are hidden all the treasures of wisdom and knowledge.* ⁴*I tell you this **so that** no one may deceive you by fine-sounding arguments.* ⁵*For though I am absent from you in body, I am present with you in spirit and **delight to see how orderly you are and how firm your faith in Christ is*** (Col. 1:28–2:5).

**Q 77** ➤ *How does Colossians 1:28–2:5 reflect Paul's purpose for writing to the Colossians?*

In Colossians 1:28–2:5 we see Paul's purpose for writing this letter. Look at the words in these verses that emphasize his ministry to the Colossians, and everywhere he went. How many times in these verses do you see words such as *so that, to this end, my purpose,* and *in order that?* Paul did not just evangelize. He did not just share the gospel message of Jesus and then move on. For he knew that Christianity is a journey—following Jesus throughout life from earth to heaven. It is a wonderful beginning when we are born into God's family. But to survive, babies need to grow and become strong. Once we experience new life, we must continue in the faith, grow in grace, put on the whole armor of God, and stand firm in Christ. False teachers at Colosse were trying to seduce believers away from Christ. Always keep this problem in mind as you read Colossians. Understanding the problems at Colosse helps us interpret and understand what Paul wrote to the Colossians.

**Q 78** ➤ *Does perfect mean A+ and 100%? Can the perfect in Christ become better? Explain.*

**Q 79** ✎ *How does a perfect believer differ from a baby Christian? Illustrate.*

Paul said that he taught with all wisdom *so that* he could present believers *perfect in Christ* (Col. 1:28). In what sense is Paul using the word *perfect?* The Greek word translated *perfect* is *telion.* It means "mature and complete." Jesus used a form of *telion* when He told His disciples to be *perfect* like our Father in heaven, by loving enemies and greeting those who are not brothers (Matt. 5:43-48). In a verse like Colossians 1:28, *perfect* does not mean there is no room to improve. Paul wants disciples to be *perfect* in the sense that we are mature, firm, and steadfast—adult believers. Those who are *perfect* in Christ are *"no longer infants, tossed back and forth by the waves, and blown here and there by every wind of teaching and by the cunning and craftiness of men in their deceitful scheming"* (Eph. 4:14). Instead, the *perfect* in Christ speak the truth in love, *"and in all things **grow up** into him who is the head, that is Christ. From him the whole body, joined and held together by every supporting ligament, **grows and builds itself up in love**, as each part does its work"* (Eph. 4:15-16).

In Colossians, Paul identifies several **aspects of perfection**—maturity of believers. This maturity develops as each member does his or her work in the body of Christ. Paul says *perfect, mature* believers are:

- Encouraged in heart (Col. 2:2a);
- United in love (Col. 2:2b);
- Complete in understanding of Christ (Col. 2:2c-3; see Col. 1:26-27);
- Steadfast against deception (Col. 2:4);
- Firm in the faith (Col. 2:5);
- Godly in morals (Col. 3:1-7);
- Godly in relationships at home and at work (Col. 3:18–4:10);
- Devoted to prayer (Col. 4:2).

In ministry, what do we seek to do? Our goal is not simply to win people to Christ—to see them raise a hand, walk an aisle, or pray a prayer. Do not be mistaken. We want to see people come to Christ in commitment. But we must want more! Our goal must include bringing them to maturity. We do not just want decisions—we want disciples! We want to see believers become more and more like Christ. This is what true perfection is all about (Col. 1:28–2:5; Eph. 4:11-16; compare Gal. 4:19).

Parents and grandparents rejoice to help their children develop. They love to see children take the first step, or say their first word. They delight to watch children imitate the good actions of adults. They love to see children grow into godly youths and adults. Likewise, let us, as believers, do our part to help new believers grow into mature disciples. And let us rejoice with every step of progress toward becoming *perfect, complete, mature, steadfast, strong,* and *fruitful* in Christ.

## D. The Power: We must live filled with the Spirit to pay the costs, proclaim the message, and fulfill our purpose of making mature disciples (Col. 1:29).

*To this end I labor, **struggling with all his energy, which so powerfully works in me*** (Col. 1:29).

Serving involves *struggling* (Col. 1:29; 2:1). Nurturing infant believers to become mature adults takes years of teaching, mentoring, leading, and shepherding. And we must do all this spiritual work *in the mighty power of the Holy Spirit*. In Ephesians, we spent an entire lesson studying the command: *"Be filled with the Spirit"* (Eph. 5:18). Here in Colossians 1:29, Paul refers to this same Holy Spirit, who works in believers "... *with all his energy, which so powerfully works in*" us (Col. 1:29).

We have studied three topics in Colossians 1:24–2:5 **the cost, the message,** and **the purpose** of spiritual ministry as we follow Jesus. But let us remember that the power of the Holy Spirit enables us to succeed in all three of these areas.

- *Living filled with the Spirit enables us to pay the costs of following Jesus.* Review what we studied in Point A above. Paul worked harder than others, sometimes lacking sleep, food, encouragement, adequate clothes, and shelter. He suffered rejection, persecution, and beatings in almost every city where he preached the gospel. And we are studying the four letters he wrote while chained in prison. How was Paul able to stand firm and continue to work for the church in all of these difficult circumstances? He depended on the power of God's Spirit within him. We are studying Paul's letter to the Ephesians in this course. But recall how difficult his ministry was there. He fought with beasts at Ephesus (1 Cor. 15:32). Scholars agree that at the least, this

**Q 80** How mature are you in Christ? In what areas is the Spirit urging you to grow?

**Q 81** In your church, what are some ways you help believers mature in Christ?

**Q 82** What is the key to paying the cost, proclaiming the message, and making mature disciples?

**Q 83** What costs did Paul pay for serving? How was he able to pay so much?

**Q 84** How has the Spirit helped you pay the cost of serving others? Illustrate.

**Q 85** ✎ *How have you, like Paul, ministered in the Spirit's power? Illustrate.*

means that Paul's enemies in Ephesus were as ferocious as wild animals.[9] At other times, Paul was pressed beyond *his* ability to endure (2 Cor. 1:8). So how did he endure? Only by the power of God's Spirit. Otherwise he would have given up, quit, or even died. Paul's letters from prison teach us that following Jesus costs us energy, hard work, and struggles. *Yet like Paul*, we can endure, overcome, and be fruitful, as we live filled with the Spirit. For His strength is made perfect in our weakness (2 Cor. 12:8-10).

- *Living filled with the Spirit enables us to proclaim the message of Jesus with spiritual power.* We do not know if Paul ever went to Colosse. But in Ephesus, Paul proclaimed the message of Christ in the power of the Spirit. He placed his hands on disciples and prayed for them. As they were filled with the Spirit—they prophesied and spoke in tongues (Acts 19:1-7). Likewise, we need to pray for the disciples we serve, and help them be filled with the Spirit. God does not intend for us to count the cost, preach the message, or fulfill our purpose without living filled with the Spirit! We will fail without the Spirit's power. Do not leave home without it! Our only hope of being fruitful for Christ is to live in the power of the Spirit. For 2 years Paul taught disciples at Ephesus in the power of the Spirit. " [11]*God did extraordinary miracles through Paul,* [12]*so that even handkerchiefs and aprons that had touched him were taken to the sick, and their illnesses were cured and the evil spirits left them"* (Acts 19:11-12). Likewise, among the Philippians, it was the power of the Spirit that enabled Paul to make converts and mature disciples (Acts 16). The Spirit that anointed Paul is the same Spirit God wants all believers to be filled with. Let us not settle for less, but live hungry for all of the Spirit that God commanded us to have (Eph. 5:18) and Jesus promised that our Father will give us (Luke 11:11-13).

**Q 86** ✎ *How is the Spirit using you to disciple and mentor others? Give examples.*

- *Living filled with the Spirit enables us to make mature disciples of those we serve.* Jesus died on the cross to make it possible for every person in the world to be reconciled to God. He trained 12 apostles and perhaps 100 disciples. He told them to go into all the world and make disciples among every ethnic group—teaching them to obey all things that He had commanded (Matt. 28:19-20). However, before Jesus ascended back to the Father, He gave them this command:

[4]*"Do not leave Jerusalem, but wait for the gift my Father promised, which you have heard me speak about.* [5]*For John baptized with water, but in a few days you will be baptized with the Holy Spirit"* (Acts 1:4-5).

**Q 87** ✎ *Do believers you know minister in the Spirit's power? Explain.*

Of those who heard this command, 120 gathered on the Day of Pentecost. As they waited on God, He filled them once with His presence. This power of the Spirit enabled them to fulfill the commission God gave to the Church. Time after time they waited on God, and He filled them again and again with His presence. Paul learned the secret of victorious living and fruitful ministry. So he passed it on to us, saying, *"Be filled with the Spirit"* (Eph. 5:18).

**Q 88** ✎ *Will you commit your life to pay the cost, proclaim the message, and make disciples in the Spirit's power?*

Do you long for God to use you in fruitful ministry? Is there something within you that cries out to make a lasting impact on your world? Think of those who have powerfully influenced your life for good and for God. What characterized their lives? Likely they had the same traits and values Paul identifies in Colossians 1:18–2:5. They were willing to pay the price, preach the message of Christ, make disciples, and depend on the power of the Holy Spirit. Are you willing to commit your life to these values in your service to the Lord?

**Q 89** ✎ *In a day when we have so much, what do we need to be more fruitful for Christ?*

In the first century, common disciples—filled with the Spirit—shook the world for Christ and expanded the kingdom of God in every direction. Today we have more believers, more money, more technology. We have more education, better transportation, and better communication. Why is it that we are not more fruitful? Is it possible that we have too much emphasis on *summa cum laude* and too little on *summa cum God*? Are we depending too much on ourselves, and too little on God? Let us come back to the basics. Once again, let us seek to live *filled with the Spirit*—as we obey His commission: to count the cost, preach the message, and make disciples in all nations.

## Lesson 22
## Four Keys to Making Heaven Our Home (Col. 2:6–3:4)
**Goal:** *Identify, illustrate, and apply 4 ways to stay on the road to heaven (Col. 2:6–3:4).*

Little by little, Paul has been developing his theme: Christ is Supreme in creation and reconciliation. Paul stated this theme in Colossians 1:15-20. Next, he applied the theme to believers whom Christ has reconciled (Col. 1:21-23). Then, the apostle wrote about the cost, message, purpose, and power of his ministry (Col. 1:24–2:5). In this lesson, we emphasize his theme that Christ is Supreme in creation and redemption. And Paul will apply the theme to believers, giving us four things to practice as we follow Jesus to heaven and our eternal inheritance. Let us look at these **four keys** (A–D), one by one.[10]

**Q 90** How does this lesson relate to Paul's theme in Colossians?

### A. Continue living in a strong relationship with Jesus Christ (Col. 2:6-7).

*4I tell you this so that no one may deceive you by fine-sounding arguments.*

*6So then, just as you received Christ Jesus as Lord, **continue to live in him**, 7rooted and built up in him, strengthened in the faith as you were taught, and overflowing with thankfulness* (Col. 2:4, 6-7).

**Q 91** What spiritual progress had the Colossians made?

*Continue* is a huge topic in the Bible. To arrive at a place we desire, we must first get on the right road. Then, we must *continue* on it to reach our destination. Believers at Colosse had made a good start. They had received Christ Jesus as Savior and Lord (Col. 2:6). Once, they were separated from God because of their evil behavior (Col. 1:21). But God reconciled them through the sacrifice of Christ on the cross (Col. 1:22). So, Paul rejoices that they have begun the journey to heaven. The have left the camp of God's enemies and have become God's children. What a wonderful change! What a glorious transformation. God rescued these Colossians from the *"dominion of darkness"* and brought them *"into the kingdom of the Son He loves"* (Col. 1:13).

The Colossian believers are on the right road. God has **qualified them** *"to share in the inheritance of the saints in the kingdom of light"* (Col. 1:12). But the Colossians must see to it that no one **disqualifies** them from the prize of their inheritance (Col. 2:18). For they have *not yet* reached heaven nor received the inheritance God wants to give them. Like us and Ephesian believers, the Colossians had the down payment of their inheritance—the Holy Spirit who entered them at conversion (Eph. 1:13-14). So Paul encourages them to **continue**. At the end of the journey, he wants them to be *presented* as a class that graduated from earth and is received into heaven. God and Paul desire the Colossians to be *presented*, at the end of their journey, *"holy in his sight without blemish and free from accusation"* (Col. 1:22). This would happen *if and only if* the Colossians **continue** in their faith, *"established and firm, **not moved** from the hope held out in the gospel"* (Col. 1:23).

**Q 92** What danger does Paul see for believers at Colosse?

**Q 93** How can we, like the Colossians, reach heaven?

Paul makes it clear that our hope is in Christ and the gospel that introduces Him to us. In other words, hope and salvation do not come by themselves. Our hope of salvation is *only* through our relationship with a person—Jesus Christ. To be saved you must *"continue to live in him, 7rooted and built up in him, strengthened in the faith as you were taught, and overflowing with thankfulness"* (Col. 2:6-7).

Paul will soon talk about the dangers of being deceived and seduced away from Christ. But here, in his first point, the apostle emphasizes the positive—*continue*.

In Ephesians, Paul likens salvation through Christ to marriage (Eph. 5:22-33). To remain in a marriage relationship, one must **continue** in it. In many marriages, spouses

**Q 94** How is salvation like marriage?

begin happy. For a few years, they are deeply in love. But in time, the emotion of love fades as the responsibility of love grows. What began as new and exciting becomes common and normal. Time for self and one's spouse decreases as time needed for others increases. There are children to raise, relatives to relate to, repairs to make, and bills to pay. Life brings illness, maintenance, suffering, accidents, disagreements, and disappointments. Dads and moms become tired from work and pressure. Their young bodies age year by year. In time, one of the spouses can begin to lack energy, motivation, and appreciation. Because of the challenges of marriage today, in many nations 50 percent of marriages end in divorce. The spouses ***Do Not Continue*** to live together, love, and serve each other. Many marriages fail because a spouse does not continue to practice what is right—things such as patience, love, kindness, thankfulness, and faithfulness. Marriages may fail from the lack of a balance between work, rest, worship, fellowship, friendship, and fun. Marriages can bend and break without a balance between taking and giving, talking and listening, understanding and being understood, being and doing. In all relationships, whether social or spiritual, we must continue to practice the things we know are right. Continuing is possible as we *walk in Christ,* put our spiritual roots down deep into Him, are built up in our relationship with Him, and live filled with His Word and His Spirit (Col. 2:6-7; 3:16; Eph. 5:18). As a branch draws its life and strength from the vine, we find all we need as we depend on Jesus Christ.

**Figure 4.29    Balance work, rest, worship, fellowship, friendship, and fun in your marriage and family.**

Continue what you are doing right. Do not look back like Lot's wife. Do not be like those who left Egypt but later longed to return to it (Exod. 16:3; Num. 4:2; 11:5). Do not put your hand to the plow and then begin looking at your past life (Luke 9:62). Keep the faith; run the race; and fight the good fight (2 Tim. 4:7). *"Let us **not** become **weary in doing good**, for at the proper time we will reap a harvest if we do **not** give up"* (Gal. 6:9). Keep on keeping on. Those who endure to the end will be saved (Matt. 24:13).

**Q 95** Complete Figure 4.30 on continuing in our relationship with Christ.

| References | Your Summaries on Verses Related to Continuing |
|---|---|
| Exod. 16:3 | |
| 1 Sam. 17:47 | |
| 2 Chron. 20:15 | |
| Matt. 24:13 | |
| Luke 9:62 | |
| Gal. 6:9 | |
| Col. 2:6 | |
| Col. 2:18 | |
| 1 Cor. 9:27 | |
| 1 Cor. 10:1-12 | |
| 2 Tim. 4:7 | |
| 2 Tim. 4:10 | |
| Heb. 2:1-3 | |
| Heb. 3:1, 12 | |
| Heb. 10:36-38 | |
| 2 Pet. 1:3-10 | |

**Figure 4.30    Practice summarizing some verses related to the huge, biblical theme of "continuing."**

## B. Danger: Watch out for false teachers (Col. 2:8, 16-19).

Some rules, like the ones in Colossians 3, are good:

*⁸See to it that no one takes you captive through hollow and deceptive philosophy, which depends on human tradition and the basic principles of this world rather than on Christ* (Col. 2:8).

Paul is concerned that believers continue to walk with Christ. A second concern he has is for believers to escape from becoming the captives of crafty teachers, those who led people astray with philosophy—mere human reasoning. Paul warns believers: *"See to it that no one takes you captive through hollow and deceptive philosophy, which depends on human tradition and the basic principles of this world rather than on Christ"* (Col. 2:8).

> PAUL IS NOT OPPOSED TO EDUCATION, REFLECTION, OR DISCUSSION ABOUT LIFE'S QUESTIONS.

Paul is not opposed to education, reflection, or discussion about life's questions. But Paul's theme is that believers keep Christ supreme—above all, as God the Son. We must evaluate everything from the cornerstone of Christ—honoring His nature, ministry, example, teachings, and values. Followers of Christ do not allow any human teaching to lessen or lead away from our relationship with Christ.

### Paul warns against those who want to lift rules up on the level with Christ (Col. 2:16-17).

*¹⁶Therefore do not let anyone judge you by what you eat or drink, or with regard to a religious festival, a New Moon celebration or a Sabbath day. ¹⁷These are a shadow of the things that were to come; the reality, however, is found in Christ.* (Col. 2:16-17).

Looking behind Paul's warning of Colossians 2:16-17, we see that some of the false teachings had Jewish roots. Some Jews wanted two saviors: Moses and Jesus. Paul's words show us that legalistic teachers were saying salvation comes by avoiding certain foods, attending feasts, celebrating the new moon, or even the Sabbath (Col. 2:16). Moses wrote about all of these rules. But Paul says they were just shadows of the things to come (Col. 2:17). In other words, the laws about food and feasts, sacrifices and priests, circumcision, and special days were all just temporary signs pointing to Jesus Christ. He is the reality—the real deal (Col. 2:17b). Some rules in God's kingdom are good—such as the rules in Colossians 3. But rules cannot save us. Only Jesus saves. Obeying God's rules of love shows that Jesus has saved us. But as we said earlier, rules are never a ladder to heaven.

**Q 96** ⌐ *How do we know that some false teachings at Colosse had Jewish roots?*

**Q 97** ⌐ *What is the role of rules in God's kindgom?*

### Paul warns against those who want to lift spiritual experiences up on the level with Christ.

*¹⁸Do not let anyone who delights in false humility and the worship of angels disqualify you for the prize. Such a person goes into great detail about what he has seen, and his unspiritual mind puffs him up with idle notions. ¹⁹He has lost connection with the Head, from whom the whole body, supported and held together by its ligaments and sinews, grows as God causes it to grow* (Col. 2:18-19).

Paul is not against spiritual experiences. He believes we must be born again. He believes we need to be filled with the Spirit. Paul himself told about his spiritual experiences. Luke and Paul wrote about some of Paul's spiritual experiences—including encounters with Christ, being caught up to heaven, encounters with angels and demons, visions, and spiritual gifts (Acts 9:1-19; 13:1-3; 16:1-10; 18:9-11; 19:1-11; 22:1-21; 23:11; 27:21-26; 2 Cor. 12:1-10). Paul had more spiritual experiences than most, and he spoke in unknown tongues more than others. But this great apostle kept focusing on CHRIST—the Supreme Creator and Reconciler of all things in heaven and on earth!

**Q 98** ⌐ *Was Paul against spiritual experiences? What warning did he give about them?*

**Q 99** Is it possible to be connected to the Head of the Church, but then lose the connection? Explain.

**Q 100** How did false teachers misuse teachings about angels?

**Q 101** In modern times, who do false teachers try to put between us and God?

He warned that anyone who lifts up spiritual experiences within a hundred miles of Jesus Christ has gotten off track—and *lost connection with the Head* of the body, the Church (Col. 2:19). Brothers and sisters, let us hide behind the cross and lift up Jesus. He alone is worthy in heaven and earth (Rev. 5:1-14). And the world is hungry and thirsty for Him, not humans like us! Let us exalt Jesus Christ with our words and with our lives as we seek to live worthy of His love.

In Paul's day, some taught that God was too holy and too far away for humans to contact directly. These false teachers taught that we must instead have spiritual experiences with angels—*intermediaries, beings between God and humans (Col. 2:18). Paul warned that people like this are just puffed up with hot air. They are full of themselves instead of the Spirit. They have been looking too much in the mirror. Throughout the history of the earth, people have tried to lead others astray to follow angels, priests, saints, false teachers, or *avatars—people who claim to be, or are said to be, God in flesh. But the Scriptures teach that the only time God became human was in Jesus Christ (Col. 1:15; 2:9; Phil. 2:8; John 1:14). And the only Mediator between God and humans is Jesus Christ (1 Tim. 2:5). So let us turn away from anything or anyone seeking to exalt self or others to the level of Jesus Christ—the Supreme Creator and Redeemer of the universe. There are *hosts* (groups of angels and people), but Jesus Christ is Lord of hosts, Lord of lords, and King of kings. Christ is the Head over every power and authority (Col. 2:10). As we keep Jesus Number One in our lives, He causes each of us and His whole body to grow (Col. 2:19).

**Q 102** Which of the false teachings at Colosse are popular where you live?

| | False Teachings at Colosse | Truth in Colossians | Col. |
|---|---|---|---|
| 1. | The spirit is good and the body is bad. | *For in Christ all the fullness of the Deity lives in bodily form.* Since Christ lives in a body, the body itself is not sinful or bad. | 1:9 |
| 2. | Salvation comes through secret knowledge, not the gospel. | *Do not let anyone who delights in false humility and the worship of angels disqualify you for the prize. Such a person goes into great detail about what he has seen, and his unspiritual mind puffs him up with idle notions.* | 2:18 |
| 3. | Jesus was only a man. The divine Spirit of Christ joined Him at His baptism. The Spirit left Him before He died. | *For God was pleased to have all his fullness dwell in him …* *For in Christ all the fullness of the Deity lives in bodily form* | 1:19 2:9 |
| 4. | Treat the body harshly, because it is evil. (This error is called *asceticism.) | *Do not let anyone judge you by what you eat or drink, or with regard to a religious festival, a New Moon celebration or a Sabbath day.* *Such regulations indeed have an appearance of wisdom, with their self-imposed worship, their false humility and their harsh treatment of the body, but they lack any value in restraining sensual indulgence.* | 2:16 2:23 |
| 5. | Sinning with the body is not wrong, because only the spirit matters. | *Put to death, therefore, whatever belongs to your earthly nature: sexual immorality, impurity, lust, evil desires and greed, which is idolatry.* | 3:5 |

**Figure 4.31   Colossians teaches the truth in contrast to the five errors of Jewish legalism and early Gnosticism.**

**Q 103** If Paul preached in your city, what warning would he give about false teachers?

Today, there are many world religions, cults, new religious teachings, and arrogant humans. Some teachings look good on the outside, but they only benefit the teachers, rather than the people who practice them. Many false teachers look good in public, but they hide their sinful private lives. What was Paul's advice? Be on guard! Do not be deceived! See to it that no one takes you captive (Col. 2:8)!

## C. Celebrate the nature and work of Christ (Col. 2:9-15).

### Transition

Paul turns from warning about false teachers to emphasizing the true teaching about Christ. In the famous passage of Colossians 2:9-15, Paul writes some of his best *Christology—teachings about Christ. He stresses two things about Christ: His nature, and His work. Let us mine both of these rich topics.

## 1. The nature of Christ (Col. 2:9, 10b)

*9 For in Christ **all the fullness of the Deity lives in bodily form**, 10 and you have been given fullness in Christ, **who is the head over every power and authority*** (Col. 2:9-10).

In Colossians 1:19 Paul wrote: *"For God was pleased to have all his fullness dwell in him...."* Colossians 2:9 repeats and explains 1:19. The key words in Colossians 2:9 are *fullness* and *Deity*. Each of these two words is rich and important. *Fullness* (Gk: *pleroma*) comes from the verb *to fill*. God poured His fullness into the human body of Christ. Christ was filled with the fullness of God. And to be sure we get the point, Paul says *all the fullness of the Deity* (God) lives (present tense) in Christ.

Why does Paul emphasize so much that Christ *is* all the fullness of God in the form of a body? Probably because the false teaching at Colosse was an early form of Gnosticism, which claimed that Christ and others were less than God, but greater than humans. As Paul teaches about Christ, he begins with the fact that Jesus Christ was the complete fullness of God in bodily form. This fact is the non-negotiable cornerstone of Christianity. To be a biblical Christian, a person must believe that Christ was fully God in human flesh.[11]

**Q 104** ⟋ *How divine was Christ? How full of God was He? Explain.*

**Q 105** ⟍ *Complete Figure 4.32 on verses that emphasize the divine nature of Jesus.*

| References | Your Summaries of Verses Stating That Jesus Reveals the Father to Us |
|---|---|
| John 1:14 | |
| John 14:9 | |
| Col. 1:15 | |
| Col. 1:19 | |
| Col. 2:9 | |
| Col. 2:10b | |
| Phil. 2:8 | |
| 1 Tim. 2:5 | |
| Heb. 1:3a | |

**Figure 4.32   Practice summarizing verses on the deity of Christ.**

## 2. The work of Christ (Col. 2:10a, 11-15)

As you study this passage in Colossians on the *work of Christ*, discern the problem that Paul is writing to solve. The heretics were attacking Christ and His followers. *First*, they tried to pull Christ down from the level of God, the Creator, to a lower level which was above angels, but below God. Paul's response to this heresy is that Christ was fully God in human form. *Next*, the false teachers tried to convince Christians that we gain salvation by keeping rules and getting secret knowledge. And of course, the false teachers claimed to have all the *secret knowledge* we need—knowledge they got through spiritual experiences with angels. These false teachers wanted in on the action. They wanted a piece of the pie. From the Colossian believers, the false teachers wanted things such as: attention, respect, prestige, position, power, and money. Paul's response to the false teachers' *special sale on secret knowledge* is that Christ Himself is the *secret mystery of God*, already revealed to the saints—the followers of Christ. Paul insists that Christ is completely God in human form. And, Paul insists that the work of salvation Christ has done is complete. As a result of Christ's nature and work, we receive the benefits of salvation. Paul emphasizes several benefits of the salvation we receive through the work of Christ. Let us inventory or count these benefits of salvation.

**Q 106** ⟋ *At what level did false teachers at Colosse put Christ?*

**Q 107** ⟋ *Why did false teachers claim to have secret knowledge?*

**Q 108** ⟍ *How is the motivation of false teachers today like those at Colosse? Illustrate.*

*10 and you have been given **fullness in Christ**, who is the head over every power and authority. 11 In him you were also circumcised, in the putting off of the sinful nature, not with a circumcision done by the hands of men but with the circumcision done by Christ, 12 having been buried with him in baptism and raised with him through your faith in the power of God, who raised him from the dead.*

*[13]When you were dead in your sins and in the uncircumcision of your sinful nature, God made you alive with Christ. He forgave us all our sins, [14]having canceled the written code, with its regulations, that was against us and that stood opposed to us; he took it away, nailing it to the cross. [15]And having disarmed the powers and authorities, he made a public spectacle of them, triumphing over them by the cross* (Col. 2:10-15).

**Q 109**  ✎  *Answer the questions in the middle column of Figure 4.33 on the benefits of salvation via the work of Christ.*

| Benefits of Believers | Your Answers to Questions on the Work of Christ | Colossians | |
|---|---|---|---|
| Fullness in Christ | In Christ, we have all we need for salvation. He is our wisdom, righteousness, sanctification and redemption (1 Cor. 1:30). As our Father, He even shares His divine nature with us, His children, and we are being renewed in His image (Col. 3:10; Eph. 4:24; Rom. 8:31; 2 Cor. 3:18; 2 Pet. 1:3-4). Why was Paul emphasizing to the Colossians that believers are full and complete in Christ? <br><br> **Q:** *In Matthew 22:15-21, what did Jesus want us to give to God, that is made in His image?* | 2:10 | |
| Circumcision by Christ | Colossians reveals that the circumcision of the Old Testament, cutting off a small piece of flesh, was a shadow. The reality is in Christ, where we remove all the dominance of the flesh, and learn to walk in the Spirit (Col. 3:5-10; Rom. 8:4, 8-10; Eph. 5:18; Gal. 5:16). Paul wrote that spiritual circumcision is *"of the heart, by the Spirit, not by the written code"* (Rom. 2:29). <br><br> **Q:** *Why did the topic of circumcision come up in Paul's letter to the Colossians?* | 2:11, 13 | |
| New Life in Christ | **Q:** *What event in the life of a believer illustrates that we died with Christ and have new life in Christ?* | 2:13 | |
| Forgiveness of sins | Although the Law was good, it was against us. For it was always accusing us of breaking commands that we lacked the power to obey (Rom. 7:7-12). <br><br> **Q:** *How was life **before** Christ different than your new life **in** Christ?* | 2:13 | |
| Freedom from regulations | The moral laws of God are forever, like those in Colossians 3:5-10. But Christ has freed us from Old Testament rules about priests, sacrifices, and diet (Eph. 2:15). These were like shadows. <br><br> **Q:** *What are some examples of rules that Christ fulfilled, cancelled, and took away?* | 2:14, 16-17 | |
| Freedom from evil rulers | Besides freeing us from ceremonial laws, Christ freed us from being under spiritual powers. Before Christ, we were under the influence of the devil, demons, the world, and the flesh (Eph. 2:1-3). But Christ conquered all the spiritual powers that are our enemies. Paul compares Christ's victory to the parade of a general who conquered his enemies. Then he stripped them of their weapons and armor, and led them in chains in a parade. Christ's victory parade over spiritual powers is a favorite theme of Paul (Col. 2:15; Eph. 4:8; 2 Cor. 2:14-16; Figure 2.10). <br><br> **Q:** *How does Paul use the metaphor of a victory parade to show that the salvation Christ won is complete— and we cannot add to it by our good deeds?* | 2:15 | |

**Figure 4.33   Practice answering questions about the benefits of salvation through the work of Christ (Col. 2:10-15).**

## D. Set your affections on Christ, rather than on the ways of the world (Col. 2:20–3:4, 12-14).

**Q 110** ⬉ *Complete Figure 4.34 on the biblical balance between too many rules and too few rules.*

| Teachings | Your Summaries |
|---|---|
| 1. Too few rules (Libertinism) | |
| 2. Too many rules (Legalism) | |
| 3. The rule of Christ over us (Christianity) | |

**Figure 4.34    Practice explaining the role of rules in God's kingdom.**

**Figure 4.35    The Prison Epistles present three paths from which to choose. Two of the paths are rules of the world, and the third path is the rule of Christ over our lives.**

**1.** The world offers the path of LIBERTINISM—TOO FEW RULES. Those who choose extreme liberty want freedom to fulfill all their desires of the flesh: sexual sins, impurity, lust, evil desires, evil behavior, greed, lying, stealing, anger, slander, fighting, malice, foul speech, drunkenness, grumbling (Col. 3:5-7). Those who choose this path are enemies of God (Col. 1:21). Libertines think only of themselves, ignoring the needs and desires of others. All of us were on the path of libertinism before we met Christ, when we were dead in our sins (Eph. 2:1-3).

**2.** A second path the world offers is LEGALISM—TOO MANY RULES. Jewish legalists at Colosse said salvation comes through obeying the laws God gave through Moses. But Paul emphasizes that the ceremonial rules of Moses, such as sacrifices and cleanliness, were shadows of the reality of Christ. Those who follow the path of legalism become slaves of rules and captives of false teachers—who make up hundreds of their own rules. Some of the rules of legalists include: do not handle; do not taste; do not touch; follow traditions; don't eat this; don't drink that; observe this holiday; be circumcised; learn secret wisdom from teachers with spiritual encounters; worship angels; pray to the saints; punish your body (Col. 2:8, 20-23).

**3.** The third path, unlike libertinism or legalism, is LIVING UNDER THE RULE OF CHRIST—BY THE POWER OF THE SPIRIT, submitting to the rule of Jesus Christ. Jesus has few rules. He summarizes all of God's command with only two: Love God with all our heart. And love your neighbor as yourself. As we are filled with God's Word and Spirit, God writes these two laws of love on our hearts. Then, His love gives us power to live in righteous relationships with Him and others. Under Christ's rule we love God; love our neighbors as ourselves; and we practice sexual purity, self-control, work, sharing, wholesome talk, love, kindness, humility, patience, compassion, forbearance, forgiveness, holiness, righteousness, thanksgiving (Col. 3:1-4,12-17; Eph. 4:25–5:20).

> [20] *Since you died with Christ to the basic principles of this world, why, as though you still belonged to it, do you submit to its rules:* [21] *"Do not handle! Do not taste! Do not touch!"?* [22] *These are all destined to perish with use, because they are based on human commands and teachings.* [23] *Such regulations indeed have an appearance of wisdom, with their self-imposed worship, their false humility and their harsh treatment of the body, but they lack any value in restraining sensual indulgence* (Col. 2:20-23).

**Q 111** ⬈ *What kind of rules were false teachers at Colosse substituting for faith in Christ?*

**Q 112** ⬉ *What types of desires must believers replace today with heavenly values?*

*¹Since, then, you have been raised with Christ, **set your hearts on things above**, where Christ is seated at the right hand of God. ²**Set your minds on things above, not on earthly things**. ³For you died, and your life is now hidden with Christ in God. ⁴When Christ, who is your life, appears, then you also will appear with him in glory. ⁵Put to death, therefore, whatever belongs to your earthly nature: sexual immorality, impurity, lust, evil desires and greed, which is idolatry. ⁶Because of these, the wrath of God is coming. ⁷You used to walk in these ways, in the life you once lived* (Col. 3:1-7).

Paul commands believers to *seek things above*. He urges us *to guide our hearts and desires* toward things above, in contrast to the evil things that our earthly nature loves—such as: *"sexual immorality, impurity, lust, evil desires and greed, which is idolatry"* (Col. 3:5).

**Q 113** ✎ *Explain: We must execute (kill) evil desires (Col. 3:5).*

What is the key to seeking things that are righteous and eternal, rather letting ourselves be pulled downward by evil desires of the flesh and the world? Paul has steered us away from just trying to keep rules such as *"Do not handle! Do not taste! Do not touch!"* He says that these may look wise and spiritual, but they *"lack any value in restraining sensual indulgence"* (Col. 2:23). In other words, mere rules may point away from evil, but they do not empower us to overcome desires of our flesh. So what is the biblical solution for winning the battles we all face with sexual temptations, lust, greed, and other evil desires? Paul says the key is **twofold**: He says we must *execute* evil desires—we must put them to death (Col. 3:5). In other words, we must be serious, stern, and severe in our attitude toward evil desires. We cannot pamper, coddle, nurse, and be gentle with evil desires we face. We must hate these desires, turn away from them, and refuse to be enslaved by evil. But it is not enough to hate what is wrong. We must love what is right (Col. 3:1-2). Think of the mind and heart as vessels, such as a glass or bowl. The best way to keep bad things out of a glass is to fill it with something that is good. Likewise, we walk in victory as we reject evil desires from our minds *and* fill our minds with good thoughts. We must turn *away from* evil and *turn toward* good. The Spirit helps us as we fill our minds with Scriptures, spiritual songs, and prayers of praise and thanksgiving. As Paul writes in another letter from prison:

**Q 114** ✎ *As we execute evil desires, what direction must we guide our desires (Col. 3:1-2)? Illustrate.*

*⁶Do not be anxious about anything, but in everything, by prayer and petition, with thanksgiving, present your requests to God. ⁷And the peace of God, which transcends all understanding, will guard your hearts and your minds in Christ Jesus. ⁸Finally, brothers, whatever is true, whatever is noble, whatever is right, whatever is pure, whatever is lovely, whatever is admirable—if anything is excellent or praiseworthy—think about such things. ⁹Whatever you have learned or received or heard from me, or seen in me—put it into practice. And the God of peace will be with you* (Phil. 4:6-9).

**Q 115** ✎ *How does Philippians 4:6-9 illustrate that victory includes turning from evil and toward good?*

**Note.**   For a helpful lesson on how to seek things above with our hearts and minds, see the *Faith & Action* course: *First & Second Corinthians, Lesson 42, Spiritual Thinking*. This is a lesson that can change your life! For what we think about stirs up either the flesh or the Spirit.

What we think about lights fires within us. *"As I meditated, the fire burned"* (Ps. 39:3). What we think about, meditate on, reflect on, and focus on affects our emotions. Musing leads to *fusing. Meditation kindles fires within—whether the fire is clean or as black as the smoke of burning oil. Thoughts create moods and emotions. We think about things, and this lights fires in us. Meditate on the wrong that someone has done to you and this will light a fire of self-pity, malice, and unforgiveness in you. Nurse a grudge and it will grow into a root of bitterness. Meditate on sexual temptations and this will light a fire of evil sexual desires. Think about a parent or teacher who believes in you and this will light a fire of encouragement that warms your heart. Focus on God's faithfulness to you and this will light a fire of faith and confidence to trust God. Meditate on God's forgiveness for your sins and this will light a fire that inspires you to forgive others. Recount past victories and this will spark courage to win again. So guide your thoughts. Censor bad thoughts and reject them like you would spit out a bitter bite of food. Welcome good thoughts and entertain them in your mind like you invite good friends into your home. *Set your mind and your heart on things above, and your life will be warm and bright with inspiring fires within.* [12]

**Figure 4.36**
Focus sunlight through a convex lens, and it will start a fire. Likewise, when we focus, ponder, and meditate on things—this process lights fires within us. Meditate on evil things and this will light fires of lust, hatred, envy, or greed within. Meditate on the love and goodness of God and this will start fires of worship and thankfulness in your heart. So set your mind on things above and this will guide your emotions and actions in the right direction.

Q 116 ✎ *Answer the questions on the effects of musing or meditating.*

| People | Your Answers to Questions on the Fires That Came From Musing | References |
|---|---|---|
| Eve | What happened because Eve focused on the fruit God forbade? | Gen. 3 |
| Abraham | What happened as Abraham meditated on the promises and nature of God? | Rom. 4 |
| Lot | What occurred as Lot gazed on the lush plains of the Jordan? | Gen. 13:10-11 |
| Israelites | What caused the Israelites to miss Canaan? | Num. 11 |
| Samson | What resulted because Samson kept thinking about Delilah? | Jud. 16 |
| David | What caused David to commit adultery and murder a woman's husband? | 2 Sam. 11 |
| David | What enabled David to lead an army to victory? | 1 Sam. 30 |
| Ananias and Sapphira | What type of thinking led to the deaths of Ananias and Sapphira? | Acts 5 |
| Paul | What type of meditation led Paul to finish the race well? | Phil. 3:13-14 |
| Saints | What type of thoughts enabled a multitude of believers to overcome? | Heb. 11 |
| A multitude | What thoughts helped faithful believers die for Christ? | Rev. 12 |

Figure 4.37   Practice answering questions on the effects of right and wrong thinking.

**Summary:** In Colossians 1:1–2:5, Paul emphasizes who Christ is and what He has accomplished through His death, burial, resurrection, and ascension. In Colossians 2:6–3:17, Paul encourages believers to continue in Christ, watch out for false teachers, celebrate the nature and work of Christ, and set their affection on things above. Much of Colossians 3 overlaps with what we studied in Ephesians 4 and 5—taking off old ways and putting on our new ways in Christ (review Figures 2.14 and 2.36).

In Colossians 3:18–4:1, Paul states rules of behavior in the family of God. Take a moment to review our earlier study of relationships in God's family (Figure 3.20).

Q 120 ✎ What stands out to you as your review Figure 4.38 on relationships?

Q 117 ➚ What does Colossians 1:1–2:5 emphasize?

Q 118 ✎ Which chapters in Colossians emphasize our responsibilities?

Q 119 ➚ In this lesson, why did we not spend much time on relationships at home and at work?

| Ephesians | What Paul Explains on Relationships in Ephesians, He Only Summarizes in Colossians | | Colossians |
|---|---|---|---|
| 5:25-33 | [25]**Husbands**, love your wives, just as Christ loved the church and gave himself up for her [26]to make her holy, cleansing her by the washing with water through the word, [27]and to present her to himself as a radiant church, without stain or wrinkle or any other blemish, but holy and blameless. [28]In this same way, husbands ought to love their wives as their own bodies. He who loves his wife loves himself. [29]After all, no one ever hated his own body, but he feeds and cares for it, just as Christ does the church— [30]for we are members of his body. [31]"For this reason a man will leave his father and mother and be united to his wife, and the two will become one flesh." [32]This is a profound mystery—but I am talking about Christ and the church. [33]However, each one of you also must love his wife as he loves himself, and the wife must respect her husband. | **Husbands**, love your wives and do not be harsh with them. | 3:19 |

Figure 4.38   Continued on next page

Continued from previous page

| Ephesians | What Paul Explains on Relationships in Ephesians, He Only Summarizes in Colossians | | Colossians |
|---|---|---|---|
| 6:1-3 | [1]***Children***, *obey your parents in the Lord, for this is right.* [2]*"Honor your father and mother"—which is the first commandment with a promise—* [3]*"that it may go well with you and that you may enjoy long life on the earth."* | ***Children***, *obey your parents in everything, for this pleases the Lord.* | 3:20 |
| 6:4 | ***Fathers***, *do not exasperate your children; instead, bring them up in the training and instruction of the Lord.* | ***Fathers***, *do not embitter your children, or they will become discouraged.* | 3:21 |
| 6:5-8 | [5]***Slaves***, *obey your earthly masters with respect and fear, and with sincerity of heart, just as you would obey Christ.* [6]*Obey them not only to win their favor when their eye is on you, but like slaves of Christ, doing the will of God from your heart.* [7]*Serve wholeheartedly, as if you were serving the Lord, not men,* [8]*because you know that the Lord will reward everyone for whatever good he does, whether he is slave or free.* | [22]***Slaves***, *obey your earthly masters in everything; and do it, not only when their eye is on you and to win their favor, but with sincerity of heart and reverence for the Lord.* [23]*Whatever you do, work at it with all your heart, as working for the Lord, not for men,* [24]*since you know that you will receive an inheritance from the Lord as a reward. It is the Lord Christ you are serving.* [25]*Anyone who does wrong will be repaid for his wrong, and there is no favoritism.* | 3:22-25 |
| 6:9 | *And* ***masters***, *treat your slaves in the same way. Do not threaten them, since you know that he who is both their Master and yours is in heaven, and there is no favoritism with him* | *Anyone who does wrong will be repaid for his wrong, and there is no favoritism.* | 3:25 |

**Figure 4.38   In this course on the four Prison Epistles, sections in Ephesians 4–6 overlap Colossians 3–4. Rather than cover the same topics twice, we include the short sections of Colossians 3–4 in the lessons on Ephesians 4–6. For example, what Paul says to wives, we cover in Ephesians 5:22-24, including the one verse from Colossians 3:18. And what Paul says to husbands, we cover in the 9 verses of Ephesians 5:25-33, including the one verse from Colossians 3:19.**

Congratulations on completing your study on the twin epistles of Ephesians and Colossians. Thank you for your work as you prepare to serve others. In the next chapter, we will have a joyful study of Philippians.

**Test Yourself:** Circle the letter by the *best* completion to each question or statement

1. Which of these cities is larger?
a) Ephesus
b) Colosse
c) Philippi
d) Thessalonica

2. What amount of Colossians overlaps with Ephesians?
a) 20 percent
b) 40 percent
c) 60 percent
d) 80 percent

3. Why did Paul give thanks for the Colossians?
a) They turned from idols to serve God.
b) They were known for their generosity.
c) They excelled in spiritual gifts.
d) They received the gospel from Epaphras.

4. Which 2 things did Paul pray for the Colossians?
a) To have unity, and avoid division
b) To know and do God's will
c) To become wise and counsel others
d) To have order and edification

5. Paul prayed for the Colossians to please God
a) with fruit, knowledge, and endurance.
b) with spiritual gifts and thankfulness.
c) with fruit and a generous offering.
d) with repentance for their divisions.

6. How did the Colossian heresy lower Christ?
a) By denying the resurrection
b) By exalting rules and angels
c) By emphasizing education
d) By replacing holy living with grace

7. Colossians 1:15-17 emphasizes that Christ is
a) Supreme as King.
b) Supreme as Priest.
c) Supreme as Mediator.
d) Supreme as Creator.

8. Which phrase describes Christ as Supreme Reconciler?
a) Head of the body
b) Firstborn over creation
c) Image of the invisible God
d) Before all things

9. What did Paul's setting illustrate?
a) The cost of spiritual ministry
b) The message of spiritual ministry
c) The purpose of spiritual ministry
d) The power of spiritual ministry

10. What is a key to overcoming false teachers?
a) Emphasize rules for every aspect of life.
b) Be willing to pay for your sins.
c) Set your affections on things above.
d) Magnify grace and avoid law.

**Essay Test Topics:** Write 50-100 words on each of these goals that you studied in this chapter (6 points each). Try to complete your writing in 2 hours.

- Analyze the authorship, date, city, purposes, theme, and outline of Colossians.
- Compare and contrast Colossians and Ephesians.
- Summarize 3 reasons why Paul gave thanks for the Colossians (Col. 1:1-8).
- Identify the 2 things Paul asked God to do for the Colossians.
- Explain 4 ways that Paul wanted the Colossians to please God.
- Summarize 6 errors of the Colossian heresy.
- Explain 4 ways Christ is Supreme as Creator (Col. 1:15-17).
- Analyze 4 ways Christ is Supreme as Reconciler (Col. 1:18-23). Apply these.
- Examine the cost, message, purpose, and power of spiritual ministry (Col. 1:24–2:5).
- Identify, illustrate, and apply 4 ways to overcome false teachings (Col. 2:6-23).

# Unit 3:
# Exploring Philippians and Philemon

Paul's letter to the Philippians is filled with the fragrance of joy. Paul writes about:

- *Joy in the places where we are—even in prison (Phil. 1:12-26)*
- *Joy in relationships with those around us (Phil. 1:27–2:30)*
- *Joy in the Lord—rather than in ourselves (Phil. 3:1–4:1)*
- *Joy in the Lord—in any circumstance (Phil. 4:2-20).*

Living in joy depends so much on the doors of life. There are always at least three doors before us. Like Paul, we can practice the principle of leaving some doors closed, and choosing to open others.

In Philippians and Philemon, Paul writes about joy in relationships and in all circumstances. As you study Unit 3, here are some goals we will help you achieve:

## Chapter 5: Philippians—A Letter of Joy (Phil. 1–4)
- *Analyze the authorship, date, recipients, city, purposes, outline, themes, background, and setting of Philippians.*
- *Sketch and explain a diagram of Paul's prayer (Phil. 1:9-11).*
- *Make a chart of key events in Acts 21–28, showing Paul's path to Rome.*
- *Explain and illustrate 3 doors that are always before us in difficult times.*
- *State the principle of Philippians 2:4, and illustrate it 7 times from Philippians 1–2. Sketch and explain the contrast between legalists, followers of Christ, and libertines (Phil. 3).*
- *Summarize factors of joy and peace (Phil. 4).*

## Chapter 6 (Philem. 1)
- *Analyze the problem of slavery in Paul's day and the biblical solution.*
- *From Philemon, explain, illustrate and apply 12 principles for resolving conflict.*

# Chapter 5:
# Philippians: A Letter of Joy
## (Phil. 1–4)

**Q 1** ✎ *Fill in the blanks with the names of the Prison Epistles.*

**Q 2** ✎ *Where should you look for joy if you are feeling low?*

Jesus is the reason we sing so much and so often. Is your joy low? Maybe you are looking in the wrong direction. Look up! Even in prison, we can sing as we turn our eyes upon Jesus.

*15 He is the image of the invisible God, the firstborn over all creation. 16 For by him all things were created: things in heaven and on earth, visible and invisible, whether thrones or powers or rulers or authorities; all things were created by him and for him. 17 He is before all things, and in him all things hold together. 18 And he is the head of the body, the church; he is the beginning and the firstborn from among the dead, so that in everything he might have the supremacy. 19 For God was pleased to have all his fullness dwell in him, 20 and through him to reconcile to himself all things, whether things on earth or things in heaven, by making peace through his blood, shed on the cross.*

*21 Once we were alienated from God and were enemies in our minds because of our evil behavior. 22 But now he has reconciled us by Christ's physical body through death to present us holy in his sight, without blemish and free from accusation...* (Col. 1:15-21).

*3 in Him are hidden all the treasures of wisdom and knowledge* (Col. 2:3).

—and He lives in our hearts! How can we keep from singing His praise?
https://www.youtube.com/watch?v=vh_8rTBpvRU

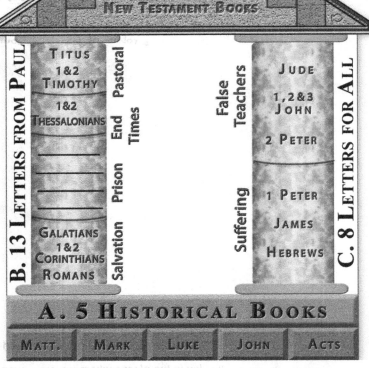

**Figure 5.1   The New Testament contains four letters that Paul wrote from prison: Ephesians, Colossians, Philippians and Philemon.**

## Lessons:

### Understanding Philippians

**Goal A:** *Analyze the authorship, date, recipients, and city of Philippians.*
**Goal B:** *Explain the purposes, outline, and 4 themes of Philippians.*
**Goal C:** *Summarize the background and setting of Philippians.*

### Introduction to Paul's Letter of Joy (Phil. 1:1-11)

**Goal A:** *Explain 3 characteristics of a good greeting to someone we love (Phil. 1:1-2).*
**Goal B:** *State and illustrate the gratitude principle (Phil. 1:3-8).*
**Goal C:** *Sketch a diagram of Paul's prayer (Phil. 1:9-11). Explain its parts, contrasting the worldly and the godly.*

## Joy in Where We Are (Phil. 1:12-26)

**25**
**Goal A:** Make a chart of key events in Acts 21–28 showing how Paul became a prisoner of Christ in Rome.
**Goal B:** Explain the door of bitterness before Paul, and how he left it closed. Apply these truths to us.
**Goal C:** Give examples of what happened as Paul opened the door of opportunity in hard times. Apply this.
**Goal D:** Summarize things that could have caused Paul to doubt. Explain how he opened the door of trust.

## Joy in Those Around Us—Part 1 (Phil. 1:27–2:11)

**26**
**Goal A:** State the principle of Philippians 2:4, and illustrate it by contrasting believing with suffering.
**Goal B:** State the principle of Philippians 2:4, and illustrate it with fruits of salvation and the kenosis.

## Joy in Those Around Us—Part 2 (Phil. 2:12-30)

**27**
**Goal A:** State the principle of Philippians 2:4, and illustrate it with working out our salvation in relationships.
**Goal B:** State the principle of Philippians 2:4, and illustrate it with Paul's attitudes toward death, Timothy, and Epaphroditus.

## Joy in the Lord (Phil. 3:1–4:1)

**28**
**Goal A:** Contrast the role of good deeds in legalists and true Christians (Phil. 3:1-11). Sketch the contrast.
**Goal B:** Illustrate the problems of bragging on the past and meditating on past failures (Phil. 3:12-14).
**Goal C:** Analyze the balance in depending on Christ, yet straining and pressing toward the goal (Phil. 3:12-14).
**Goal D:** Contrast and illustrate legalists, followers of Christ, and libertines in Paul's writings (Phil. 3:12-21).

## Joy in the Lord—in Any Circumstance (Phil. 4:2-23)

**29**
**Goal A:** Summarize how joy and peace depend on agreeing in the Lord and rejoicing in the Lord (Phil. 4:2-4).
**Goal B:** Analyze and illustrate the relationship of joy and peace to prayer, right thinking, and right living (Phil. 4:6-9).
**Goal C:** Explain and illustrate a principle about joy for each of these: contentment, thankfulness, and generosity (Phil. 4:10-19).

---

## Key Words

**kenosis**—a Greek word that refers to Christ *emptying* Himself of His privileges, to become a servant, and save us by dying on the cross

**Legalists**—those who emphasize salvation by rules, as some Jewish teachers; Paul refers to these as dogs, because of their harsh nature.

**Libertines**—those who ignore laws or claim to be free from obeying God's laws; Paul says their god is their appetite, and destruction is their destiny. Scripture compares libertines to hogs, who wallow in the mud.

**Euodia and Syntyche**—two beloved ladies among the church leaders in Philippi

---

**Lesson 23** **Understanding Philippians**
**Goal A:** Analyze the authorship, date, recipients, and city of Philippians.
**Goal B:** Explain the purposes, outline, and 4 themes of Philippians.
**Goal C:** Summarize the background and setting of Philippians.

**Q 3** Which 4 letters do we call the Prison Epistles?

## A. Author and date

We are studying the four letters that Paul wrote from prison: Ephesians, Colossians, Philippians, and Philemon. Each of these four letters begins with Paul's name, showing that he is the author. Also, all four letters refer to Paul's chains or bonds (Col. 1:24; Eph. 3:1; 4:1; 6:20; Phil. 1:1-13; Philem 1, 9-10). Most believe that Paul wrote these letters from Rome. He probably wrote the four prison epistles about A.D. 60–61. His time in prison was difficult, but fruitful. In Rome, a Roman soldier was guarding Paul at all times and may have been chained to him.[1] He lived in a house he rented for 2 years and received visitors (Acts 28:16, 30-31). This enabled him to hear reports from churches. As a result, he wrote letters to encourage, solve problems, teach, and guide believers. His ministry of prayer and evangelism continued in spite of his chains (Col. 1:3-14; Eph. 1:15-23; Phil. 1:3-6, 12-18; Philem 4-6).

*Q 4* ➚ *For which famous king was Philippi named? On what highway was Philippi?*

We have reviewed the authorship, date, and setting of the Prison Epistles. Now let us consider several key things about Paul's letter to the Philippians.

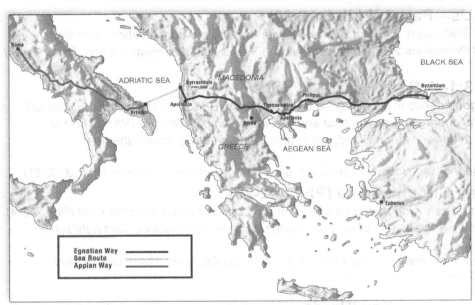

Figure 5.2    The Egnatian Way

## B. The recipients and their city

Philippi was named after King Philip the Second, father of Alexander the Great. It was located on the Egnatian Way—a stone road built in the second century B.C., that stretched about 1,100 kilometers (700 miles). The Egnatian Way began on the east side of the Adriatic Sea at the city of Dyrrachium (now Durrës). It stretched across the Roman provinces of Illyricum, Macedonia, and Thrace. This important road connected the Adriatic and Aegean Seas—going through modern Albania, Macedonia, Greece, and European Turkey (Figure 5.2).[2] This stone road helped Philippi be a prosperous colony of Rome. People in Rome called Philippi "the gateway to the east." It was a Gentile city with few Jews. There was no synagogue in Philippi when Paul was there (Acts 16:12). This probably means there were less than ten Jewish men there and explains why Paul does not quote the Old Testament in his letter to the Philippians. Politically, Philippi was like Rome in every way—with Roman laws, Roman styles, and Roman citizens with all the rights and privileges of Rome! Paul contrasted being a citizen of Rome with being a citizen of heaven (Phil. 3:20-21).

*Q 5* ➚ *How was Philippi like Rome? Were the citizens Jews or Gentiles?*

*Q 6* ➚ *Which 3 conversions began the church in Philippi?*

Acts 16 tells the story of three conversions that led to the church in Philippi: **Lydia**, a successful businesswoman; a **girl with a demon**; and a **jailer** with his family. Believers in Philippi were special to Paul. They sent gifts to him on several occasions (see Phil. 1:3-5; 2:25-30; 4:10-20). And Paul boasted about their generosity to other churches (2 Cor. 8:1-5). Philippian believers sent Epaphroditus, their personal representative, to help care for Paul while he was in prison. This letter reflects the warmth of a close friendship!

*Q 7* ➚ *What are 4 reasons that Paul wrote Philippians?*

## C. Purposes of the letter:

- *To say "thank you"* for the gift they gave and concern they showed to Paul in prison (Phil. 1:5; 4:10-19);

- *To report on his circumstances* that God was using to spread the gospel (Phil. 1:12-26; 4:10-19). The Philippians had sent Epaphroditus to Paul with money, but he had not returned. So they wondered what had happened. Paul writes to tell them that Epaphroditus was sick, and almost died. But God had mercy and restored him, sparing Paul sorrow upon sorrow (Phil. 2:27).

- *To encourage believers* to rejoice and stand firm in spite of circumstances (Phil. 1:27-30; 4:4);
- *To exhort them to unity* in relationships through love and humility (Phil. 2:1-11; 4:2-5);
- *To commend Timothy and Ephaphroditus* to the church;
- *To warn believers* to avoid errors of Judaizers (legalists) and the worldly (libertines, Phil. 3).

## D. Outline and themes of Philippians

| Themes | Philippians |
|---|---|
| **Introduction** | **1:1-11** |
| Greeting | 1:1-2 |
| Thanksgiving | 1:9-8 |
| Prayer for believers | 1:3-11 |
| **A. Joy in the Places Where We Are—Even in Prison** | **1:12-26** |
| **B. Joy in Relationships With Those Around Us** | **1:27–2:30** |
| Live a life worthy of the gospel. | 1:27-30 |
| Follow the servant-example of Christ | 2:1-18 |
| Paul's Messengers: Timothy and Epaphroditus | 2:19-30 |
| **C. Joy in the Lord** | **3:1–4:1** |
| Avoiding the sorrow of the Judaizers, who emphasize rules too much | 3:1-16 |
| Avoiding the sorrow of the worldly, who emphasize the flesh too much | 3:17–4:1 |
| **D. Joy in the Lord—in Any Circumstance** | **4:2-20** |
| Teachings about unity, joy, gentleness, and peace | 4:2-9 |
| Testimony and thanks to the Philippians | 4:10-20 |
| **Conclusion** | **4:21-23** |

**Figure 5.3   Outline of Philippians**

We will spend at least one lesson on each main point of the outline, A–D.

> **Q 8** ↗ *What word stands out in the outline of Philippians?*

## E. Background and setting

The founding of the church at Philippi was on Paul's second missionary journey (Figure 5.5). After the Jerusalem Council of Acts 15, Paul and Barnabas returned to minister in Antioch Syria. In about A.D. 50, Paul said to Barnabas,

> **Q 9** ↗ *Which chapters in Acts give us the background of the church in Philippi?*

> *"... Let us go back and visit the brothers in all the towns where we preached the word of the Lord and see how they are doing."* [37] *Barnabas wanted to take John, also called Mark, with them,* [38] *but Paul did not think it wise to take him, because he had deserted them in Pamphylia and had not continued with them in the work.* [39] *They had such a sharp disagreement that they parted company. Barnabas took Mark and sailed for Cyprus,* [40] *but Paul chose Silas and left, commended by the brothers to the grace of the Lord.* [41] *He went through Syria and Cilicia, strengthening the churches* (Acts 15:36-41).

On the second missionary trip, Paul and Silas walked north in Syria. When they got to the north coast of the Mediterranean Sea, they turned west and continue walking—through Paul's home city of Tarsus. They continued west, following in the steps of Paul's first missionary journey. They passed through Derbe and on to Lystra—where a young man named Timothy joined them. From Lystra, they walked on to Iconium, and then Antioch in Pisidia. By this time, they had walked at least 565 kilometers (350 miles), not counting all the ups, downs, and arounds of the mountains (Figures 5.4 and 5.5). And keep in mind that they were not wearing Nike shoes!

| Description | Kilometers | Miles |
|---|---|---|
| Antioch, Syria to Tarsus | 241 | 150 |
| Tarsus to Derbe | 145 | 90 |
| Derbe to Lystra | 48 | 30 |
| Lystra to Iconium | 48 | 30 |
| Iconium to Antioch in Pisidia | 137 | 85 |
| Antioch in Pisidia to Dorylaeum | 241 | 150 |
| Dorylaeum to Troas | 402 | 250 |
| **Totals** | 1263 | 785 |

**Q 10** ⊁ *How far did a traveler like Paul walk in a day?*

**Figure 5.4　Some distances Paul walked on his second missionary journey through Philippi in Macedonia.**

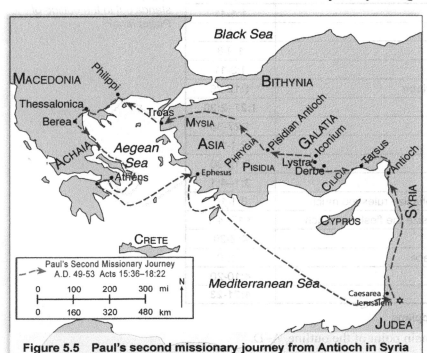

**Figure 5.5　Paul's second missionary journey from Antioch in Syria**

Horses were faster than walking. But horses were for the wealthy. Remember that Paul had little income and even sewed tents to earn enough money for the basics. A fast Roman courier on horseback changed horses every 16-48 kilometers (10-30 miles), and went about 80 kilometers (50 miles) per day. But a walker, like the apostle Paul, traveled 5 km (3 miles) in an hour, and about 32 kilometers (20 miles) per day.[3] So to walk from Antioch, Syria to Antioch, Pisidia—at least 565 km (350 miles)—took Paul and Silas 20 days of walking, depending on things such as food, health, rest, wind, rain, snow, or robbers. And of course, they spent many days ministering in the young churches planted on the first missionary journey.

**Q 11** ⊁ *Fill in the blanks beside Figure 5.6 that identify seven large provinces, four smaller districts like the three in ASIA, and 15 cities.*

*A–G are for provinces, H–K for districts, and 1–15 for cities.*

A. _____　　1. _____

B. _____　　2. _____

C. _____　　3. _____

D. _____　　4. _____

E. _____　　5. _____

F. _____　　6. _____

G. _____　　7. _____

　　　　　　　8. _____

H. _____　　9. _____

I. _____　　10. _____

J. _____　　11. _____

K. _____　　12. _____

　　　　　　　13. _____

　　　　　　　14. _____

　　　　　　　15. _____

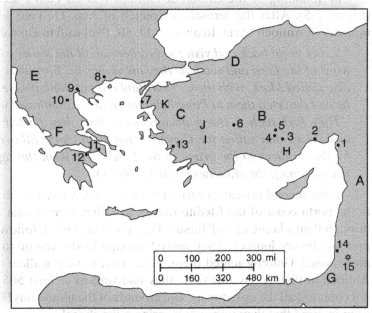

**Figure 5.6　Practice map of Paul's second trip**

In Antioch, Pisidia, even though they have walked at least 20 days, Paul is not content to stay where churches already exist. So he, Silas, and Timothy start walking west toward the Roman province of Asia, which is western Turkey. One wonders if Silas knew what he had signed up for. No doubt, Paul is headed for the capital city of Ephesus. But the Spirit says they cannot go there. So they turned north, at the border of Mysia, trying to go into Bithynia (northern Turkey, south of today's Russian border). Again, the Spirit says they cannot go there. Luke writes, *[7]When they came to the border of Mysia, they tried to enter Bithynia, but the Spirit of Jesus would not allow them to. [8]So they passed by Mysia and went down to Troas* (Acts 16:7-8).

**Q 12** *On Paul's second missionary trip, how far did they walk to reach Philippi?*

By this time, they have walked an additional 650 km (400 miles). Probably, if he had walked straight and never retraced his steps or never taken a curving mountain route, he would have walked straight 800 miles. But in all likelihood, by that time he had walked 1,200 miles. During that long trip, he had with him Silas, and he picked up Timothy at Lystra. He did not know where he was going, but the Spirit was telling him where not to go.

Some of you have had the experience of the Lord saying you should *not* to do something—and you wish He would tell you what you *should* do. But all He seems to be saying is, "No, you can't do this," "No, you can't do that." The wonderful thing about the apostle Paul on this trip is that he never lies down in the path and starts complaining to God, saying, "I'm not going to take another step until You tell me what to do!" I imagine there were times when the young missionary Timothy said, "Where are we going?" And Paul said, "I don't know where we are going. I just know where we are *not* going." So with a good attitude, he continued to walk those hundreds of miles.

**Q 13** *Have you ever needed to walk by faith, without knowing where you were going? Explain.*

Paul finally gets where he can walk no further because there is the sea. While there, at the city of **Troas,** *"During the night Paul had a vision of a man of Macedonia standing and begging him, 'Come over to Macedonia and help us'"* (Acts 16:9). Macedonia is Northern Greece. So on the basis of that man of Macedonia, they board a ship. By this time Luke has joined them, so there are four men going to evangelize where there is not even one believer. That is a lot of faith—four people going into a place where there are no Christians, to plant the church.

The journey by boat is another 320 km (200 miles). When they reach Philippi, there is no man from Macedonia to meet him! No mayor greets them with the key to the city. Philippi was a proud and prosperous Roman colony—planted right in the middle of Greek culture.

**Q 14** *In Philippi, why was there no synagogue?*

**Q 15** *What does Paul's preaching in Philippi show about his attitude toward women?*

So Paul arrives in Philippi and, as was Paul's custom, they looked first for a synagogue—to find Jews worshiping. Paul liked to enter the synagogue and explain the Scriptures on the Sabbath Day. But Philippi did not have a synagogue. That means it did not have ten Jewish men 20 years or older. So, Paul looks for a river. For where there were few Jews, they would gather to worship by a river outside of the city. Paul finds the Gangites River and discovers a small company of women.[4] Some think of Paul as a person who did not like women. But this is not true. So Paul explains the gospel of Jesus to the group of ladies by the river in Philippi. *One* of them opens her heart to the Lord. Her name is Lydia. She became the first convert in Europe. Then she opens her home to Paul and the three men with him.

Later, Paul begins walking the streets of the city—still no action. No man of Macedonia meets him. Luke records no male converts to the church at this point. In the market, they encounter a slave girl who has a spirit that enables her to predict the future. For many days, she follows them, mocking and shouting,

**Figure 5.7**
**The Gangites River where Paul met Lydia**

**Q 16** ✎ *What are some questions Satan might have whispered to Paul in prison, in Philippi?*

**Figure 5.8　Paul and Silas prayed and sang in prison at Philippi.**

**Q 17** ➚ *In prison, what did Paul do instead of complaining?*

**Q 18** ✎ *Do you think the jailer would have been saved if Paul had been complaining instead of singing? Explain.*

**Q 19** ✎ *What lesson can we learn from Paul's humility and rejoicing in Philippi?*

[17b] *"These men are servants of the Most High God, who are telling you the way to be saved." She kept this up for many days.* [18] *Finally Paul became so troubled that he turned around and said to the spirit, "In the name of Jesus Christ I command you to come out of her!" At that moment the spirit left her.* [19] *When the owners of the slave girl realized that their hope of making money was gone, they seized Paul and Silas and dragged them into the marketplace to face the authorities.* [20] *They brought them before the magistrates and said, "These men are Jews, and are throwing our city into an uproar* [21] *by advocating customs unlawful for us Romans to accept or practice."* [22] *The crowd joined in the attack against Paul and Silas, and the magistrates ordered them to be stripped and beaten.* [23] *After they had been severely flogged, they were thrown into prison, and the jailer was commanded to guard them carefully.* [24] *Upon receiving such orders, he put them in the inner cell and fastened their feet in the stocks* (Acts 16:17b-24).

As Paul and Silas were bleeding in prison at Philippi, Satan might have whispered questions to Paul, like these:

- Did you miss the will of God because you argued with Barnabas, your best friend?

- Have you walked all those miles outside the will of God?

- Since no man met you in Macedonia, was your vision just a bad dream?

- If God loves you, why did He let you walk all these miles to meet a man who is not here, and then get a beating and be locked in prison? Is this how God treats those He loves?

- Was it fair of God to let Luke and Timothy go free, and let you and Silas be beaten and jailed?

Satan may have whispered questions like these. But Paul and Silas did not pay any attention to them. They knew whom they had believed. The pain in their backs and the stocks on their feet made it impossible to sleep. *But they made an important decision.* Instead of complaining, they started singing a song of praise to God. So there is this beautiful moment at midnight in the jail at Philippi. Their joyful song of praise to God is a key to their victory. This habit Paul had of rejoicing, like a star shining in the night, was a key to his fruitful life.

> SATAN MAY HAVE WHISPERED QUESTIONS LIKE THESE. BUT PAUL AND SILAS DID NOT PAY ANY ATTENTION TO THEM. THEY KNEW WHOM THEY HAD BELIEVED.

**Application.** There are moments when life is hard. Things fall in on us. We want to lie down, cover ourselves with pity, and blame God for our troubles. But in those moments, when we feel the lowest, like Paul, we need to release a hymn of praise to God.

That song at midnight in the jail was a special moment for Paul, because suddenly everything changed. God sent an earthquake. Soon the strong Roman jailer is kneeling and trembling before Paul and Silas—asking how he can be saved. Perhaps he was the man God showed Paul in a vision. The jailer and his family, Lydia, and probably many she knew, and perhaps the slave girl that had been delivered from a demon—all these became members of the new church in Philippi. Why? Because Paul and his team lived as *servants* of the Lord. They went where the Lord sent them. And they practiced being joyful, even though the journey was difficult. God is able to bless others through us as we see ourselves as servants and practice the habit of rejoicing.

## Introduction to Paul's Letter of Joy (Phil. 1:1-11).

Lesson 24

**Goal A:** *Explain 3 characteristics of a good greeting to someone we love (Phil. 1:1-2).*
**Goal B:** *State and illustrate the gratitude principle (Phil. 1:3-8).*
**Goal C:** *Sketch a diagram of Paul's prayer (Phil. 1:9-11). Explain its parts, contrasting the worldly and the godly.*

Paul and Silas planted the church in Philippi about A.D. 50 on Paul's second missionary trip. We have studied this background. About 10 years later, in A.D. 61, Paul wrote to the Philippians—as he sat chained in Rome.

**The introduction to Philippians includes three parts:** A. Paul's greeting (Phil. 1:1-2); B. His gratitude (Phil. 1:3-8); and C. His prayer (Phil. 1:9-11). Let us study each of these.

### A. Our greeting to believers should be personal, courteous, and complimentary (Phil. 1:1-2).

[1]*Paul and Timothy, servants* of Christ Jesus, To all the *saints in Christ Jesus at Philippi, together with the overseers and deacons:* [2]*Grace and peace to you from God our Father and the Lord Jesus Christ* (Phil. 1:1-2).

Paul's letters always begin with the courtesy of a greeting. He does not just rush into conversation without saying, "hello" and expressing a desire for all to go well with his readers. In other words, he is less direct and more indirect than much of Western culture. Paul's letters reflect a strong value on relationships. People, and their well-being, are near the top of Paul's priorities. And unlike some letters today, where people sign their names at the end, ancient people had a good idea. They put the author's name at the beginning. This makes the letter more personal, and lets the reader know at once who is writing. Note that Timothy is still with Paul, as he was when they planted the church at Philippi. So Paul sends greetings from himself and from Timothy, his son in the faith. Like Paul, we should greet others in ways that are courteous and personal.

Paul emphasizes that he and Timothy are servants of Christ Jesus. Acts 16 underlines the fact that Paul saw himself as a servant. Recall that he walked about 800 miles over mountains, and traveled another 200 miles by ship to reach Philippi. And when he was unfairly beaten and jailed, he did not pout, sulk, or complain. Instead, he sang a song of joy to God. May the Lord help all of us to see ourselves as servants—thinking more of others than we do ourselves. Paul will illustrate this point in the life of Jesus in Philippians 2:1-11. Thinking of others as well as self is a major principle we will study in Philippians 2.

Besides being courteous and personal, Paul included a compliment in his greeting. He referred to believers in Philippi as *saints*. This was not flattery, but truth; for all believers are saints—which means *holy*. Like God, we are holy in three ways: our position, our actions, and our condition (See the *Faith & Action* book *Romans & Galatians*, Figure 5.4, with its discussion.) **There are more saints living on earth than in heaven.** Some err by saying that we do not become saints until we reach heaven. Before he met Christ, Paul put many of the saints in prison (Acts 26:29). And as God's apostle, Paul wrote to **the saints at Philippi** (Phil. 1:1). These were not people who had lived and died on earth, then suffered through hundreds of years of purgatory, and finally been promoted to be saints in

**Q 20** *How many years passed between Paul's trip to Philippi and his letter to the Philippians?*

**Q 21** *What are the 3 parts of this lesson?*

**Q 22** *In your culture, do people take time to greet with courtesy?*

**Q 23** *What makes Paul's letters more personal than many letters today?*

**Q 24** *What are some ways Paul showed he was a servant?*

**Q 25** *How can we recognize a servant in the church today?*

**Q 26** *What does the word "saints" mean? Do we become saints on earth or in heaven? Explain.*

**Q 27** *When and how do we become saints?*

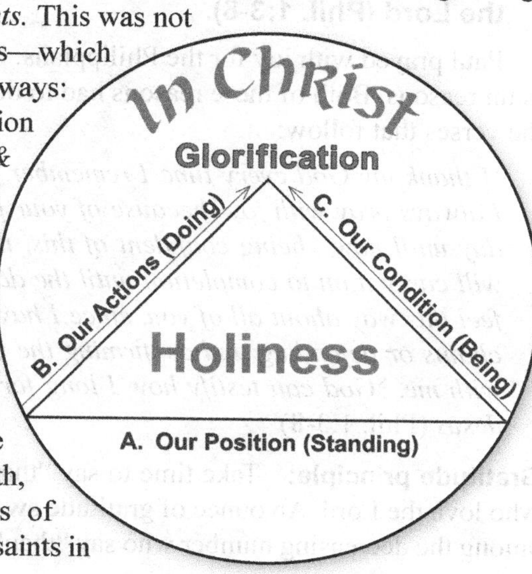

**Figure 5.9
Holiness (sanctification) includes three aspects: our position, our actions, and our condition.**

heaven. No! The *saints* that Paul wrote to were living on the earth. They were members of a church in Philippi that was only about 10 years old. Who were the saints in the church at Philippi? The word saint means *holy*. Throughout his letters Paul refers to all believers in Christ as *saints*. When Paul writes "*to all the saints in Christ Jesus at Philippi* including *the overseers and deacons*," (Phil. 1:1)we can picture three people. There was Lydia, a businesswoman; there was an unnamed girl that had been delivered from a demon; and an unnamed Roman jailer. These three *saints* remind us of the nature of the church of Jesus Christ. The Church is NOT a club where people gather because they have the same income, the same personalities, or the same interests. Rather, the church of Jesus Christ unites people who may be very different from one another. Yet when we discover Jesus Christ—when He forgives our sins and calls us *holy*, we have something in common. We are all forgiven, redeemed by His blood, and alive in Jesus Christ—for by His blood and His grace He has *qualified us to share in the inheritance of the saints in the kingdom of light* (Eph. 1:7; 2:1-3; Col. 1:12). The *saints* are not people we pray to in heaven. The *saints* Paul wrote to were common people on earth whom God had already qualified to be *citizens of heaven* (Phil. 3:20; Eph. 2:19). Paul defines *saints* as those who have discovered new life in Christ. The saints at Philippi included a local businesswoman, a girl delivered from demon possession, and a jailer! Likewise today, saints on earth are not people perfected through hundreds of years of living and suffering. *Saints* are just plain people. We are the body of Christ on earth, growing in His likeness in righteousness and holiness, and being renewed in the image of our Creator day by day (Phil. 1:1; Eph. 4:23; Col. 3:10; 2 Cor. 3:18). In heaven too, there are saints—all the believers who walked with God when they lived on earth. For to be absent from the body is to be present with the Lord (2 Cor. 5:8; Rev. 6:9-11). But there are more people living on the earth in this generation than all the previous generations combined. So there must be more saints living on earth than there are in heaven.

**Q 28** Which always comes first, grace or peace? Explain.

In his greeting to the saints, Paul says, "*Grace and peace to you from God our Father, and the Lord Jesus Christ*" (Phil. 1:2). Grace always precedes peace. People search in vain for peace if they do not first find God's grace. But rejoice, for you have peace knowing that God is your Father and Jesus is your Lord! The day is coming when we will celebrate our inheritance with all the saints—from Philippi and other places—because God is our Father and Jesus is our Lord. Paul packed a lot into his greeting—we are servants and saints, blessed with grace and peace, because God is our Father and Jesus rules over our lives.

### B. Say "thank you" to those who are kind to you, and to those who love the Lord (Phil. 1:3-8).

Paul prayed with joy for the Philippians. He gave **thanks** for these believers for *two* main reasons. Both of these reasons had to do with sharing. See if you can spot them in the verses that follow:

> [3]*I thank my God every time I remember you.* [4]*In all my prayers for all of you, I always pray with joy* [5]*because of your partnership in the gospel from the first day until now,* [6]*being confident of this, that he who began a good work in you will carry it on to completion until the day of Christ Jesus.* [7]*It is right for me to feel this way about all of you, since I have you in my heart; for whether I am in chains or defending and confirming the gospel, all of you share in God's grace with me.* [8]*God can testify how I long for all of you with the affection of Christ Jesus* (Phil. 1:3-8).

**Q 29** Where you live, do most people express thanks to those who deserve it? Explain.

**Gratitude principle:**    Take time to say "thank you" to those who are kind to you, and who love the Lord. An ounce of gratitude sweetens the attitude. Distinguish yourself: be among the decreasing number who say "thank you" when others do something for them.

Make someone's day. Show a little appreciation for the work and thoughtfulness of others. Jesus healed ten lepers, but nine did not even say "thank you" (Luke 17:11-19)! Be like the one leper who said "thank you." Show some gratitude. Some estimate that even today, nine people out of 10 do *not* say "thank you" very often. Say "thank you" to a parent, a teacher, a pastor, a spouse, a child, or a friend. Say "thank you" whenever someone does something for you, whether it is big or small. Giving thanks costs us nothing, but it is worth a fortune to the people who receive it. We feel empty when we are thoughtful of others, but they show no gratefulness. But when we serve others and hear them say "thank you," this puts a smile on our faces and a song in our hearts. It makes us feel that our work was worthwhile.

**Q 30** *Why should believers practice the habit of saying "thank you"?*

The Philippians were partners with Paul in spreading the gospel. With their missionary, these believers shared the responsibility of sharing Jesus Christ with the lost. Paul saw their love in action. This gave him confidence that God would finish what He started in the believers at Philippi. In those early days, Lydia, the slave girl, and the jailer first began to share in the grace of God. Ten years had passed, and the grace they received had been overflowing year after year. It is truly a joy to pray for believers who continue in the grace of God, and who pass it on to others with their daily lives and through their offerings to missionaries. The prophet Jeremiah wept because the people to whom he he ministered were selfish and sinful. In contrast, Paul rejoiced that the Word of God took root in the Philippians and was producing a harvest of good deeds to others.

### C. Paul's prayer: may we grow in Christ, so that our love overflows in discernment and righteous living—to glorify God (Phil. 1:9-11).

Paul was joyful for the Philippians. But like any good leader, he urged the saints to continue growing in love. History reveals that believers never stand still for long. Our love for God and others either slides backward or moves forward. Love decreases or increases. Lukewarm love must chill to cold or heat to hot. Forward or backward is a law of life. We either grow to be more like Christ or we shrivel to be less like our Savior. So all of Paul's letters coach us to grow in love from good, to better, to best.

The introduction to Philippians includes a greeting, gratitude, and a prayer (Phil. 1:1-11). The focus of Paul's prayer is: *"...that your love may abound more and more"* (Phil. 1:9). Look closely at Paul's prayer.

**Q 31** *What is the focus of Paul's prayer (Phil. 1:9)?*

**Q 32** *What is the first way that mature love reveals itself? Give an example.*

**Q 33** *How do discerning and perceiving affect living? Illustrate.*

*⁹And this is my prayer: that your **love** may abound **more and more** in knowledge and depth of insight, ¹⁰so that you may be able to **discern** what is **best** and may be **pure and blameless** until the day of Christ, ¹¹**filled** with the fruit of righteousness that comes through Jesus Christ—**to the glory and praise of God** (Phil. 1:9-11).*

**Figure 5.10  Paul prayed for believers to *love* God and others more and more (Phil. 1:9-11). Mature love reveals itself in two ways: *First*, we know God and His will, which enables us to discern and do what is best. *Second*, we perceive the nature and true value of things, which guides us to live pure and blameless. The result of mature love is that we choose what is best, and live pure and blameless, to glorify God.**

Our greatest need is to grow in love. All God requires of us is to love Him and others (Rom. 13:8-10; Matt. 7:12; 22:34-40). As our love matures, it reveals itself in two ways (Figure 5.10). Much of what Paul explains about righteous living in Ephesians 2 and 4–6, he packs into three verses in his prayer of Philippians 1:9-11! So let us look more closely at how mature love for God expresses itself.

**Q 34** ⬉ *How does knowing God's will enlighten our choices?*

**Knowing God and His will.**    In Figure 5.10 look at the *top* row, to the right of the heart. Mature love knows God and His will. Mature love understands what pleases God and what displeases Him. Mature love **knows** what God says is right and wrong. Knowing God and His will enlightens us to discern what to hate and what to love in this world. Mature love enlightens us to turn away from evil desires of the flesh and choose what is best—to please and glorify God. Earlier, we studied what Paul wrote about the way we lived *when we did not love God or know His will.*

> [1]*As for you, you were dead in your transgressions and sins,* [2]*in which you used to live when you followed the ways of this world and of the ruler of the kingdom of the air, the spirit who is now at work in those who are disobedient.* [3]*All of us also lived among them at one time, gratifying the cravings of our sinful nature and following its desires and thoughts. Like the rest, we were by nature objects of wrath* (Eph. 2:1-3).

Before we knew God and His will, we lived in sin. We were disobedient to the will of God. We followed the sinful desires of the flesh and the ways of the world. We were children of darkness.

**Q 35** ⬉ *How does a baby Christian differ from a mature one?*

In contrast, when we met God in Christ, we became children of light. Paul's prayer is for us to grow and mature in love—knowing God and His will (Phil. 1:9-11). *Agape* love discerns what is *best* for God's kingdom, *best* for our relationship with Him, and *best* for others—now and forever. *Biblical love is not blind, it has perfect spiritual vision.* Mature love discerns and chooses what

> WHEN WE MET GOD IN CHRIST, WE BECAME CHILDREN OF LIGHT.

pleases God. As God's love fills our heart, we turn away from the ways of darkness and walk as children of light—discerning and choosing the best decisions, attitudes, and actions to glorify God. Biblical love says "no" to disobeying God, and "yes" to obeying His will. This is the highest purpose of humans—to know, love, praise, and glorify God.

**Q 36** ⬉ *How can we recognize those without love for God?*

**Perceiving the nature and value of things.**    In Figure 5.10, look at the *bottom* row to the right of the heart. Without love for God in the heart, people lack insight. They are enemies of God and children of wrath. They love the world and the things of the world. They walk through life guided by lust of the flesh, lust of the eyes, and the pride of life (1 John 2:15-17). Satan and worldly businessmen deceive those who lack spiritual perception. They advertise products and pleasures that appeal to the flesh.

**Q 37** ⬈ *Why did the pigs follow the man?*

One man led a group of pigs to the slaughter by dropping beans on the path. The pigs ate the beans and followed the man to the slaughter. Like the pigs, those without the love of God lack discernment. James says they nourish their hearts, as in a *day of slaughter* (James 5:5). Paul also writes about those who lack perception. They are unable to discern the value of things in life. Paul says of these people who lack the love of God that they do not walk in the pattern or path of godliness. He calls them *"enemies of the cross of Christ. Their destiny is destruction, their god is their stomach, and their glory is in their shame. Their mind is on earthly things"* (Phil. 3:18-19).

**Q 38** ⬉ *Why do we obey God's commands? Why do people disobey God's commands?*

In contrast, those of us who *love* God keep His commands. We obey our Father because we love Him. And His love gives us perception. We perceive and turn away from the vile and worthless choices of life. We live *"pure and blameless until the day of*

*Christ"* (Phil. 1:10). In Ephesians 4–6 and Colossians 3–4 Paul explains what it means to walk worthy, living pure and blameless until the day of Christ.

A wise man described those who lack judgment and are without perception as *spiritually brain-dead.*

<sup>27</sup>*Can a man scoop fire into his lap without his clothes being burned?* <sup>28</sup>*Can a man walk on hot coals without his feet being scorched?* <sup>29</sup>*So is he who sleeps with another man's wife; no one who touches her will go unpunished...* <sup>32</sup>*But a man who commits adultery **lacks judgment**; whoever does so destroys himself.* <sup>33</sup>*Blows and disgrace are his lot, and his shame will never be wiped away* (Prov. 6:27-29; 32-33).

<sup>6</sup>*At the window of my house I looked out through the lattice.* <sup>7</sup>***I saw among the simple, I noticed among the young men, a youth who lacked judgment.*** <sup>8</sup>*He was going down the street near her corner, walking along in the direction of her house* <sup>9</sup>*at twilight, as the day was fading, as the dark of night set in.* <sup>10</sup>*Then out came a woman to meet him, dressed like a prostitute and with crafty intent.* <sup>11</sup>*(She is loud and defiant, her feet never stay at home;* <sup>12</sup>*now in the street, now in the squares, at every corner she lurks.)*

**Q 39** How does Proverbs describe a youth who is foolish and spiritually brain-dead?

<sup>13</sup>*She took hold of him and kissed him and with a brazen face she said:*

<sup>14</sup>*"I have fellowship offerings at home; today I fulfilled my vows.* <sup>15</sup>*So I came out to meet you; I looked for you and have found you!* <sup>16</sup>*I have covered my bed with colored linens from Egypt.* <sup>17</sup>*I have perfumed my bed with myrrh, aloes and cinnamon.* <sup>18</sup>*Come, let's drink deep of love till morning; let's enjoy ourselves with love!* <sup>19</sup>*My husband is not at home; he has gone on a long journey.* <sup>20</sup>*He took his purse filled with money and will not be home till full moon."*

<sup>21</sup>*With persuasive words she led him astray; she seduced him with her smooth talk.* <sup>22</sup>*All at once he followed her like an ox going to the slaughter, like a deer stepping into a noose* <sup>23</sup>*till an arrow pierces his liver, like a bird darting into a snare, little knowing it will cost him his life.* <sup>24</sup>*Now then, my sons, listen to me; pay attention to what I say.* <sup>25</sup>*Do not let your heart turn to her ways or stray into her paths.* <sup>26</sup>*Many are the victims she has brought down; her slain are a mighty throng.* <sup>27</sup>*Her house is a highway to the grave, leading down to the chambers of death* (Prov. 7:6-27).

<sup>7</sup>*Do not be deceived: God cannot be mocked. A man reaps what he sows.* <sup>8</sup>*The one who sows to please his sinful nature, from that nature will reap destruction; the one who sows to please the Spirit, from the Spirit will reap eternal life.* <sup>9</sup>*Let us not become weary in doing good, for at the proper time we will reap a harvest if we do not give up* (Gal. 6:7-9).

**Summary.**  The heart of Paul's prayers was for believers to grow in love. For as the love of God fills us, it inspires us to love Him and overflows in loving behavior to others. Paul links love to *knowing* God. As we know and experience God's love—its width, length, height, and depth—then we have all the fuel and energy we need to live worthy, please Him, and fulfill His will for our lives. *Little children* have little love, and they have shallow desires, thinking mostly of themselves—what they like and want. But *as we mature*, we learn to love God *more* than self. Our discernment deepens, and we balance personal desires with loving God and others. Biblical love says "yes" to sharing our time, energy, and money for His kingdom and those in need. Biblical love says "no" to fulfilling desires of the flesh that rebel against God and violate others. A lack of love is the root of every sin we commit. And a heart filled with love is the source of every good deed we do. Our greatest need is not to be smarter, stronger, or richer—but to overflow with God's love more and more (Phil. 1:9).

**How** does our love increase? Paul answers this question in his prayer (Phil. 1:9-11). God is love, so our love increases as our relationship with Him deepens. Thus, Paul prays that our knowledge (knowing God) may increase. Likewise, love expresses itself as the fruit of righteous living—which *comes through Jesus Christ* as we are *filled with the Spirit* (Phil. 1:11; Eph. 5:18). Our relationship with the *God of love* is the key to having all the love we need flowing through us. So let us meet our Father in devotions each morning; have an attitude of prayer throughout each day; sing to Him with spiritual songs; walk softly with Him in obedience; live in unity and fellowship with His other children; and live *filled with the Spirit*, seeking to please Him always.

In the Prison Epistles, let us review some prayers and desires of Paul for believers to *grow in love* (Figure 5.11).

**Q 40**    *Complete Figure 5.11, summarizing verses about growing in love for God and others.*

| Reference | Your Summaries |
|---|---|
| Eph. 1:17 | |
| Eph. 3:17-19 | |
| Eph. 4:14-16 | |
| Eph. 6:24 | |
| Col. 1:10 | |
| Col. 2:2 | |
| Col. 2:6-7 | |
| Col. 2:19 | |
| Col. 3:10 | |
| Col. 4:5 | |
| Phil. 1:9-11 | |
| Phil. 2:14 | |
| Phil. 3:12-15 | |
| Philem. 1:5-6 | Mature love shares the faith with *all* the saints—even slaves. For in Christ we are one family. |

**Figure 5.11**    **Practice summarizing Scriptures in the Prison Epistles about growing in love for God and others.**

After Paul's greeting, gratitude for the Philippians, and prayer for their increasing love, Paul begins to reveal his joy in difficult circumstances. We will study about Paul's joy in the next five lessons on Philippians.

## Joy in the Places Where We Are (Phil. 1:12-26)

Lesson 25

**Goal A:** *Make a chart of key events in Acts 21–28 showing how Paul became a prisoner of Christ in Rome.*

**Goal B:** *Explain the door of bitterness before Paul and how he left it closed. Apply these truths to us.*

**Goal C:** *Give examples of what happened as Paul opened the door of opportunity in hard times. Apply this.*

**Goal D:** *Summarize things that could have caused Paul to doubt. Explain how he opened the door of trust.*

**Q 41**  *Did Paul's joy depend on his circumstances?*

**Q 42**  *How can we have joy in hard times? What is the secret?*

Paul wrote Philippians from prison. Yet Philippians is one of the most positive letters in the Bible. It is a letter that overflows with joy. This joyful letter from a man in chains buries the idea that we must be in pleasant circumstances to be cheerful. A key to Paul's joy is that in the first 30 verses he mentions Jesus Christ 17 times. Get a grip on this truth. Paul mentions Jesus in 17 out of 30 verses. This has a lot to do with his attitude. For when we begin to speak the name of Jesus, we begin to look up instead of down. When we turn our eyes and our thoughts on Jesus, the Spirit lifts our emotions. As we study Philippians 1:12-26, let us look at three possibilities in difficult circumstances—like three closed doors we can open.

**Figure 5.12** In difficult circumstances, there are always three closed doors before us: bitterness, opportunity, and trust.

## A. The door of Bitterness is always before us in the difficult places of life.

Bitterness is a robber of joy. As a thief will steal your money, bitterness will steal your joy. No bitter person is happy or joyful. Bitterness is a cancer of the soul. It eats away joy, love, and spiritual life. And bitterness is a poison that curses those around us. Ask Esau. After selling his birthright to Jacob, he opened the door of bitterness. Four thousand years later, the descendants of Esau and Jacob still hate each other. So let us beware of planting the seed of bitterness lest it become a root below the ground and a tree with sour fruit above it (Heb. 12:15-17). Surely, if we discerned the fate that bitterness brings, we would leave this door closed and choose to never open it—no matter how difficult our circumstances. Opening the door of bitterness in hard times is like inviting a robber to protect you.

Paul had a good reason to be bitter. It was not fair for him to be in prison or in chains. Paul was *a prisoner of Christ Jesus* for **the sake of the Gentiles** (Col. 1:24; Eph. 3:1; 4:1; 6:20; Phil. 1:1-13; Philem 1, 9-10). In other words, prison was a part of what it cost Paul to love and serve the Gentiles. Paul was chained because he was faithful to God's call to preach to the Gentiles. To understand that Paul was in prison for his Gentile ministry, we must review Acts 21–28! Recall that you studied these in Chapter 1, Lesson 7. But these final chapters of Acts are a lot of material. To help you learn the big picture, and remember Paul's path to prison, we are asking you to review this final fourth of Acts again (Figure 5.13). Learning the overview of Acts 21–28 will help you for the rest of your life, so please take time to learn it well.

**Q 43** Which 3 doors are always before us in difficult times?

**Q 44** How is bitterness like a thief?

**Q 45** How does Esau illustrate the fruit of bitterness?

**Q 46** What reasons did Paul have to be bitter in prison?

**Q 47** Complete Figure 5.13, summarizing trials that led to Paul's imprisonment for the Gentiles.

| Acts 21 → | Acts 22 | Acts 23 | Acts 24 | Acts 25 | Acts 26 | Acts 27 | Acts 28 |
|---|---|---|---|---|---|---|---|
| In Jerusalem | Jews | The Sanhedrin | In Caesarea | Gov. Festus | King Agrippa | Chained on a ship | In Rome, Paul writes to |

**Figure 5.13** Practice summarizing the trials in Acts 21–28 that led to Paul's imprisonment for his ministry to Gentiles.

**Q 48** ➤ *How many years did Paul suffer unjustly at Caesarea and in Rome?*

It was not fair or just for Paul to be in prison for 2 years in Philippi or in prison in Rome. The Roman Commander, Claudius Lysius, wrote to Governor Felix in Caesarea that Paul did not deserve to be in prison (Acts 23:29). Yet Paul suffered in prison for 2 years in Caesarea, under Governor Felix. Then Felix was relocated to Rome. The new Governor, Festus, and King Agrippa agreed that Paul did not deserve to be in prison (Acts 26:31). Paul's years in prison were a result of injustice. He was arrested in Jerusalem while doing a good deed. He had brought to the saints of Jerusalem a large offering—to help them in their poverty. During his time in Jerusalem, he was arrested. This was not fair. Imagine how Paul felt about being put in prison while bringing an offering for the poor! He spent years in a cold, dingy, stinking prison cell in Caesarea. Next, they took Paul as a prisoner by ship, which cracked to pieces in the Mediterranean Sea. God's apostle swam to the island of Malta—where he spents the winter as a prisoner. When he reached Rome, they locked him in chains for two more years. Still, Paul left the door of bitterness closed and wrote the Prison Epistles: Ephesians, Colossians, Philippians, and Philemon.

**Q 49** ➤ *Has life brought you some reasons to be bitter? Illustrate.*

**Application.** Often, the trials of life are not fair. They come when we are serving God and His children. People may not appreciate your service; or they may misunderstand your motives. Some may hate you just as Cain hated Able because you are more righteous than they are. Joseph's brothers hated him for being so good and so favored by his father. Some Pharisees hated Jesus because the people loved Him so much. As Christians, we must cope with unfairness that comes to us. All of us can think of unfair things that have happened to us. Throughout the centuries, God's people have suffered injustice (2 Thess. 1:3-12). Often, we did not deserve the harsh treatment we received. No one cared for us when we needed help. We did not get the credit we deserved. We had an accident or became sick while serving God and others. Resentment can seep in like a poison if we allow it. Lots of things in life are not fair. But how we respond to unfair times determines the quality of person we become. Often, we cannot change our circumstances. Sometimes the only influence we have is on our own response. Paul chose to leave the door of bitterness shut tight. Perhaps you are the victim of an unfair situation that even a dog on the street should not have happen to him. Will you choose to open the door of bitterness when life is unfair?

**Q 50** ➤ *What can you do if a root of bitterness is already growing inside you?*

But what if you have already opened the door of bitterness? What if a root of bitterness is already growing in your heart? Then ask the Lord to forgive you for nursing a grudge. Accept His forgiveness and inner healing. And remember, you must forgive the person you are bitter against. The Bible teaches that God only forgives us as we forgive others (Matt. 6.15). When we forgive a person, it does not mean that person will go free. God remains the judge of all who sin. As the Scripture says, "*Do not take revenge, my friends, but leave room for God's wrath, for it is written: 'It is mine to avenge; I will repay,' says the Lord*" (Rom. 12:19). So forgiving others does not release them from God's judgment. **Sabio** says, "He who forgives another releases a person from prison only to discover that the prisoner was himself."[5]

**Q 51** ➤ *How did Paul rule over his own thoughts?*

**B. A second door that we face in hard times is the door of Opportunity—a source of joy (Phil. 1:12-18a).**

Paul ruled over his own mind. He practiced being aware of what he was thinking. As a man knows what is on a table in front of him, Paul knew what was on his mind. He was selective. He did not choose his thoughts from the world's menu. Rather, he depended on the Spirit to guide his mind. Paul censored bad thoughts that came to him. So he turned away from the door of bitterness, and he turned toward the door of opportunity. It was closed. But the apostle wanted to know what was behind that door in his prison. So he reached out his hand and opened it. That is when he discovered joy in a wonderful opportunity—in the worst of circumstances.

**Q 52** ➤ *How did Paul discover opportunity while suffering unjustly in chains?*

Caesar's best soldiers guarded his palace in Rome. There were about 16,000 soldiers in the palace guard. And Rome was their headquarters. These were elite military men. They served 16 years and then retired with the free gift of citizenship and a large sum of money. What an opportunity Paul discovered. These soldiers would probably never have attended a synagogue or a house church. But one by one, two by two, or even in groups of four, soldiers guarded Paul. Recall that when Peter was in prison in Jerusalem, 16 soldiers guarded him each night. They divided the night into four parts, and there were four soldiers to guard each part or shift. When soldiers guarded Peter, two were chained to him and two guarded the entrance (Acts 12:4-6). We do not know exactly how many soldiers guarded Paul. But he was an important prisoner whom Caesar did not want to escape. So every day of his 2 years in a Roman prison, Paul had soldiers guarding him in shifts of four hours. Every day, Paul had the opportunity to witness to several soldiers. And you can be sure Paul was talking about Jesus. Paul reports the results:

*12Now I want you to know, brothers, that what has happened to me has really served to advance the gospel. 13As a result, it has become clear throughout the whole palace guard and to everyone else that I am in chains for Christ* (Phil. 1:12-13).

A soldier would get curious and ask Paul, "Why are you here?" Paul did *not* say, "Because everyone has been unfair to me. I do not deserve this. God has deserted me. Who knows why I am here! It makes no sense."

**Instead,** Paul said something like, "God has allowed me to be here to tell you about the Lord Jesus. He came to earth to save us from the penalty and power of our sins. He was crucified and rose from the dead." By the time Paul was through witnessing one-on-one, he was able to say that the gospel had come even into Caesar's household (Phil. 4:22). The gospel entered and bore fruit in surprising places—like the seed that enters a tiny crack in a boulder, and grows into a large tree—because Paul looked for opportunity in prison. And Paul rejoiced in a prison cell because of the opportunity God gave him to witness for Christ.

**Application.** Maybe you are in a place saying, "I do not want to live here. I hate it. I do not want to be doing what I'm doing." But if we will all look around us, we will see that there is an opportunity in that place to witness for Jesus Christ. Life has negative and positive circumstances. And in difficult experiences, we can choose what our response will be—whether we blame God and become bitter, or look for opportunities to glorify Him. There are times when God does not change our circumstances and we must ask Him, "God, change me in the circumstance. Give me an opportunity to be a blessing to someone during this difficult time." And often, as we use opportunities to help others, we experience joy when we least expect it.

**Another opportunity** Paul discovered in prison was encouraging believers in Rome to be bold witnesses. He writes:

*14Because of my chains, most of the brothers in the Lord have been encouraged to speak the word of God more courageously and fearlessly. 15It is true that some preach Christ out of envy and rivalry, but others out of goodwill. 16The latter do so in love, knowing that I am put here for the defense of the gospel. 17The former preach Christ out of selfish ambition, not sincerely, supposing that they can stir up trouble for me while I am in chains. 18But what does it matter? The important thing is that in every way, whether from false motives or true, Christ is preached. And because of this I rejoice* (Phil. 1:14-18a).

Q 53 How many soldiers guarded Paul?

Q 54 How did all the guards of Caesar's palace learn why Paul was chained in Rome?

Q 55 Do you think complaints were the center of Paul's testimony? Explain.

**Figure 5.14** Sometimes people are amazed to see a tree growing out of rock, where it looks impossible for a tree to grow. Likewise, as we look for opportunities to witness in difficult circumstances, the gospel takes root in places that surprise us.

Q 56 Are you willing to look for opportunities to serve when life is tough? Explain.

Q 57 Besides testifying to soldiers, what other opportunity did Paul discover in chains?

**Q 58**  *What is the message of 2 Corinthians 1:4?*

**Q 59**  *How can you use your sufferings to minister to others? Illustrate.*

In his trial of prison, Paul discovered the opportunity to minister to other believers. We sometimes think that if we let anyone know our struggles and our weaknesses, it will lessen their courage. We may fear that knowing our trials will discourage others. But this is not true. As others know our trials and see us standing firm, it encourages them to stand firm with us. We do not feel so alone in our struggles when we hear of the struggles of others. Through our testimonies of persevering through trials we encourage one another. As Paul said, we comfort others with the comfort we receive in our trials (2 Cor. 1:4). Paul found that his imprisonment, instead of scaring other believers, gave them new boldness to witness. They watched his boldness in trials and became bolder themselves. Paul models what he earlier wrote to believers in Rome:

> We also rejoice in our sufferings, because we know that suffering produces perserverence; ⁴perserverence, character; and character, hope. ⁵And hope does not disappoint us" (Rom. 5:3-5).

Opportunities to minister to others increase in our times of trials and suffering.

**Q 60**  *Why do some preach with the wrong motives?*

**Q 61**  *How can we avoid becoming cynical about fleshly preachers?*

Paul notes that some preach Christ with the wrong motives, like envy, rivalry, and selfish ambition (Phil. 1:15, 17). Why would anyone do that? Some workers are always trying to climb higher on the ladder of success than others. Perhaps some thought Paul would be martyred soon. Maybe they were arguing over who would take Paul's title as an apostle. Some were jealous of his position and influence in the church. Paul knew that there are people who preach mainly to get money, fame, and power. Preachers like this were trying to elbow Paul out of the way. And even today, there are some who preach for the wrong reasons. But remember Paul's attitude. Even when a preacher's motives are bad, Paul sees an opportunity to rejoice—because Christ is preached (Phil. 1:18). Of course, we are sorrowful when false preachers lead people astray and destroy whole families for money (Titus 1:11). But one way we can avoid being cynical is to **rejoice** like Paul when anyone preaches Jesus Christ. Sometimes, good comes even from bad preaching. For the Word of God creates faith—and people can connect with God—even when the preacher is separated from Him. There is a time to correct false teaching in the church as when Paul corrected the heresies at Colosse. And there is a time to rejoice that Christ is being preached and leave the rest to God. Paul turned away from the door of bitterness. He looked for opportunities to minister and rejoice—even when he was chained in a prison cell with no window.

### C. A third door before Paul and us in hard times is the door of Trust in God—the source of all joy (Phil. 1:18b-26).

> **Yes, and I will continue to rejoice,** ¹⁹*for I know that through your prayers and the help given by the Spirit of Jesus Christ, what has happened to me will turn out for my deliverance.* ²⁰*I eagerly expect and hope that I will in no way be ashamed, but will have sufficient courage so that now as always Christ will be exalted in my body, whether by life or by death.* ²¹**For to me, to live is Christ and to die is gain.** ²²*If I am to go on living in the body, this will mean fruitful labor for me. Yet what shall I choose? I do not know!* ²³*I am torn between the two: I desire to depart and be with Christ, which is better by far;* ²⁴*but it is more necessary for you that I remain in the body.* ²⁵*Convinced of this, I know that I will remain, and I will continue with all of you for your progress and joy in the faith,* ²⁶*so that through my being with you again your joy in Christ Jesus will overflow on account of me* (Phil. 1:18b-26).

**Q 62**  *Why do we treat trust as its own door?*

We could consider *trust* behind the door of opportunity. For we always have the opportunity *to doubt* God or *to trust* Him. But we are treating trust as a door in itself because it is such a big and vital topic. Our entire journey with God, from start to finish, is based on trusting in Him.

**Q 63**  *Did Paul have reasons to doubt God? Explain.*

Paul could have fanned coals of doubt by focusing on his circumstances instead of on God. He could have stumbled over the apparent unfaithfulness of his Lord. He was a prisoner in Jerusalem for two long years. He was in a shipwreck at sea. He wrote the Prison Epistles while in chains in Rome. Surely people were praying for him—praying for his release. And Paul was praying for his own release. But in spite of the prayers, Paul was still in prison for 2 years in Rome (Acts 28:16, 30). God allowed Paul to suffer. It is no wonder that Paul is not popular with the positive confession movement. Many negative things happened in his life—which, in spite of prayer, did not change. It seemed as though God was being unfair to Paul. The Lord could have at any time released Paul from chains. Perhaps Paul had moments when he wondered if the Lord was still with him.

But note Paul's words of trust. His main concern is to have the courage to remain faithful in life or death (Phil. 1:20; 2:17). Paul makes no demands on God. He is willing to live and keep on serving. His whole life was dedicated to serving others. Even at death's door, he desires the joy of the Philippians to be complete (Phil. 1:26). Yet he knows that dying would be better for him—for then he would be face to face with Christ (Phil. 1:23). So the apostle just rests in trust. He is content to let God decide whether he lives or dies (Phil. 1:20, 27; 2:17).

**Q 64** How did Paul avoid fanning coals of doubt?

**Q 65** Complete Figure 5.15, summarizing verses on peace and joy that come from trusting God.

| References | Your Summaries on Peace and Joy That come From Trusting God |
|------------|------------------------------------------------------------|
| Job 13:15 | |
| Job 19:25-26 | |
| Job 23:10 | |
| Acts 16:25-26 | |
| 2 Cor. 6:9-10 | |

Figure 5.15   Practice summarizing Scriptures on the peace and joy that come from trusting God in hard times.

Paul's attitude reminds us of the three Hebrew children. King Nebuchadnezzar threatened to throw them into the fiery furnace if they would not bow down and worship him. They knew God was able to deliver them. But they were not sure what the Almighty would decide. Still, they stood firm, trusting in God and resting in whatever outcome He allowed (Dan. 3:17-18). Paul's outcome reminds us of Job, who said: *"Though he slay me, yet will I hope in him"* (Job 13:15). *" 25 I know that my Redeemer lives, and that in the end he will stand upon the earth. 26 And after my skin has been destroyed, yet in my flesh I will see God"* (Job 19:25-26). *"When he has tested me I will come forth as gold"* (Job 23:10). There is great peace and joy as we trust in God (Phil. 4:8-9). As we focus our trust on God, the Spirit gives us songs of joy in the darkest night—as He did for Paul and Silas in the jail at Philippi (Acts 16:25-26; Gal. 5:22). God can give us joy, even in the midst of pain, sorrow, and suffering. Consider the paradox of Paul's words to the Corinthians: *"...dying, and yet we live on; beaten, and yet not killed; 10 sorrowful, yet always rejoicing; poor, yet making many rich; having nothing, and yet possessing everything"* (2 Cor. 6:9-10). As we rest in God and trust Him, we discover peace that passes understanding; we experience joy, even in times of sorrow.

**Application.**   Perhaps you are in a difficult situation. You may be asking, "What good can come out of this?" But stand firm in the Lord. Keep your heart open to God. Remain sweet and humble in your attitude instead of blaming God or others. Avoid saying things that will hurt you and others. Keep calm. Wait on the Lord. Say with Job, *"Though he slay me, yet will I hope in him"* (Job 13:15). As you trust God, strength will flow into your life. It is a wonderful thing to be able to go through the worst that you can imagine and find, when you have gone through it, that God was holding you above the waters. Anyone can trust when the sun is shining and all is going well. But trust is our privilege and calling in *all* circumstances. If we open the door of trust, God will give us a song to sing in the darkest night.

**Q 66** Are you willing to open the door of trust when life is dark?

**Closing prayer**

"Father, we pray that Your Spirit in us will help us to resist and overcome the temptations of hard times. Help us to leave the door of bitterness closed. Help us to be joyful in the places where we are and, like Paul, to seek opportunities to bless others, even in tough times."

---

## Lesson 26   Joy in Those Around Us—Part 1 (Phil. 1:27–2:11)

**Goal A:** *State the principle of Philippians 2:4, and illustrate it by contrasting believing with suffering.*
**Goal B:** *State the principle of Philippians 2:4, and illustrate it with fruits of salvation and the kenosis.*

---

**Q 67** ⌦ *What are 4 types of relationships in Philippians?*

Philippians is a letter that deals with several relationships.

- The letter emphasizes the relationship of Philippian *believers to God*. Paul writes *"to all the saints in Christ Jesus at Philippi"* (Phil. 1:1). Paul reminds them of the encouragement they have received from being united with Christ Jesus; and the fellowship of the Spirit they have because of their relationship with God (Phil. 2:1).

- This letter also stresses *Paul's relationship with the Philippians*. He loved them and they loved him. Paul thanks them for their prayers and the financial gifts sent via Epaphroditus (Phil. 1:3-8; 4:10-18). The apostle tells them about his situation.

- Philippians is concerned about the relationship of *believers to the lost*. Paul wants us to *"shine like stars in the universe."* He wants us to live *"without complaining or arguing…in a crooked and depraved generation"* as we *"hold out the word of life"* (Phil. 2:14-16).

- Finally, Paul spends a lot of time on the relationship between believers. He wants believers to live without *arguing* (Phil. 4:2). There is an argument between two women named Euodia and Syntyche. These are beloved leaders in the house church. Most scholars think Paul's goal in writing Philippians 2:1-11 is to restore unity and humility between these two ladies. Paul wants these leaders—***and all believers***—to work out our common salvation and relationships *"with fear and trembling"* (Phil. 2:12). This relationship of a believer to other believers is the focus of this lesson on Philippians 1:27–2:30.

**Q 68** ⌦ *What is the one principle we will study in this lesson?*

A big theme in Philippians and all of Christianity is: **"not only me—but also others"** (Figure 5.16). This theme provides a good lens for us to study Philippians 1:27–2:30, about *joy* in our relationships. In this lesson and the next one we can identify seven illustrations (A–G) on Paul's theme: ***"Each of you should look not only to your own interests, but also to the interests of others"*** (Phil. 2:4).

**Q 69** ⌦ *How many times does Paul illustrate the one principle in this lesson?*

| Phil. | Not Only My Interests | But Also the Interests of Others |
|---|---|---|
| 1:27-30 | **A.** *Not only* for me to believe in Christ and be saved | *But also* to suffer for Him, so I can relate to others and they can relate to me |
| 2:1-4 | **B.** *Not only* my interests about being united with Christ | *But also* the interests and salvation of others |
| 2:5-11 | **C.** *Not only* was Christ God by nature | *But also* He became nothing—a human servant to redeem us |
| 2:12-16 4:2-3 | **D.** *Not only* concerned about my *vertical* relationship with God | *But also* concerned about my *horizontal* relationships with others |
| 2:17-18 4:4,10-13 | **E.** *Not only* joyful when I get what is best for me | *But also* joyful when others, like Paul, get what is best for them |
| 2:19-24 | **F.** *Not only* does Timothy care for his own interests | *But also* for the interests of Jesus Christ |
| 2:25-30 | **G.** *Not only* what Epaphroditus can do for me | *But also* what he can do for himself and for other believers in Philippi |

**Figure 5.16   In Philippians 1:27–2:30 we see seven examples (A–G) illustrating the principle:**
*"Each of you should look not only to your own interests, but also to the interests of others"* (Phil. 2:4).

In Lessons 26 and 27 we will study how Paul illustrates one principle seven times (A–G).

> **Principle:** *Each of you should look not only to your own interests, but also to the interests of others* (Phil. 2:4).

## A. First illustration: Believing is for *our own* salvation, but suffering helps bring salvation to *others* (Phil. 1:27-30).

*[27] Whatever happens, conduct yourselves in a manner worthy of the gospel of Christ. Then, whether I come and see you or only hear about you in my absence, I will know that you **stand firm in one spirit**, contending **as one man** for the faith of the gospel [28] **without being frightened in any way by those who oppose you.** This is a sign to them that they will be destroyed, but that you will be saved—and that by God. [29] For it has been granted to you on behalf of Christ **not only to believe on him, but also to suffer for him**, [30] since you are going through the same struggle you saw I had, and now hear that I still have* (Phil. 1:27-30).

**Q 70** *What are our interests in believing in Christ? What do we gain?*

Paul's words in Philippians 1:27 reveal that he is uncertain about his future. He may be set free from prison; or he may be martyred. Paul's main concern is not himself, but the Philippians. Epaphroditus has told Paul about a division among believers (Phil. 4:2). So, Paul emphasizes the need to stand firm *"in one spirit... as one man for the faith of the gospel"* (Phil. 1:27). He wants believers in Philippi to be united and to witness for Christ with courage and boldness (Phil. 1:14; 28). This is because standing united and witnessing without fear is a **sign** to unbelievers (Phil. 1:28). Unity and courage reveal that Christ truly lives within us. In contrast, unbelievers already know the emptiness and lack of assurance they have in themselves. A united, bold church in the face of persecution is a powerful light to the lost. Some estimate that the church in Northern Asia has grown to over 60 million believers during persecution.[6] As believers stand firm in suffering, their faith shines like stars in the darkness—and many other people come to Christ through their testimonies. Paul calls on believers to embrace suffering as a part of following Christ. The apostle writes: *"For it has been granted to you on behalf of Christ not only to believe on him, but also to suffer for him"* (Phil. 1:29).

**Q 71** *What has resulted in Northern Asia as believers have suffered?*

Following Jesus in Philippi was a rocky road. Recall that when Paul first went to Philippi, the local businessmen had him beaten and jailed. They were angry because he cast a demon out of a slave girl who prophesied for money. Once the demon left her, she had no spiritual source of information. Her owners saw that their path to money was gone. So they hated Paul and anyone who accepted his gospel. **As we see in Philippians 1:28, some in Philippi continued to hate and oppose followers of Jesus.** Paul explains that following Jesus brings *not only* salvation, *but also* suffering. Believers in Philippi were suffering in ways similar to Paul's suffering in Philippi and also in Rome. A servant is not above his master. As Jesus suffered, His followers also suffer. Believing in Jesus Christ does not come by itself. Believing comes with suffering. As Paul wrote elsewhere, *"In fact, everyone who wants to live a godly life in Christ Jesus will be persecuted"* (2 Tim. 3:12). It is a **fact** that believing in Christ includes suffering for Him.

**Q 72** *Why did some hate and persecute believers in Philippi?*

We are all interested in believing because this brings salvation. But not many of us have an interest in suffering. Yet suffering is necessary for us to relate to others. Why does God allow believers to suffer for Christ? Let us look at **three reasons why it is God's will for believers to suffer at times**.

- *Suffering perfects us.* It draws us closer to Jesus. It makes us more like Him, and deepens our fellowship with Him (Phil. 3:10; Col. 3:2; John 15:20; 1 Pet. 2:21). It unites us with all believers who have suffered, from Abel to the end of time. Suffering perfects us in many ways. Discover and summarize some personal blessings of suffering as you complete Figure 5.17.

**Q 73** *How is suffering in our own interest? How does it help us?*

**Q 74** ✎ *Complete Figure 5.17 on the personal blessings of suffering.*

| References | The Blessings From Suffering for Christ |
|---|---|
| Matt. 5:11-12 | |
| John 15:20 | |
| 1 Cor. 11:30-32 | |
| Col. 3:2 | |
| Heb. 5:8 | |
| Heb. 12:3-11 | |
| James 1:2-4 | |
| 1 Pet. 1:6-7 | |
| 1 Pet. 2:21 | |
| 1 Pet. 4:1-2 | |

**Figure 5.17   Suffering for Christ is a blessing in many ways.**

**Q 75** ✎ *How do our sufferings help us relate to others?*

- *Suffering helps us relate to others.* When we suffer, God comforts us. We receive comfort to pass on to others who suffer (2 Cor. 1:4). But if we did not suffer, we would not receive comfort from God because we would not need it. In other words, suffering qualifies and equips us with comfort to share with others. This is a big principle in Scripture. Paul writes:

  ³*Praise be to the God and Father of our Lord Jesus Christ, the Father of compassion and the God of all comfort,* ⁴***who comforts us in all our troubles, so that we can comfort those in any trouble with the comfort we ourselves have received from God.*** ⁵***For just as the sufferings of Christ flow over into our lives, so also through Christ our comfort overflows.*** ⁶*If we are distressed, it is for your comfort and salvation; if we are comforted, it is for your comfort, which produces in you patient endurance of the same sufferings we suffer* (2 Cor. 1:3-6).

  Comfort is proportional to suffering. The comfort we have to give others is the same comfort that God gives us when we suffer. Only as we suffer do we receive comfort to pass on to others. Suffering enables us to relate to others.

**Q 76** ✎ *How do our sufferings help others relate to us?*

- *Suffering helps others relate to us.* Common people relate to others who have suffered. Hearing about the patience of Job encourages us. To whom do you relate better: Solomon or David? Most people relate better to David. Solomon grew up in a palace with a silver spoon in his hand. He had more money than he could spend. He gave us the book of Ecclesiastes, which we appreciate but do not read often. In contrast, David worked hard, cared for a flock of sheep, fought battles, and suffered much. He gave us many Psalms that everyone loves. Likewise, when common people see believers suffer, they can relate to them. Why? Because all people suffer in many ways. And we relate to those who cry tears just as we do.

We should not be foolish by bringing suffering on ourselves. As Peter writes, there is no value in suffering for doing wrong (1 Pet. 2:20). But when we suffer for Christ, let us encourage ourselves that God is perfecting us, helping us relate to others, and enabling others to relate to us.

**Principle:**   *Each of you should look not only to your own interests, but also to the interests of others* (Phil. 2:4).

## B. Second illustration: The blessings we receive from God, we must share with others (Phil. 2:1-4).

Paul urges believers to pass on to others the kindness God has given us. He lists four blessings that all believers have received (Phil. 2:1-3).

[1] *If you have **any** encouragement from being united with Christ, **if any** comfort from his love, **if any** fellowship with the Spirit, **if any** tenderness and compassion,* [2] *then make my joy complete by being like-minded, having the same love, being one in spirit and purpose.* [3] *Do nothing out of selfish ambition or vain conceit, but in humility consider others better than yourselves.* [4] ***Each of you should look not only to your own interests, but also to the interests of others*** (Phil. 2:1-4).

| Phil. | Our Interests<br>ROOTS: Blessings We Have Received From God | | |
|---|---|---|---|
| 2:1 | If you have any _____ from being united with Christ | | |
| 2:1 | If you have any _____ from his love | | |
| 2:1 | If you have any _____ with the Spirit | | |
| 2:1 | If you have any _____ and compassion | | |

**Figure 5.18   The roots of our behavior are the blessings we have from God.**

Q 77 ↖ *Complete Figure 5.18 on blessings we have received from God.*

| Interests of Others, Including Paul<br>FRUITS: Our Love, Humility, and Concern for Others | Phil. |
|---|---|
| Make *my* _____ complete by being _____. | 2:2 |
| Sharing the same _____ | 2:2 |
| Being *one* in _____ and _____ | 2:2 |
| Do nothing out of _____ _____ or _____ _____. | 2:3 |
| In _____ consider *others* better than yourself. | 2:3 |
| Look also on the _____ of others. | 2:4 |

**Figure 5.19   Paul wants the blessings we have from God to result in the fruits of good relationships with others.**

Q 78 ↖ *Complete Figure 5.19 on the fruits that should grow from blessings we have received from God.*

We each have great interest in what *we* receive from God such as: *encouragement* from being united in Christ; *comfort* from His love; *fellowship* with God through His Spirit in us; His *love and tenderness* in forgiving our sins and adopting us as His children. All of these things are *our interests*. Paul wants us to be concerned about our own interests. Receiving our own spiritual interests provides the roots of our salvation. But Paul wants us to mature—growing **from selfish children to mature adults** who are also concerned about the interests of others.

Q 79 ↖ *Does Paul want us to ignore our own interests? Explain.*

Selfish people rarely recognize their own selfishness. They think sermons on selfishness are for others in the church, not them. But there are several *signs of selfishness.* Boasting is a mark of selfishness. Selfish people talk all the time rather than listen some of the time. Likewise, selfish people tend to be stingy. Selfish people find it difficult to be generous. They give very little unless someone important is watching. Also, selfish people are critical. They are quick to mention changes they want to see in others—but slow to evaluate their own faults. And many selfish people are two-faced—deceitful and sneaky, because they are out for number one. They speak evil of others behind their backs. Their attitude is often, "What have you done for me lately?"[7]

Q 80 ↖ *What are some signs of selfishness—thinking only about our own interests?*

Paul requests believers to make *his joy* complete by living in harmony with each other. His joy overflows *if* they live *worthy* of the gospel (Phil. 1:27) and the blessings God has given them (Phil. 2:1). His labors in Philippi are *not useless* if the believers there obey the Word and live *pure and blameless—shining like stars* in a dark universe (Phil. 2:16). This is a strong appeal from an apostle in chains. *If* his spiritual children obey him, he will rejoice and brag on them *on the day of Christ*—when our Lord returns (Phil. 2:16).

Q 81 ↗ *What would cause Paul's joy to overflow? Why?*

**Application.**   Paul connects *his joy* to the behavior of the Philippians. Every pastor and Christian parent shares the feelings of Paul. Our joy is bound up in our physical and spiritual children. Like Jacob, our gray hairs go down in sorrow to the grave if things do not go well with our children (Gen. 44:29). And like Paul, our joy overflows and is *complete* **as our children pass on the love God has given them** (Phil. 2:1-4).

Q 82 ↖ *Does your life cause your parents and leaders to rejoice? Explain.*

**Q 83** *How is Christ the supreme model of Philippians 2:4? Summarize.*

**Principle:** *Each of you should look not only to your own interests, but also to the interests of others* (Phil. 2:4).

### C. Third illustration: Christ is our model for thinking of the interests of others (Phil. 2:5-11).

*[5] Your attitude should be the same as that of Christ Jesus: [6] Who, being in very nature God, did not consider equality with God something to be grasped, [7] but made himself nothing, taking the very nature of a servant, being made in human likeness. [8] And being found in appearance as a man, he humbled himself and became obedient to death—even death on a cross! [9] Therefore God exalted him to the highest place and gave him the name that is above every name, [10] that at the name of Jesus every knee should bow, in heaven and on earth and under the earth, [11] and every tongue confess that Jesus Christ is Lord, to the glory of God the Father* (Phil. 2:5-11).

**Q 84** *What does kenosis mean?*

Paul uses Jesus as the **supreme example** of **looking out for the interests of others**. Philippians 2:5-11 is one of the most famous passages in the New Testament. Many think this was a hymn of the early church. This passage is called the "Emptying of Christ," based on the Greek word *kenosis*, which means "to empty or make void" (Phil. 2:7).[8]

**Q 85** *On the kenosis of Christ, answer the questions in column two of Figure 5.20.*

As the Son of God in heaven, Christ was divine, and equal to God the Father. But to redeem us, Christ greatly humbled himself. Figure 5.20 shows five steps of humility Christ took to save us—from the throne to the cross.

| Five Steps of Humility Jesus Took for Us | Comments and Questions |
|---|---|
| 1. Christ came all the way down the ladder from heaven to earth. | Q: *Can you imagine the number of steps to climb down a ladder from heaven to earth?* |
| 2. He emptied Himself of divine privileges, and became a human, Jesus. | **Jesus was fully God and fully man.**<br>Q: *What are some divine privileges Christ emptied Himself of on earth?* (Matt. 4:1-7; 26:53; 27:42, 50) |
| 3. He stepped down from the throne of a king, and became a servant. | Q: *How did Jesus serve us?* (Matt. 20:28) |
| 4. He humbled Himself and became obedient, even unto death. | Q: *What are some lesser ways that God asks us to obey and humble ourselves, that are far short of death?* |
| 5. He humbled Himself to the most humiliating death possible—death on a cross. | Q: *Since Jesus died to free you from the penalty and power of sin, are you willing to humble yourself and obey Him as Lord?* |

**Figure 5.20    Christ took at least five steps of humility down from the throne to the cross. Does your life sing a worthy response to the price Jesus paid to have you in His family?**

(English students visit: https://www.youtube.com/watch?v=393OSwfDTb4)

On any step down, as Christ emptied Himself, He could have said, "This is as far as I am willing to go. There is a limit to how much I will humble myself." He could have said, "I don't mind leaving the glories of heaven, although it's difficult, but don't send Me as a servant. If I leave heaven, the least I should be is an earthly king." But when Jesus descends to earth, He becomes a servant. He could have said, "If I am going to become a servant, that is the bottom of the ladder. I will be a servant, but I will not suffer." But He did not stop at serving. Nor did He say, "I will suffer, but I am unwilling to die—especially not the humiliating, shameful death of crucifixion that is for criminals." But Christ put no boundaries on emptying Himself. He went all the way. There were no limits to His love.[9]

**Q 86** *What are some limits Christ could have put on humbling Himself?*

**Q 87** *Do you put limits on humbling yourself to preserve unity with believers? Explain.*

**Application.**    There is glory in humbling ourselves to preserve a relationship. There are times when the Spirit and the Word guide us to stand our ground. But the attitude of being crucified with Christ is beautiful. It enables us to look at our motives and ask,

"Why am I holding out for this?" "Why am I so strong in this position?" "Is Christ calling me, at this moment, to die to self and to follow Him to the cross?" "Is this a time for me to humble myself for this relationship?" "Is this a time to remove boundaries from my love?" "Is this a time to give or forgive with no limits?"

Philippians 2:5-11 is Paul's version of the incarnation. It is so profound and famous that we can miss the point. When we think of how Christ humbled Himself to redeem us—from the throne to the cross—our eyes fill with tears. Thinking of the Son of God, stripped, beaten, and nailed to a cross fills us with wonder. Our salvation was so expensive! How could God love us SOOOOO much? It is fitting for us to kneel and worship at the foot of the empty cross. And to remember that humility leads to exaltation. *"Everyone who exalts himself will be humbled, and the one who humbles himself will be exalted"* (Luke 14:11). Jesus returned to His throne, as God exalted Him. And some day, every knee in heaven and on earth will bow to him, *"and every tongue confess that Jesus Christ is Lord, to the glory of God the Father"*—with joy or with sorrow (Phil. 2:10-11). The incarnation, crucifixion, resurrection, ascension, and exaltation of Christ inspire us to worship whenever we pause to reflect on these truths. These themes are the source of many songs we sing. Our moments of praise and worship are fitting and wonderful. *But let us remember the main reason Paul gave us the example of Christ in Philippians 2:5-11.* **Paul wants us to follow the example of Christ by thinking of others, not just ourselves.** Believers in the church at Philippi were arguing with each other. They were acting proud and thinking of their own interests. As a result, the unity of the Spirit was broken and the death of Jesus for the lost was being ignored. A selfish spirit destroys fellowship and silences the gospel.

So Paul takes arrogant believers back to the Incarnation and the Crucifixion. The apostle says, *"Your attitude should be the same as that of Christ Jesus"* (Phil. 2:5). He did not think *only* of Himself, *but also of others.* " ⁴*Each of you should look not only to your own interests, but also to the interests of others"* (Phil. 2:4). There are no footprints of Christ that lead believers to fight with each other. Following in the steps of Christ inspires us to practice humility, considering the needs and interests of others. Whenever we are tempted to hate, fight, and argue with others, God calls us back to the cross. The attitude Christ showed from the throne to the cross is not just to admire, but to imitate.

> OUR *ATTITUDE SHOULD BE THE SAME AS THAT OF* CHRIST JESUS—WHO HUMBLED HIMSELF TO BRING PEACE (PHIL. 2:5). AS WE PRACTICE HUMILITY, WE EXALT CHRIST, AND HE WILL ONE DAY EXALT US.

**Lesson 27**

## Joy in Those Around Us—Part 2 (Phil. 2:12-30)

**Goal A:** *State the principle of Philippians 2:4 and illustrate it with working out our salvation in relationships.*

**Goal B:** *State the principle of Philippians 2:4 and illustrate it with Paul's attitudes toward death, Timothy, and Epaphroditus.*

**Principle:** *Each of you should look not only to your own interests, but also to the interests of others* (Phil. 2:4).

### D. Fourth illustration: We believers must work out our salvation with fear and trembling, thinking of the interests of others (Phil. 2:12-16).

¹²*Therefore, my dear friends, as you have always obeyed—not only in my presence, but now much more in my absence—continue to* **work out your salvation with fear and trembling,** ¹³*for it is God who works in you to will and to act according to his good purpose.* (Phil. 2:12-13)

---

**Q 88** ➚ *What is the main reason why Paul summarizes the servant heart of Jesus (Phil. 2:5-11)?*

**Q 89** ✎ *How does the example of Christ inspire you to think of others as well as self? Explain.*

**Q 90** ✎ *Why does Paul command believers to be obedient, working out their salvation with fear and trembling?*

**Q 91** *If salvation is a free gift, why must we work out our salvation with fear and trembling?*

**Q 92** *In what sense is salvation vertical and horizontal?*

**Figure 5.21**
**Salvation has vertical and horizontal aspects. The *first* and greatest commandment is *vertical*: "Love the Lord your God with all your heart and with all your soul and with all your mind" (Matt. 22:37). But the *second* great commandment is *horizontal*: "Love your neighbor as yourself" (Matt. 22:39).**

**Q 93** *Have you heard preachers who ignore the horizontal responsibilities of salvation? Explain.*

**Q 94** *How is salvation a group process?*

**Q 95** *Will God save us without our cooperation? Explain.*

Again, Paul illustrates and applies the principle: *Each of you should look not only to your own interests, **but also to the interests of others*** (Phil. 2:4). He tells them: ***Work out your* [plural] *salvation with fear and trembling*** (Phil. 2:12). The word *your* is plural in Philippians 2:12. Personal salvation is related to the salvation of the group. Each believer is not only to think of his or her personal salvation, but is also to be concerned about the salvation of all other believers in the church.

Salvation is both vertical and horizontal. To have a good relationship with God we **must** have good relationships with those around us. This is Paul's gospel. In all of his

letters, Paul insists that saving faith reveals itself in godly living toward others. Those who hate others, refuse to forgive others, lie to others, slander others, steal from others, sin against others through sexual immorality—Paul insists that such people have NO inheritance in the kingdom of God (1 Cor. 6:9-11; Gal. 5:19-21; Eph. 4:17–5:18; Phil. 4:12). Our faith in God **must** reveal itself in the way we relate to others. God forgives our sins through the blood of Christ, *only as* we forgive those who sin against us (Matt. 6:12; 18:21-35).

Beware of cheap, counterfeit grace that promises you heaven without insisting that you live in righteous relationships with others. Some cultures value the individual more than the group. And some cultures value the group more than the individual. But the Bible values both. It teaches us that to be saved as individuals, we must obey God's guidelines for relationships in the group. We must *work out our salvation with fear and trembling.* We must be concerned about the interests of others, not just our own. For God Himself is in our midst (Phil. 2:12-13). Will God welcome into heaven those who slander their neighbors?

Salvation is a [8] *"gift of God—*[9]*not by works, so that no one can boast."* (Eph. 2:8-9). Paul often uses the *first half* of his letters to emphasize the free gift of salvation that comes to us because of God's love. Then, in the *second half* of his letter, Paul emphasizes that we must live a life worthy of the gift of salvation in Christ. For salvation is not a gift in a box; it is a gift in a relationship with Jesus Christ—and in relationships with others. Salvation belongs to those who meet Jesus Christ, then become and remain His disciples. **In Philippians 2:12-13, Paul is emphasizing salvation as a group process,** with a beginning, a middle, and an end—a past, present, and future. We were saved; we are being saved; and, we will be saved. Salvation is a gift that involves our continuing participation. We begin the journey of salvation at the new birth. At this time, we repent of past sins and accept God's offer of forgiveness in Jesus. God forgives our sins, and puts His Spirit within us—so we partake of His divine nature and have power to overcome sinful desires of the flesh (Rom. 8:1-17; 2 Pet. 1:4). He writes our names in the book of life. And we begin the process of following Jesus, obeying His teachings, and being transformed into His image (Eph 4:24; Col. 3:9-10; Rom. 8:29; 2 Cor. 3:18).

Paul often emphasizes that our full cooperation for salvation is essential. He urges the Philippians to obey his teachings, lest his labors among them were in vain (Phil. 2:16). And later in this letter, Paul compares himself to a runner, straining to attain to the resurrection which is *before* us (Phil. 3:12-15). Paul does not want himself or others, such as the Colossians, to be disqualified from the prize of heaven ahead (Col. 2:18; 1 Cor. 9:24-27). Paul means what he says about our cooperation in the salvation of our souls—we must *work out **our** salvation **with fear and trembling*** (Phil. 2:12). For salvation includes what Jesus Christ did *for us* and also what He does *in us*. As individuals—and as a group—we must walk humbly with the Spirit of God who lives **in us**.

Those who refuse to humble themselves to maintain relationships lack discernment. They have lost sight of the truth that the Church belongs to God and He lives among His people by the Holy Spirit. God's presence among the wise causes them to relate to others with humility, fear, and trembling—because God is working in and through us for His purposes. The Church is not just about us! God has big plans for the Church. When we cooperate with Him, we shine like stars in a dark night. When we are obedient children, we are pure and blameless in God's eyes. But notice the contrast in God's obedient children and sinners. We shine like stars, but sinners are crooked and depraved.

**Q 96** What have proud believers who fight and argue forgotten? Explain.

[14]*Do everything without complaining or arguing,* [15]*so that you may become blameless and pure, children of God without fault in a crooked and depraved generation, in which you* **shine like stars** *in the universe* [16]*as you hold out the word of life—in order that I may boast on the day of Christ that I did not run or labor for nothing* (Phil. 2:12-16).

**Principle:** *Each of you should look not only to your own interests, but also to the interests of others* (Phil. 2:4).

**Q 97** Why did Paul want believers to think of his interests?

### E. Fifth illustration: Paul encourages the Philippians to think of his best interests, not just their own (Phil. 2:17-18).

It is *far* better for Paul to depart from this world and be with Christ (Phil. 1:23). He is willing to remain and serve the interests of the Church in any way possible. But he is unsure that his life on earth will continue. His blood may be poured out on the ground if he is beheaded—as the priests poured out wine around the altar, as *a drink offering to God* (Num. 15:1-12) " [17]*But even if I am being poured out like a drink offering on the sacrifice and service coming from your faith, I am glad and rejoice with all of you.* [18]*So you too should be glad and rejoice with me*" (Phil. 2:17-18). Looking back on history, we see that Paul was not martyred in A.D. 62/63 when he wrote the Prison Epistles. But a few years later, perhaps under the Roman Emperor Nero, Paul was again imprisoned and then beheaded. At that time he wrote to Timothy that his race was over, his crown was ready, his departure was at hand—and he was being poured out like a drink offering (2 Tim. 4:6). For those who follow Jesus Christ, death is not a threat, but a promotion. It is never easy to say good night to those at death's door. But God can give us the grace to rejoice in what is best for them, rather than focusing on our own interests.

**Figure 5.22** My mother saw a vision of an old, bony horse that lacked the strength to pull a wagon. Yet those nearby were urging the horse to continue working.

My great-grandmother in the faith, 101 years old, lay in a hospital bed. She was tired, weak, and pale. Her eyes were no longer clear. She did not want food when we offered it to her. When she talked, her lips barely moved. Her words were very slow, and no louder than a whisper. As a little boy, I stood beside her, with my head no higher than her bed. With me were my godly mother and grandmother. We were all praying that God would heal this elderly loved one, who was so special to us. As we prayed, my mother saw a vision of an old, bony horse hitched to a wagon that it no longer had the strength

**Q 98** When saints are at death's door, how can we think of their interests, not just our own?

to pull. Still, several people standing around the horse were urging it to keep trying to work. With this simple vision, the Lord spoke peace to my mother. As she shared the vision with us, we all agreed, and God gave us the grace to tell her good night. In that very moment, her spirit departed from this world and entered the next. There comes a time for us to release our loved ones into the hands of our Heavenly Father—for this is better for them. *"Blessed are the dead who die in the Lord... 'Yes', says the Spirit, 'they will rest from their labor, for their deeds will follow them' "* (Rev. 14:13).

**Q 99** ⟩ *How was Timothy an example of Philippians 2:4?*

> FOR HUMAN RELATIONSHIPS TO WORK WELL, PEOPLE MUST LOVE ENOUGH TO THINK OF THE NEEDS AND VIEWS OF OTHERS.

**Principle:**  *Each of you should look not only to your own interests, but also to the interests of others* (Phil. 2:4).

### F.  Sixth illustration: Timothy was a rare model of unselfishness (Phil. 2:19-24).

Paul continues to illustrate the principle. As he writes about sending Timothy to minister to the Philippians, notice the godly characteristic in Timothy that Paul emphasizes (Phil. 2:19-24):

> [19] *I hope in the Lord Jesus to send Timothy to you soon, that I also may be cheered when I receive news about you.* [20] **I have no one else like him, who takes a genuine interest in your welfare.** [21] **For everyone looks out for his own interests, not those of Jesus Christ.** [22] *But you know that Timothy has proved himself, because as a son with his father he has served with me in the work of the gospel.* [23] *I hope, therefore, to send him as soon as I see how things go with me.* [24] *And I am confident in the Lord that I myself will come soon* (Phil. 2:19-24).

For human relationships to work well, people must love enough to think of the needs and views of others. Timothy was an outstanding example of unselfish living. The attitude of Christ Jesus was truly in Timothy (Phil. 2:5-11).

**Principle:**  *Each of you should look not only to your own interests, but also to the interests of others* (Phil. 2:4).

**Q 100** ⟩ *Who was Epaphroditus?*

**Q 101** ⟩ *How did Paul's attitude toward Epaphroditus illustrate Philippians 2:4?*

**Q 102** ⟩ *How did Paul's attitude toward Epaphroditus illustrate Philippians 2:4?*

### G.  Seventh illustration: Paul cared as much about Epaphroditus as he cared for himself (Phil. 2:25-30).

Again, Paul illustrates his principle: In prison, Paul enjoys the fellowship of Epaphroditus. But the apostle senses that this brother longs to return to the church in Philippi, to assure them that he has recovered from a deadly illness (Phil. 2:26).

> [25] *But I think it is necessary to send back to you Epaphroditus, my brother, fellow worker and fellow soldier, who is also your messenger, whom you sent to take care of my needs.* [26] **For he longs for all of you and is distressed because you heard he was ill.** [27] *Indeed he was ill, and almost died. But God had mercy on him, and not on him only but also on me, to spare me sorrow upon sorrow.* [28] *Therefore I am all the more eager to send him, **so that when you see him again you may be glad and I may have less anxiety.*** [29] *Welcome him in the Lord with great joy, and honor men like him,* [30] *because he almost died for the work of Christ, risking his life to make up for the help you could not give me* (Phil. 2:25-30).

**Q 103** ⟨ *What were the 2 layers of sorrow Paul referred to (Phil. 2:27)?*

**Q 104** ⟨ *What is an example of how God in His mercy has delivered you from sorrow upon sorrow?*

Paul referred to *sorrow upon sorrow* (Phil. 2:27). Would the sorrow have been prison, and the death of Epaphroditus, or the sorrow of the Philippians if their representative died? Defend your answer.

***Sabio*** says: "The most important principle in relationships is learning to see things from the other person's point of view, and to care about what you see."

**Q 105**   *Complete Figure 5.23 on thinking **not only** of your needs, **but also** of the needs of others* (Phil.2:4).

| References | Your Summaries on How Each Passage Restates, Illustrates, or Applies the Principle of "Thinking of Others; and Seeing Life Through Their Eyes." |
|---|---|
| Exod. 23:4 | |
| Judg. 8:1-2 | |
| 1 Kings 12:1-16 | |
| Matt. 7:12 | |
| Matt. 10:41-42 | |
| Matt. 25:31-46 | |
| Luke 6:38 | |
| Luke 10:25-37 | |
| Acts 6:1-6 | |
| Acts 15:36-41 | |
| Acts 21:17-25 | |
| Rom. 12:10 | |
| Rom. 13:9 | |
| Rom. 14:21 | |
| 1 Cor. 8:13 | |
| 2 Cor. 9:6-11 | |
| Gal. 6:3 | |
| Phil. 2:4 | |
| 1 Tim. 5:9-10 | |
| Heb. 10:34 | |
| James 1:27 | |
| 1 John 3:16-20 | |

**Figure 5.23   Practice summarizing verses that emphasize the biblical theme of thinking about others. Note that a key to practicing this principle is *seeing life through the other person's eyes or point of view*. As we go through life, God wants us to practice asking ourselves, "What does life look like to the person in front of me? What needs does this person have? How can I respect and encourage this person? How can I edify him or her?" (1 Cor. 14:4-6).**

**Conclusion.**   As we read Philippians 1:27–2:30, it is clear that Paul has a joyful relationship with believers at Philippi. They have often prayed for him, sent offerings, and even sent Epaphroditus to share their love with him in prison. Believers in Philippi are some of Paul's favorite people. But they are no more perfect than we are. So Paul writes to encourage them to keep growing in the Lord. He cares enough to repair the damage in their relationships with one another. All relationships require humility, love, communication, unselfishness, and maintenance.

Part of the joy in living is repairing and cleaning house. When we see bad habits in our lives—such as grumbling, complaining, or arguing, the Spirit guides us to sweep these away. Then, as we look *not only* on our own interests, *but also* on the interests of others, we experience joy with the people around us. The Spirit fills us with the attitude that was in Christ—who humbled Himself to bring peace.

If you had different people close to you, would you be happier? Probably not. For the roots of joy are in our own relationship with Christ. There is joy with the people around us as the love of God in us overflows and we practice showing concern for their needs. May the Lord help us to avoid blaming our problems on others. And, may we practice letting Jesus Christ be the Lord of our attitudes toward others. Then we will treat them with dignity, respect, and love. And we will realize that many relationships will improve as we improve.

**Prayer:**   "Lord, help our relationships sparkle with Your presence. Take away the tones of harshness and criticism in our words. Deliver us from selfishness. Fill us with humility and Your love. And let us always reflect gratitude for the encouragement, comfort, compassion, and tenderness we have discovered in You."[10]

## Joy in the Lord (Phil. 3:1–4:1)

**Lesson 28**

**Goal A:** *Contrast the role of good deeds in legalists and true Christians (Phil. 3:1-11). Sketch the contrast.*

**Goal B:** *Illustrate the problems of bragging on the past and meditating on past failures (Phil. 3:12-14).*

**Goal C:** *Analyze the balance in depending on Christ, yet straining and pressing toward the goal (Phil. 3:12-14).*

**Goal D:** *Contrast and illustrate legalists, followers of Christ, and libertines in Paul's writings (Phil. 3:12-21).*

The theme of Philippians is *continuous joy in Jesus Christ*. We have studied:

- **Lesson 24**—Introduction to Paul's Letter of Joy (Phil. 1:1-11);
- **Lesson 25**—Joy in Where We Are (Phil. 1:12-26);
- **Lessons 26 and 27**—Joy in Those Around Us (Phil. 1:27–2:30).

And now we have come to:

- **Lesson 28**—Joy in the Lord (Phil. 3:1–4:1).

**Q 106** *Why do we sometimes lack joy?*

Sometimes we let our joy rise or fall with circumstances, or with the people around us. But Paul reminds us, through this letter from prison, that the roots of joy are not in our circumstances or the people with whom we live. Paul emphasizes that we can discover a level of joy that is deeper than places or people. We may have good circumstances and kind people on every side—yet still lack joy within. In this lesson we will focus on looking to Jesus, our constant source of joy. Let us look at three principles that help us *rejoice in the Lord, always* (Phil. 3:1; 4:4).

### A. Rejoice in the Lord, not in your own human efforts (Phil. 3:1-11).

**Q 107** *Explain the contrast in Figure 5.24.*

¹*Finally, my brothers, **rejoice in the Lord!** It is no trouble for me to write the same things to you again, and it is a safeguard for you.* ²*Watch out for those dogs, those men who do evil, those mutilators of the flesh.* ³*For it is we who are the circumcision, we who worship by the Spirit of God, **who glory in Christ Jesus**, and who put no confidence in the flesh* (Phil. 3:1-3).

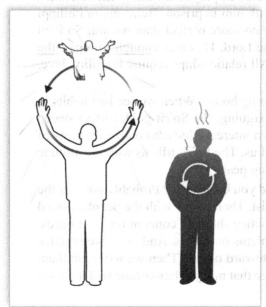

**Figure 5.24   Paul contrasts rejoicing in Christ, with rejoicing in ourselves. He wants us to be Christocentric, not egocentric.**

Paul contrasts rejoicing in the Lord with rejoicing in ourselves (Phil. 3:1-3). Throughout the Prison Epistles the apostle emphasizes that *God* has made us alive *in Christ* (Eph. 2:8; Col. 2:13; Phil. 3:1, 3). The roots of Paul's joy, and ours, are *in Jesus Christ*. Earlier we saw that Paul mentioned *Jesus* 17 times in Philippians 1:1-30. Again, here in Philippians 3, Paul mentions *Jesus, Jesus Christ, Lord,* or *Lord Jesus Christ* 11 times in 21 verses. Jesus is the fountain of joy.

Fans go to sports games and cheer for their team. At the end of the game, if their team wins, the fans proclaim, "We won!" These fans had little or nothing to do with the victory. They did not even compete or participate in the contest on the field. Yet they are claiming and celebrating the victory of those who represented them. Likewise, we rejoice in the victory of Jesus over sin, Satan, and the world. We trust in Him, not in ourselves. All of our claims to salvation and heaven are based on the ministry of Jesus Christ, not on ourselves.

**Q 108** *How are we like fans who rejoice that their team wins?*

Figure 5.25    Beware of Dogs

Paul guides believers away from trusting in religious rites—such as circumcision, which was important for males (but never females) under the old covenant. Today, circumcision for males has some fleshly benefits. It lowers the risk of infection in the urinary tract, and lowers the risk of sexual diseases. [11] But physical circumcision has no spiritual benefits. In Colossians, Paul—battling against the Judaizers—considers circumcision as one of the shadows of things to come (Col. 2:17). In other words, outward circumcision for Jews was a symbol of the inner, spiritual circumcision that we all need. Paul teaches that when we accept Jesus as Savior, we receive an inner, spiritual circumcision of the heart, not done by human hands, but by Christ (Col. 2:11). Paul also writes that circumcision is *"of the heart, by the Spirit, not by the written code"* (Rom. 2:29).

Scripture sometimes compares people to animals, such as sheep, goats, pigs, and dogs. The Bible even compares Jesus to a lamb. Paul compares the Judaizers to *dogs* because of their fierce nature. These Jewish *legalists said salvation was by keeping rules such as circumcision, feasts, diet guidelines, a new moon celebration, or a Sabbath day (Col. 3:16). Many of these practices under the old covenant were shadows—pointing to Christ and the new covenant through His blood (Col. 2:17).

**Application.**    Today, most of us do not have a Jewish background and there are fewer Judaizers pressing us to obey the laws God gave through Moses. Still, we must be careful to center our trust and rejoicing in Christ. As Paul wrote, we *"glory in Christ Jesus, and...put no confidence in the flesh"* (Phil. 3:3). We do not glory in our good deeds, our good abilities, good looks, or good luck. Our confidence is in Christ (Figure 5.24)! He is our Savior. Our confidence is not in circumstances, friends, or water baptism. Our hope is not in church membership, giving, a Christian name, or purgatory. JESUS is our Savior and Deliverer. He is our Lord, Master, and Coming King! The Lord Jesus Christ has become to us wisdom, righteousness, holiness, and redemption (1 Cor. 1:30). He is the pearl of great price that makes our hearts sing. He is the Author and the Finisher of our faith (Heb. 12:2). We fix our hope on Christ alone! Any acts of obedience or good deeds we do are not to earn our salvation, but only to show respect and thankfulness to Jesus Christ and to pass on His love. "On Christ the solid rock we stand, all other ground is sinking sand." [12] O may we never boast, except in the cross of Christ—and our Savior who died in our place (Gal. 6:14). We *glory in Christ Jesus, and...put no confidence* in ourselves, our efforts, our accomplishments, or our human relationships.

Paul uses himself as an example of trusting and glorying in Christ—and putting no confidence in the flesh. Read his testimony again:

| 1. | 2. | 3. | 4. |
|---|---|---|---|
| 5. | 6. | 7. | |

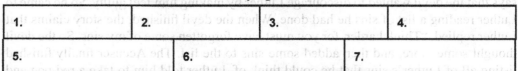

Figure 5.26    **Practice identifying seven reasons why Paul could have trusted in the flesh for salvation.**

Q 109  *In Paul's day, what were false teachers substituting for faith in Christ? Give examples.*

Q 110  *How was physical circumcision a shadow of spiritual circumcision?*

Q 111  *Does physical circumcision have any spiritual value today? Explain.*

Q 112  *Why does Paul compare the legalists to dogs?*

Q 113  *Do our good deeds or suffering help us earn our salvation? Explain.*

Q 114  *What happens to the joy of those who think they earn salvation?*

Q 115  *What are 7 religious reasons why Paul could have trusted in the flesh (Phil. 3:5-6)?*

*¹Finally, my brothers, **rejoice in the Lord!** It is no trouble for me to write the same things to you again, and it is a safeguard for you. ²Watch out for those dogs, those men who do evil, those mutilators of the flesh. ³For it is we who are the circumcision, we who worship by the Spirit of God, **who glory in Christ Jesus**, and who put no confidence in the flesh ⁴though I myself have reasons for such confidence. If anyone else thinks he has reasons to put confidence in the flesh, I have more: ⁵circumcised on the eighth day, of the people of Israel, of the tribe of Benjamin, a Hebrew of Hebrews; in regard to the law, a Pharisee; ⁶as for zeal, persecuting the church; as for legalistic righteousness, faultless. ⁷But whatever was to my profit I now consider loss for the sake of Christ.* (Phil. 3:1-7)

Paul put no confidence in the seven reasons above; for trusting in these was like building on a spider's web (Job 8:14).

**Q 116** *Compared to knowing Christ, what was the total value Paul put on ALL of his fleshly deeds and claims (Phil. 3:8)?*

*"What is more, I consider everything a loss compared to the surpassing greatness of knowing Christ Jesus my Lord, for whose sake I have lost all things. I consider them rubbish, that I may gain Christ"* (Phil. 3:8). Paul's total hope was in his relationship with Jesus Christ! That's what kept him smiling. His joy bubbled like a spring from his fellowship with Jesus.

Paul's hope of salvation did NOT depend on his genealogy or his religious rites (such as circumcision, fasting, or giving). His hope of salvation was not in his education, his spiritual gifts, his visions and dreams, or his ministry. Paul wrote:

*⁹I want to be found in him, not having a righteousness of my own that comes from the law, but that which is through faith in Christ—the righteousness that comes from God and is by faith. ¹⁰I want to know Christ and the power of his resurrection and the fellowship of sharing in his sufferings, becoming like him in his death, ¹¹and so, somehow, to attain to the resurrection from the dead* (Phil. 3:9-11).

Paul's identity was in Christ. He wanted the righteousness Christ gives us by faith. He wanted to stand firm as a messenger of Christ—even if this meant *suffering* like Christ. He wanted to be faithful unto *death* just like Jesus was. He wanted to be *resurrected* from the grave just like Jesus was with a new, glorious body (Phil. 3:11). Paul wanted to be like Jesus in life, death, and beyond.

**Q 117** *How does rejoicing in the Lord, instead of our own performance, keep our joy consistent?*

**Application.**    Paul overflowed with joy **because** his focus and trust were in Jesus Christ. And Jesus never disappoints us. *"Anyone who trusts in him will never be put to shame"* (Rom. 10:11). It is "so sweet to trust in Jesus, just from sin and self to cease. Just from Jesus simply taking life and rest, and joy and peace."¹³ If we trust in ourselves, money, power, positions, parents, or friends, we will be disappointed and discouraged sooner or later. But the more we trust in Jesus and depend on Him, the happier we remain.

**Q 118** *Do you celebrate the joy of the value Jesus places on you?*

A dad and mom had a son born to them, and later adopted another child. Once, when the two children were talking, the adopted son said to the son born into the family, "I feel sorry for you, because you did not have the chance to be chosen." Paul reflects this kind of self-worth when he recalls that Jesus Christ chose us. Rejoice in the Lord, who chose us to be in His family! Delight in the One who places a high value on us!

**Q 119** *What lesson can we learn from the story about Martin Luther?*

Martin Luther is famous as the person who helped bring about the *Reformation. An old story about Luther illustrates that he trusted in Jesus Christ, not himself. The story says that the devil wanted to discourage Luther by making him feel guilty. So he came to Luther reading a list of sins he had done. When the devil finished, the story claims that Luther replied, "Think harder, for you must have forgotten some of my sins. So the devil thought some more, and then added some sins to the list. The Accuser finally finished listing all of Luther's sins that he could think of. Luther told him to take a red pen and write across the list: *"The blood of Jesus, his Son, purifies us from all sin"* (1 John 1:7). The devil had nothing to say, so he left.¹⁴ Other versions of this story say that Luther quoted 1 John 1:7, and then threw a bottle of ink at the devil. This story may be only a legend. But it illustrates Luther's discovery and belief that we are saved by trusting in Jesus Christ and not in ourselves.

We are studying three principles that help us live full of joy. The first principle is: Rejoice in the Lord—not in your own human efforts (Phil. 3:1-11). Now let us look at the second principle.

## B. Face the future—not the past (Phil. 3:12-14).

[12]*Not that I have already obtained all this, or have already been made perfect, but I press on to take hold of that for which Christ Jesus took hold of me.* [13]*Brothers, I do not consider myself yet to have taken hold of it.* **But one thing I do: Forgetting what is behind and straining toward what is ahead,** [14]**I press on toward the goal to win the prize for which God has called me heavenward in Christ Jesus** (Phil. 3:12-14).

**Q 120** What was the prize that Paul pressed forward to win (Phil. 3:14)?

A key to having joy is facing the future, not the past. As the old proverbs say, "Don't saw the sawdust." "Don't cry over spilt milk."

Some of the past can be valuable. It encourages us to recall God's faithfulness. He saved Noah and his family through the flood. He fulfilled His promises to Abraham. He delivered the Israelites from Egypt, the most powerful nation in the world. He delivered and restored Job. He gave Moses the power to lead millions of Israelites. He heard the prayers of women like Leah, Hannah, and Deborah. He heard the final prayer of Samson. He delivered David from the paw of a bear and the mouth of a lion; He empowered young David to defeat Goliath, and then anointed him as king and promised the Messiah through his lineage. He delivered Daniel from the lions, the three Hebrews through the fiery furnace, and restored a nation from captivity in Babylon. It inspires us to recall these stories and a hundred others from Old Testament times. Likewise, it lifts our spirits to think of ways God blessed the apostles, the 120 at Pentecost, and thousands of Gentile believers. And there is great value in remembering that in the recent past, God has forgiven *our* sins through Jesus Christ, filled us with His Spirit, and promised us an inheritance. He has helped *us* through sickness, to cross rivers, to climb mountains, to overcome temptations, and to endure fiery trials. There is much in the past to strengthen us and for us to learn from. Like Samuel, we can raise an Ebenezer stone, and write on it: *"Thus far has the Lord helped us"* (1 Sam. 7:12).[15] (For a tremendous sermon on God's help in past days, see https://www.blueletterbible.org/comm/spurgeon_charles/sermons/0500.cfm).

**Q 121** Interpret the proverb: "Don't saw the sawdust."

**Q 122** How can we use the past to encourage ourselves in the Lord?

**The Problems.** There can be value in recalling the past. Yet there are several types of *looking back* that we should avoid—as we avoid a disease. Let us consider two aspects of the **past** to turn away from.

*We should avoid bragging about **past** successes and good deeds.* Paul is saying that if you try to find joy in keeping *all* the rules or *always* being your best, you will find that *we all* fall short of perfection. Our salvation is not based on our performance. But if our goal is to know Christ and His sufferings and His resurrection, we will find joy in our experiences.

**Q 123** Why should we avoid bragging about our past successes?

There is no one more addicted than the person who is drunk on his own success. The person wrapped up in himself makes a small package. Those who walk looking backwards soon stumble and fall. Better to focus on the present and future than to relive the "good old days." God struck down a multitude among the Israelites who complained that the fish and melons *back in Egypt* were better than the manna in the wilderness (Num. 11:1-35). A few days later, this fascination for the past prevented a nation from entering Canaan (Num. 14:2). Paul has just written about the need to turn away from our good deeds, good luck, and good old days. He has listed seven reasons why he could have

**Q 124** What happens to those who walk looking backwards? Apply this.

had confidence in the flesh, and compared these to rubbish—trash (Phil. 3:8)! Good deeds we have done for Christ are good. But we should not spend much time thinking about our good deeds of the past. Jesus said that when we have done all He has commanded and enabled us to do, we should count ourselves as *"unworthy servants"* (Luke 17:10).

Paul counsels us not to think of ourselves more highly than we should (Rom. 12:3). *"God opposes the proud but gives grace to the humble"* (James 4.6). Looking at the strutting Pharisees, Jesus warned that whoever exalts himself will be humbled (Matt. 23:12). When King Nebuchadnezzar claimed the credit for his great kingdom, God struck him insane for 7 years (Dan. 4). God used King Saul while he was small in his own eyes, but replaced him when he became arrogant (1 Sam. 15:17; 13:13-14). And when King Herod did not give God the glory for his success, God struck him down with worms (Acts 12). Let us not be like the house cat that looked in a mirror and thought he saw a lion. Let us not be like the donkey who thought the crowds were cheering for him, rather than the King who was riding him. And let us not be like the rooster who thought his crowing caused the sun to rise each morning. A pastor and his people must avoid being conceited, lest they *"fall under the same judgment as the devil"* (1 Tim. 3:6; Luke 10:18). Paul asks: *"⁷For who makes you different from anyone else? What do you have that you did not receive? And if you did receive it, why do you boast as though you did not?"* (1 Cor. 4:7). Better to *glory in Christ* for any success He gives us, but avoid gloating over past victories. Better to trust in Christ and Him alone for our salvation. Those who trust in themselves will fall short. But whoever trusts in Christ will never be ashamed.

**Q 125** ⟍ *Besides avoiding bragging, what is a second error to avoid in regard to the past?*

*To have joy, we should also avoid meditating on our past sins, failures, mistakes, and sorrows.* In his zeal, Paul persecuted the church (Phil. 3:8). He dragged men and women to prison for following Jesus (Acts 22:4). He was probably the leader of those who stoned Stephen (Acts 8:58). Then Paul discovered that these beloved children of God whom he persecuted were right and he was wrong. After Paul met Jesus, these past evil deeds were a source of guilt and sorrow to Paul. He referred to himself as *less than the least of God's people* (Eph. 3:8). His remorse caused him to write: *"I am the least of the apostles and do not even deserve to be called an apostle, because I persecuted the church of God"* (1 Cor. 15:9). But the Holy Spirit led Paul to look away from these past sins. The Spirit assured Paul that God had forgiven and forgotten these sins. And the Spirit guided Paul to face the future and think on good things (Phil. 3:14; 4:8-9). Never look back to mourn over sins that God has removed as far as the east is from the west (Ps. 103:12).

**Q 126** ⟍ *Does God remember our past sins that He has forgiven?*

**Application.**   None of us is perfect, even on our best day. And none of us wants others to know or recall our worst days. God Word urges us to let the past be the past. For surely our sins are buried in the sea of God's forgetfulness. As He promises us under the new covenant by the blood of Christ: *"I will forgive their wickedness and will remember their sins no more"* (Heb. 8:12; 1 John 1:9). God does not have a bad memory. But He chooses to forget our sins that He has forgiven. So let us forget those evil things behind us and forgive ourselves as God has forgiven us. Whenever we feel guilty for past sins and mistakes, let us remember that it is NOT God who makes us feel guilty for sins He has forgotten. He forgives our sins and remembers them no more. Likewise, let us not recall the sins of other believers after repentance, church discipline, and restoration. Let us do unto others as we want them to do unto us.

**Q 127** ⟍ *How are those who recall past sins like the boy who kept pulling a dead dog out of the grave?*

One of the rules of marriage is that spouses should never dig up sins of the past that they agreed to bury. This is especially true in moments of anger, when Satan tempts us to silence others by reminding them of past faults. A boy buried his dog when it died, but left the tail sticking out. From time to time, the boy visited the dog's grave, and pulled the dead animal out. Yuk! What a terrible odor and horrible sight. After a few minutes the boy buried the dog again, leaving the tail out as before. Whenever he did this, people did not want to be near him, because of the stench on his hands and clothes. Finally his father learned of this stinky practice, buried the dog completely, and stopped the son from digging it up again. Likewise, when a spouse or a child digs up past mistakes of another, it makes the room stink and causes those nearby to want to get away from the person who dug up the past. May our Heavenly Father convict us of this terrible sin of "grave-digging", which is a worse sin than anything we may dig up.

In one nation, two groups of people fought against each other in a fierce war. Thousands were killed and many others were wounded. Many homes were burned to the ground, and there was damage to much property. One widow complained to a leader about a beautiful tree that was damaged in front of her house. She wept with bitterness

**Figure 5.27   Those who bring up the past mistakes of others are like the boy who kept digging up his dead dog.**

that the trunk and limbs were broken. She wanted the leader to condemn those who destroyed the tree or at least speak words of sympathy to her. After a brief silence, the leader replied, "Dear woman, give thanks that you still have a house. Cut the tree down and forget it. Better to forget the past, than to let its memory poison the present."[16]

*Q 128* ➤ *What lesson can we learn from the widow who mourned over a damaged tree?*

Paul counsels us to forget the past. We have considered two types of "looking back" that we should avoid. We should never look back to brag about past success through our own efforts. And we should not look back and feel guilty about sins God has forgiven and forgotten. Now let us look at Paul's solution to avoid looking back. How do we avoid the errors of facing the past?

**The Solution.**   [13b]*But one thing I do: Forgetting what is behind and straining toward what is ahead,* [14]*I press on toward the goal to win the prize for which God has called me heavenward in Christ Jesus* (Phil. 3:13b-14).

*Q 129* ➤ *How did Paul avoid the error of meditating on his past successes and failures?*

Earlier, we considered the Ebenezer stone and praise: *"Thus far has the Lord helped us"* (1 Sam. 7:12). This verse suggests the assurance: "And God will continue to help us to the end of our journey." There is much ahead. We must face: more trials, more joys; more temptations, more triumphs; more prayers, more answers; more toils, more strength; more battles, more victories; more slanders, more comforts; more deep waters, more high mountains; more demons, and more angels. And then come sickness, old age, disease, and death. Are the challenges over? Not yet! *We will raise one stone more just before we enter the cold waters of death* or just after the Rapture! We will shout our final Ebenezer: *"Thus far has the Lord helped us"* for the best is yet to come. Our eternal inheritance of living with God in heaven is ahead. We shall awaken in His likeness. We shall soar through the stars. We shall behold Jesus face to face. Our joyful praises will echo through the ages. We shall fellowship with the saints and enjoy the presence of God forever—in an atmosphere beyond human imagination. It will be a kingdom with no sin and no darkness and Jesus will wipe all tears from our eyes. Yes, as surely as God has helped us so far until this day, He will help us to the end. The Lord has promised us: "I will never leave you, I will never forsake you; I have been with you, and I will be with you to the end." So let us have courage and faith, *facing the future* with confidence.

*Q 130* ➤ *How does 1 Samuel 7:12 encourage us for the future?*

As Paul says, let us *practice* doing the things that we know are right (Phil. 3:15-16; Col. 3). Let us *live up to* the truth we have already learned—and the maturity we have already reached and attained. Paul encourages us: " [15]*All of us who are mature should take such a view of things. And if on some point you think differently, that too God will make clear to you.* [16]*Only let us live up to what we have already attained"* (Phil. 3:15-16).

*Q 131* ➤ *State Philippians 3:16 in your own words.*

**Q 132** ⬋ *Do we trust in Christ to save us, but in ourselves to live right? Explain.*

The *roots* of Paul's hope of salvation are in Jesus Christ. But the *fruits* of salvation are in the life of Jesus that flows *through us*. So throughout Paul's letters, there is a twofold emphasis. *First,* we trust in Christ, not ourselves to save us. *Second,* we trust in Christ to enable us to live lives that are worthy of the gift of salvation—lives that glorify God and shine the light to those still in darkness. So, although Paul places no confidence in himself, we do not see him just taking a nap. Rather, we see him *practicing forgetting the past, straining toward* the future like a runner in a race, and *pressing toward* the goal to win the prize of heaven ahead. Paul's confidence is in Jesus Christ and the power of the Spirit—but he does all that he knows to cooperate with God. Likewise, we trust in Christ and are led by the Spirit, not by evil desires of the flesh.

*Sabio* **says**: "The gift becomes the task. Salvation is free, but we must live to show we appreciate the blood of Christ that paid our debt." This is possible as we rest in the truth that God loves us, wants us, and accepts us. As earthly parents cheer for their children who are growing, God delights to have us in His family and cheers for us as we mature in Christ. Knowing the love of God deep within, we have joy, security, and encouragement.

### C. Follow a godly example—not a worldly one whose destiny is destruction (Phil. 3:12-21).

**¹⁷***Join with others in following my example, brothers, and take note of those who live according to the pattern we gave you.* **¹⁸*For, as I have often told you before and now say again even with tears, many live as enemies of the cross of Christ.* ¹⁹*Their destiny is destruction, their god is their stomach, and their glory is in their shame. Their mind is on earthly things*** (Phil. 3:17-19).

**Figure 5.28**
**We win or lose by who we choose to follow. In most of his letters, Paul identifies three types of people we may follow: Legalists (dogs, like some Jews who teach that obeying rules brings salvation—Phil. 3:2; Col. 2:16-17); the Godly (sheep, like Paul, who trust in Christ for salvation—Phil. 3:17); and Libertines (hogs, who wallow in sin, yet may claim to know Christ—Phil. 3:18-19; Eph. 2:1-3; see also 2 Pet. 2:2).**

**Q 133** ⬈ *Are biblical writers being rude when they compare people to animals? Explain.*

**Q 134** ⬋ *How were the Jewish legalists like dogs?*

Scripture and other books often compare people to animals and other things in nature, using similes and metaphors. The prophet Hosea compared Israel to a backsliding heifer (Hos. 4:16). Jesus compared people to sheep and goats; wolves, snakes, and doves; pigs and dogs; chickens and vultures (Matt. 25:33; 10:16; 7:6; 23:37; 24:28). These comparisons use figurative language to emphasize a truth or characteristic. For example, snakes are known for being shrewd. Wolves are fierce and destructive. Some dogs are harsh and vicious. When biblical writers use comparisons to clarify a truth, we should recognize that they are not being rude or insulting. Jesus compared Himself to a door; He compared Himself to a grapevine, and His followers to branches. Throughout the book of Revelation, John compares Jesus to a lamb. Such comparisons reflect literary style, not bad manners. Paul compares legalists to mean dogs, because they are harsh and injure people (Phil. 3:2). Such dogs are always barking, growling, snarling, snapping, or biting. Peter compares believers who return to old, sinful ways to pigs that return to the mud (2 Pet. 2:2).

Q 135 ⬲ Complete Figure 5.29 on comparisons in Scripture.

| References | Comparison | Explanation |
|---|---|---|
| Hos. 4:16 | | |
| Matt. 7:6 | | |
| Matt. 10:16 | | |
| Matt. 23:37 | | |
| Matt. 24:28 | | |
| Matt. 25:33 | | |
| Acts 20:29 | | |
| Eph. 2:20 | Stones | |
| Eph. 2:21 | A temple | |
| Phil. 2:15 | | |
| Phil. 3:2 | | |
| Col. 1:15 | The firstborn | |
| Col. 2:19 | The body | |
| 2 Pet. 2:2 | | |
| 2 Pet. 2:12 | | |
| Jude 12 | Trees without fruit | |
| Jude 13 | Wild waves of the sea | |
| Rev. 12:9 | A dragon and a serpent | |

**Figure 5.29   Biblical writers often compare people to animals, other things in nature, or objects.**

Let us review three types of people in Philippians.

**Dogs.  In Philippians 3:1-11**, Paul warns against following the bad examples of the *legalists*. Various religions, including some branches of Christianity, Judaism, Islam, and Hinduism, are versions of legalism. They teach that our relationship with God is based on how well we obey rules and do our duties. Since none of us is perfect, following a legalist makes us feel *insecure* and *guilty*. Those who think their relationship with God is based on obeying rules often condemn themselves. Legalists may pray five times a day, give offerings, and make sacrifices. They may hope to be reincarnated and do better in the next life; or think they must suffer in purgatory to pay for their own sins. Most legalists, except for Pharisees and hypocrites, seldom feel they are good enough. After many good deeds and sacrifices, they still lack the assurance of a good relationship with God. The legalists are bad examples because they seek salvation from the wrong direction. They put the fruit before the root. They turn the tree of salvation upside down as if our relationship with God is based on the fruit we bear! God does not love us *because* we do good deeds. God loves us when we are yet sinners, before we even know Him. And He still loves us, even when we sin—although He must discipline all of His children who go astray. We are not saved by good works. Rather, the good works we do are the fruit of a new heart and a new relationship with God. So Paul guides believers away from legalists who put our performance as the basis for our relationship with God. **We are saved by grace, through faith in what Christ did for us—not by what we do for Him!** The legalists are bad examples to follow. They are on a road that leads away from the cross where, in love, Jesus paid every penny of our debt.

Q 136 ⬲ *In what sense do legalists have the tree of salvation upside down?*

Q 137 ⬲ *How do legalists insult the ministry of Christ?*

**Sheep.  In Philippians 3:12-17**, Paul urges believers to follow godly examples. He writes: *"Join with others in following my example, brothers, and take note of those who live according to the pattern we gave you"* (Phil. 3:17). *"Whatever you have learned or received or heard from me, or seen in me—put it into practice. And the God of peace will be with you"* (Phil. 4:9).

Q 138 ⬲ *Do you have a good example to follow?*

Q 139 ⬲ *Are you a good example to follow? Explain.*

There is wisdom in following godly examples. In contrast, *"Bad company corrupts good character"* (1 Cor. 15:33). We avoid many temptations by walking on godly

**Figure 5.30   Be a good example—raise the standards of those watching you.**

paths with godly friends. Lot led his family into Sodom, which had a bad influence on his wife and daughters. Paul counseled Timothy: *"Don't let anyone look down on you because you are young, but **set an example** for the believers in speech, in life, in love, in faith and in purity"* (1 Tim. 4:12). All believers should follow good examples so that we are good examples to follow. Let your light shine like stars in a dark world (Phil. 2:15). Those who follow Jesus and godly examples are as secure as a lamb in the lap of the Good Shepherd.

**Hogs.   In Philippians 3:18**, Paul warns against following the ***libertines** (Figure 5.31), those in the church who say, "Do anything you want and rely on the grace of God." In our world, Mr. or Miss Popular may not be good examples to follow. Those who claim to know Christ, yet follow the desires of the flesh, believe *false security*. God's grace is amazing. But just as the Gnostics made a heresy out of knowledge, the *Gracetics transform grace into filth. Paul asks: *" ¹Shall we go on sinning so that grace may increase? ²By no means! We died to sin; how can we live in it any longer?"* (Rom. 6:1-2). He warns that the wrath of God is coming on those who live in sin (Col. 3:6). The apostle insists that no one who follows the desires of the flesh has any inheritance in God's kingdom (1 Cor. 6:9-11; Gal. 5:21). Concerning those who follow sinful desires, Paul writes with tears:

**Q 140** ✎ *Do you know some who claim to be Christians, but are enemies of the cross (Phil. 3:18)? Explain.*

> ¹⁸*For, as I have often told you before and now say again even with tears, many live as enemies of the cross of Christ. ¹⁹Their destiny is destruction, their god is their stomach, and their glory is in their shame. Their mind is on earthly things* (Phil. 3:18-19).

Some begin to follow Jesus, but later return to their sins. Peter compares these backsliders to hogs, as he writes: *" ²²A sow that is washed goes back to her wallowing in the mud"* (1 Pet. 2:22).

**Q 141** ✎ *In what sense do legalists and libertines follow the ways of the world?*

Legalists and libertines are bad examples to follow. They *walk in the ways of this world*, not the next (Eph. 2:2). *Their minds are on earthly things* (Phil. 3:19; Col. 2:10-23). Paul contrasts those *of the world* with believers:

> ²⁰*But our citizenship is in heaven. And we eagerly await a Savior from there, the Lord Jesus Christ, ²¹who, by the power that enables him to bring everything under his control, will transform our lowly bodies so that they will be like his glorious body* (Phil. 3:17-21).

| Paul's Letters | Dogs (Legalists) | Sheep (Followers of Jesus) | Hogs (Libertines) |
|---|---|---|---|
| Rom. | 2:1–3:20 | 1:16-17; 3:21-22 | 6:1-2 |
| 1 Cor. | | 1:4-9 | 6:9-11 |
| 2 Cor. | 5:22 | 5:11-21 | |
| Gal. | 1:1–5:12 | 1:3-5; 3:15; 5:18, 22-26 | 5:19-21 |
| Eph. | 2:14-15 | Most of 1–6 | 4:17-20; 5:5-7, 11-12 |
| Phil. | 3:2-11 | 1–2; 3:12-17; 3:20–4:23 | 3:18-19 |
| Col. | 2:4, 8-23 | Most of 1–4 | 3:5-6 |
| 1 Thess. | | Most of 1–5 | 4:3-8 |
| 2 Thess. | | Most of 1–3 | 3:14-15 |
| 1 Tim. | 1:3-11; 4:1-5; 6:3-5, 20-21 | Most of 1–6 | 1:19-20 |
| 2 Tim. | 3:3-4 | Most of 1–4 | 2:14-19; 3:1-9 |
| Titus | 1:10-16 | Most of 1–3 | |
| Philem. | | 1:1-25 | |

**Figure 5.31   Throughout Paul's letters, he often refers to three groups of people: legalists (dogs), true Christians (sheep), libertines (hogs).**

**Conclusion.** ¹*Therefore, my brothers, you whom I love and long for, my joy and crown, that is how you should stand firm in the Lord, dear friends!* (Phil. 4:1).

A. Rejoice in the Lord—not in your own human efforts (Phil. 3:1-11).

B. Face the future—not the past (Phil. 3:12-14).

C. Follow a godly example—not a worldly one whose destiny is destruction (Phil. 3:12-21).

---

## Joy in the Lord—in any circumstance (Phil. 4:2-23)

**Lesson 29**

**Goal A:** *Summarize how joy and peace depend on agreeing in the Lord and rejoicing in the Lord (Phil. 4:2-4).*

**Goal B:** *Analyze and illustrate the relationship of joy and peace to prayer, right thinking, and right living (Phil. 4:6-9).*

**Goal C:** *Explain and illustrate a principle about joy for each of these: contentment, thankfulness, and generosity (Phil. 4:10-19).*

---

**Review of Philippians 1–3.** As we enter the last lesson of Philippians, let us review lessons we have studied.

**Q 142** ➚ *What is the theme of Philippians?*

### Lesson 24—Introduction to Paul's letter of joy (Phil. 1:1-11)

- Paul's greeting teaches us to be personal, courteous, and complimentary. He loves the *saints* in Philippi.

- He opens and closes his letter saying, "Thank you." Thanking others should be a habit of all believers.

- Paul prayed for all believers to grow in Christ so that our love overflows in discernment and righteous living—to glorify God.

### Lesson 25—Joy in where we are (Phil. 1:12-26)

- In hard times, the three doors of bitterness, opportunity, and trust are always before us. What happens *in* us is more important than what happens *to* us.

### Lessons 26 and 27—Joy in those around us (Phil. 1:27–2:30)

- We do not need to move to discover joy. We can increase our joy by discerning two principles:
  - The Christian life includes: not only believing in Christ—but suffering for Him.
  - The Christian life includes: not only your own interests—but also the interests of others.

### Lesson 28—Joy in the Lord (Phil. 3:1–4:1)

- Beware of dogs. Rejoice in the Lord—not in your own human efforts.

- Face the future—not the past.

- Follow the example of a sheep—not a dog or a hog.

**Lesson 29** is our final study in Paul's letter of joy. It covers **Philippians 4:2-23.** The theme of this lesson is: *Rejoice in the Lord, always*—in any circumstance (Phil. 4:4). This final chapter contains several principles, commands, and exhortations. We will study these (A–G) under the theme of *joy and peace in any circumstance.* **Joy and peace** are like a married couple—most of the time we see them together. In Paul's list of the Spirit's fruit, we see joy and peace side by side. It is helpful to realize that there are three dimensions of these spiritual fruits (Figure 5.32). We will structure our lesson around these three dimensions of peace and joy.

**Q 143** ➚ *How are joy and peace like a married couple?*

**Q 144** ➘ *What are 3 dimensions or aspects of joy?*

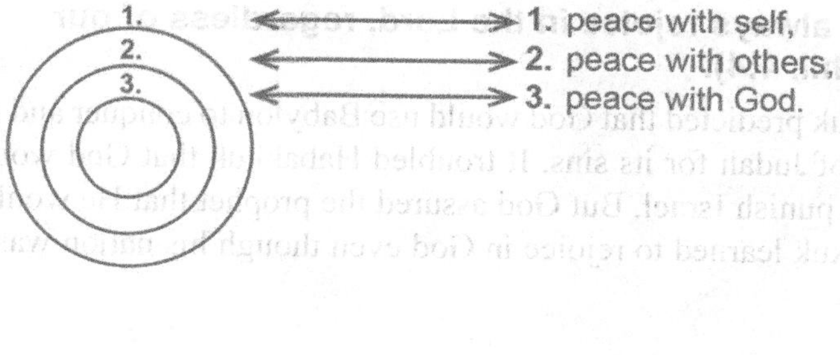

1. peace with self,
2. peace with others,
3. peace with God.

**Figure 5.32**
**Fruits of the Spirit, such as peace and joy, have three dimensions.**

This final chapter of Philippians reminds us of 1 Thessalonians 5:12-22, where Paul gives at least 16 exhortations in 11 verses. Paul says so much, so fast, that grasping it can be like trying to drink water from a fire hose. We will focus on seven principles (A–G) related to having joy and peace in all circumstances. And we will *briefly* explain, illustrate, and apply each of these principles.

Q 145 ⟋ Who were Euodia and Syntyche?

## A. Principle: We have peace and joy with others as we agree in the Lord (Phil. 4:2-3).

*2I plead with Euodia and I plead with Syntyche to **agree with each other in the Lord**. 3 Yes, and I ask you, loyal yokefellow, help these women who have contended at my side in the cause of the gospel, along with Clement and the rest of my fellow workers, whose names are in the book of life* (Phil. 4:2-3).

Q 146 ⟋ What does it mean to "agree in the Lord"?

*Euodia and *Syntyche were two leading ladies at the church in Philippi. When two main people in a church argue, the disharmony spreads. Some follow one leader, and some follow the other leader. As we noted earlier, Paul probably wrote Philippians 2, emphasizing the humility of Christ, as a step toward uniting these sisters in Christ. He did not insult or condemn anyone. He did not try to make them feel guilty. And he did not say that both need to have the same opinion about topics. Rather, Paul pleaded with them in love to *agree in the Lord*. In other words, he asked them to lay aside their differences and focus on the things they agreed about Christ. There are always topics that stir up controversy. There are always many differing opinions about politics, how to raise children, and how to cook. But the main things in life that matter are the truths of the gospel of Christ. So when we are tempted to quarrel, let us recall that God blesses the peacemakers (Matt. 5:8). God requires us to *walk worthy* of the love He has shown us. Christ gave us an example, and teaches us to *"be completely humble and gentle; be patient, bearing with one another in love"* (Eph. 4:2). God is watching us, and Jesus is coming soon. So Paul writes: *"Let your gentleness be evident to all. The Lord is near"* (Phil. 4:5). God means it when He says: *"Make every effort to keep the unity of the Spirit through the bond of peace"* (Eph. 4:3).

Q 147 ⟍ How big should we draw the circle of fellowship in Christ? Give examples.

**Application.**    As Euodia and Syntyche humbled themselves and agreed in the Lord, the unity of the Spirit was restored. The reputation of love among believers was protected. The light and love of the church could influence the community. So it is with us. God hates those who cause division among brothers (Prov. 6:19). But His joy and peace flow through us as we step over disagreements and agree in the Lord.

Too often, believers draw a smaller circle within the body of Christ and say, "We know that you must belong to Christ, but you also must fit within this smaller circle in order to have any relationship with us." But as believers, we should not draw the circle of peace and relationships any smaller than Jesus Himself has drawn it. Can we be critical and joyful at the same time? There are always some personal differences and points of view among believers. It is a wonderful thing to *agree in the Lord* on the major doctrines of the Bible and to allow diversity on little details that do not affect salvation. In this way, we can have peace, joy and unity. We are one in the Spirit. We are one in the Lord. As Paul reminded the arguing Philippians, the names of all believers are *in the book of life* (Phil. 4:3). So surely we can find a way to *agree in our Lord* and live in peace and harmony.[17]

Q 148 ⟍ How does rejoicing in the Lord differ from rejoicing in circumstances? Illustrate.

## B. Principle: We can always rejoice in the Lord, regardless of our circumstances (Phil. 4:4).

Q 149 ⟋ What enabled Habakkuk to rejoice in hard times?

The prophet Habakkuk predicted that God would use Babylon to conquer and punish the Southern Kingdom of Judah for its sins. It troubled Habakkuk that God would use a fierce, pagan nation to punish Israel. But God assured the prophet that He would later punish Babylon. Habakkuk learned to rejoice in God even though his nation was about to be conquered by a nation that did not know or serve God at all. In the worst of times, the prophet lifted up his voice in praise, singing:

> [17]*Though the fig tree does not bud and there are no grapes on the vines, though the olive crop fails and the fields produce no food, though there are no sheep in the pen and no cattle in the stalls,* [18]*yet I will rejoice in the LORD, I will be joyful in God my Savior* (Hab. 3:17-18).

**Q 150** ⟋ *What enabled Paul and Silas to sing in prison?*

Paul and Silas sang in Philippi, in prison and in the stocks, with their backs raw and bleeding from a beating (Acts 16). And Paul wrote *"Rejoice in the Lord always"* while in prison, not knowing if he would live or be executed (Phil. 4:4).

**Q 151** ⟍ *What lesson can we learn from the carpenter?*

A carpenter was building a wooden wall to extend a house. After many hours of work, the wall was almost ready to connect to the house. Suddenly, a strong wind blew the wall to the ground, damaging much of the carpenter's work. The owner of the house saw what happened and said, "O my, this is terrible." But the carpenter replied with a smile, "We cannot let something like this get us down." This carpenter's attitude reminds us of Paul, a good example for us. No matter what happened, Paul's response was: "We cannot let something like this get us down." Whether Paul was stoned, bitten by a snake, shipwrecked, sleepless, or lacked food, Paul's response was to rejoice in the Lord. May we learn to follow in Paul's steps, rejoicing in our Lord in sunshine or rain, comfort or pain.

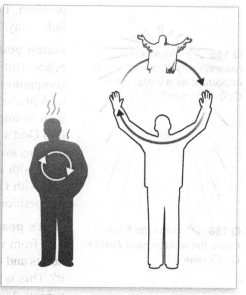

*"Rejoice in the Lord always. I will say it again: Rejoice!"* (Phil. 4:4).

**Figure 5.33** We can always rejoice in the Lord, regardless of circumstances.

**Application.** If the only times we rejoice in the Lord are when the sun is shining, we will live at least half of life without singing. To obey Philippians 4:4, we must learn the habit of *choosing* to praise God *in heaven*, *regardless* of what is happening *on earth*. Rejoicing, like loving or forgiving, is a choice—a closed door before us that we can open at any time. Some go through life guided by their emotions and feelings. Others, like Paul, are led by the Spirit and guide their emotions to glorify God.

**Q 152** ⟍ *When do those who guide their emotions rejoice? Explain.*

## C. Principle: The cure for anxiety is prayer, which brings the peace of God (Phil. 4:6-7).

> [6]*Do not be anxious about anything, but in everything, by prayer and petition, with thanksgiving, present your requests to God.* [7]*And the peace of God, which transcends all understanding, will guard your hearts and your minds in Christ Jesus* (Phil. 4:6-7).

**Q 153** ⟋ *What are 3 reasons why anxiety is an enemy?*

(For a sermon on this passage, see the *Faith & Action Series* book, *Homiletics 1*, Lesson 28, point B).

Worrying wastes our time. It is like digging to get out of a pit. The more we dig, the further we are from a solution. Anxiety and worry are our enemies. They waste our time and harm our health. Being anxious causes tooth decay, ulcers, high blood pressure, and insomnia. And worrying dishonors our Heavenly Father. When we worry, we are acting as orphans who have no father to love and care for them. So Jesus taught us not to worry about the things we need in life. Rather, He counseled us to put God's kingdom first and to trust our Heavenly Father to care for us (Matt. 6:33).

The sun is so big that 1,300,000 earths could fit inside it.[18] But if you hold a small coin near your eye, it can prevent you from seeing the sun. What we see depends on what we put close to our eyes. When we focus on our problems, they can seem like a mountain in front of us. But Paul knew the secret of putting God between him and his

**Q 154** ⟋ *How can a penny hide the sun? Apply this.*

problem. For as we focus on God, His love, faithfulness, and power cause anxiety to fade away. So instead of worrying, pray your problems.

**Q 155** *What are 3 reasons why thanksgiving is important as we approach God in prayer?*

**Watch your attitude as you pray.** Paul promises that as we pray, God will give us peace. But the apostle guides us to come to God with the attitude of thanksgiving, not complaining. As the Psalmist says, *"Enter his gates with thanksgiving and his courts with praise; give thanks to him and praise his name"* (Ps. 100:4). If you had a meeting with an important person, would you greet him with a complaint? Likewise, as we enter into God's presence let us count our blessings rather than our problems. Thanksgiving turns us away from a problem and toward a solution. Thanksgiving causes us to look up with faith instead of down with doubt. So let us prepare our attitudes as we prepare to talk with God. Let us recall some of the blessings God has poured out on us as we lay our petitions and requests at the throne of grace.

**Q 156** *How did Paul relate the soldier near him to God's peace?*

**God's peace is like a guard.** Paul gives us a marvelous promise. He says that as we turn from worry to God and pray to our Father with thanksgiving, peace will **guard** our hearts and minds. Have you ever seen a guard or a policeman standing by a door to guard it? This is the picture Paul is seeing. As he wrote from prison, there was at least one soldier standing beside him as a guard. Paul is saying that as we pray with thanksgiving, God's peace comes to stand at the door of our mind and at the door of our heart. As Paul's guard prevented people from entering Paul's cell in prison, God's peace prevents fear, worry, and anxiety from entering our hearts and minds. And this peace of God is powerful! It is stronger than logic. It transcends circumstances. Even when reason and circumstances would cause us to be anxious, God's peace that transcends them both guards our hearts and minds. For through prayer, we connect with the great power of God who rules the universe. And we trust in the One who transcends the tiny thoughts of men and views the circumstances that ripple across the earth like water shaking in a coffee cup. As a child feels at peace sitting in a dad's lap, our hearts and minds enjoy a peace that surpasses understanding in the bosom of our Heavenly Father. During a fierce storm, Jesus slept in the boat like a baby being rocked in a cradle (Matt. 8). Likewise, there is peace in the midst of a storm when we dwell in the shadow of the Most High.

### D. Principle: Peace from God flows through right thinking and right living (Phil. 4:8-9).

*[8] Finally, brothers, whatever is true, whatever is noble, whatever is right, whatever is pure, whatever is lovely, whatever is admirable—if anything is excellent or praiseworthy—**think about such things**. [9] Whatever you have learned or received or heard from me, or seen in me—**put it into practice**. And the God of peace will be with you* (Phil. 4:8-9).

**Q 157** *How do our thoughts affect our emotions?*

**Q 158** *How can beliefs be like a rider on a bicycle?*

**What we think about affects our peace.** Our emotions and feelings do not just happen. They are a result of what we fix our thoughts on. The person who feeds his mind a diet of bad news, insults, and criticism will sour his emotions. Those who meditate on problems, past grievances, past sins, and the rise of evil must suffer from another gloomy day. Those who practice doubt are like the waves of the sea. Their emotions are mixed with turmoil, discouragement, and anxiety. Thinking affects feeling. So we must pay attention to our thoughts. As a rider steers a bicycle, we must turn our minds away from useless and harmful thoughts.

**Q 159** *What key does Paul give us to conquer bad thoughts? Illustrate.*

It is not enough to turn away from bad thoughts—such as temptations, unforgiveness, worry, wickedness, and fleshly desires. Enjoying God's peace requires avoiding negative patterns of thinking *and* practicing right thinking. As a person pours dirty water from a bucket and fills it with clean water, we must replace harmful thoughts with helpful thoughts. Paul tells us what to fill our minds with. *"Finally, brothers, whatever is true, whatever is noble, whatever is right, whatever is pure, whatever is lovely, whatever* *is admirable—if anything is excellent or praiseworthy—**think about such things***" (Phil. 4:8). The heart is a reflection of the mind. As we think about good things, our hearts reflect the peace of God. (For a powerful sermon on *Spiritual Thinking,* see the *Faith & Action* book, *1 & 2 Corinthians,* Lesson 42.)

Spiritual thinking includes fixing our thoughts and affections on things above (Col. 3:1-4). This includes spiritual self-talk. Paul tells us to speak to ourselves in psalms, hymns, and spiritual songs (Col. 3:16). The author of Hebrews counsels us to fix our eyes and thoughts on "*Jesus, the author and perfecter of our faith*" (Heb. 12:2). Let us not be like the Israelites who magnified the giants, instead of magnifying the Lord. Let us count our blessings, rather than our problems. Surely there are a thousand reasons for us to rejoice in the Lord!

**Q 160** *What does Paul teach us about self-talk? Give an example.*

**Paul links peace to right thinking and right living (Phil. 4:8-9).** Right thinking and right living are like the two feet we need to walk on. So besides thinking good thoughts, we need to put into practice the things we know are good and righteous. Right thinking and right living are like two sides of a coin—you can't have one without the other.

**Q 161** *How are right thinking and right living like two sides of a coin?*

## E. Principle: Personal peace and joy depend on learning to be content in Christ with a little or a lot (Phil. 4:10-13).

*¹⁰I rejoice greatly in the Lord that at last you have renewed your concern for me. Indeed, you have been concerned, but you had no opportunity to show it. ¹¹I am not saying this because I am in need, for I have learned to be content whatever the circumstances. ¹²I know what it is to be in need, and I know what it is to have plenty. I have learned the secret of being content in any and every situation, whether well fed or hungry, whether living in plenty or in want. ¹³I can do everything through him who gives me strength* (Phil. 4:10-13).

Money is a good servant, but a poor master. Jesus warned that we cannot serve God and money—we must choose one or the other (Matt. 6:24). The love of money is a root of many evils, such as lying, stealing, murder, greed, and covetousness. Ask people such as Balaam, Achan, Gehazi, Ananias and Sapphira, or Demas about the fruit that comes from the root of loving money.

*Sabio* says: "Contentment makes much of little; but greed makes little of much. Contentment is the poor man's riches; but greed is the rich man's poverty."[19]

**Q 162** *How does **Sabio** say contentment and greed differ?*

"To many people wealth and comfort are like a shoe: if what they have seems too small, it pinches and irritates; but if their wealth and comfort are too large, they cause them to stumble and fall."[20]

## F. Principle: Peace and joy in relationships requires saying "thank you" (Phil. 4:10-19).

**Q 163** *Why is saying "Thank you" so important in relationships?*

*¹⁴Yet it was good of you to share in my troubles. ¹⁵Moreover, as you Philippians know, in the early days of your acquaintance with the gospel, when I set out from Macedonia, not one church shared with me in the matter of giving and receiving, except you only; ¹⁶for even when I was in Thessalonica, you sent me aid again and again when I was in need* (Phil. 4:14-16).

Showing gratitude in relationships is so important that Paul opens and closes Philippians with "thank you." We studied about showing appreciation in Philippians 1:3-8. So we will not spend much time on it here. Take time to review the two paragraphs on *saying "thank you"* (Lesson 22, point B). *Thank you* are two of the most important words you can ever speak. Notice that Paul does not just say *thank you* for the *most recent* gifts from the Philippians. Rather, he takes time to remember and thank them for gifts they had sent him in previous years. When we give to help others, it leaves us with an empty feeling *if* they do not show appreciation. In contrast, when the receiver of a gift takes time to say "thank you" and explains how the gift helped, it makes the giver feel like the gift was worthwhile.

### G. Principle: Peace and joy in the Lord flourish as we are generous to others (Phil. 4:17-19)

[17] *Not that I am looking for a gift, but I am looking for what may be credited to your account.* [18] *I have received full payment and even more; I am amply supplied, now that I have received from Epaphroditus the gifts you sent. They are a fragrant offering, an acceptable sacrifice, pleasing to God.* [19] *And my God will meet all your needs according to his glorious riches in Christ Jesus* (Phil. 4:17-19).

**Q 164** *How did the generosity of the Philippians increase their peace and joy?*

> GOD KEEPS RECORDS.

God keeps records. His *book of life* records the name of each person who is born again. He knows all the *citizens of heaven* (Phil. 3:20). Paul refers to the heavenly *account* of believers in Philippi. God sees each sparrow when it falls. He knows the number of hairs on each believer's head. He is a personal God who lives within each believer. He listens to our conversations (Matt. 12:36). God knows whether every person is generous or stingy. So when the Spirit urges us to share, we should be generous knowing that the Lord is watching and keeping records.

Besides keeping records, God has created laws that govern the earth. The law of gravity applies to all, whether or not people are aware of it. And the law of sowing and reaping applies to all, even if people are unaware. Whatever a person sows, he or she will reap. Those who sow little reap little. Those who sow much reap much. Because the Philippians were generous to help Paul, he assures them that God will meet all of their needs (Phil. 4:17-19; 2 Cor. 9:6-11; Gal. 6:7; Deut. 28).

**Q 165** *How does being generous bless those who give?*

The plain truth is that no one ever loses by giving what the Spirit says to give. As surely as day follows night, we reap what we sow. So do not eat the seeds God tells you to plant or you will miss the harvest He wants you to reap. Peace and joy overflow as we let the Spirit lead us to be generous.

**Q 166** *Does God love the generous more than the stingy? Explain.*

Does God love generous givers more than He loves those who are stingy? Does God seek generous givers and set them aside to bless in a special way. Yes! It is God's will to bless everyone. But those who give generously cooperate with God's plan—which enables God to bless them. The sunshine always warms those who stand in it more than it warms those in the shade. It is God's will to bless all people. But each one of us decides if we will allow Him to bless us. Obey God when He speaks to you. This is the path of blessing throughout the old and new covenants!

**Q 167** *What lesson can we learn from Aunt Denice?*

Someone asked Aunt Denice, "Why do you love and bless that child more than other children?" She replied, "I am not partial to that child: he is partial to me! He comes and sits on my lap. He smiles at me and sings to me. He reaches out his hands and asks me to pick him up. He brings me little pictures and flowers he has picked. He always gets the closest to me. He obeys me when I speak to him. He allows me to love him more than I can love other children."[21] (See *Faith & Action, 1 & 2 Corinthians*, Lesson 41, Point D, *The Harvest Principle: We reap in proportion to what we sow.*)

**Q 168** *What promise does God give the generous, like the Philippians?*

God's apostle assures the Philippians that God will meet all of their needs, *from the storehouse of riches He has in Christ Jesus* (Phil. 4:19). God never runs short. He creates wealth. He owns all the wealth in the universe. God did not run short on bread when He decided to feed more than two million Israelites in the wilderness twice a day for 40 years. He just sprinkled a little bread from heaven's kitchen. And our Creator did not find it difficult to send meat for two million Israelites who wanted meat. He just sent a few million quail to their camp, until the birds were piled up 3 feet deep in every direction. Show faith in God by responding when your heart tells you to share.

Trusting God and obeying His Word and Spirit allow God to meet *all* our needs. He delights to meet our physical needs. *And* He delights to meet the needs of our souls for peace and joy. Please God with your giving and you will experience the joy of our Father supplying all your needs. This is God's promise to you (Phil. 4:17-19). We reap what we sow. This is God's law of the harvest illustrated by over 100 Scriptures.

[38] *Give, and it will be given to you. A good measure, pressed down, shaken together and running over, will be poured into your lap. For with the measure you use, it will be measured to you"* (Luke 6:38).

## Conclusion

[20] *To our God and Father be glory for ever and ever. Amen.* [21] *Greet all the saints in Christ Jesus. The brothers who are with me send greetings.* [22] *All the saints send you greetings, especially those who belong to Caesar's household.* [23] *The grace of the Lord Jesus Christ be with your spirit. Amen* (Phil. 4:20-23).

As a follower of Christ, Paul never neglects the basic *courtesies of life*. He begins and ends his letter to the Philippians with greetings of courtesy. His letter opens and closes with grace and graciousness in Christ. Paul knows that his letter will be read to the church in public. It would probably not have been safe for him to name all the *saints* in Rome. But do not miss the joyful message Paul is sending with his final words to the Philippians. *"The saints here send you greetings, especially those who belong to Caesar's household"* (Phil. 4:22). Paul is overflowing with joy and reminding the Philippians that in his time of being imprisoned by Caesar, he has loved members of Caesar's administration to Christ. He has led Caesar's soldiers and perhaps others to Christ. So now, because Paul was in chains in Rome, new Roman believers are able to greet their fellow saints in Philippi. God has accomplished a work of fruitfulness in Paul's time of difficulty.

**Application.** I do not know where this letter to the Philippians has found you. Perhaps you are living in a time of difficulty. As you reflect on your circumstances, there may not be much joy or sunshine. But with iron chains on Paul's wrists in prison, he chose **to reflect on things he had gained because of his circumstances.** Likewise, God is at work doing things in and through us in our hard times. As we trust the Lord, rest contented in Him and practice rejoicing in the Lord—it will strengthen us and encourage others to live for Christ. Joy! Joy in where we are! Joy in those around us! Joy in the Lord! Joy in any circumstances! These are the big lessons in Paul's letter to the Philippians: joy in the deep, quiet rest of knowing Christ and growing in His grace.

Q 169 What final message of joy does the apostle in chains send to the Philippians?

⚖️ **Test Yourself:** Circle the letter by the *best* completion to each question or statement.

1. How far did Paul walk from Syria to Philippi?
a) 200 km
b) 1200 km
c) 2200 km
d) 3200 km

2. How should our greetings be like Paul's?
a) Be brief and to the point.
b) Include a compliment.
c) Mention prayer requests.
d) Hug or shake hands.

3. How does mature love reveal itself (Phil. 1:9-11)?
a) Giving and receiving
b) Praising and thanking
c) Knowing and perceiving
d) Being and doing

4. Which chapters trace Paul's steps to prison?
a) Acts 15–16
b) 2 Cor. 10–12
c) Titus 1–3
d) Acts 21–28

5. The principle of Philippians 2:4 emphasizes
a) thinking of self, and also of others.
b) Jesus dying on the cross for us.
c) Paul suffering in prison for the Gentiles.
d) thinking on things that are pure.

6. In most of his letters Paul contrasts
a) sheep and goats.
b) wolves and doves.
c) dogs and hogs.
d) eagles and snakes.

7. How could Paul rejoice in prison?
a) He rejoiced in the past.
b) He gloried in the future.
c) He was joyful for the present.
d) He rejoiced in the Lord.

8. Why was Paul joyful for the Philippians' gifts?
a) They brought him contentment.
b) He was in great need.
c) Their offering was generous.
d) God credited them for their giving.

9. Paul urged unity through
a) agreeing in the Lord.
b) finding points of compromise.
c) sacrificing our own concerns.
d) putting the whole church first.

10. Philippians 4:8-9 teaches that a key to peace is
a) right thinking and praying.
b) right thinking and behaving.
c) right relationships and reactions.
d) right praying and singing.

**Essay Test Topics:** Write 50-100 words on each of these 20 goals you studied. Try to complete this test in 2 hours. On the final exam, we will combine some of these goals and ask you to write on a few of them. As you practice writing on each of these goals now, you are preparing well for the final test. (5 points for each goal)

- Analyze the authorship, date, recipients, and city of Philippians.
- Explain the purposes, outline, and 4 themes of Philippians.
- Summarize the background and setting of Philippians.
- Explain 3 characteristics of a good greeting to someone we love (Phil. 1:1-2).
- State and illustrate the gratitude principle (Phil. 1:3-8).
- Sketch a diagram of Paul's prayer (Phil. 1:9-11). Explain its parts, contrasting the worldly and the godly.
- Make a chart of key events in Acts 21–28, showing how Paul became a prisoner of Christ in Rome.
- Explain the door of bitterness before Paul, and how he left it closed. Apply these truths to us.
- Give examples of what happened as Paul opened the door of opportunity in hard times. Apply this.
- Summarize things that could have caused Paul to doubt. Explain how he opened the door of trust.
- State the principle of Philippians 2:4, and illustrate it by contrasting believing with suffering.
- State the principle of Philippians 2:4, and illustrate it with fruits of salvation, and the kenosis.
- State the principle of Philippians 2:4, and illustrate it with working out our salvation in relationships.
- State the principle of Philippians 2:4, and illustrate it with Paul's attitudes toward death, Timothy, and Epaphroditus.
- Contrast the role of good deeds in legalists and true Christians (Phil. 3:1-11). Sketch the contrast.
- Illustrate the problems of bragging on the past and meditating on past failures (Phil. 3:12-14).
- Analyze the balance in depending on Christ, yet straining and pressing toward the goal (Phil. 3:12-14).
- Contrast and illustrate legalists, followers of Christ, and libertines in Paul's writings (Phil. 3:12-21).
- Summarize how joy and peace depend on agreeing in the Lord and rejoicing in the Lord (Phil. 4:2-4).
- Analyze and illustrate the relationship of joy and peace to prayer, right thinking, and right living (Phil. 4:6-9).
- Explain and illustrate a principle about joy for each of these: contentment, thankfulness, and generosity (Phil. 4:10-19).

# Chapter 6:
# Paul's Love for a Slave
## (Philem. 1-25)

**Q 1** ➤ *Who was Onesimus? Why did he flee from Colosse to Rome?*

Philemon is Paul's shortest letter—just 335 words in the *Nestle-Aland Greek text. It is a personal letter Paul wrote for a slave, Onesimus, who had stolen from his master, Philemon, in Colosse. To escape, Onesimus fled about 2,100 km/1,300 miles to hide in the big city of Rome. But God was watching. And somehow, this slave who had run away from his master met Paul the apostle in Rome. Then, as Paul

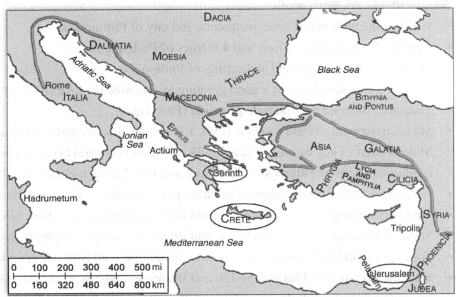

**Figure 6.1**
**Map showing the journey of Onesimus from Colosse to Rome**

had once led Philemon to Christ, he led Onesimus to Christ. In Philippians, we saw Paul in chains praising God for the many good things that were happening in such difficult circumstances. Now we can add the salvation of Onesimus to Paul's list of blessings in prison. But the story gets even better.

**Q 2** ➤ *Why did prisoners in Rome need friends?*

Living as a prisoner in Rome was not easy or fun. The Romans provided nothing for prisoners under house arrest—no food, clothes, or blankets.[1] But Onesimus was among those who helped care for Paul while he was in chains. He could bring Paul some of the basic things the apostle needed. Perhaps he used money from the Philippians to buy bread for Paul.

**Q 3** ➤ *What was the purpose of Paul's letter to Philemon?*

Onesimus was valuable to Paul. But he was also valuable to Philemon, his owner. In Roman times, the average price of a slave was about 500 denari—the wages of a common worker for 500 days![2] As we study Philemon, we will discover how Paul's letter brought reconciliation between an angry slave owner and a fearful slave. And we will marvel in the way that the gospel lifts believing slaves and masters to the same spiritual level—for a few years on earth and for eternity (Philem. 15).

## Lessons:

### Philemon—12 Biblical Steps to Resolve Conflict in a Relationship—Part 1

**Goal A:** *Describe the 4 main characters of Philemon, the setting, and the outline.*
**Goal B:** *Analyze the problem of slavery in Paul's day, and the biblical solution.*
**Goal C:** *From Philemon, explain and illustrate principles on the conflict, the solution, and the goal.*
**Goal D:** *From Philemon, explain and illustrate principles on humility and family language.*

### Philemon—12 Biblical Steps to Resolve Conflict in a Relationship—Part 2

**Goal A:** *From Philemon, explain and illustrate principles on prayer, appreciation, and love.*
**Goal B:** *From Philemon, explain and illustrate principles on associating and investing.*
**Goal C:** *From Philemon, explain and illustrate principles on recalling and envisioning.*

**Philemon**—a beloved brother who refreshed the saints in Colosse, yet owned a slave named Onessimus

**Onesimus**—a slave who fled from Colosse and his owner, Philemon, to Rome, where he was saved under Paul's ministry as a prisoner in Rome

**restitution**—making right the wrongs we have done to people; paying the debts we owe

---

**Lesson 30**

## Philemon—12 Biblical Steps to Resolve Conflict in a Relationship—Part 1

**Goal A:** *Describe the 4 main characters of Philemon, the setting, and the outline.*
**Goal B:** *Analyze the problem of slavery in Paul's day, and the biblical solution.*
**Goal C:** *From Philemon, explain and illustrate principles on the conflict, the solution, and the goal.*
**Goal D:** *From Philemon, explain and illustrate principles on humility and family language.*

---

**Q 4** *Who are the 4 main characters in Philemon? Describe each.*

| Four Main People | Explanation |
|---|---|
| 1. Paul | God's apostle who was in prison |
| 2. Philemon | A believer who lived in Colosse; he owned at least one slave (Philem. 15-16). |
| 3. *Onesimus | A slave who ran away from Philemon; he was saved when he met Paul, probably in Rome. In Greek, the name *Onesimus* means "useful" (See Philem. 11). |
| 4. Christ Jesus | The One who paid the debt we owed and freed us from slavery; our beloved Redeemer in whom we are all equal brothers and sisters in the family of God. |

**Figure 6.2   There are four main people in Paul's letter to Philemon.**

## A. The setting of Philemon

Five times in this little letter, the apostle refers to being a prisoner or in chains (Philem. 1, 9, 10, 13 and 23). Paul probably wrote all four Prison Epistles from Rome (Acts 28:16-31). The letter is to a wealthy believer named Philemon who was saved under Paul's ministry. (**Please read the first two paragraphs in your text, at the beginning of this chapter.**) Paul had never been to Colosse (Col. 2:1). Perhaps he led Philemon to Christ during his ministry in Ephesus, on the coast of the Aegean Sea about 160 km/100 miles west of Colosse.

Some time later, Paul leads Onesimus to Christ. Imagine how surprised Paul and Onesimus are to discover that they both know Philemon, who lives 2,100 km/1,300 miles away in the small town of Colosse! Now what? Paul was benefiting from the help Onesimus gave him in prison. But what about the responsibilities of Onesimus to Philemon, his owner? The law permitted Philemon to execute or punish Onesimus. But now, Onesimus had become a believer. If Onesimus dared to return to Colosse, what would Philemon's attitude be? Would he expect Onesimus to pay back what he had stolen? Would Philemon ever be able to trust Onesimus again? And if Philemon forgave Onesimus and took him back without punishment, would this encourage other slaves to steal and run away from their masters? Or what would other masters say if Philemon did not execute Onesimus? There were many scary questions to consider before Onesimus decided whether he would return to work for Philemon.

## B. The problem of slavery in New Testament times.

Slavery was a huge problem in the days of Paul. Some scholars estimate that there were 60 million slaves in the Roman Empire.[3] The Romans conquered many nations. They acquired slaves from the regions of Europe and Africa.

**Q 5** *Which letters are the Prison Epistles? Where was Paul when he wrote them?*

**Q 6** *Where is Colosse? How far did Onesimus flee to reach Rome?*

**Q 7** *As believers, what types of questions about reconciliation troubled Onesimus and Philemon?*

**Q 8** *How many slaves were in the Roman kingdom?*

**Q 9**  *In the Prison Epistles, what guidelines does Paul give to slaves and masters?*

To modern readers, it may be shocking that the Bible does not condemn slavery. Slavery is an issue we have seen three times in the Prison Epistles. Review these in the verses that follow.

### Ephesians 6:5-9

*⁵Slaves, obey your earthly masters with respect and fear, and with sincerity of heart, just as you would obey Christ. ⁶Obey them not only to win their favor when their eye is on you, but like slaves of Christ, doing the will of God from your heart. ⁷Serve wholeheartedly, as if you were serving the Lord, not men, ⁸because you know that the Lord will reward everyone for whatever good he does, whether he is slave or free. ⁹And masters, treat your slaves in the same way. Do not threaten them, since you know that he who is both their Master and yours is in heaven, and there is no favoritism with him.*

### Colossians 3:22–4:1

*²²Slaves, obey your earthly masters in everything; and do it, not only when their eye is on you and to win their favor, but with sincerity of heart and reverence for the Lord. ²³Whatever you do, work at it with all your heart, as working for the Lord, not for men, ²⁴since you know that you will receive an inheritance from the Lord as a reward. It is the Lord Christ you are serving. ²⁵Anyone who does wrong will be repaid for his wrong, and there is no favoritism. ¹Masters, provide your slaves with what is right and fair, because you know that you also have a Master in heaven.*

### Philemon 12-16

*¹²I am sending him—who is my very heart—back to you. ¹³I would have liked to keep him with me so that he could take your place in helping me while I am in chains for the gospel. ¹⁴But I did not want to do anything without your consent, so that any favor you do will be spontaneous and not forced. ¹⁵Perhaps the reason he was separated from you for a little while was that you might have him back for good—¹⁶no longer as a slave, but better than a slave, as a dear brother. He is very dear to me but even dearer to you, both as a man and as a brother in the Lord.*

**Q 10**  *What would have happened in Paul's day if the church had tried to abolish slavery?*

The gospel brings change into society. But it does not bring change by force or rebellion. Jesus and the apostles hated violence and taught submission to authority. If Christians had tried to abolish slavery in Roman times, the government would have crushed them. Likewise, the message of the gospel would have been confused with political and social issues.

**Q 11**  *How does the Golden Rule affect the relationship between masters and slaves who are believers?*

The gospel is directly for individuals and indirectly for nations. It is true that God has used some believers to have great influence on nations. Joseph had a godly influence in Egypt. Jonah brought revival to Assyria, modern Iraq. Esther and Nehemiah helped shape the history of Persia. Daniel was highly respected in Babylon. Even so, the gospel is person to person. It brings change by transforming hearts, one at a time. It teaches believers to live by the Golden Rule (Matt. 7:12). It teaches us to love others as we love ourselves (Matt. 22:39). Those who obey the teachings of Christ become solutions to the problems of society, such as slavery. Under the Emperor Constantine, 306–337 A.D., Christianity began to transition to be the main religion of the empire. But to enter God's kingdom, each person must be born again. Unless a person has a living relationship with Jesus Christ, it is impossible to obey the Savior's teachings.

**Q 12**  *If a Christian slave rebelled against his master, how would this give the gospel a bad name?*

Paul does not want the gospel to get a bad name. So he tells slaves to remain under their masters. This fulfills God's will and ensures that the gospel will not be slandered (Titus 2:5).

Paul encourages slaves to gain their freedom in a legal manner, if possible (1 Cor. 7:21). A social principle for Paul is that all should remain in the situation they are in when they become believers.

> *Nevertheless, each one should retain the place in life that the Lord assigned to him and to which God has called him. This is the rule I lay down in all the churches* (1 Cor. 7:17).

**Q 13** *How are Peter's words to believing slaves more pastoral than Paul's counsel?*

Unlike Paul, Peter writes to slaves, but not masters. Peter's advice to slaves who become believers is similar to Paul's counsel, yet more pastoral. Peter writes to Christian slaves as a pastor, saying:

> [18] *Slaves, submit yourselves to your masters with all respect, not only to those who are good and considerate, but also to those who are harsh.* [19] *For it is commendable if a man bears up under the pain of unjust suffering because he is conscious of God.* [20] *But how is it to your credit if you receive a beating for doing wrong and endure it? But if you suffer for doing good and you endure it, this is commendable before God.* [21] *To this you were called, because Christ suffered for you, leaving you an example, that you should follow in his steps.* [22] *"He committed no sin, and no deceit was found in his mouth."* [23] *When they hurled their insults at him, he did not retaliate; when he suffered, he made no threats. Instead, he entrusted himself to him who judges justly.* [24] *He himself bore our sins in his body on the tree, so that we might die to sins and live for righteousness; by his wounds you have been healed.* [25] *For you were like sheep going astray, but now you have returned to the Shepherd and Overseer of your souls* (1 Pet. 2:18-25).

In religion, Gentiles should not seek to be circumcised for religious purposes. They should live as Gentiles and not try to become Jewish. In the home, wives should be subject to their husbands, and children should obey their parents. In society, slaves should not run away or rebel. And all believers should submit to the government (Rom. 13:1). The gospel does not cause confusion or disorder in society. Rather, it makes society a better place.

**Q 14** *Give some examples of Paul's social principle in 1 Corinthians 7:17.*

> ### ACCEPTING THE GOSPEL MAKES PEOPLE BETTER.

Accepting the gospel makes people better. The Greek word *onesimus* means "useful." As a slave who ran away, Onesimus was *useless* to Philemon. But because of the gospel, Onesimus became *useful*. He was useful to Paul as a helper (Philem. 11). And the gospel made Onesimus *"better than a slave"* (Philem. 16). God's love causes us to treat people with love and respect. Accepting the gospel makes us better citizens.

**Q 15** *What does "onesimus" mean? How was he more useful after he became a follower of Christ?*

So Paul talked to Onesimus about returning to his master, Philemon. Onesimus was fearful, but willing—although he had already spent or traded the things he had stolen from Philemon (Philem. 15-16, 18-19). So to help restore and improve the relationship between the master and the slave, Paul wrote a short letter to Philemon. We think Philemon lived in Colosse, since many of the same names are in Colossians and Philemon (Philem. 1-2, 10, 23-24; Col. 4:9-10, 12, 14, 17); and we know Onesimus was from Colosse (Col. 4:9). Paul sent the letter to the Colossians and the letter to Philemon together. It appears that Tychicus, a fellow worker of Paul, carried the two letters to Colosse (Col. 4:7-9).

**Q 16** *Why did Paul write the letter to Philemon?*

**Q 17** *Have you ever tried to help resolve a conflict between believers? Explain.*

Philemon is a letter of love and intimacy. It has the fragrance of tact and diplomacy. The main themes of Philemon are forgiveness and restoration. Slavery is a hot topic. Paul's letter to Philemon is a Spirit-led masterpiece on the art of how to treat people and restore relationships. As we study Philemon, we will look at principles the Spirit led Paul to weave into the letter.

## C. Outline of Philemon

**Q 18** *What are the 4 parts of the letter to Philemon?*

| Sections in Philemon | Philemon |
|---|---|
| Greeting | 1-3 |
| Thanksgiving and Prayer for Philemon | 4-7 |
| Request for Philemon to Restore Onesimus | 8-22 |
| Conclusion | 23-25 |

Figure 6.3  Outline of Philemon

**Q 19** *Read Philemon. How long did it take you?*

Take a few minutes and read Paul's letter to Philemon and those who met in his house. Try to imagine how Philemon felt when he saw Onesimus coming down the road home. And try to imagine how Philemon and Onesimus felt as Philemon read Paul's letter with Onesimus beside him. Then, we will study through the letter, identifying 12 steps to solve conflict in a relationship.

**Greeting:** ¹*Paul, a prisoner of Christ Jesus, and Timothy our brother, To Philemon our dear friend and fellow worker, ²to Apphia our sister, to Archippus our fellow soldier and to the church that meets in your home: ³Grace to you and peace from God our Father and the Lord Jesus Christ* (Philem. 1-3)

**Thanksgiving and prayer:** ⁴*I always thank my God as I remember you in my prayers, ⁵because I hear about your faith in the Lord Jesus and your love for all the saints. ⁶I pray that you may be active in sharing your faith, so that you will have a full understanding of every good thing we have in Christ. ⁷Your love has given me great joy and encouragement, because you, brother, have refreshed the hearts of the saints* (Philem. 4-7).

**Q 20** *In one sentence, what did Paul want Philemon to do?*

**Request:** ⁸*Therefore, although in Christ I could be bold and order you to do what you ought to do, ⁹yet I appeal to you on the basis of love. I then, as Paul—an old man and now also a prisoner of Christ Jesus—¹⁰I appeal to you for my son Onesimus, who became my son while I was in chains. ¹¹Formerly he was useless to you, but now he has become useful both to you and to me. ¹²I am sending him—who is my very heart—back to you. ¹³I would have liked to keep him with me so that he could take your place in helping me while I am in chains for the gospel. ¹⁴But I did not want to do anything without your consent, so that any favor you do will be spontaneous and not forced. ¹⁵Perhaps the reason he was separated from you for a little while was that you might have him back for good—¹⁶no longer as a slave, but better than a slave, as a dear brother. He is very dear to me but even dearer to you, both as a man and as a brother in the Lord. ¹⁷So if you consider me a partner, welcome him as you would welcome me. ¹⁸If he has done you any wrong or owes you anything, charge it to me. ¹⁹I, Paul, am writing this with my own hand. I will pay it back—not to mention that you owe me your very self. ²⁰I do wish, brother, that I may have some benefit from you in the Lord; refresh my heart in Christ. ²¹Confident of your obedience, I write to you, knowing that you will do even more than I ask. ²²And one thing more: Prepare a guest room for me, because I hope to be restored to you in answer to your prayers* (Philem. 8-22).

**Conclusion:** ²³*Epaphras, my fellow prisoner in Christ Jesus, sends you greetings. ²⁴And so do Mark, Aristarchus, Demas and Luke, my fellow workers. ²⁵The grace of the Lord Jesus Christ be with your spirit* (Philem. 23-25).

## D. 12 biblical steps to resolve conflict in a relationship (Philem. 1-22)

**Q 21** *What are 2 ways you can use the 12 steps to resolve conflict?*

These are steps that Paul took to resolve the conflict between Philemon and Onesimus. You can follow these steps to resolve a conflict you have with someone. Or you can use these steps to help two other people or groups resolve a conflict between them.

**Step 1:** **Examine and summarize the conflict.** Identify it. Discuss it. Analyze it. Summarize it in one sentence. The first step in answering a question is to understand the question. Paul discussed the conflict with Onesimus. The problem was that Onesimus had wronged Philemon, his master.

Yes, slavery itself was an evil problem. In most of its forms, slavery is sinful—whether it is slavery to drugs, slavery to pornography, slavery to a master who owns sex slaves, or slavery in which one does good work, like Onesimus, but is owned by another person. In contrast, Paul urges us, as followers of Christ, to be slaves of righteousness—servants of Jesus Christ, doing what is right (Rom. 6:18-20). Onesimus was a slave, owned by Philemon. This type of slavery is terrible. But we cannot just put a stick of dynamite under slavery and blow it up without killing both slaves and masters. A revolution may solve one problem, but it creates a hundred others. So there had to be laws to govern slavery. Otherwise, there would have been *anarchy—a state of rioting, looting, killing, chaos, confusion, and lawlessness.

Q 22 *Even with a sinful problem like slavery that should be abolished, why are laws necessary?*

Q 23 *What are some forms of slavery where you live?*

So even when a practice like slavery is bad, it is better to have laws that govern it, than to have total chaos in society. And in time, the government can abolish an evil practice such as slavery. In the meantime, Onesimus had broken the law by running away from his master. And he had broken another law by stealing. So Paul and Onesimus identified the conflict and discussed it. Their discussion included the need to make *restitution—to repay those we have wronged if we can. God forgives our sins so far as heaven is concerned. But on earth, He still expects us to repay wrongs we have done in society, if possible. Elsewhere Paul writes: *"Let no debt remain outstanding, except the debt to love one another"* (Rom. 13:8; Philem. 18-19; see also, Luke 19:8). Trying to make right the wrongs you did before meeting Christ helps people believe your testimony for Christ. Restitution is some of the first fruit we bear as followers of Jesus. Some people may just forgive your debts as God has done in Christ. But others will appreciate your restitution and respect you for it. Heaven's grace is not a substitute for being a responsible citizen on earth.

Q 24 *Which 2 laws had Onesimus broken?*

Q 25 *When sinners become believers, does God expect us to make restitution? Explain.*

Do not ignore Step 1. It is a small, but important step. A journey always begins with the first step. But you will not take the journey to a solution until you take this first step. So in many ways, this first step is the most important.

Q 26 *Why is step 1 perhaps the most important?*

**Step 2:** **State the goal to resolve the conflict—as a specific response that you want.** After Paul led Onesimus to Christ, he spent time talking with him. Paul learned that Onesimus had a conflict with another believer named Philemon. This knowledge of the problem helped Paul see the goal clearly. His goal was to bring Onesimus and Philemon together in Christ as brothers in God's family (Philem. 17).

Q 27 *In one sentence, summarize Paul's goal for Philemon and Onesimus.*

Paul does not state his goal in the first sentence of his letter. He is more indirect and polite than that. But Paul saw his goal clearly—even before he started praying about a path to reach the goal. The apostle has his goal in mind before he ever starts writing. Otherwise, how would he know what to write? Paul states his goal in one sentence, in verse 17.

Q 28 *Why did Paul not state his goal in the first sentence of his letter to Philemon?*

[10]*I appeal to you for my son Onesimus, who became my son while I was in chains.* [11]*Formerly he was useless to you, but now he has become useful both to you and to me.* [12]*I am sending him—who is my very heart—back to you.* [13]*I would have liked to keep him with me so that he could take your place in helping me while I am in chains for the gospel.* [14]*But I did not want to do anything without your consent, so that any favor you do will be spontaneous and not forced.* [15]*Perhaps the reason he was separated from you for a little while was that you might have him back for good—*[16]*no longer as a slave, but better than a slave, as a dear brother. He is very dear to me but even dearer to you, both as a man and as a brother in the Lord.* [17]***So if you consider me a partner, welcome him as you would welcome me*** (Philem. 10-17).

Before Paul states his goal in the letter, there must be bonding: his expression of humility, greetings, family language, affirmation, and love. Paul does not even mention Onesimus until verse 10. Even so, he knows where he is going, before he begins the journey to go there.

**Q 29** ✎ *Why is it unwise to try to resolve conflict **before** seeing the goal clearly?*

To resolve a conflict, we must first understand the conflict and see the goal we want to reach. There is no point in kicking the soccer ball until we know where the goal is. Throughout this book, we begin each lesson with the end in mind. We aim at a target

before we shoot the arrow. We state the goals *before* we write a lesson. We bring our goal into clear focus. Then we write the content and create graphics to help students reach the goals. At the end of the chapter, we put tests to evaluate whether students have reached the goals. Likewise, when you want to resolve a conflict, you must first see the goal clearly. If you do not know where you want to go, how will you know when you get there? Seeing your goal clearly makes it possible for you to discover a way to reach the goal.

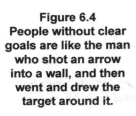

**Figure 6.4**
**People without clear goals are like the man who shot an arrow into a wall, and then went and drew the target around it.**

Before the Son of God was born in Bethlehem, the goal of heaven was clear. Through the sacrifice of Christ, God was reconciling the world to Himself, not counting their sins against them (2 Cor. 5:19; John 3:16). Before the beginning of time, God had a plan and a goal to save us in Christ (1 Tim. 1:9; Rev. 13:8).

**Q 30** ↗ *What goal did God have long before sending His Son to earth?*

**Step 3:** **Approach the conflict and the goal with faith and hope to find a solution.** Choose not to ignore the conflict. Decide to face it and find a solution with God's help. Conflicts in relationships are normal. They happen to everyone. But conflicts do not disappear if we ignore them. To resolve a conflict in a relationship, we must identify it and begin to seek a solution. Paul did not just lead Onesimus to Christ, turn his back on the problem, and say, "Welcome to the family of God." Paul took Step 2. After he talked with Onesimus and identified a conflict, **Paul chose to write a letter to Philemon.**

**Q 31** ✎ *Complete Figure 6.5 on moving forward in faith to find a solution to the conflict.*

| References | Your Summaries of Steps 1–3 in Conflict Resolution |
|---|---|
| Matt. 5:23-24 | |
| Acts 6:1-7 | |

**Figure 6.5   Practice summarizing Steps 1–3 in biblical passages.**

Jesus teaches all who follow him to take this first step. Our Lord says:

" ²³*Therefore, if you are offering your gift at the altar and there remember that your brother has something against you,* ²⁴*leave your gift there in front of the altar. First **go and be reconciled to your brother**; then come and offer your gift*" (Matt. 5:23-24).

Notice that our Lord's word includes Steps 1 and 2: Identify the conflict, face it, and move forward to solve it with God's help.

The early church took Step 1 when they became aware of a conflict. In Acts 6, the leaders discovered a conflict between two types of believers—the Hellenistic (related to Greek language and culture) and Hebraic Jews. Many of the believers in Jerusalem were Hebraic Jews. They spoke Hebrew and passed it on to their children. But some Jews had been influenced a lot by Greek (Hellenistic) culture. Perhaps these had been scattered and lived among Gentiles who spoke Greek. These Hellenistic Jews spoke more Greek than Hebrew. The apostles identified the problem. Some of the widows among the

Hellenistic Jews were being neglected when food was distributed. The apostles did not ignore the problem. They did not just tell the widows to give thanks and stop complaining. They did not just say, "Oh, we should be more careful about distributing food." Rather, they owned the problem, faced it, and took a step forward to solve it—having the people appoint seven Hellenistic deacons to distribute the food.

**Step 4:** **Humble yourself.** *"Be completely humble and gentle"* (Eph. 4:2). Set your titles and position aside. Leave your formal clothes in the closet, and put on your friendly, plain clothes for a while. Notice how Paul begins the letter to Philemon. He does not begin as usual with *Paul, an apostle*. Rather, he starts with no title—just *"Paul, a prisoner of Christ Jesus"* (Philem. 1). When we want to resolve conflict, it is important to avoid looking down on people. Talk eye to eye, face to face, and heart to heart with them.

When Jesus came to resolve the conflict between God and humans, He laid aside His privileges and became a servant. Let this attitude that was in Christ, who *humbled himself*, be in us as we seek to serve others and be peacemakers (Phil. 2:5-8).

**Step 5:** **Emphasize family words and relationships.** Notice how many times in this short letter Paul uses words such as *brother, sister,* and *dear friend* (Greek: *beloved*), *home, grace, peace.*

> ¹ *Paul, a prisoner of Christ Jesus, and Timothy our* **brother,** *To Philemon our* **dear friend** *and fellow worker,* ² *to Apphia our* **sister,** *to Archippus our fellow soldier and to the church that meets in your* **home.** ³ **Grace** *to you and* **peace** *from God our Father and the Lord Jesus Christ* (Philem. 1-3).

Paul's greeting is warm with affection. He refers to himself as *a prisoner of Jesus Christ,* the head of the family. He calls Philemon *beloved* (a Greek form of *agape*); and refers to Apphia as *sister.* Apphia was probably Philemon's wife since Paul mentions her next to Philemon and before Archippus, a fellow soldier or minister (see Col. 4:17). Archippus was probably one of the house pastors in Colosse. Look at all the close, family ties Paul mentions in his greeting. Paul mentions things that the family members have in common such as grace, peace, faith, love—and *"every good thing* **we have in** *Christ"* (Philem. 4-6). The rest of the letter is also salted with family language such as *brother, old man, my son, my very heart, brother in the Lord,* and *partner.* Take a colored pen and underline all the family words Paul uses in Philemon.

**Q 35** Complete Figure 6.6, identifying family words and phrases in Philemon. Some verses have several.

**Q 32** How did Paul show humility toward Philemon?

**Q 33** As you have watched leaders deal with conflict, did they show humility? Give an example.

**Q 34** Why do you think Paul uses so many family words in Philemon?

| Philemon | Family Words Paul Uses in Philemon |
|---|---|
| 1 | |
| 2 | |
| 3 | |
| 5 | |
| 6 | |
| 7 | |
| 9 | |
| 10 | |
| 12 | |
| 16 | |
| 17 | |
| 20 | |
| 23 | |
| 25 | |

**Figure 6.6  Practice identifying family language in Philemon.**

**Q 36** ✎ *Why do family members love each other so much? Give some reasons.*

In all of his letters, Paul uses family language to help strengthen our relationships. He refers often to God our Father, our Lord Jesus Christ, our unity, our gifts to help each other, our faith, our love, our hope. The apostle often exhorts us to keep the unity of the Spirit; to put up with one another; to forgive each other as God has forgiven us. He reminds us that we are all saints. As brothers and sisters, we are members of the household of faith. There is one body, one Spirit, one hope; one Lord, one faith, and one baptism. There is one God and Father of us all (Eph. 4:4-6). The names of all believers are in God's book of life. We are citizens of heaven. We all have the same destiny. Paul believed what our Lord taught: The world will know we are followers of Christ by our love for one another. That we are members of one family is one of Paul's biggest themes. Let us remember and affirm this often—and especially in times of conflict. Remembering that we are members of one family draws us closer together.

## Lesson 31  Philemon—12 Biblical Steps to Resolve Conflict in a Relationship—Part 2

**Goal A:** *From Philemon, explain and illustrate principles on prayer, appreciation, and love.*
**Goal B:** *From Philemon, explain and illustrate principles on associating and investing.*
**Goal C:** *From Philemon, explain and illustrate principles on recalling and envisioning.*

In the previous lesson based on Philemon, we studied Steps 1–5 for resolving a conflict.

### D. 12 biblical steps to resolve conflict in a relationship (Philem. 1:1-22)

**Step 1.** Examine and summarize the conflict.
**Step 2.** Approach the conflict with faith and hope to find a solution.
**Step 3.** State the goal to resolve the conflict—as a specific response that you want.
**Step 4.** Humble yourself.
**Step 5.** Emphasize family words and relationships.

**Q 37** ✎ *Write a brief comment or explanation on each Steps 1–5.*

| Steps | Your Comments and Explanations on Steps 1–5 |
|---|---|
| 1. | |
| 2. | |
| 3. | |
| 4. | |
| 5. | |

**Figure 6.7**   Practice summarizing Steps 1–5 for resolving conflict in a relationship.

In this final lesson on Philemon, we will continue with Point D, studying Steps 6–12 on resolving conflict in a relationship.

**Q 38** ✎ *As Paul prayed, why did he thank God for Philemon?*

**Step 6:** 👣 **Pray for the person you want to see reconciled.**

⁴*I always thank my God as I remember you in my prayers,* ⁵*because I hear about your faith in the Lord Jesus and your love for* **all** *the saints.* ⁶*I pray that you may be active in* **sharing your faith***, so that you will have a full understanding of every good thing we have in Christ.* ⁷*Your love has given me great joy and encouragement, because you, brother, have refreshed the hearts of the saints* (Philem. 4-7).

Prayer changes people, beginning with the one who prays. Through our prayers, God *first* tunes our hearts to be in harmony with Him. Through our prayers, God can soften and open the heart of a person who is offended. The words we speak have more power and anointing as we soak our lives in prayer. If a picture is worth a thousand words, an hour of prayer is worth ten thousand words.

Paul talked with God about Philemon *before* he talked with Philemon. Paul's prayer included *thanksgiving* for the faith and love of Philemon. The apostle thanked God that Philemon was generous with brothers and sisters in the family of God. Philemon was known for his *love for **all** the saints*. He made a habit of refreshing *the hearts of the saints,* probably by sharing his wealth with those in need.

A key phrase in Paul's prayer is in Philemon, verse 6—*sharing your faith* (Greek: *koinonia*). By *sharing your faith,* Paul does not mean "witnessing to others about what you believe"—although witnessing is important. In Philemon 6, *sharing* faith means "fellowshipping with all saints." For as we fellowship with all other believers, we gain *"a full understanding of every good thing we have in Christ"* (Philem. 6). In other words, to fully understand the blessing God pours out in Christ, we need to fellowship with the full range of believers, including a slave like Onesimus. If Philemon only fellowshipped with believers of his social level, his understanding of the blessings of Christ would be very narrow. So in this prayer, Paul is not just asking Philemon to forgive Onesimus. That would have been much easier than what Paul is praying. Paul wants Philemon to fellowship with Onesimus in the faith—to welcome him as a brother and equal joint heir in Christ. We see this thought more clearly later in Paul's letter: *"no longer as a slave, but better than a slave, as a dear brother"* (Philem. 16). When God helps us remove the boundaries of our fellowship, we gain the full understanding of the scope of our faith. God has the same love for people of all ages, all colors, and all levels of society. In Christ, the lowest slave is as worthy of the love of God as the wealthiest master. The ground is level at the foot of the cross. There are no big and small people in the Lord. All of us are equal family members in the body of Christ. In the letter to Philemon, there is a subtle and indirect challenge to slavery. But Paul believes *regeneration* is better than revolution. For through being born again in Christ, Paul sees Onesimus freed from slavery to sin and slavery to Philemon. Onesimus may continue to work for Philemon in society, but in the Lord, it must be *as a brother,* and *no longer as a slave.*[4]

> **Q 39** How does the phrase "sharing your faith" relate to the conflict Paul hopes to solve (Philem. 6)?

Paul emphasized *equality in Christ* in Ephesians, saying that Jews and Gentiles are fellow citizens and members of God's household (Eph. 2:11-20). And here he is emphasizing once again that our fellowship in Christ is with believers at all social levels. *"There is neither Jew nor Greek, slave nor free, male nor female, for you are all one in Christ Jesus"* (Gal. 3:28). Paul was *praying* for Philemon to grasp this truth *before* he ever wrote the letter to Philemon. As we marvel at the *sensitivity* and *diplomacy* of the letter to Philemon, let us recall that these qualities are a result of Paul's habit of praying. And let us be sure that Paul's prayers helped open Philemon's heart.

> **Q 40** What role did prayer have in the letter Paul wrote and sent to Philemon?

**Application.** God does not just want us to humble ourselves. He wants us to lift others up. When there is a conflict between two believers, it is important to remind ourselves that no one is higher or lower than another. Through the blood of Christ, we are all family members at the same table. This does not mean that believers live on the same levels of power, prestige, and position. But we need to understand that believers with whom we have a conflict are as dear to God as we are. This truth becomes clearer as we kneel in prayer.

> **Q 41** Which was harder for Philemon—to forgive Onesimus or to embrace him as a brother? Explain.

**Step 7:** **Share appreciation.** Paul showed public appreciation to Philemon several times in this letter. This was a letter for reading to the church that met in Philemon's home. So everyone in the house church heard the words of praise Paul wrote about Philemon. Likewise, this is a letter that has made thousands of generations appreciate Philemon. Paul acknowledged Philemon for opening his home so other believers could have a place to meet (Philem. 2). For there were no church buildings in the first century of the church. The apostle also complimented Philemon for expressing his faith and love by often *refreshing the saints* (Philem. 5-7). And in an indirect way, Paul showed appreciation for Philemon by showing confidence in him. Paul wrote:

> **Q 42** In the letter to Philemon, what are some ways Paul showed appreciation to him?

*"Confident of your obedience, I write to you, knowing that you will do even more than I ask"* (Philem. 21). Showing confidence in a person is one of the greatest compliments and forms of appreciation we can ever express.

**Q 43** *What are five reasons we should show appreciation when seeking to resolve conflict?*

Why do we show appreciation to people? Show appreciation because people *deserve it* and they *need it*. Being appreciated is one of our greatest needs. As humans, we all have many needs. Physically, we need air to breath, bread to eat, and water to drink. Each day we need several hours of rest for our bodies. Likewise, we have emotional and spiritual needs. God has created every person with the need to feel appreciated and worthwhile. Life can be hard, and people can be thankless. A word of appreciation brightens the heart and lifts the head. Appreciation is free, but worth a fortune. As you take the time to show appreciation, you will *encourage* people and lift their spirits. How long do you remember the appreciation others have shown you? For some, receiving appreciation is so rare that it may encourage them for a year—or even a lifetime. Also, people will love and appreciate you for noticing their hard work, sacrifices, and efforts to bless others. Criticism closes doors, but gratitude *opens hearts* and *strengthens relationships*.

**Q 44** *What are some examples of times that Jesus and Paul showed appreciation?*

**Q 45** *How often do you encourage those near you with appreciation? Give examples.*

In every letter he writes, Paul includes words of appreciation for his readers. Jesus looked for opportunities to show appreciation. He commended the widow who gave a small offering, the women who washed His feet with tears (Luke 7:39-48), and Mary for pouring her inheritance on his feet (John 12:7-8), the Centurion for his faith (Matt. 8), Peter for receiving a revelation from God (Matt. 16:17). And when Jesus sent messages to the seven churches in Asia, He greeted each church with words of appreciation—except for Laodicea (Rev. 2–3). God loves to express His approval and appreciation to us with words such as, "Well done, good and faithful servant." God is the great encourager—through His Word, His Spirit, and His deeds. And when we encourage others with appreciation, we are following the example of the Father, the Son, and the Spirit.

*Sabio* **says:** "A *small gift* of appreciation to a living person means 100 times more to him than a *truck full of gifts* at his grave. Appreciation is always appreciated. Be a wise peacemaker. Share *sincere* appreciation with people, and this will help *open their hearts* wide to the message God sent you to share with them.

**Q 46** *How is Paul's appeal based on love, not force? Explain.*

(Step 8:) **Appeal to love, not force.** At the start of the letter, we see Paul introducing himself in a *humble* manner, as a prisoner of Jesus Christ—without mentioning that he was a powerful apostle. And further into the letter he writes: " [8]*Although in Christ* **I could be bold and order you to do what you ought to do**, [9]*yet I appeal to you on the basis of love. I then, as Paul—an old man and now also a prisoner of Christ Jesus—*[10]*I appeal to you for my son Onesimus, who became my son while I was in chains"* (Philem. 8-10).

Paul is very patient in approaching the conflict. He has taken a third of the letter to emphasize family terms and show appreciation to Philemon. Not until verse 10 does he even mention the conflict. And when Paul does identify the conflict, he does **not** seek a solution based on the power and force of *apostolic authority*. Rather, Paul refers to himself as *an old man in prison*, asking Philemon to *love* a son that Paul begat while in chains. Paul does not use his rank or his title. He does not bark orders like a big boss. The tone of his voice echoes no command. Rather, as an elder in chains, he softly *requests* Philemon *to love* his new son, Onesimus.

**Q 47** *Does God seek to resolve the conflict between us and Him by force or love? Explain.*

Paul is following the example of God, who has all the power and authority in the world. Yet the Almighty never uses His power to force us. Rather, one by one, He loves people out of sin and into His family. He loves us and invites us to love Him in return. There are laws and commands in God's kingdom, for every kingdom must have law and order. But during our years on earth, God does not enforce His laws by force. Instead, He appeals to love, saying: *"If you love me, keep my commandments"* (John 15).

Love succeeds where force fails. Powerful rulers have tried to conquer the world by force. They command mighty armies and threaten those they want to force to submit. But kingdoms built by force crumble into the dust. Meanwhile, the kingdom of God expands by love until it will one day fill the whole earth.

Figure 6.8

The wind and the sun had a contest to see who could get a man to take off his coat. The wind blew with a great force, but this force caused the traveler to grip the coat more firmly than ever. Then the sun shone upon the man with a warmth of friendship. With no effort, the man loosened his grip and removed the coat. Love never fails (1 Cor. 13:8). It is eternal. And it will open many doors that force will only close tighter.

Paul had a conflict with Peter in Antioch, Syria. Peter was being two-faced.

*¹¹ When Peter came to Antioch, I opposed him to his face, because he was clearly in the wrong. ¹² Before certain men came from James, he used to eat with the Gentiles. But when they arrived, he began to draw back and separate himself from the Gentiles because he was afraid of those who belonged to the circumcision group. ¹³ The other Jews joined him in his hypocrisy, so that by their hypocrisy even Barnabas was led astray* (Gal. 2:11-13).

**Q 48** *Why do you think Paul used more love to Philemon than he showed to Peter (Gal. 2:11-13)?*

Wow! Look at the pressure a group can put on a believer. In case you have not discovered it yet, you should know that even apostles can become hypocrites to save their own reputations and relationships! Sorry, but the best of humans have times of weakness. I could tell you some personal stories to illustrate this, and you probably have a few stories of your own, but we had better move on. Paul identifies the problem of hypocrisy and chooses to seek a solution. In his early years as an apostle, Paul was less diplomatic. He probably wrote Galatians in 51–53 A.D. And salvation apart from the law of Moses was a hot topic for him since his ministry was mostly to the Gentiles. So in this illustration from Galatians 2, many of the steps we see in Philemon are missing. Galatians 2 runs deep with conviction, but lacks the love, tenderness, affirmation, and prayer we see in Philemon (written as much as 9 years later, in 60 A.D.). Even the best apostles become better, grow, and develop new skills with years. And we all do better when we can take time to write a letter rather than when we respond face to face while emotions are hot. Still, in Galatians 2, we see Paul taking Steps 1 and 2. There is hope for us. Do you lack patience, love, and tact in times of conflict? We can improve day by day if we choose to keep growing in grace and in the skills of relating to people. Is there an area in your life that you want to improve? If so, take a few minutes to talk to God about it. Ask Him to fill you with more of His love and to strengthen you where you are weak. It is God's plan for His children to become more and more like Jesus. What we are today does not need to be what we are tomorrow.

**Q 49** *As you are growing in grace, are you growing in the love you show others? Illustrate.*

(Step 9: Associate yourself with the person you want to reconcile.** Paul did not talk with cold or neutral words about some slave at a distance. He called Onesimus by name. He spoke for Onesimus in a personal way, referring to him as *my son Onesimus*; and, *my son*, whom I begat in chains (Philem. 10). Paul associated himself closely with Onesimus. He identified himself with the slave. Paul wrote: *"So if you consider me a partner, welcome him as you would welcome me"* (Philem. 17). Paul bound himself to Onesimus in such a way that whatever happened to the slave was happening to Paul. The apostle yoked himself to the slave in need. Paul said, "If you

**Q 50** *What are some ways Paul associated himself closely with Onesimus?*

want *to refresh my heart in Christ,* then receive Onesimus *as you would receive me."* Paul was not indifferent about the outcome. His joy was attached to how Philemon treated Onesimus, his son in the faith.

Jesus used this principle to refer to those in need, whom He wanted us to help. Our Lord associated Himself with the people He wants others to befriend. Christ said, *"He who receives you receives me"* (Matt. 10:40). Jesus also said:

> [34] *"Then the King will say to those on his right, 'Come, you who are blessed by my Father; take your inheritance, the kingdom prepared for you since the creation of the world.* [35] *For I was hungry and you gave me something to eat, I was thirsty and you gave me something to drink, I was a stranger and you invited me in,* [36] *I needed clothes and you clothed me, I was sick and you looked after me, I was in prison and you came to visit me.'*

> [37] *"Then the righteous will answer him, 'Lord, when did we see you hungry and feed you, or thirsty and give you something to drink?* [38] *When did we see you a stranger and invite you in, or needing clothes and clothe you?* [39] *When did we see you sick or in prison and go to visit you?'*

> [40] *"The King will reply, 'I tell you the truth, whatever you did for one of the least of these brothers of mine, you did for me'"* (Matt. 25:34-40).

Associate yourself with the person in need. Express personal emotion and appreciation for the response you are requesting. Be sure people know how much the outcome means to you.

So many things divide people: race, color, culture, the nation you are from, your background, economics, possessions, education, social status, sex, religion, and abilities or lack of them! These become prisons of prejudice. We judge people based upon our opinions—and put them in their place. But Jesus tore down the barriers of prejudice through His sacrifice on the cross (Eph. 2:14-16)! The gospel is for the whole world and everyone in it. He reached out to, accepted, forgave, and ate with sinners. He ignored prejudice by associating with Samaritans. He welcomed outcasts. He loved and died so every person in the world—rich or poor, educated or illiterate, enslaved or free, famous or unknown—could come back to the Father!

**Step 10** **Invest in the solution. Pay a price.** Sacrifice. Don't just ask others to bear the burden of reconciliation. Lead the way. Set an example. As the proverb says, "Put some of your skin in the game."

Look at how much Paul was willing to invest in the solution—the reconciliation and brotherhood of Onesimus and Philemon.

Paul's first sacrifice and investment in the solution was sending Onesimus back.

> [12] *I am sending him—who is my very heart—back to you.* [13] *I would have liked to keep him with me so that he could take your place in helping me while I am in chains for the gospel* (Philem. 12-13).

Prison was lonely, and visitors came and went. It would have been wonderful for Paul to have a constant brother like Onesimus to be sure he had food and other things he needed. But Paul cared more about Onesimus and Philemon than he cared about his own comfort. So he sent Onesimus back to Philemon.

The second investment Paul made in the solution amazes us. Paul wrote: [18] *If he has done you any wrong or owes you anything, charge it to me.* [19] *I, Paul, am writing this with my own hand. I will pay it back...* (Philem. 18-19).

Paul offers to repay whatever Onesimus stole. Imagine that! The apostle says he will pay the full debt the slave owes. It is doubtful that a wealthy man like Philemon would allow an old, poor, imprisoned apostle to send him money. But Paul is not joking or

**Q 51** *Did Jesus associate Himself with those He wanted to help? Give examples?*

**Q 52** *Do you follow the example of Jesus by associating with those in conflict with God and others? Illustrate.*

**Q 53** *What are 2 ways that Paul invested in the solution for Onesimus?*

**Q 54** *What have you done to invest in resolving the conflict that people have with God or others?*

trying to manipulate Philemon. Paul means what he says. If it is necessary for him to lead in love, he is willing to pay the price. Paul does not just point in the direction he wants Philemon to go. The apostle sets an example. As the proverb says, "People would rather see a sermon than just hear one." The eye is a better pupil than the ear. What we do speaks louder than what we say. If the goal you want is giving, then be the first to give. If the goal you want is forgiving, be the first to forgive. For few of the people God calls you to help are leaders, but many will follow your good example.

**Step 11:** **Recall the debt Jesus paid for us, and the forgiveness He so freely gives us.**

Paul offers to pay the debt Onesimus owes. But he also reminds Philemon of a debt that he once owed. For like all of us, Philemon was once a slave to sin who owed God a debt that he could never repay. But Paul met Philemon and preached the gospel to him. Philemon repented of his sins and received the forgiveness that Jesus purchased for him with His own blood. So Paul writes: *"I, Paul, am writing this with my own hand. I will pay it back—**not to mention that you owe me your very self**"* (Philem. 19). Philemon was indebted to Paul for introducing him to Jesus. How much was that worth to Philemon? And all of us were once in shoes like Onesimus wore. All of us believers sing: "I owed a debt I could not pay; He paid a debt He did not owe." [5]

When there is a conflict and we need to forgive someone, it is good for us to remember that God has forgiven us. And it is important to remember that God forgives us as we forgive others.

Jesus taught us to pray: *"Forgive us our debts, as* [in the same way] *we have forgiven our debtors"* (Matt. 6:12). Take 2 minutes to review the parable of the unmerciful servant (Matt. 18:21-35). To keep the forgiveness God gives us, we must pass it along to those who sin against us (Matt. 6:16; 18:21-35). Those who refuse to forgive others forfeit their own pardon. *"Judgment without mercy will be shown to anyone who has not been merciful. Mercy triumphs over judgment!"* (James 2:13). We do ourselves a favor when we forgive those who do us wrong.

**Step 12:** **Envision future fellowship after the conflict has been solved.**

[21] *Confident of your obedience, I write to you, knowing that you will do even more than I ask* [22] *And one thing more: Prepare a guest room for me, because I hope to be restored to you in answer to your prayers* (Philem. 21-22).

Paul expressed confidence that Philemon will do all the apostle is asking, and more. What does the *more* include? Is Paul hinting for Philemon to free Onesimus? Is Paul hoping that Philemon will send Onesimus back to Rome to help the old apostle during his time in chains? We cannot be sure what he is thinking when he says, *"I write to you, knowing that you will do even more than I ask"* (Philem. 21). But notice that Paul looks beyond the conflict and envisions a joyful reunion with Philemon (Philem. 22).

Visualizing a blessed future is often Step 4 of a sermon that has five steps. (See the *Faith & Action* course: *Preach the Word: Preparing Biblical Messages—Homiletics 1,* Chapter 12: The Choice, Lesson 32, Point A).

In this final step, select a definite situation in the future. Picture your listeners there. Describe them enjoying safety, peace, honor, pleasure, joy, and satisfaction. They are happy because they chose to accept God's solution to the problem.

Jesus emphasized a future good result in Matthew 19. The rich young ruler had refused to forsake all to follow Christ. Peter asked, *"What then will there be for us?"* (Matt. 19:27). Jesus wanted to encourage Peter and the other disciples. They had made the difficult choice of following Him. So the Master took them into the future. He did this by using words to paint a picture of that future:

**Q 55** *How were all of us in a situation like Onesimus was in?*

**Q 56** *How does recalling the debt Jesus paid for us affect resolving conflicts with others?*

**Q 57** ⟋ *How did Jesus emphasize a future good result in Matthew 19:28-29?*

[28]*Jesus said to them, "I tell you the truth, at the renewal of all things, when the Son of Man sits on his glorious throne, you who have followed me will also sit on twelve thrones, judging the twelve tribes of Israel.* [29]*And everyone who has left houses or brothers or sisters or father or mother or children or fields for my sake will receive a hundred times as much and will inherit eternal life"* (Matt. 19:28-29).

**Q 58** ⟋ *What helped Jesus endure the cross?*

Jesus helped His followers feel the honor they would receive in the future. He guided them to think about the thrones they would sit upon. Jesus showed the future good result of the choice the disciples were making. Emphasizing the future good result encourages people to make hard decisions in the present. We might not have the strength to carry the cross *today* if we think only about its weight. But thinking about the joy ahead (future) inspires and motivates us. How was Jesus able to choose the cross? He thought of the future good result.

[2]*Let us fix our eyes on Jesus, the author and perfecter of our faith, who **for the joy set before him** endured the cross, scorning its shame, and sat down at the right hand of the throne of God* (Heb. 12:2).

## Conclusion

**Q 59** ⟋ *What do you think helped resolve the conflict between Paul and Mark?*

[23]*Epaphras, my fellow prisoner in Christ Jesus, sends you greetings.* [24]*And so do Mark, Aristarchus, Demas and Luke, my fellow workers.* [25]*The grace of the Lord Jesus Christ be with your spirit* (Philem. 23-25).

Paul ends his letter as he began, with a loving greeting. We are not sure if Epaphras (Epaphroditus) was in prison as a visitor, or if he had been arrested. Among the names Paul mentions, note Mark, who has been reconciled to Paul after a hot split in relationship (Acts 13:13; 15:36-41). What brought about the reconciliation? Had Mark become stronger, or had Paul become more diplomatic? Perhaps both.

⚖️ **Test Yourself:** Circle the letter by the *best* completion to each question or statement.

1. In Philemon, who is the owner of a slave?
   a) Philemon
   b) Onesimus
   c) Epaphras
   d) Aristarchus

2. When Paul wrote Philemon, how far away was he from Colosse?
   a) 100 km
   b) 700 km
   c) 1400 km
   d) 2100 km

3. Which letter from prison does NOT mention slavery?
   a) Ephesians
   b) Colossians
   c) Philippians
   d) Philemon

4. How many slaves were in the Roman Empire when Paul wrote?
   a) 100 million
   b) 60 million
   c) 20 million
   d) 1 million

5. How does the gospel affect slavery?
   a) It frees slaves from masters.
   b) It changes nations.
   c) It changes one heart at a time.
   d) It causes masters to free slaves.

6. The first step to solve a conflict is:
   a) Identify the conflict.
   b) State the goal.
   c) Humble yourself.
   d) Approach the problem with faith.

7. What does Paul emphasize more than 10 times in Philemon?
   a) Appreciation
   b) Family language
   c) Envisioning
   d) The goal

8. Whom did Paul commend?
   a) The saints
   b) Aristarchus
   c) Philemon
   d) Apphia

9. Offering to pay a debt illustrates
   a) seed faith.
   b) envisioning harvest.
   c) accounting.
   d) investing.

10. Recalling which city helps us resolve conflict?
    a) Samaria
    b) Bethlehem
    c) Jerusalem
    d) The New Jerusalem

✍️ **Essay Test Topics:** Write 50-100 words on each of these goals that you studied in this chapter on Philemon (14 points each plus 2 free).

- Describe the 4 main characters of Philemon, the setting, and the outline.
- Analyze the problem of slavery in Paul's day, and the biblical solution.
- From Philemon, explain and illustrate principles on the conflict, the solution, and the goal.
- From Philemon, explain and illustrate principles on humility and family language.
- From Philemon, explain and illustrate principles on prayer, appreciation, and love.
- From Philemon, explain and illustrate principles on associating and investing.
- From Philemon, explain and illustrate principles on recalling and envisioning.

# Definitions

The right-hand column lists the chapter in the textbook in which the word is used.

Chapter

**abstinence**—choosing to do without something, such as avoiding drinking alcohol — 2

**adoption**—the legal process of bringing a person into a family, and giving that person all the status and privileges of sons and daughters who were born in the family — 1

*agape*—a Greek word used in the Bible for the highest form of love; the supernatural love of God that flows from Him to and through humans — 5

**anarchy**—a state of rioting, looting, killing, chaos, confusion, and lawlessness — 6

**armor of God**—the six pieces of armor that God provides for us (Eph. 6:14-17) — 3

**Artemis**—a Greek goddess of the moon. Her Roman name was Diana. She was associated with becoming pregnant. Her statues had many breasts., daughter of Zeus and sister of Apollo. — 1

**asceticism**—harsh treatment of the body through denial of all forms of pleasure, especially for religious or spiritual reasons — 4

**avatars**—people who claim to be, or are said to be, God in flesh. — 4

*chiasms*—a Greek word used to describe forms of parallel thoughts — 4

**Christology**—the study of Christ; beliefs about who Jesus Christ is — 4

**Colosse**—the city in the old province of Asia (modern Turkey) where the Colossians lived — 4

**Colossian Heresy**—the false teaching at Colosse that was pulling Jesus down and lifting humans up — 4

**compass**—an instrument containing a magnetized pointer that shows the direction of magnetic north and bearings from it. — 4

**debauchery**—shame; sin, fleshly indulgence; the opposite of self-control — 2

**deposit**—a partial, initial payment to assure that someone will receive the full amount; God deposited His Spirit in us to assure us that we will receive all He has promised. — 1

**doxology**—a word of praise to God; a song, prayer, or praise glorifying God, often at the end of a section of writing, or at the end of a church service — 1

**election**—the act or process of choosing; God elects or chooses all who choose to receive and follow Jesus. — 1

**Euodia**—a beloved lady among the church leaders in Philippi

**filled with the Spirit**—the process of living full of God's Spirit. When we are born again, the presence of God's Spirit in us gives new life. But when the Spirit fills us as He did the 120 believers at Pentecost, He brings us power to serve, and to live a holy life. Being filled *once* with the Spirit is *not* enough. We need to live filled day by day (Eph. 5:18). — 2

**firstborn**—first in order, importance, or position. As God, Christ is the firstborn over the creation He created; also, he is the firstborn from the dead—the first to permanently rise from and conquer death. — 4

**fusing**—join or blend to form a single entity — 5

**gentiles**—the ethnic groups and nations of earth; non-Jews — 1

**gnosticism**—a false teaching based on secret knowledge that some claimed we need for salvation — 4

**grace gifts**—the talents, skills, and abilities God gives to each member of His family to serve and strengthen others. — 2

**'grace-tics'**—modern heretics who walk in darkness but claim that God does not see their sins because they are covered by grace; these deny their sins by claiming that their sins do not matter.

**imparted righteousness**— holiness we experience (sanctification) as we partake of the nature of God at regeneration, and as we grow in the likeness of Christ (Rom. 8:29)

**imputed righteousness**—right standing (justification) that God credits to us as we trust in Jesus as Savior and Lord

**in Christ**—the boundary, realm, and sphere of God's plan of redemption; salvation is available as we abide *in Christ. In Christ* occurs seven times in Ephesians and over 160 times in Paul's 13 letters.   1

**inheritance**—wealth and riches that one person gives to another; the inheritance of those who follow Jesus is all that God has promised us in Christ.   1

**intermediaries**—beings between God and humans   4

*Kenosis*—a Greek word that refers to Christ *emptying* Himself of His privileges, to become a servant, and save us by dying on the cross   5

**legalists**—those who emphasize salvation by rules, as some Jewish teachers; Paul refers to these as dogs, because of their harsh nature.   5

**libertines**—those who ignore laws or claim to be free from obeying God's laws; Paul says their god is their appetite, and destruction is their destiny. Scripture compares libertines to hogs, who wallow in the mud.   5

**literary context**—the written setting that surrounds a biblical passage, including the subdivision, section of a book, the book itself, and the entire Bible   4

**Marriage Encounter**—the name of a weekend program for married couples, first made popular in the US, but now available in many countries; the goal is to enable people to discover God's vision of marriage and family life so they can better understand their relationship with each other and with God   3

**masterpiece**—a work of outstanding artistry, skill, or workmanship   1

**moorings**—ropes, chains, or anchors by or to which a boat, ship, or buoy is moored   1

**Nestle-Aland Greek text**—Today the designation *Novum Testamentum Graece* normally refers to the Nestle-Aland editions, named after the scholars who led the critical editing work.   6

**odious**—extremely unpleasant; repulsive.   2

**Onesimus**—a slave who fled from Colosse and his owner, Philemon, to Rome, where he was saved under Paul's ministry as a prisoner in Rome   6

**parallel passages**—passages on the same subject or topic; used to compare the same author in a different book, a different author of the same Testament, or an author in the other Testament.   4

**Parthenon**—a former temple on the Athenian Acropolis in Greece that was dedicated to the goddess Athena, whom the people of Athens considered their patron.   1

**Philemon**—a beloved brother who refreshed the saints in Colosse, yet owned a slave named Onessimus   6

**predestination**—to plan a destiny; God has planned for all who receive Jesus to become like Him and be with Him.   1

**Prison Epistles**—the four letters Paul wrote as a prisoner in Rome, about A.D. 60-61; Ephesians, Colossians, Philippians, and Philemon   1, 4

**redemption**—the act or process of buying back a person who has become a slave   1

**Reformation**—(also called The Protestant Reformation) the religious movement of the 16th century that began as an attempt to reform the Roman Catholic Church and resulted in the creation of Protestant churches   5

**restitution**—making right the wrongs we have done to people; paying the debts we owe   6

**seal**—a mark, emblem, or other way to show validity or ownership; God put the Holy Spirit in us to assure us that His promises to us are valid, and to show that we belong to Him.   1

**Spiritual warfare**—the process of standing firm in Christ to remain faithful to the gospel, and live worthy of our calling, as we face temptations of the world, evil desires of the flesh, and the influence of evil spirits.   3

**submission**—the attitudes and actions of honoring a person in authority. Examples: children submit to the authority of their parents; all citizens submit to government leaders.   3

**supreme**—At the top, above all others; number one. Christ is Supreme as Creator, far above all that has
    been created; and He is Supreme as Reconciler—the One who through His sacrifice brought God and            4
    humans together in peace.

**syncretism**—mixing good and bad beliefs of religions into one                                                4

**Syntyche**—a beloved lady among the church leaders in Philippi                                                5

*telion*—the Greek word translated "perfect," it means mature and complete                                      4

**Trinitarian**—a person who believes the Father, Son, and Holy Spirit are equal and work together to provide   1
    salvation

**worthy**—appropriate and fitting. We respond to the salvation God gives us in Christ, by living in ways that  2
    please God, and show we are grateful to be members of His family.

# Scripture List

# Bibliography

Abbott, T. K. *New International Commentary, Epistles to the Ephesians and Colossians,* Edinburg, Scotland: T. & T. Clark, 1977.

Arrington, French L. and Roger Stronstad, eds. *Life in the Spirit New Testament Commentary—Ephesians,* Grand Rapids, Michigan: Zondervan Publishing House, 2003.

Barclay, William. *The Daily Study Bible: Galatians and Ephesians,* Philadelphia, Pennsylvania: The Westminster Press, 1976.

Barclay, William. *Daily Study Bible: The Letters to the Galatians and the Ephesians,* Philadelphia, Pennsylvania: The Westminster Press, 1976.

Barker, Kenneth, gen. ed. *The NIV Study Bible.* Grand Rapics, Michigan: Zondervan Publishing House, 1985.

Barrett, David. International Bulletin of Missionary Research, January 1997.

Barton, Bruce B. and others. "Philippians, Colossians, Philemon," in the *Life Application Bible Commentary*, eds. Grant Osborne and Philip Comfort, Wheaton, Illinois: Tyndale House Publishers, 1995.

Beggs, Jimmy. interview, December, 2007.

Borthwick, Christie and Paul. "Don't Give Up on Your Family," *Discipleship Journal,* 149:32.

Bruce, F. F. *The Epistles to the Colossians, to Philemon, and to the Ephesians,* in The New International Commentary on the New Testament. Grand Rapids, Michigan: Wm. B. Eerdmans Publishing Company, 1984.

Cooley, Robert E. "The Apocalypse: 7 Letters to the Church," *The Pentecostal Evangel*, April 11, 1999.

Crum, Ellis J. Adapted from: "He Paid a Debt He Did Not Owe," Ellis J. Crum Publisher, 1977.

Cushman, Ralph Spaulding. Adapted from: "The Secret" *I Met God in the Morning,* Spiritual Hilltops, 1932,

Draper, Edythe, ed. *Draper's Book of Quotations for the Christian World.* Wheaton, Illinois: Tyndale House Publishers, Inc., 1992.

Elliott, Charlotte, "Just as I Am," 1835, Public Domain.

Fee, Gordon D. *God's Empowering Presence: The Holy Spirit in the Letters of Paul*, Peabody, Massachusetts: Hendrickson Publishers, 1994.

Gilbrandt, Thoralf, ed. *The Complete Biblical Library: The New Testament Greek-English Dictionary, Delta-Epsilon.* Springfield, Missouri: World Library Press, 1990.

Gingrich, Wilbur F. *Shorter Lexicon of the Greek New Testament, 2nd ed.*, rev. by Frederick W. Danker. Chicago, Illinois: University of Chicago Press, 1983.

Harris, Ralph W. *The Complete Biblical Library: The New Testament Study Bible, Galatians–Philemon,* vol. 8. Springfield, Missouri: World Library Press, 1989.

Horton, Stanley M. *The Ultimate Victory.* Springfield, Missouri: Gospel Publishing House,1991.

Jowett, J. H. *Springs in the Desert; Studies in the Psalms.* New York: George H. Doran Company, 1924.

Knight, John A. *Beacon Bible Expositions,* Vol. 9, *Philippians, Colossians, Philemon.* Kansas City, Missouri: Beacon Hill Press, 1985.

Meyer, F. B. Adapted from http://www.worthychristianlibrary.com/fb-meyer/the-secret-of-guidance/chapter-9-the-fullness-of-the-spirit/

Meyer, Joyce. *Help Me I'm Married.* Tulsa, Oklahoma: Harrison House, 2000.

Mote, Edward. Adapted from: "My Hope is Built on Nothing Less," 1863, Public Domain.

O'Brien, Peter T. "Colossians, Philemon," in *Word Biblical Commentary*, gen. eds. David A. Hubbard and Glenn W. Barker, no. 44. Waco, Texas: Word Books, 1982.

Reese, Thomas. "Adoption," in *The International Standard Bible Encyclopedia*, volume 1, ed. Geoffrey W. Bromiley. Grand Rapids, Michigan: Wm. B. Eerdmans Publishing Company, 1979.

Robinson, J. Haddon. "Sermon on Philemon," *Put That on Master Charge*. https://www.youtube.com/watch?v=HhKyl7tVsaI.

Spurgeon, Charles Haddon. Adapted from https://www.studylight.org/commentaries/spe/ephesians-6.html.

Stamps, Donald C. Adapted from, *Life in the Spirit Study Bible* (formerly *The Full Life Study Bible*). Grand Rapids, Michigan: Zondervan Publishing Company, 1992.

Stead , Louisa M. R. "'Tis So Sweet to Trust in Jesus," 1882, Public Domain.

Strobel, Lee. From sermon "The Case for Christ." Lake Forest, California: Saddleback Church

Tan, Paul Lee. *Encyclopedia of 15'000 Sermon Illustrations: Signs of theTimes*. Dallas, Texas: Bible Communications Inc., 1998.

Tenney, Merrill C. *New Testament Survey.* Grand Rapids, Michigan: Wm. B. Eerdmans Publishing Co., 1961.

Toplady, Augustus Montague. "Rock of Ages, cleft for me," 1776, Public Domain.

Watts, Isaac. "When I Survey the Wondrous Cross," from *Hymns and Spiritual Songs*, 1707.

Wiersbe, Warren. *The Bible Expository Commentary,* Vol. 2. Wheaton, Illinois: Victor Books, 1992.

Williams, Morrris. *Declare His Righteousness*. Springfield, Missouri: Gospel Publishing House, 1975.

Wilson, Bill. *Streets of Pain.* Waco, Texas: Word Publishing, 1992.

Wood, George O. Sermons ... various. Costa Mesa, California: Newport-Mesa Christian Center (see below).

Yancey, Philip. *What's So Amazing about Grace?* Grand Rapids, Michigan: Zondervan Publishing House, 1997.

Youngblood, R. F. "Peace," in *The International Standard Bible Encyclopedia,* gen. ed. Geoffrey W. Bromiley, No. 3. Grand Rapids, Michigan: Wm. B. Eerdmans Publishing Company, 1986.

**ALL George O. Wood sermons can be found on the website http://georgeowood.com.** *Look under Expositional Sermons, New Testament, and choose book.*

Wood, George O. Sermon on Ephesians 1:1-14, "God's Wealthy Church."

_____. "Sermon on Philippians 1:27-2:30, "Joy and the People I'm With."

_____. "Sermon on Philippians 3:1-4:1, "Joy and the Person I Am."

_____. "Sermon on Philippians 4:2-23, "Joy in Any Circumstance."

_____. "Sermon on Ephesians 5:18–6:9, "Marks of a Spirit-Filled Christian."

http://anitamathias.com/2011/11/29/martin-luther-didnt-say-that-did-he-yes-he-did/

https://carm.org/manuscript-evidence

https://cccmidland.com/missions/regions/northern-asia/

http://coolcosmos.ipac.caltech.edu/ask/5-How-large-is-the-Sun-compared-to-Earth-

http://discoveryseries.org/discovery-series/moses-his-anger-and-what-it-cost-him/

https://en.wikipedia.org/wiki/Abraham%27s_family_tree

https://en.wikipedia.org/wiki/Attributes_of_God_in_Christianity

http://en.wikipedia.org/wiki/Herod%27s_Temple#Herod.27s_Temple

https://en.wikipedia.org/wiki/Jewish_population_by_country

https://en.wikipedia.org/wiki/Via_Egnatia

https://www.blueletterbible.org/comm/spurgeon_charles/sermons/0500.cfm

https://www.cdc.gov/features/alcoholconsumption/ (National Council of Alcoholism, 2006).

http://www.christianitytoday.com/history/issues/issue-47/on-road-with-paul.html

https://www.guideposts.org/better-living/positive-living/guideposts-classics-corrie-ten-boom-on-forgiveness

http://www.npr.org/sections/health-shots/2012/08/27/159955340/pediatricians-decide-boys-are-better-off-circumcised-than-not

http://www.pewforum.org/files/2011/12/ChristianityAppendixC.pdf

http://www.redeemer-lutheran.net/Articles/1000039345/Redeemer_Lutheran_Church/Media_Center/Pastors_Articles/Throwing_Ink_at.aspx

https://www.space.com/33903-most-distant-galaxy-cluster-found.html

http://www.worldinvisible.com/library/fbmeyer/ch9.htm

# Endnotes

## Chapter 1

1  F. F. Bruce, *The Epistles to the Colossians, to Philemon, and to the Ephesians*, in The New International Commentary on the New Testament (Grand Rapids, Michigan: Wm. B. Eerdmans Publishing Company, 1984), p. 229.

2  https://carm.org/manuscript-evidence

3  Robert E. Cooley, "The Apocalypse: 7 Letters to the Church," *The Pentecostal Evangel* (April 11, 1999), p. 22.

4  Stanley M. Horton, *The Ultimate Victory* (Springfield, Missouri; Gospel Publishing House, 1991), p. 41.

5  French L. Arrington and Roger Stronstad, *Life in the Spirit New Testament Commentary— Ephesians,* (Grand Rapids, Michigan: Zondervan Publishing House, 1999), p. 1026.

6  George O. Wood, "God's Wealthy Church," sermon on Ephesians 1:1-14. http://georgeowood.com.

7  Adapted from Stamps, *Life in the Spirit Study Bible*, p. 1855.

8  Thomas Reese, "Adoption," in *The International Standard Bible Encyclopedia*, volume 1, ed. Geoffrey W. Bromiley (Grand Rapids, Michigan: Wm. B. Eerdmans Publishing Company, 1979), p. 53.

9  Arrington and Stronstad, pp. 1030-1032.

10  Isaac Watts, "When I Survey the Wondrous Cross," from *Hymns and Spiritual Songs*, 1707.

11  T. K. Abbott, *New International Commentary, Epistles to the Ephesians and Colossians,* (Edinburg, Scotland: T. & T. Clark, 1977), p. 30.

12  Bruce, p. 69.

13  http://www.worldinvisible.com/library/fbmeyer/ch9.htm

14  Ralph W. Harris, ed., *The Complete Biblical Library: The New Testament*, Galatians—Philemon, p. 106.

15  Gordon D. Fee, *God's Empowering Presence: The Holy Spirit in the Letters of Paul.* (Peabody, Massachusetts: Hendrickson Publishers, 1994), p. 678.

16  Lee Strobel, author and teaching pastor at Saddleback Church, Lake Forest, California, from sermon "The Case for Christ."

17  Philip Yancey, *What's So Amazing about Grace?* (Grand Rapids, Michigan: Zondervan Publishing House, 1997), p. 11.

18  This list is adapted from Phoenix First Assembly of God, which has over 200 ministries by church members.

19  Arrington and Stronstad, pp. 1042-1043.

201  Augustus Montague Toplady, "Rock of Ages, cleft for me," 1776, Public Domain.

21  Charlotte Elliott, "Just as I Am," 1835, Public Domain.

22  Merrill C. Tenney, *New Testament Survey* (Grand Rapids, Michigan: Wm. B. Eerdmans Publishing Co., 1961), p. 91. Dr. C. Schick's model of Herod's Temple, based on his research.

23  Arrington and Stronstad, pp. 1044-1045.

24  https://en.wikipedia.org/wiki/Second_Temple#Herod.27s_Temple

25  Wilbur F. Gingrich, Shorter Lexicon of the Greek New Testament, 2nd ed., rev. by Frederick W. Danker (Chicago, Illinois: University of Chicago Press, 1983), p. 46.

26  https://en.wikipedia.org/wiki/Jewish_population_by_country

27  https://en.wikipedia.org/wiki/Abraham%27s_family_tree

28  Gilbrandt, *The Complete Biblical Library: The New Testament Greek-English Dictionary, Delta-Epsilon,* p. 233.

29  Gingrich and Danker, p. 55.

30  https://www.space.com/33903-most-distant-galaxy-cluster-found.html

31  https://cccmidland.com/missions/regions/northern-asia/

32  Bruce, p. 69.

33  Adapted from: Ralph Spaulding Cushman, "The Secret" *I Met God in the Morning,* from Spiritual Hilltops, 1932, https://www.youtube.com/watch?v=3PIBge37J9k

## Chapter 2

1  Fee, pp. 698-705.

2  Arrington and Stronstad, p. 1061.

3  This list is adapted from Phoenix First Assembly of God, which has over 200 ministries by church members.

4  http://discoveryseries.org/discovery-series/moses-his-anger-and-what-it-cost-him/

5  NIV Study Bible, Ephesians 4:26

6  National Council of Alcoholism, 2006, https://www.cdc.gov/features/alcoholconsumption/.

7  Adapted from F. B. Meyer, http://www.worthychristianlibrary.com/fb-meyer/the-secret-of-guidance/chapter-9-the-fullness-of-the-spirit/

8  *ibid*

9  Wood, "Marks of a Spirit-FIlled Christian," Ephesians 5:18-6:9. http://georgewood.com.

## Chapter 3

1  Joyce Meyer, *Help Me I'm Married* (Tulsa, Oklahoma: Harrison House, 2000), p. 69.

2  *ibid*, p. 69.

3  Harris, p. 161.

4  William Barclay, *The Daily Study Bible: Galatians and Ephesians* (Philadelphia, Pennsylvania: The Westminster Press, 1976), p. 173.

5  Adapted from Spurgeon, https://www.studylight.org/commentaries/spe/ephesians-6.html

6  Edythe Draper, ed. *Draper's Book of Quotations for the Christian World* (Wheaton, Illinois: Tyndale House Publishers, Inc., 1992), p. 62.

7  https://anitamathias.com/?s=Martin+luther+didn%27t+say+that

[8] William Barclay, *Daily Study Bible: The Letters to the Galatians and the Ephesians,* (Westminster, 1976), p. 178.

[9] *ibid,* p. 178.

[10] *ibid,* p. 179.

[11] Diagram adapted from Morrris Williams, *Declare His Righteousness* (Springfield, Missouri, Gospel Publishing House, 1975), p. 50.

[12] Arrington and Stronstad, p. 1083.

[13] *ibid,* p. 1083.

[14] Fee, pp. 575-586.

## Chapter 4

[1] Peter T. O'Brien, *Colossians, Philemon,* in Word Biblical Commentary, gen. eds. David A. Hubbard and Glenn W. Barker, no. 44 (Waco, TX: Word Books, 1982), p. 27.

[2] Bruce B. Barton and others, *Philippians, Colossians, Philemon,* in the Life Application Bible Commentary, eds. Grant Osborne and Philip Comfort (Wheaton, IL: Tyndale House Publishers, 1995), 145.

[3] R. F. Youngblood, "Peace," in *The International Standard Bible Encyclopedia,* gen. ed. Geoffrey W. Bromiley, no. 3 (Grand Rapids, MI: Eerdmans Publishing, 1986) 732-33.

[4] Bill Wilson, *Streets of Pain* (Waco, TX: Word Publishing, 1992) 123-24.

[5] https://en.wikipedia.org/wiki/Attributes_of_God_in_Christianity

[6] David Barrett, International Bulletin of Missionary Research, January 1997, p. 25.

[7] *ibid,* p. 25.

[8] Christie and Paul Borthwick, "Don't Give Up on Your Family," *Discipleship Journal,* 149:32.

[9] NIV Study Bible, 1 Cor. 15:32

[10] Arrington and Stronstad, p. 1141

[11] *ibid,* p. 1144.

[12] J. H. Jowett, *Springs in the Desert,* nd., London: Hodder and Stroughton, pp. 76-80.

## Chapter 5

[1] NIV Study Bible note on Acts 28:16.

[2] https://en.wikipedia.org/wiki/Via_Egnatia

[3] http://www.christianitytoday.com/history/issues/issue-47/on-road-with-paul.html

[4] NIV Study Bible note on Acts 16.13.

[5] https://www.guideposts.org/better-living/positive-living/guideposts-classics-corrie-ten-boom-on-forgiveness

[6] http://www.pewforum.org/files/2011/12/Christianity AppendixC.pdf

[7] Wood, "Joy and the People I'm With," sermon on Philippians 1:27–2:30. http://georgewood.com.

[8] Harris, ed., pp. 198-199.

[9] Wood, "Joy and the People I'm With," sermon on Philippians 1:27–2:30. http://georgewood.com.

[10] *ibid*

[11] http://www.npr.org/sections/health-shots/2012/08/27/159955340/pediatricians-decide-boys-are-better-off-circumcised-than-not

[12] Adapted from: Edward Mote, "My Hope is Built on Nothing Less," 1863, Public Domain.

[13] Louisa M. R. Stead, lyrics from the gospel song 'Tis So Sweet to Trust in Jesus, 1882 [in public domain] https://www.hymnal.net/en/hymn/h/568

[14] http://www.redeemer-lutheran.net/Articles/1000039345/Redeemer_Lutheran_Church/Media_Center/Pastors_Articles/Throwing_Ink_at.aspx

[15] Charles Haddon Spurgeon, www.spurgeon.org/sermons/0500.php

[16] Wood, "Joy and the Person I Am," sermon on Philippians 3:1–4:1. http://georgewood.com.

[17] Wood, "Joy in Any Circumstance," sermon on Philippians 4:2-23. http://georgewood.com.

[18] http://coolcosmos.ipac.caltech.edu/ask/5-How-large-is-the-Sun-compared-to-Earth-

[19] Adapted from *Encyclopedia of Sermon Illustrations*, p. 50.

[20] ibid, p. 143.

[21] Jimmy Beggs, interview, December, 2007.

## Chapter 6

[1] J. Haddon Robinson sermon on Philemon, *Put That on Master Charge,* https://www.youtube.com/watch?v=HhKyl7tVsaI

[2] Warren Wiersbe, *The Bible Expository Commentary,* Vol. 2 (Wheaton, Illinois: Victor Books, 1992), p. 270.

[3] *ibid,* p. 270.

[4] John A. Knight, *Beacon Bible Expositions,* Vol. 9, *Philippians, Colossians, Philemon* (Kansas City, Missouri: Beacon Hill Press, 1985), p. 266.

[5] Adapted from: Ellis J. Crum, "He Paid a Debt He Did Not Owe," 1977, Ellis J. Crum, Publisher (Admin. by Sacred Selections R.E. Winsett LLC).

# God's Plan of Salvation

**1. Introduction:**   God is holy, good, and pure—completely righteous. *"God is light; in him there is no darkness at all"* (1 John 1:5).

**2. The Problem:**   Our sins have separated us from God. Because we have sinned—done things we know are wrong—we cannot fellowship with God. Our sins make us too dirty to come into God's holy presence. As we cannot enter a clean room with muddy shoes, we cannot come into God's presence with our sins. *"All have sinned"* (Rom. 3:23). The wages for our sin is death—spiritual death—which is separation from God, now and forever. Those who reject Jesus will die in their sins. They will spend eternity tormented in the flames of hell, away from the presence of God.

**3. God's Solution:**   God loves us so much that he sent Jesus to rescue us. Jesus said, *"I am the way and the truth and the life. No one comes to the Father except through me"* (John 14:6). His name is Jesus, which means Savior, because He saves us from our sins (Matt. 1:21). Jesus saves us from both the penalty and the power of sin–now and forever. Jesus, the Son of God, became a man and lived a perfect, sinless life (Jn. 1:14; Heb. 4:15). He died on the cross as our substitute—He took the penalty for our sins (Rom. 6:23; 2 Cor. 5:21; 1 Pet. 2:24-25. Those who submit their lives to Jesus—God declares to be forgiven, clean and righteous (Rom. 5:1-2).

**4. God's Invitation:**   Jesus says, *"Here I am! I stand at the door (of your heart) and knock. If anyone hears my voice and opens the door, I will come in"* (Rev. 3:20). God's favorite word is "Come". He wants to come to all people, and He wants them to come to him. *"The Spirit and the bride say, "Come!" And let him who hears say, "Come!" Whoever is thirsty, let him come; and whoever wishes, let him take the free gift of the water of life"* (Rev. 22:17). Accept God's invitation. Come to Jesus. Repent of your sins, that is, turn away from what you know is wrong. Put your trust in Jesus as your Savior and Lord. Believe that He died to save you from your sins. Ask Him to forgive your past sins and free you from being a slave to sin. *"If we confess our sins, He is faithful and just and will forgive us our sins, and cleanse us from all unrighteousness"* (1 John 1:9). Welcome Jesus into your life and He will enter. To all who receive Him, He gives the right to become God's children (1 John 1:12).

**5. Your Commitment:**   Welcome to the family of God! God's plan of salvation has a beginning, a middle, and a completion–when we reach heaven. By walking through steps 1-4 above, you have begun to follow God's plan of salvation. Your name is now written in God's book of life (Ph. 4:3; Rev. 3:5; 20:12). The middle part of God's plan is following Jesus as we live on earth. As a child of God, seek to obey the teachings of Jesus in the Bible (Mt. 28:19-20). As you follow Him, He will lead and strengthen you in your relationship with God. As a baby grows into an adult, you will grow from a new child of God into to a mature family member. Be baptized in water (Mt 28:19; Acts 8:36-38; Rom. 6:4; Mk. 16:16). Become part of a local church that preaches and teaches the Bible (Acts 2:41; 9:31). Seek to be filled with the Holy Spirit (Acts 1:8; 2:4; 4:31; 8:17; 10:44-46; 19:1-7; Eph. 5:18-20). Learn to walk in the Spirit, so you can overcome sinful desires that come through the flesh (Rom. 8:5; Gal. 5:16). Grow in grace, and in the knowledge of our Lord and Savior Jesus Christ, and in maturity (2 Pet. 3:18; 2 Pet. 1:5-18). Fellowship with other believers who will encourage you. Share your testimony with others, and lead them to Jesus (Jn. 1:40-42; 4:39). The completion of salvation occurs when Jesus Christ returns. At that time, He will give you a new body, and complete His glorious plan of salvation in your life (Rom. 8:18-25; 1 Cor. 15:20-58; 1 Th. 4:13-17). We do not know the exact time Jesus will return. For now, enjoy the presence of God, and His Spirit in you, as you grow in grace. You have been saved from your past sins. You are being saved daily, as you abide and grow in Christ. And your salvation has a glorious completion ahead.